Beauty, Art, and the Polis

American Maritain Association Publications

General Editor: Anthony O. Simon

Jacques Maritain: The Man and His Metaphysics
Edited by John F.X. Knasas, 1988
★ ISBN 0-268-01205-9 (out of print)

Freedom in the Modern World: Jacques Maritain, Yves R. Simon, Mortimer J. Adler
Edited by Michael D. Torre, 1989, Second Printing 1990
★ ISBN 0-268-00978-3

From Twilight to Dawn: The Cultural Vision of Jacques Maritain
Edited by Peter A. Redpath, 1990
★ ISBN 0-268-00979-1

The Future of Thomism
Edited by Deal W. Hudson and Dennis Wm. Moran, 1992
★ ISBN 0-268-00986-4

Jacques Maritain and the Jews
Edited by Robert Royal, 1994
★ ISBN 0-268-01193-1

Freedom, Virtue, and the Common Good
Edited by Curtis L. Hancock and Anthony O. Simon, 1995
★ ISBN 0-268-00991-0

Postmodernism and Christian Philosophy
Edited by Roman T. Ciapolo, 1997
◆ ISBN 0-8132-0881-5

The Common Things: Essays on Thomism and Education
Edited by Daniel McInerny, 1999
◆ ISBN 0-9669226-0-3

The Failure of Modernism: The Cartesian Legacy and Contemporary Pluralism
Edited by Brendan Sweetman, 1999
◆ ISBN 0-9669226-1-1

Beauty, Art, and the Polis
Edited by Alice Ramos, 2000
◆ ISBN 0-9669226-2-X

★ Distributed by the University of Notre Dame Press
◆ Distributed by The Catholic University of America Press

Beauty, Art, and the Polis

Alice Ramos
Editor

With an Introduction by
Ralph McInerny

AMERICAN MARITAIN ASSOCIATION
Distributed by The Catholic University of America Press
Washington, D.C. 20064

Library of Congress Cataloging-in-Publication Data

Beauty, art, and the polis / edited by Alice Ramos ; with an introduction by Ralph McInerny.
    p. cm. — (American Maritain Association publications)
Includes bibliographical references and index.
ISBN 0-9669226-2-X (alk. paper)
    1. Aesthetics. 2. Neo-Scholasticism. 3. Maritain, Jacques, 1882–1973. 4. Art—Philosophy. I. Ramos, Alice. II. Series.

BH39.B3827 2000
111'.85—dc21   00-021847

Manufactured in the
United States of America

Distributed by The Catholic University of America Press

Contents

PART III ART, MORALITY, AND THE POLIS

Editor's Note

In his fine introductory essay Ralph McInerny tells us that aesthetics for Maritain was not accidental to his philosophy but rather essential to it. Both Maritain and the Scholastics knew that beauty is not a social construct or a purely subjective experience, as some would have it today, but that beauty is intrinsic to things themselves. Beauty has been called the "splendor of the form," its radiance; we are captivated by that radiance, and we thirst for it. The aesthetic experience is thus similar to the philosophical experience. As we desire to know, to be united to the truth, we also desire to be united with beauty. Our desire for happiness is often expressed in aesthetic terms: contemplation, with enjoyment, of the ultimately Intelligible and Beautiful. The aesthetic experience calls us beyond the self, beyond what we see and touch. As Michelangelo once wrote: "The soul of man winging its way towards the heavens whence it descended cannot rest in the contemplation of the fragile and deceptive beauty which allures the bodily senses, but in its sublime flight it seeks to attain to the universal principle of beauty."

The essays in this volume recognize in the beautiful a call to the transcendent, to an order not of man's making, as they also recognize in the arts the power to elevate man or degrade him, to dispose him toward the good or to alienate him from the good. Thus, although Maritain distinguishes, as Aquinas had done before him, artistic from moral excellence, art from prudence, he also clearly sees that the artist as a man has a responsibility toward the truth and his fellowmen. A study of the arts brings us then to ethical and political considerations, for the good lawgiver, if called to act in artistic matters, will want to promote virtue and the common good. The arts which uplift man and enable him to live a good and virtuous life will become, as it were, a window onto the transcendent. Seen in this way, the arts and beauty cannot but have an essential role in the life of the human person and in the *polis*. And so, this volume has an important contribution to make in discussions of art and beauty.

The essays herein have been arranged in three parts. Those in the first part provide us with the metaphysical and epistemological foundations for a consideration of beauty in art, as well as in nature, and of creative activity, both human and divine. The second part deals specifically with different forms of art and interpretations of the artist and his work; the "usefulness" of art and beauty in, for example, religious experience and liturgy, is but one of the ways in which art is shown here to serve human life. The third and final section of the volume presents us with moral and political questions concerning the arts, such as censorship, public funding and the educational role of the arts. This last part also paves the way for a broad understanding of aesthetic principles and their application to the well-being of the human person and of life in society.

Throughout the editing process of this volume, I have received encouragement and advice from many friends and colleagues. I would like first of all to thank Curtis Hancock, President of the American Maritain Association, along with Anthony O. Simon and Peter Redpath, both dedicated members of the Executive Committee of the Association, for their moral support. A special thanks goes to Willard Gingerich, Provost of Research at St. John's University, and to Salvatore Spizzirri, Associate Dean of St. John's College, for their help in securing intramural funds for the publication of this volume. Dr. Gingerich was not only supportive of the project, but also enthusiastic about previous volumes published under the auspices of the American Maritain Association. I hope that he will be equally pleased with the outcome of this present volume. I also wish to thank Jamie Manson for her help in the initial formatting of the essays, and Grace Wu, as well as Katherine Osenga, for their suggestions on the design of the cover. Last but not least, I would like to thank all the contributors for their insightful work; I am very appreciative to Ralph McInerny for agreeing to write the introductory essay. I could think of no one more qualified than he—a Thomist, Maritainian scholar, and author of the well-known Father Dowling books—to write the introduction to this volume.

Finally, I would like to say a word about the cover. I chose Rodin's *Pensée—Thought*—not only for its beauty, but also as a reminder of what Thomas Aquinas knew only too well: that beauty is essentially found in the contemplative life, in the act of reason. I hope that the reader of this volume will experience something of the beautiful in the thoughts expressed by the contributors, and that their reflections may serve some of us who by profession engage in the contemplative life to journey along with Aquinas, Maritain, and others in the elaboration of an aesthetics, so necessary for the perfection of human life.

Introduction
"A Bracelet of Bright Hair About the Bone"

Ralph McInerny

The purpose of an introduction is to say what need not be said and very likely will not be read. One can seek to stave of this unsavory fate by choosing an arresting title. But over and beyond this ploy, the line from Donne is meant to recall the profound spiritual and withal romantic love that linked Jacques and Raïssa, to whom he applied Horace's phrase, *dimidium animae meae*. He deferred to her in many things, but particularly when it was a question of aesthetics, and if I do not show this in the lines that follow, let mentioning it here, if not suffice, excuse. They have lain together in their common grave at Kolbsheim many decades now, but they are joined eternally elsewhere.

Among the many attractions of Jacques Maritain as a thinker is the range and depth of his interests. From metaphysics to the philosophy of history, from political philosophy to the philosophy of nature and its offspring modern science, from mysticism to morals—has anything escaped him? Is there any area of culture on which he has not written? Looked at in this way, Maritain's aesthetics may seem the final fillip, sprinkles on the waffle cone of his remarkable genius. But it is not so. Art is not an incidental add-on; it is of the essence.

When Chesterton, in *The Everlasting Man*, compared the God in the Cave and the Man in the Cave, he was taking up the dispute that had arisen about the prehistoric inhabitants of southern France. Had they been human? Typically, Chesterton went to the heart of the matter. Look at the drawings on the walls of the caves. There is your answer. Where there is art, there is man. Of course, *homo faber* has long been a designation of our ancient for-

1

bears, but the making involved had been tools and weapons. The line draw-ings of animals on the cave walls are something more. With them the move from the useful to the fine arts was already made.

One of the earliest discussions—letting the Bekker numbers establish chronology—of art in Aristotle occurs in Book Two of the *Physics*. His aim is to clarify nature by contrasting it with art. Nature is a first principle of motion and rest in that to which it belongs as such and not incidentally. This definition is illustrated by the two constituents of physical things that Aristotle had established in the previous book. Both matter and form, in their different ways, save the definition of nature. Some activities of the thing have their origin in its matter, others in its form. But the common mark of the natural is that it proceeds from what is intrinsic to the thing. Art by contrast is an extrinsic principle of change.

Since every efficient cause is extrinsic, this seems to have the unsettling effect of making every efficient cause artful. This is avoided by requiring that the cause that is art be intelligent and endowed with will. The alter-ation of the natural by the human agent, by design and for his own pur-poses, that is art. Elsewhere, Aristotle observes that, compared with other animals, man seems to have been ill-provided for by nature. Turtles and porcupines are armored; all animals are clothed and most species are programmed to find shelter. Watching ovenbirds or even wrens construct their nests or muskrats build their watery homes, who has not felt a Walt Disney impulse to see more than an analogy with human art? And of course there is intelligence involved, but it resides in the one who fash-ioned their nature, the artist *par excellence*. Against these fully endowed species stands man, the poor forked animal, naked, defenseless, homeless. And yet, Aristotle sees him as the most richly endowed of all. He has a prehensile hand, the instrument of instruments, and what it is an instru-ment of is reason. Art is necessary for man if he is to survive: art is natural to him.

Clearly then when art is opposed to nature, it is not nature in the nar-rower sense of human nature that is meant. The panoramic description of human life with which the *Metaphysics* begins, glossing its opening gener-alization—"All men by nature desire to know"—characterizes man first of all as the one who from experience can acquire an art. One might by luck or inadvertence produce something and be unable to repeat the feat. One might be able to repeat the feat and not know why certain actions of ours have the effect that they do. Aristotle is thinking of medicine—more than once we are reminded of the fact that his father was a physician, and there is a tradition that he was too—and the difference between a midwife and a physician. Experience guides the midwife and she can give anecdotal reasons for doing what she does, referring to Mrs. Smith and Mrs. Brown, but why this procedure worked with Mrs. Smith and Brown she does not know. Art appears when the Why is grasped.

It is no accident that such an art as medicine enters into the discussion here. A little later, the art of building illustrates a point. We are confronted, in other words, with the practical arts, man's use of natural materials to provide for himself—clothing, shelter, food, tools, weapons. We are first occupied with the necessities of life and art is necessary if we are to secure them. But the artful ordering to satisfy our needs—agriculture, fishing, hunting, trade—creates conditions for something more. Earlier when Aristotle illustrated his initial generalization about our natural pursuit of knowledge, he pointed to seeing. Seeing is along with the other senses indispensable to our getting along in the world, but Aristotle notes that we take pleasure in seeing "even when it has no purpose beyond itself." This is an adumbration of the theoretical. Hugh of St. Victor, in his *Didascalion*, gives such a list of seven practical arts as contrast to the liberal arts.

ART IMITATES NATURE

Art relates to nature as imitation, and imitation can be grasped in a first and obvious meaning in this connection through the example of medicine. The art of medicine seeks to aid nature in doing what it can often do unaided. Wounds heal, fevers subside, bruises fade away, bones knit. The physician's acts seek to imitate nature in these various effects. Clearly, imitation does not mean replicating identically what nature can do unaided. A broken bone that knits naturally might very well leave a person permanently handicapped. Imitation takes into account the end of nature's self-healing, which is the fitness and health of the person. It is the end that governs the medical procedure; the means are sometimes suggested by nature, but increasingly medicine employs means to the end of health that nature herself could not supply. Open-heart surgery could not of course take place without a surgeon. But however sophisticated the procedures become, they are guided by knowledge of nature, of what in the nature of things the healthy condition of a person is with all the variations that age and gender introduce into the concept. The experience of the physician provides an ever-broadening empirical base for increased knowledge of health.

MAN IS BY NATURE A POLITICAL ANIMAL

This relation of practical reason to the given can also be seen in the Aristotelian dictum that man is by nature a political animal. Nature in the phrase suggests the given, not the elective. Aristotle is not suggesting that we are such that we have a tendency to enter into groups contractually, to form associations. There is a community which is necessary for our existence and survival, the family. Any reflection on the good of man which overlooks the given truth about its subject will produce fantastic theories. The contract theory of society may seem to be merely a heuristic device, something like Rawls's Veil of Ignorance, but it leads all too easily to the supposition that human beings are isolated individuals which show up in an adult condition and then, out of self-interest, decide that the trade-offs involved in forming a community are such that advantages outweigh the disadvantages. Of course, there are no such human individuals. Humans begin as infants, helpless, totally dependent on parents, in need of years of nurture and education before they are recognizably responsible persons. Man's natural condition therefore is as a member of a community. The good for man must of necessity concern his fulfillment or perfection as a member of a society. The moral dimension then is not some putative choice to live or not to live in society, but how to do this well. The willy-nilly is always a presupposition of responsible acts of will.

Much the same is true of the initial claim of the *Metaphysics*: "All men by nature desire to know." The desire is natural, that is, it is not initially a choice. The senses and the mind are fashioned to know, and they perform those actions independently of any choice. The cognitive is ordered to the true and the mind cannot fail to reach that goal. But the natural beginnings of the life of the mind are truths known by all. Thus, Thomas will distinguish between *ratio ut natura* and *ratio ut ratio*, just as he distinguished between *voluntas ut natura* and *voluntas ut voluntas*. The will cannot not will the good, that is its nature; the mind cannot not grasp the true. But these natural grasps provide only the beginnings of rational activity; principles are inchoative starting-points, and moving out from them carries with it no guarantee that one will hit upon further truths, anymore than deliberate will-acts always relate to the true good. The art of logic elevates the hit or miss activity of mind as it moves off from principles in search of more specific truths.

The sense of "natural" in natural law is clear against the background of such considerations. The first precepts of practical reason are those a person cannot fail to know, and they are followed by others which can be grasped *cum modica consideratione*. Discussions of whether *synderesis* is a habit stir up considerations of the kind in which we have been engaged.

ART AS A VIRTUE

Man's characteristic activity, that which sets him off from every other agent in the cosmos, is rational activity. In this he engages naturally and necessarily, but he does not necessarily do so well. The modification or perfection of this activity, so that it achieves its naturally given end surely, is its excellence or virtue, and because rational activity has an ordered set of meanings, there is an ordered set of virtues. Insofar as what is sought is the perfection of rational activity as such, the achievement of truth, virtues of speculative reasoning are distinguished. Sometimes we use our mind, not to perfect mental activity as such, but to gain truths which enable mind to govern activities other than mental activity. Aristotle distinguished two virtues of the practical intellect, art and prudence, calling art the perfecting of practical reason with regard to things to be made, and prudence the perfection of practical reason with respect to things to be done. *Agenda*. The doing of things to be done, when perfected, is the perfection of the doer. Prudence guides choices in the light of our given appetite for pleasure and given aversion to pain. The cardinal virtue bearing on the former is Temperance, the cardinal virtue bearing on the latter is Fortitude. Unlike the activities that art directs, those directed by prudence are immanent; when perfected they perfect the agent as such. Art in its first sense involves transitive activity: it modifies a material external to man, and its perfection will be the perfection of the thing made. It comes within the ambit of the moral in the way in which other commanded voluntary acts do, such as walking, throwing, striking, on and on.

LIBERAL ARTS

The art of logic is a liberal art, liberal as opposed to art in a more basic and practical sense. Art is used here in an extended or analogous sense of the term. In its first sense, *techne* or *ars* involves the production of some artifact which mimics the composition of something produced by nature. The result of natural becoming is a compound of matter and form. The result of artful making is a compound of a natural material and a humanly induced form. This is done with an eye to the necessities of human life. The liberal art has an *opus* only in a sense: not an *opus* external to mind but rather internal to it. The affirmations and denials, the arguments, studied in logic are products of thought which organize and direct thought more surely to the end of truth. The arts of language and the arts of quantity all have *opera* of this not extra-mental sort. As the *artes humaniores*, they perfect the man, but partially. One is not thought to be a good man *tout court* because he is a good logician or a good geometer. These virtues concern a partial good of the agent and do not as such relate themselves to man's overall or total good. Insofar as they are so related it will be by another virtue, prudence, and then an activity can receive two appraisals, one as mathematical, say, and another as moral. One can be a good mathematician and a morally bad man, one can be a morally good man and a poor mathematician. While the moral virtues are more fundamentally virtues and more necessary for us, they do not substitute for nor render less fulfilling of us as rational agents the liberal arts and the sciences.

THE FINE ARTS

Where do the fine arts fall in this schema? The things recalled provide the context within which Jacques Maritain takes up the discussion of the fine arts. The *beaux arts*, the arts of the beautiful. Maritain had to fashion from implications and suggestions in the texts of Thomas what we have come to call an aesthetics. The Thomistic context does not easily accommodate the fine arts as a distinct consideration. It will occur to us that music is mentioned among the liberal arts, whereas house-building (architecture) falls to the practical arts. It seems clear that the fine arts will cut across the division of arts into practical and liberal. It is no easy matter to say what they have in common and what would distinguish them.

The example of architecture makes clear that being useful to our material needs can characterize a fine art, but then how does shoemaking or industrial design fall short of being a fine art. *Ars gratia artis*? But architecture is irredeemably connected with providing shelter. Sculpture may be the sweatiest of the fine arts and we would doubtless group it with painting. Music as the quantification of sound which when heard somehow structures our emotions seems ethereal by comparison, and the old question whether music is music when it is not being played or performed is not the same question as whether a statue or painting are achieved works of art when unobserved. The arts of language begin with grammar but scientific treatises do not seek the same effect as fiction or poetry, and in opera we have that fusion of music and poetry that struck Kierkegaard's pseudonym as the apex of art.

This is the area in which Maritain made one of his greatest contributions to philosophy done in the tradition of Aristotle and Thomas Aquinas. Readers can argue about the degree, or indeed whether what he has to say can be traced back to his philosophical mentors, but it is clear that he has gone far beyond them. There is nothing comparable to the *Poetics* in Thomas—a work which had not yet in Thomas's lifetime been translated into Latin—but we can be sure that the discussions of music in the *Politics* and *Republic* had their effect on Maritain's truly original aesthetic work.

NOVA ET VETERA

It is pleasant for an old Thomist to rehearse the matters that make up the first part of this essay, matters that provide the backdrop for Maritain's aesthetics. But unsettling questions must arise with respect to that background. It is of course Aristotelian, it is pre-Copernican, and it is even more distant from the situation in which we find ourselves, what Rémi Brague has called *la perte du monde*: the loss of the world. The Aristotelian cosmos, like the world of the Middle Ages, provided a sustaining matrix for moral philosophy as well as for reflections on human artistic activity. The universe no longer functions in that way for the modern mind. The almost cozy cosmos that provided Dante with an astronomical metaphor of the inner life has been replaced by accounts which seem almost more poetic than scientific. Our solar system has long since been swallowed up in a galaxy which in turn is recognized as one of innumerable others in a universe that is rushing ever outward toward God knows what. It looks as if the nature which grounded both morality and art simply isn't there anymore.

One of the fascinations of Maritain's aesthetics, particularly as we find it in *Creative Intuition in Art and Poetry*, is his response to modern art. Only a cynic would attribute this to his many friendships with contemporary artists. One detects unease before Picasso, and not because they were not friends. The distortions of the human figure bother Maritain, an apparent hostility toward the natural. Reed Armstrong has developed an unflattering interpretation of modernity with Picasso's *Demoiselles d'Avignon* providing the bridge from then to now. It is not of course the function of the artist to convey contemporary scientific accounts of the universe, but the discarded image of a cosmos and world necessarily affect the artist, whether or not the new astronomy is *toto caelo* different from the old. It feels that way. Already with Pascal *le silence de ces espaces infinis m'effraie*, and we can imagine the artist in that interiority where Maritain locates the *fons et origo* of art having to deal with being lost in space. Read the Mellon lectures with this in mind. Remember Maritain's lifelong effort to put together the philosophy of nature of Aristotle and Aquinas and the science of his day. But however the philosopher might resolve the apparent quantum jump from old to new, the creative membrane of the poet's soul will respond to the current vision of the universe to which chaos theory is another response. Auden spoke of the poet's as a secondary world. But what if the primary world is gone? Maritain's work is a first step in an unfinished journey for Thomistic aesthetics.

PART I

THE FOUNDATIONS OF
BEAUTY, ART, AND CREATIVITY

"Radiance":
The Metaphysical Foundations of
Maritain's Aesthetics

John G. Trapani, Jr.

"Poetry is in love with beauty, and beauty in love with poetry,"[1] Maritain says in the chapter "Poetry and Beauty," from *Creative Intuition in Art and Poetry*. In order to understand the relationship indicated by this puzzling claim, one needs to situate this remark within the context of a whole host of metaphysical distinctions that extend from the ordinary to the specialized. Examples of the ordinary include: the relation of the Creator to the universe with its resultant inherent intelligibility, the divine likeness of human nature, and the cognitive/creative dimensions of the intellect; examples of the specialized include: Maritain's unique claims regarding "poetry," "spiritualized emotion," "intelligentiated sense," and beauty as the "radiance of a mystery."

By exploring these metaphysical underpinnings, we will see how the "radiance" of beauty and "poetry" found in genuine works of art (and manifested throughout creation) leads us to a glimpse of the Divine, who is the source of all being. It is for this reason that Maritain includes the following passage from Baudelaire in no less than six of his works—works which include discussions about God as well as art, beauty, and "poetry":

> It is the instinct for beauty which makes us consider the world and its pageants as a glimpse of, a *correspondence* with, Heaven. . . . It is at once by poetry and *through* poetry, by music and *through* music, that the soul divines what splendors shine behind the tomb; and when an exquisite poem brings tears to the eyes, such tears are not the sign of

---

[1] Jacques Maritain, *Creative Intuition in Art and Poetry* (New York: Pantheon Books, 1953), p. 173.

an excess of joy, they are rather a witness to an irritated melancholy, an exigency of nerves, a nature exiled in the imperfect which would possess immediately, on this very earth, a paradise revealed.[2]

In this paper, we will articulate the metaphysical foundations of Maritain's aesthetics and explore the early development of his thought. In particular, we will find that the philosophical notion of "radiance" is of special significance metaphysically, aesthetically, and even emotionally. The paper will conclude with some brief remarks about the tragedy of the human condition which results if one is cut off from the ability to delight in and share the aesthetic experience of radiance.

THE METAPHYSICAL FOUNDATIONS
OF MARITAIN'S AESTHETICS

> Earth's crammed with heaven
> And every common bush afire with God;
> But only he who sees takes off his shoes—
> the rest sit 'round it and pluck blackberries.[3]

There are at least two contrasting views of reality. One of these conforms to the above lines from Elizabeth Barrett Browning: there is a supreme Creator-God whose creation is "crammed" with divine intelligibility—less apparent in inanimate, material things and more apparent in those created beings (including humans) which manifest, progressively by degrees, higher and higher aspects of life and of immanent, self-perfecting activities. For those creatures that sentiently and intellectually experience the divinely created, material universe, the crowning radiance occurs when the intelligibility of creation is variously revealed and concealed through the cognitive and creative activity of human participated intelligence.

The other opposing view of reality would maintain neither a notion of a Divine Creator nor any "heaven in a grain of sand"—the material universe is simply "there" (*de trop*); it is neither meaningful in itself nor is it in any sense purposeful. Human beings, on this reckoning, are neither endowed with any spiritual intellect, nor is the universe "flooded with intelligibility." Rather, intelligence is understood as a function of a highly developed and

---

[2] Ibid., p. 166. See also Jacques Maritain, *Art and Scholasticism and The Frontiers of Poetry*, trans. Joseph W. Evans (New York: Charles Scribner's Sons, 1962), p. 32; *Art and Faith* (New York: Philosophical Library, 1948), p. 91; *The Situation of Poetry* (New York: Philosophical Library, 1955), p. 43; *Approaches to God* (New York: The Macmillan Company, 1965), p. 80; and *Man's Approach to God* (Latrobe, Pennsylvania: The Archabbey Press, 1960), p. 18.

[3] "Aurora Leigh," in *The Poetical Works of Elizabeth Barrett Browning*, ed. Ruth M. Adams (New York: Houghton Mifflin, 1974), p. 372.

complex central nervous system. As a result, any notion of "intelligible meaning" is thus seen as the result of an essentially Kantian or post-modern construction of reality; perhaps less true for the derivation of the laws of the physical and natural sciences, where the structure of reality, while somewhat fixed and discoverable, is nonetheless a product of the random and arbitrary forces that govern the physical universe, and more true of all the other "interpretive" sciences—the humanities, history, and the social and political sciences—all of which "construct" the basic insights and meanings found in their respective fields.

The consequences of these two contrasting metaphysical foundations are significant. Does the intelligible structure of the universe derive from some essentially arbitrary evolution controlled by the physical/chemical laws of nature and the natural selection of living beings, or does this intelligible structure go beyond those physical/chemical natural laws to include the meaningful intelligibility that derives from its Creator-God? This distinction between these two fundamentally different starting points is a dramatic example of St. Thomas's "small mistake in the beginning." From it will come the foundational principles of every branch of one's philosophical thinking, including aesthetics.

With this in mind, it is easy to trace the essential pieces in Maritain's aesthetics. Maritain recognizes the metaphysical importance of the Creator/Creation relationship when he talks about the created universe in which artists find themselves. "I need to designate the secretive depths and the implacable advance of the infinite host of beings, aspects, events, physical and moral tangles of horror and beauty—of that world, that undecipherable Other—with which . . . the artist is faced; and I have no word for that except the poorest and tritest word of the human language; I shall say: the things of the world, the Things."[4] But these "things," he goes on to say later,

> are not only what they are. They ceaselessly pass beyond themselves, and give more than they have because from all sides they are permeated by the activating influx of the Prime Cause. They are better and worse than themselves, because being superabounds. . . .[5]

Those familiar with Maritain's aesthetics know that this understanding of the superabundant, inexhaustible, and intelligible richness of the universe is complemented by the "infinite depths of this flesh-and-blood and spiritual existent, the artist,"[6] and that both together provide the ingredients

[4] Maritain, *Creative Intuition in Art and Poetry*, p. 10.

[5] Ibid., p. 127.

[6] Ibid., p. 10.

for Maritain's signature use of the notion of "poetry"; it is "that intercommunication between the inner being of things and the inner being of the human self which is a kind of divination." "Poetry," on this reading, is "the secret life of each and all the arts. . . ."[7]

Careful attention to his notion of "poetry" reveals two distinguishable senses of the term "things" which are, so to speak, wrapped up together. On the one hand, there are the "things" of the natural universe which derive their inexhaustible intelligibility from their Creator, while on the other hand, there are also those "things" of the artist's making (works of art) which derive their intelligibility from the richness of the artist's own subjectivity or "Self." Considered all together, they form that classic, analogous relationship between God the Creator and the works of creation on the one hand, and the human creator-artist and the works of art on the other; the analogy *is* found in Maritain's earliest writing in aesthetics, *Art and Scholasticism* (1920).[8] But there is more.

In *Creative Intuition* (1953), Maritain describes his unique notion of "poetry" as possessing two distinguishable moments: "poetic knowledge as cognitive" and "poetic knowledge as creative."[9] Both of these moments, Maritain makes clear, are the unique knowledge proper to the creative, work-producing artist. As such, however, they only tell half of "poetry's" story. With the original 1920 publication of *Art and Scholasticism*, one may be surprised to learn that his special use of the term "poetry" does not appear. Instead, Maritain's initial aim was to discuss the metaphysical fundamentals of art and beauty. And since beauty is primarily a transcendental, it is not limited to aesthetics alone. Manifested in both natural creation and art, it always involves a relation to an intelligence, either God's or our own. This discussion of the perception of beauty is especially significant since it opens the way to a broader treatment of the triadic relationship of "artist/work/audience," and does not limit the discussion to the creative artist alone.

MARITAIN ON "POETRY"
AND THE PERCEPTION OF BEAUTY

In Maritain's two detailed discussions of the perception of beauty, the chapters "Art and Beauty" from *Art and Scholasticism* and "Poetry and

---

[7] Ibid., p. 3.

[8] See Maritain, *Art and Scholasticism and The Frontiers of Poetry*, especially pp. 30–35.

[9] For the discussion of these two moments, see Maritain's *Creative Intuition in Art and Poetry*, pp. 117–41.

Beauty" from *Creative Intuition*, his method of proceeding is initially the same in both cases: he begins with the fundamentals of St. Thomas's claim that the beautiful is "that which, being seen, pleases: *id quod visum placet*."[10] Maritain is quick to point out, of course, that the kind of seeing implied here is not confined to the senses. But he is also prudent in his claim that it is not an exclusively intellectual seeing either; rather, it is a unique mode of *intuitive* intellectual knowledge. What distinguishes this mode of intuition from others is the part that the senses play in the act of knowing. Only in sense knowledge do we "possess perfectly . . . the intuitiveness required for the perception of beauty. . . . [It] delights the intellect through the senses and through their intuition."[11]

Maritain uses the term *intelligentiated sense* to identify this interdependent union of sense and intellectual intuition. Although prominent in *Creative Intuition*, his use of that term actually first appears in a celebrated footnote from *Art and Scholasticism*.[12] A careful examination of the original French edition reveals that the paragraph containing it was inserted in the 1927 edition. Like the notion of "poetry," it too did not appear in the original 1920 publication. Maritain is at pains to make clear the contrast between that intellectual knowledge which terminates in a concept, and that intellectual knowledge which does not. Concerning the joy which an encounter with the beautiful gives us, we are placed, Maritain says, "*through the means of the sensible intuition itself*, in the presence of a radiant intelligibility . . . which . . . cannot be disengaged or separated from its sense matrix and consequently does not procure an intellectual knowledge expressible in a concept."[13] And in the 1927 insertion, he adds, "it is intellect and sense as forming but one . . . *intelligentiated sense*, which gives rise in the heart to aesthetic joy."[14]

This special relationship between beauty, the senses, and the intellect provides the context for understanding the three classic characteristics of beauty: integrity ("because the intellect is pleased in the fullness of Being"), proportion ("because the intellect is pleased in order and unity"), and radiance or clarity ("because the intellect is pleased in light and intelligibility").[15] It is here that we encounter "radiance"; Maritain says that, of the three characteristics of beauty, radiance is the most important because it

[10] Maritain, *Art and Scholasticism*, p. 23.
[11] Ibid., pp. 23–24.
[12] Ibid., pp. 162–67, n. 56.
[13] Ibid., pp. 163–64.
[14] Ibid., p. 164.
[15] Ibid., p. 24.

is the proper principle of intelligibility. It is the splendor of the form, the splendor of intelligibility. This form is "a vestige or a ray of the creative Intelligence imprinted at the heart of created being."[16] Beauty is thus "a flashing of intelligence [either God's or the artist's] on a matter intelligibly arranged"[17] or, as Maritain adds in the 1927 edition of *Art and Scholasticism*, it is "the ontological secret that [things] bear within them[selves], their spiritual being, their operating mystery."[18]

Maritain the metaphysician is quick to remind us that this aesthetic beauty is primarily a participation in ontological beauty. He cautions us in a different inserted note, also in the 1927 edition, that it is all too easy to misunderstand words like *clarity, radiance, intelligibility,* and *light,* if we attempt to understand these terms in relation *to ourselves,* rather than as something clear and luminous *in themselves.* For this reason, beauty is often obscure to us though not in itself. "The more substantial and the more profound this secret sense is, the more hidden it is from us; so that, . . . to define the beautiful by the radiance of the form is in reality to define it by the radiance of a mystery."[19] Accordingly, our intelligence must be equipped with some means of being able to apprehend these mysteries and spiritual secrets as they are obscurely radiant in matter, or all would be lost to us, and it would make no sense to speak of them at all. In this context, we can appreciate the genius of Maritain's notion of "poetry" as a purely natural, human means of "divining" the "spiritual in the things of sense. . . ."[20]

Although a detailed discussion of this relation between "poetry" and the perception of beauty appears in *Creative Intuition,* there are several occasions in Maritain's earlier writings where he does give us a clear indication of "poetry's" purely contemplative function. "Artistic [or poetic] contemplation," he tells us, "affects the heart with a joy that is above all *intellectual.* . . ."[21] Other references include:

> Poetry . . . is clearly no longer the privilege of poets.[22]
> One can be a poet and still produce nothing.[23]
> Poetry . . . can also be found in a boy who knows only how to look and to say ah, ah, ah, like Jeremiah. . . .[24]

[16] Ibid., p. 25.
[17] Ibid.
[18] Ibid., p. 24.
[19] Ibid., p. 28.
[20] Maritain, "The Frontiers of Poetry," in *Art and Scholasticism,* p. 128.
[21] Maritain, *Art and Scholasticism,* p. 164, n. 56.
[22] Maritain, "The Frontiers of Poetry," in *Art and Scholasticism,* p. 129.
[23] Maritain, *Art and Faith,* p. 90.
[24] Maritain, *The Situation of Poetry,* p. 44.

Thus we find: on the metaphysical side, a universe flooded with radiant intelligibility, whether created by God in the beauty of nature or made by the human artist in the beauty of the art work. On the epistemological side, we observe that human intellectual knowledge can (1) result in abstract understanding (where the term of the intellect's activity is a concept or *verbum mentis*), or that it can (2) function non-conceptually and manifest itself in either: (a) the *creative* intuition of "poetry" (where the term of the intellect's activity is a work made or *objet d'art*), or (b) the *contemplative* intuition of "poetry" (where the term of the intellect's activity is an aesthetic delight that finds its rest in a joy of the heart or *verbum cordis*). Of course, the fundamental Thomistic insight that is at work here concerns the cognitive and creative functions of the human intellect, both of which pass beyond themselves on account of their spiritual energies. What unites them is the intelligible radiance of "things" on the one hand, and the unified, intuitive, intellectual/affective nature of the human person on the other; a person capable of grasping this radiance in a non-conceptual way and of beaming in ecstasy with a joy and delight that spills over and expands the heart with a love that is at once natural and divine.

CONCLUSION: THE RADIANCE OF LOVE AND THE LOVE OF RADIANCE

The more you love, the more you see . . .
The more you see, the more you love.

When we speak of love philosophically, we may place our emphasis on either its cognitive/intellectual aspect or on its affective/emotive aspect. On different occasions, Maritain writes about each. On the one hand, he had learned from Bergson the necessity of using the term "intuition" to identify those non-conceptual human experiences not adequately expressible in concepts. From St. Thomas, he learned that all senses of "intuition" are always and primarily intellectual.[25] But Maritain also recognized that love too can become a vehicle for non-conceptual knowledge. He writes:

> By love, finally, is shattered the impossibility of knowing another except as object. . . . To the degree that we truly love (. . . when . . . the intellect within us becomes passive as regards love, and, allowing its concepts to slumber, thereby renders love a formal means of knowl-

---

[25] See Jacques Maritain, *Bergsonian Philosophy and Thomism* (New York: Philosophical Library, 1955), pp. 148–52.

edge), to this degree we acquire an obscure knowledge of the being we love. . . .[26]

Maritain occasionally refers to such love/knowledge as an affect of the heart: "This eye-covered love of intelligence, this is what you call the heart, isn't it? *The illuminated eyes of the heart*, say the Scriptures."[27] Surprisingly perhaps, this use of the notion of the "heart," as regrettably metaphorical as some may find it, does have its root in St. Thomas himself. In the *Summa Contra Gentiles*, St. Thomas writes: "For love proceeds from a word: we are able to love nothing but that which a word of the heart [*verbum cordis*] conceives."[28]

On the other hand, it is often the emotive dimension of our affective experiences that receives his attention. When discussing this topic, Maritain is careful to distinguish genuine affective experiences from brute emotion and the sentimentality of feelings (which "sends a chill down the spine," so to speak). Always permeated by intellectual light, love can also stir "affective resonance,"[29] or what Maritain also calls "spiritualized, intentional, or significant emotion"; it too can function as a determining means of genuine intellectual knowledge. Like the terms "poetry" and "intelligentiated sense," his use of "spiritualized emotion" is his own unique contribution to Thomistic epistemology and aesthetics. Reminiscent of the earlier passage where love becomes a means of knowledge, Maritain tells us that this significant or spiritualized emotion also can become

> for the intellect a determining means . . . through which the things which have impressed this emotion on the soul, and the deeper, invisible things that are contained in them . . . are grasped and known obscurely.
>
> It is by means of such a spiritualized emotion that poetic intuition, which in itself is an intellective flash, is born in the unconscious of the spirit.[30]

Radiance, then, is the luminosity and beauty of all being and of the fullness of being, our Creator-God. The *love of radiance* is manifested in our aesthetic or emotional love/experiences of the mysterious and ineffable, transcendent secrets of being which shine forth in works of art, of nature,

---

[26] Jacques Maritain, *Existence and the Existent* (New York: Pantheon Books, 1948), p. 84.

[27] Maritain, *Art and Faith*, p. 109.

[28] St. Thomas Aquinas, *Summa Contra Gentiles* (*On the Truth of the Catholic Faith*) (New York: Image Books, 1957), p. 140.

[29] For the discussion of "significant, intentional, or spiritualized emotion," see Maritain's *Creative Intuition in Art and Poetry*, pp. 118–25.

[30] Ibid., p. 123.

and ultimately, *when we shall see face to face*, of the Divine radiance itself (recall the quotation from Baudelaire). The *radiance of love* is manifested by the creative expressions of love and goodness found proportionately in God and creatures; for "God's love causes the beauty of what He loves, whereas our love is caused by the beauty of what we love."[31] To perceive that radiance and beauty is to glimpse paradise even on this earth; but to be cut off from it, even while the creative artist may be participating in it unaware, is to know the pain and suffering of isolation. Maritain notes how remarkable it is that we communicate with one another at all, given our human limitations. And yet only through genuine communication do we pass beyond ourselves and "escape from the individuality in which matter encloses us."[32] If we remain on the level of our sense-needs and sentimentality only, then we may tell or sing or yell or scream our stories, but each remains alone, and we do not understand one another. Maritain says: "[We] observe each other without seeing each other, each one of [us] infinitely alone, even though work or sense pleasures bind [us] together."[33] But enter love, "poetry," beauty, and radiance, and all the walls are broken. For "the moment one touches a transcendental, one touches being itself, a likeness of God, an absolute, that which ennobles and delights our life; one enters into the domain of the spirit." For we know that we "are really united only by the spirit; light [Radiance!] alone brings [us] together."[34]

[31] Maritain, *Art and Scholasticism*, p. 27.
[32] Ibid., p. 32.
[33] Ibid., pp. 32–33.
[34] Ibid.

The Agent Intellect and the Energies of Intelligence

Donald Haggerty

The technical language of medieval scholasticism can pose a stylistic burden, especially on first encounter. The conceptual apparatus may seem heavy to carry and lacking all suppleness, and suggestive even of a certain inaccessibility. There are times the abstract verbalism dependent on precise definition insinuates almost a note of inflexibility, as though closed to nuance, insulated in its impersonality by the linguistic armor of esoteric terms. Despite the Thomistic insistence that all knowledge has its origin in the simplicity of sense experience, the prevalence of abstract terminology can indeed convey the opposite impression—a disengagement from concrete realities and a preference for complexity.

While discussing the vocabulary and language of St. Thomas Aquinas in his invaluable introduction to the Angelic Doctor's writings, M.-D. Chenu alluded to another issue in this regard—namely, the difficulty in the medieval period of translating Aristotelian conceptual categories into Latin. Simply put, the Greek texts confronted a semantic indigence in Latin philosophical vocabulary. This poverty in language combined, moreover, with the tendency of scholastic philosophical discussion to display in Latin a "disturbing deviation from the concrete to the abstract, with a consequent disappearance of realistic original meanings."[1] A literal appropriation of terms from Aristotle was a natural option; yet this only accentuated the abstractive quality of the work. Chenu specifically invoked the *intellectus agens*, i.e., the agent intellect, as an example of an expression translated in a strictly literal manner from an Aristotelian context, but so tied down

---

[1] M.-D. Chenu, *Toward Understanding Saint Thomas*, trans. A.-M. Landry and D. Hughes (Chicago: Henry Regnery Company, 1964), p. 113.

thereby by the heaviness of an abstractive association that it had "no buoyancy right from the start."[2]

Be that as it may, the insertion of such a concept as the agent intellect into the broader context of contemporary associations invites further reflection on its meaning. Our effort here is to reconsider the agent intellect in order to grant an epistemological value unexamined in any full manner by St. Thomas, but nonetheless consistent with his writings. In particular, Jacques Maritain's grasp of the agent intellect's catalyzing role in creative intuition is worth revisiting not only for the sake of exposing a crucial portion of Maritain's epistemology of artistic intuition as rooted in the spiritual unconscious, but more interestingly perhaps, because his ideas are corroborated in the experience of creative thinkers who have testified to the spontaneous emergence of creative intuitions into consciousness.

With that purpose in mind we will first examine St. Thomas's understanding of the agent intellect both as a preliminary function in conceptual formation and as a principle of light in the intellect, then take up Maritain's extension of St. Thomas's thought, and finally look at one striking account of creative intuition that would seem to provide an empirical confirmation for the theoretical positions of Maritain on the role of the agent intellect in creativity.

ST. THOMAS ON THE AGENT INTELLECT

St. Thomas ascribed an indispensable action to the agent intellect in the initial stage of the knowing process; this can be illustrated most simply and briefly in the case of sense knowledge. In themselves the senses are primarily passive powers acted upon by extramental phenomena. By their natural operation they are open to modification by encounter with external realities. While sensation in itself exhibits this passive aspect of receptivity, human knowledge of a sensible object requires an active power within the soul to make what is extramental become actually intelligible within the mind. There must be an active process in the mind to move from an initially receptive encounter with an external object through the senses to a grasp of that object's intelligibility within the mind.

The immediate result of the senses' passive receptivity to a sensible phenomenon is the production of the phantasm, i.e., an image of that which is encountered through sensation. The role of the agent intellect is to operate as an active spiritual power in the intellect after the phantasm has been formed. The agent intellect acts upon the initially produced phantasm of a

[2] Ibid.

sensible object, "lighting up the phantasm, as it were,"[3] and thereby rendering it intelligible within the mind. This initial act of illumination involves taking hold of a spiritual content by abstracting an immaterial essence from the materiality of a sensible object conveyed in the phantasm.

Such a step is necessary because knowledge of extramental things filtered through the senses requires that they be received by the intellect in a manner suitable to an immaterial spiritual power. And indeed, everything known depends on an intellectual penetration into the immaterial content of things. At this point, however, the process of intellection is still prior to the formation of the concept. Yet without this initial production of a spiritual content culled from sense knowledge, no concept would eventually convey an intelligibility that reflects an exact similitude to extramental being. And it is only by the medium of the concept identified with extramental being that an act of judgment can grasp the existent actuality of an extramental object, allowing the knower to be truly assimilated to the known.

Nonetheless, this association of the agent intellect with a provisional role in the formation of concepts is liable to overlook a more important aspect of the agent intellect as a force of energy within the intellect. Although St. Thomas's treatment of the agent intellect is generally restricted to the rather technical operation just summarized, he also conceived the agent intellect as a primal source of energy within the very structure of intellect, a subsisting principle of light affecting the entire range of the intellect's operations. There are implications in a few allusive descriptions St. Thomas makes that can be a point of departure for further consideration. He thus affirmed as well in the *Summa Theologiae* that the agent intellect is a power which "derives from the supreme intellect"[4] of the divine creator. It is a dynamic principle "flowing from the essence of the soul,"[5] a power "essentially in act."[6] From these references, it is proper to call it an active and activating presence of light within the intellect which participates in the divine light shed by the divine intelligence upon created things.

Such descriptions of the agent intellect as a basic power of illumination within the soul certainly stretches its importance beyond merely an initial phase of activity in the formation of concepts. This larger import was clearly suggested when St. Thomas affirmed the continuing activity of the agent intellect even after death.[7] His position was that even after the sepa-

---

[3] *Summa Theologiae* I, q. 79, a. 4.
[4] *Summa Theologiae* I, q. 79, a. 4, ad 5.
[5] Ibid.
[6] *Commentary on Aristotle's De Anima*, III, 10, 431a17.
[7] Cf. *Quaestio Disputata De Anima*, a. 15, ad 9.

ration of the soul from the body, the agent intellect still functions as an activating impetus within the intellect, a principle of light still actualizing the intellect's potency to the act of knowing. On the other hand, after death and the cessation of bodily activity, the abstractive process dependent on the union of body and soul is no longer operative. If the agent intellect operates as a power only after the senses introduce a phantasm intramentally, the agent intellect would not function after death, inasmuch as there is no body to filter sensations of extramental reality to the mind. Clearly then, the agent intellect is not limited to a merely functional role in the formation of concepts upon contact by the senses with extramental being.

That the agent intellect operates as a power always in act, even after death, makes it akin to a type of preconscious disposition within the intellect. The metaphor of light applied to the agent intellect is therefore a fitting one not only for the agent intellect's early role in the process of forming concepts. Even more fundamental to the metaphor is the notion of a spontaneity of preconscious intelligence at work, amounting to a type of abiding disposition at the ground of the intellectual operations. For it is by a natural and spontaneous cast of light turned on the phantasms culled from sense experience that the agent intellect forges the intelligible content of an extramental thing that was only potentially intelligible prior to sensation. To the extent that the mind's penetration into the spiritual intelligibility of extramental things is piercing and sharp in this initial stage of the knowing process, a greater possibility exists for deeper knowing of extramental being in an eventual act of judgment.

The identification of the agent intellect with an intrinsic principle of light subsisting within the intellect suggests that there is a dynamic tendency in the agent intellect akin to a type of intellectual *habitus*. And this is precisely what St. Thomas argues in his *Commentary on Aristotle's De Anima*, offering a quite subtle analogy while refuting the notion that the agent intellect could be a faculty in itself separate from the intellect, or reified as a separated substance. There he writes: "The agent intellect is to ideas in act in the mind as art is to the ideas it works by."[8] Careful examination of this analogy can lead to the more important understanding of the agent intellect as an intrinsic power of light within the intellect.

The analogy Thomas draws is with art as an intellectual virtue, a *habitus* of the practical intellect which inheres as an abiding disposition of intelligence before it manifests itself in actual works of art. Precisely as a *habitus* of the practical intellect, art is, as it were, an abiding potency for vision.

---

[8] *Commentary on Aristotle's De Anima*, III, 10, 431a18.

Not only is the *habitus* of art the original source for the initially inchoate notion of a work-to-be-made at early moments of inspiration. The *habitus* of art also identifies the person possessed of it with every moment of artistic inspiration. From the original preconscious inspiration to a completed work, the virtue of art functions as a *habitus* of the practical intellect in transmuting inspiration from a preconscious stage of inchoate notions into a concrete object externalized in some artistic medium. Even at a preconscious stage, therefore, the identification of the artist with his original inspiration, however inchoate or unformed it may at first be, is due to the presence of the *habitus* of art in the intelligence.

Thomas continues with the analogy: "Obviously the things on which art impresses such ideas do not themselves produce the art."[9] Thomas makes a play on the word art here. In one sense art refers to the intellectual *habitus* which is the source and continuing animator of inspiration; in the other sense, art refers to the finished artistic product. He is affirming that the ideas the virtue of art works by have no precedence or primacy over the *habitus* itself of art which inheres in the practical intellect of the artist as a disposition.

Thus, in the statement just quoted the term "things" refers to the artistic medium for the artist's imaging. A block of stone, or a canvas, or language itself, receives the external expression of an interior drive toward capturing in a concretized image some inchoate inspiration whose original source is due to the *habitus* of art. But the finished product objectified in an external work of art is the result of an internal *habitus* of intelligence that has animated an ongoing process from some original notion of a work-to-be-made to the completed work. In rejecting the notion that art could be some thing separate from the personhood of the artist, St. Thomas is emphasizing that it is the artist who is the source of the work through a process internal to the artist's very being.

"Hence," writes Thomas in reference now to the agent intellect as a *habitus* analogous to art, "even granted that we were the subjects of ideas made actually intelligible in us, it would not follow that it is we who produce them by means of an agent intellect in ourselves."[10] The suggestion here is that the agent intellect functions in a similiar manner to the *habitus* of art. Like the inspiration that flows from the intellectual *habitus* of art, the agent intellect is an internal animator of intelligent operations from the beginning to the end of the knowing process. This power known as the agent intellect is not to be reified as though it functioned as an independent and

---

[9] *Commentary on Aristotle's De Anima*, III, 10, 430a18.
[10] Ibid.

autonomous faculty in itself which the subject of ideas would then make use of. Rather, the agent intellect inheres as a dispositive quality of the intelligence animating the natural tendency of intelligence to seek intelligibility in extramental being. While the agent intellect is a power intrinsic to the intellect, its existence as a primal energy underlying all intelligent operations resembles a type of *habitus* inhering in the very nature of the intellect.

Some reflections on St. Thomas's link between the agent intellect and the *habitus* of art may be useful for a moment. In light of his analogy between the agent intellect as an intellectual *habitus* and the intellectual *habitus* of art, one can arguably posit a dynamic ordination in the agent intellect similar to the appetitive desire for making things inherent in the artistic *habitus*. The dynamic ordination in this case would involve a constitutive drive toward the illumination of extramental being. As noted earlier, the agent intellect activates the knowing process by dispensing a kind of immediate light on phantasms culled from sense experience. But it does so as a principle of spontaneous light intrinsic to the intellect and "ceaselessly in act." In this manner the agent intellect not only provides a particular intervention necessary for the intellective process to "jump-start," so to speak. The operative illuminating energy of the agent intellect manifests as well a dynamic tendency in the intellect toward the grasp of intelligibility in extramental things. This essential ordination toward the grasp of intelligibility can be conceived as a primary condition for the rational intelligence of the human subject.

MARITAIN'S MORE EXTENSIVE
NOTION OF THE AGENT INTELLECT

Maritain will affirm this understanding of the agent intellect as a pervasive power of active energy underlying human intelligence. In *Creative Intuition in Art and Poetry*, for example, Maritain referred to the agent intellect as "an inner spiritual light which is a participation in the uncreated divine light, but which is in every man, through its pure spirituality ceaselessly in act, the primal quickening source of all intellectual energy."[11] This conception of the agent intellect disposed to act as a primordial energy within the hidden structure of the intellect is consistent with St. Thomas's view of the agent intellect as analogous in operation to a type of intellectual *habitus*. But Maritain adds an original dimension to St. Thomas's treatment

---

[11] Jacques Maritain, *Creative Intuition in Art and Poetry*, The A. W. Mellon Lectures in the Fine Arts (Princeton, New Jersey: Princeton University Press, 1953), p. 71.

by positing a vast substratum of active intelligence in the so-called spiritual unconscious. In Maritain's treatment the abiding energies of the agent intellect can be understood only in tandem with the existence of the spiritual unconscious. Some reflections on Maritain's notion of the spiritual unconscious are therefore of importance inasmuch as Maritain's idea differs from the description of the unconscious commonly assumed in the literature of clinical psychology.

For Maritain, then, the spiritual unconscious is a subliminal locus of preconscious activity marked by purposive movements and an implicit intelligence. In this sense it is clearly distinct from the Freudian unconscious of uncontrolled instincts and irrational drives, of fears and complexes linked to repressed memories. Rather than envisioning the unconscious as chaotic and turbulent in its vitality, Maritain's idea is that there is a primordial capacity of active intelligence within the undercurrents of the spiritual unconscious which shapes consciousness prior to the reflexive grasp of knowledge. By positing the spiritual unconscious as a primal source of intelligent operations beneath consciousness, the very notion of rational intelligence is broadened and stretched, extending now into activity taking place within the enclosed world of the unconscious. As Maritain writes:

> Reason does not only consist of its conscious logical tools and manifestations, nor does the will consist only of its deliberate conscious determinations. Far beneath the sunlit surface thronged with explicit concepts and judgments, words and expressed resolutions or movements of the will, are the sources of knowledge and creativity, of love and supra-sensuous desires, hidden in the primordial translucid night of the intimate vitality of the soul. Thus it is that we must recognize the existence of an unconscious or preconscious which pertains to the spiritual powers of the human soul and to the inner abyss of personal freedom, and of the personal thirst and striving for knowing and seeing, grasping and expressing: a spiritual or musical unconscious which is specifically different from the automatic or deaf unconscious.[12]

More importantly for our own discussion, the spiritual unconscious is a locus of rational tendencies precisely because it is animated by the energies of the agent intellect. Active intelligent operations can be posited below the threshold of consciousness due to the existence of an activating light within the hidden structure of the spiritual unconscious. Inasmuch as the agent intellect triggers the intellect's natural dynamism toward the grasp of intelligibility in things, it reflects a constitutive ordination pervading the intellect even at a preconscious level, "ceaselessly radiating," as Maritain writes,

---

[12] Ibid., p. 69.

"which activates everything in intelligence, and whose light causes all our ideas to arise in us, and whose energy permeates every operation of our mind."[13] As a power rooted in the spiritual unconscious of the intellect, the agent intellect is therefore less a function than the primordial energy behind every tendential movement toward intelligent activity.

The impact of this hidden power of illumination upon the interior dynamisms of the spiritual unconscious persists at all times, but always beneath consciousness. While inhering in the very structure of the intellect as the catalyzing source of all intelligent activity, the agent intellect remains always an energy within the spiritual unconscious and operates within a realm of preconscious activity. This activating spiritual light remains therefore always inaccessible to observation, cut off from a reflexive grasp of consciousness. "This primal source of light cannot be seen by us," writes Maritain, "it remains concealed in the unconscious of the spirit."[14] Nonetheless, despite its hidden presence within the spiritual unconscious, it energizes the intellect's natural dynamism toward all intelligent activity. It is an ever-present impetus for the natural dynamisms of all intelligent operations, inhering in the very structure of the intellect as a "perpetually active intellectual energy."[15]

It should be remarked that such a stress on the hidden activity of the agent intellect in the spiritual unconscious moves us beyond the common conception that knowing is a process which begins only when conceptual formulations commence. On the one hand, Maritain noted that the concept once formed does not necessarily lead to an act of explicit knowledge self-consciously achieved by the intellect. There can be incomplete or half-realized acts of knowing that do not cross the threshold of consciousness even when such an object of thought is potentially realizable. As a consequence, "there can exist," argues Maritain, "unconscious acts of thought and unconscious ideas."[16] On the other hand, some degree of knowing engagement with the intelligible content of extramental being occurs even below the threshold of consciousness. This statement may appear to contain a self-contradiction in description. On the contrary, while it acknowledges an absence of reflexive grasp by the intellect of its own preconscious formulations, it affirms another critical point. The process of knowledge displays concealed aspects of intermediate activity, intelligent in operation, which

[13] Ibid., p. 73.
[14] Ibid.
[15] Ibid., p. 70.
[16] Ibid., p. 72.

do not always lead to an act of conceptual apprehension. Maritain's position on this is quite clear:

> Thus it is that we know (not always, to be sure!) what we are thinking, but we don't know how we are thinking; and that before being formed and expressed in concepts and judgments, intellectual knowledge is at first a beginning of insight, still unformulated, a kind of many-eyed cloud which is born from the impact of the light of the Illuminating Intellect [the agent intellect] on the world of images, and which is but a humble and trembling inchoation, yet invaluable, tending toward an intelligible content to be grasped.[17]

Maritain thus most typically calls the agent intellect "the *activator* of intelligence in all its operations."[18] This raises the question of the agent intellect's role in creative thought. Creative activity amounts to a particular instance of the intellect tending toward a grasp of intelligibility in the encounter with extramental being. Clearly, all creative inspiration assumes at its origin some level of preconceptual activity taking place within the unconscious. And indeed, the creative artist's or thinker's experience of being sparked into sudden moments of recognition at unexpected junctures suggests a definite triggering of intuition whose source lies beneath conscious awareness. Necessarily, then, from what we have proposed thus far, the agent intellect must exercise a key role in such creative moments, inasmuch as the agent intellect is associated with a pervasive energy inhabiting the spiritual unconscious.

If the agent intellect exists in a way consistent with these descriptions, it will exercise itself in creative thought as an active power which lights up with intelligibility some inchoate idea which remains initially preconceptual in mode. According to Maritain, this triggering action in the psyche occurs precisely where the powers of the soul are mutually interpenetrating. What he meant was the necessity of appetitive desire and sense experience accompanying the movement toward creative insight. Creative intuitions have their source in the intelligent preconceptual life of spiritual unconscious, and thus they flow "from the totality of man, sense, imagination, intellect, love, desire, instinct, blood and spirit together."[19] While the spontaneity of creative moments indicates a certain effect of affectivity on preconceptual activity in the depths of the spiritual unconscious, the suddenness of their breaking through into consciousness should not be identified with an absence of all guiding direction at their origin. Rather, the fol-

---

[17] Ibid., p. 73.
[18] Ibid., p. 308, n. 24.
[19] Ibid., p. 80.

lowing statement of Maritain on the vital intelligence present within the spiritual unconscious should be read in light of the agent intellect's purposive energies dynamically orienting the intellect to the grasp of intelligibility in creative moments.

> There is still for the intellect another kind of life, which makes use of other resources and another reserve of vitality, and which is free . . . from the engendering of abstract concepts and ideas, free from the workings of rational knowledge and the disciplines of logical thought. . . . This free life of the intellect is also cognitive and productive, it obeys an inner law of expansion and generosity, which carries it along toward the manifestation of the creativity of the spirit; and it is shaped and quickened by creative intuition.[20]

The essential implication, then, of Maritain's position is that the spiritual unconscious, where the agent intellect stirs and activates the intellectual appetite of the soul, cannot be simply an inert "holding station" in the structure of the intellect. It rather possesses a life of its own which is animated by the energies inherent in the agent intellect. The existence of the agent intellect as an "uninterrupted irradiation"[21] within the spiritual unconscious not only energizes the active thrust of the intellect toward conceptual knowledge. This pervasive force of light tending to the grasp of intelligibility is "the highest point of spiritual tension naturally present within us."[22] While it is impossible to attain a reflexive grasp of the agent intellect's energies, this inaccessibility merely signifies that the illuminative activity ascribable to the agent intellect is preconceptual in mode, rather than without rational direction. Despite its concealment below the threshold of consciousness, the power of illumination intrinsic to the agent intellect is the fundamental directive cause of all intelligent movements within the spiritual unconscious, including that of creative intuition. Maritain writes about poetic creation in such terms:

> Thus, when it comes to poetry, we must admit that in the spiritual unconscious of the intellect, at the single root of the soul's powers, there is, apart from the process which tends to knowledge by means of concepts and abstract ideas, something which is preconceptual or nonconceptual and nevertheless in a state of definite intellectual actuation: not, therefore, a mere way to the concept . . . but another kind of germ, which does not tend toward a concept to be formed, and which is already an intellective form or act fully determined though enveloped in

[20] Ibid., p. 79.
[21] Jacques Maritain, *The Degrees of Knowledge*, trans. Gerald Phelan (New York: Charles Scribner's Sons, 1959), p. 126.
[22] Ibid.

the night of the spiritual unconscious. In other words, such a thing is knowledge in act, but nonconceptual knowledge.[23]

EXPERIENTIAL CONFIRMATION

We move now to an empirical testimony that would seem to support aptly the previous philosophical descriptions. It is our contention that the existence of preconscious intelligent activity triggered by the action of the agent intellect is implicit in the mathematician Henri Poincaré's account analyzing the process of creative discovery in mathematics. He relates that in a number of instances, after a period of strenuous effort and no gain of insight, usually followed by some degree of frustration, an answer to a mathematical problem arrived in a sudden burst of intuitive certainty while engaged in an activity of relaxation far removed from the work that preceded it. This assertion offers a concrete substantiation for the reality of preconscious intelligent activity in the spiritual unconscious. It supports Maritain's position that the spiritual unconscious "does not necessarily mean a purely unconscious activity. It means most often an activity which is principally unconscious, but the point of which emerges into consciousness."[24] The following description by Poincaré emphasizes both the immediacy of the creative inspiration, which flows with apparent ease into awareness, and on the other hand its link to prior conscious work which has thus far proven unavailing:

> Most striking at first is this appearance of sudden illumination, a manifest sign of long, unconscious prior work. The role of this unconscious work in mathematical invention appears to me incontestable, and traces of it would be found in other cases where it is less evident. Often when one works at a hard question, nothing good is accomplished at the first attack. Then one takes a rest, longer or shorter, and sits down anew to the work. During the first half-hour, as before, nothing is found, and then all of a sudden the decisive idea presents itself to the mind. It might be said that the conscious work has been more fruitful because it has been interrupted and the rest has given back to the mind its force and freshness. But it is more probable that this rest has been filled out with unconscious work and that the result of this work has afterward revealed itself.[25]

[23] Maritain, *Creative Intuition in Art and Poetry*, p. 80.
[24] Ibid., p. 67.
[25] Henri Poincaré, "Mathematical Creation," in *The Creative Process*, ed. Brewster Ghiselin (Berkeley: University of California Press, 1952), p. 27. The article is translated by George B. Halsted. The book was re-published by the University of California Press in 1985.

For one thing, then, he affirms that dedicated effort and conscious work is a necessary condition for the emergence of such creative ideas:

> These sudden inspirations never happen except after some days of voluntary effort which has appeared absolutely fruitless and whence nothing good seems to have come, where the way taken seems totally astray. These efforts then have not been as sterile as one thinks; they have set agoing the unconscious machine and without them it would not have moved and would have produced nothing.[26]

Nonetheless, the arrival of the decisive idea is independent of work. Conscious work in and of itself "plays at most the role of excitant as if it were the goad stimulating the results already reached during rest, but remaining unconscious, to assume the conscious form."[27] Finally, he makes mention of a further critical element at work in preconscious activity, the link between affectivity and the particular ideas that eventually cross the threshold of consciousness, as decisive for the realization of one idea rather than of another:

> What is the cause that, among the thousand products of our unconscious activity, some are called to pass the threshold, while others remain below? Is it simple chance which confers this privilege? Evidently not; among all the stimuli of our senses, for example, only the most intense fix our attention, unless it has been drawn to them by other causes. More generally the privileged unconscious phenomena, those susceptible of becoming conscious, are those which, directly or indirectly, affect most profoundly our emotional sensibility.[28]

Poincaré's account would seem to illustrate well Maritain's position that from the depths of the spiritual unconscious emerge insights that had their gestation in a preconceptual life of active intelligence beneath the threshold of consciousness. Maritain's stress on the dynamic presence of the agent intellect within the spiritual unconscious seems more than justified in the light of such a testimony to creative intuition. For a creative gestation in the unconscious as described by Poincaré is understandable in light of the dynamisms implicit in the activity of the agent intellect. Creative intuitions arising out of preconceptual activity require some activating catalyst, of which the natural energy of the agent intellect is a plausible explanation. Insofar, then, as creative intuition has its gestation in the active preconceptual life of the spiritual unconscious, the agent intellect or some capacity akin to it would seem a necessary component in all creative inspiration.

---

[26] Ibid.
[27] Ibid.
[28] Ibid., pp. 28–29.

CONCLUSION

While the term agent intellect may always retain something of an abstract scholastic association, it is to be hoped from these reflections that something of the dynamic implication inherent in discussing energies and orientations within the intellect has enlivened the expression. Whatever choice of terminology is employed, it would seem important to acknowledge an essential ordination to the grasp of intelligibility within the intellectual power. Indeed, much of what has been proposed in regard to the agent intellect is consistent with any observation of basic intellectual desire. For it is experientially evident that the mind has a natural desire to take hold of and assimilate all that confronts it, and even to hurl light on objects with redoubled vigor when some complexity leaves the conscious mind stammering in frustration. Whenever extramental reality confronts the human person, an interior intellectual urge is initiated which will find its completion only in the attainment of insight and clarity. Even prior to a conscious act of knowledge, then, the intellectual life is animated by a natural inclination to reach out spontaneously toward a grasp of intelligibility in things. The identification of the agent intellect as a kind of fulcrum of energy within the intellect offers an explanation for such spontaneous drives to the grasp of intelligibility experienced by the intellectual power.

One parting question that might be asked is the value of an exposition that defies verification. The stress on the hidden dimension of the agent intellect's existence in the spiritual unconscious suggests an obscurity in activity that parallels the abstractive inaccessibility of it as a scholastic term. But the emphasis here has been that the preconscious intelligent movements stirred by the energies of the agent intellect reflect a vital tendency of the intellect toward the grasp of intelligibility. While the agent intellect is not a power capable of being consciously cultivated, one reason for the variation of intelligence among individuals is due to intrinsic differences in such a power residing within the intellect. If it is true that the possibility for discovery of new and richer aspects of reality is linked to the light emitted by the agent intellect, then the most common function of the agent intellect to cast light on phantasms culled from sense experience should encourage us to cultivate precisely what can be a deliberate endeavor—a sensitive engagement with concrete realities experienced through the senses. The interior energies of intellectual life exercise themselves and flourish to the degree extramental reality is engaged in a fuller way.

In sum, we should affirm that the epistemological realism long defended by Thomist thinkers has its salutary justification in the sound development of human faculties. The acknowledgement of the agent intellect as an abiding energy orienting the human intellect to extramental being is not so important for the terminology it presents, as much as for the recognition of a power within human intelligence thrusting the human person in a natural orientation beyond self to what is other than self. If the energy descriptive of the agent intellect leads us to discern this truth more readily, the term itself is a more than useful legacy of scholastic technical language.

Form and Fluidity:
The Aquinian Roots of Maritain's
Doctrine of the Spiritual Preconscious

Matthew Cuddeback

In *Creative Intuition in Art and Poetry* Jacques Maritain roots his notion of poetic intuition in a philosophic doctrine of the human intellect's preconscious life. This life that is found in the highest part of the intellective soul. Here, says Maritain, aesthetic creativity begins in a flash of intuitive insight. In an effort to provide a philosophic foundation for his teaching on the spiritual preconscious, Maritain calls upon two teachings of St. Thomas Aquinas: Aquinas's teaching on the agent intellect, and his teaching that the powers of the soul flow from the soul's essence. It is this teaching on the flow of powers from the soul that particularly interests me in this paper. After a brief account of Maritain's appropriation of these two teachings in *Creative Intuition*, I shall examine Aquinas's teaching on the flow of powers, so as to lay bare the Aquinian roots of Maritain's teaching.

I

At the highest reaches of our intellective life, says Maritain, the illuminating intellect is ceaselessly in act. It does not itself know, but it is the source of our knowing. It is "the primal quickening source of all intellectual activity";[1] its light activates and permeates every operation of the mind.[2] While this illuminating activity of the agent intellect is above the level of awareness, and thus not immediately known to us, it is a legitimate target of philosophic inquiry. If we would grasp the full scope of the do-

---

[1] Jacques Maritain, *Creative Intuition in Art and Poetry* (New York: Pantheon, 1953), p. 97.
[2] Ibid., p. 99.

34

main of intellect, we must look "beneath the sunlit surface thronged with explicit concepts and judgments," to the "primordial translucid night of the intimate vitality of the soul,"[3] to the intellect's living springs.[4]

Maritain next appeals to Aquinas's teaching that the powers of the soul flow from its essence. In this "ontological procession," as Maritain calls it, one power of the soul proceeds from the soul's essence through the mediation of another. There is an order to this procession: the more perfect powers are the efficient and final cause of the powers they beget: from the power of intellect flows the imaginative power, and from the imaginative power flow the sense powers. The ontologically posterior power *serves* the prior power: the senses serve the imagination, and through the imagination, the intellect. Maritain says this teaching of Aquinas shows that there is an "immense dynamism working upwards and downwards along the depths of the soul."[5]

Maritain asserts that it is at the common root of the soul's powers, in the soul's essence—where all of these powers are active in common[6] and are quickened and enveloped by reason[7]—that we find the home of creative intuition. From the common root of the soul's powers there is outflow to the sense powers, and the reflow of the harvests of imagination and sense upward to the depths of the soul, fecundating creative intuition.

Maritain's teaching follows Aquinas's teaching on the flow of powers from the soul in question 77 of the *prima pars*. I shall now examine Aquinas's own teaching. I shall first endeavor to place Aquinas's teaching in its historical context, by summarizing the teachings of several other thirteenth-century thinkers on the relation of the powers of the soul to the soul's essence. This will allow appreciation of the originality of Aquinas's teaching. I shall then examine the teaching of Aquinas himself.

II

Aquinas has two *ex professo* treatments of the question of the order and flow of powers from the soul: one is in *ST* I, q. 77, a. 4–7, which we have already mentioned; the other is found in I *Sent.*, d. 3, q. 4, a. 2–3. In both treatments the question of the flow of powers is forerun by a more fundamental question, namely, whether the soul *is* its own power, or put another way, whether the essence of the soul is identical to its powers. By the time

---

[3] Ibid., pp. 94, 100.
[4] Ibid., p. 91.
[5] Ibid., p. 109.
[6] Ibid., p. 110.
[7] Ibid., p. 99.

Aquinas takes up this question, it has a long history. An important line of that history—perhaps the most important one for the thirteenth-century scholastics—begins with Augustine. In an objection at the very start of the *Summa's* treatment of the identity of soul and power, Aquinas cites Augustine's *De Trinitate*: "Augustine says that memory, intelligence, and will are one life, one mind, one essence."[8] The critical point is that Augustine finds in the union of these powers the image of the union of the three divine Persons.

Centuries later, when in his *Sentences* Peter Lombard discusses the assignation of the image of God in man, Augustine's formula is prominent. The Lombard asks how the three faculties of memory, intelligence, and will can constitute one essence, and yet be distinguished. He concludes the three faculties are *one substance* because they inhere in the soul substantially, not as accidents that can be present or not present.[9] The weighty *auctoritas* of Augustine, and the influence of the Lombard as author of the *Sentences*, assure that any thirteenth-century discussion of the identity of power and essence must reckon with Augustine's formula that this triad of powers is one essence, and thus with the yoking of this question with the question of the *imago Dei* in man. These will profoundly influence the way the question is posed and answered up to and beyond Aquinas.

In the early part of the thirteenth century this Augustinian, Trinitarian psychology confronts—in the newly translated works of Aristotle—an Aristotelian psychology that cooly distinguishes powers without adverting to theological teaching. Finding themselves in the confluence of these two doctrinal streams, the great thinkers of the day join issue on the question of the relation of essence to power. Some oppose Aristotle, while others attempt somehow to graft the teachings of Aristotle and Augustine.

We pick up this story in the 1230s, in the twenty years or so before Aquinas writes his commentary on the *Sentences*. At this time we may discern two basic positions on the relation of the soul to its powers.[10] The first position maintains that the soul and its powers are one identical reality. Perhaps the most stalwart defender of this position, and certainly the most influential, is William of Auvergne, Bishop of Paris beginning in 1228, and

---

[8] *ST* I, q. 77, a. 1, obj. 1.

[9] Peter Lombard, I *Sent.*, d. 3., c. 2 (ed. Quaracchi).

[10] In this division I have followed Odon Lottin, "L'Identité de l'âme et de ses facultés pendant la première moitié du XIIIème siècle," *Revue néoscolastique de philosophie* 36 (1934), pp. 195–204. The same basic division is described in the scholion of the Quaracchi editors at Bonaventure's I *Sent.*, d. 3, p. 2, a. 1, q. 3 (ed. Quaracchi, vol. 1, p. 87).

chancellor of the University of Paris.[11] William holds that the soul is a sub-stance that is absolutely simple and one. It can have no composition what-soever. The soul cannot possess faculties that are essentially distinct from it, for this would destroy its absolute unity. To the extent that we speak of an intellect or will or sense power, we are speaking of various "offices" that the one, selfsame soul performs. *Ego sum quae intelligo*, says William; *I am the one who understands*. It is I who know, I who will and desire. It is I who remain one and undivided through these acts. He translates this expe-rience of the person's unity in acting into the language of substance and ac-cident: if these acts are *mine*, they are the acts of my substance. These acts are not mine if they are the acts of accidents—an imbecility, for every man knows within that it is he who acts.[12] The conclusion to be drawn from this is that memory, intelligence, will, and all other powers are really the soul it-self: *anima humana et una est, et unum est*. Again, to the extent that we speak of different powers we really mean that the one soul has diverse ob-jects of action, not that there is any diversity in the soul itself.

We can see how those who hold this position would find in Augustine's words—that memory, intelligence, and will and one life, one mind, one essence—the affirmation of their position, and of the profound unity of man. They would worry that the application of the term "accident" to the powers of the soul (particularly the triad) makes these powers adventitious or incidental.

The second position—still in the twenty years before Aquinas—is repre-sented by the Franciscans Alexander of Hales, John de la Rochelle, and Odo Rigaldus. These thinkers distinguish three ways in which the powers

---

[11] On the importance of William of Auvergne see Étienne Gilson, *La Philosophie au moyen âge*, 3rd ed. (Paris: Payot, 1947), pp. 414–15; and Fernand van Steen-berghen, *La Philosophie au XIIIe siècle* (Louvain: Publications Universitaires, 1966), pp. 155–56.

[12] "Et quamquam intelligere virtuti intellectivae attribuatur, velleque et deside-rare virtuti desiderativae atque voluntati, ipsa tamen anima una est qua intelligit, vult atque desiderat, et hoc omnis anima humana sentit in semetipsa, cognoscit cer-tissime, atque testificatur, nec possibile est ei ut mentiatur super hoc. Absque enim ulla dubitatione constantissimeque asserit apud semetipsam et in seipsa: Ego sum quae intelligo, quae scio, quae cognosco, quae volo, quae appeto, quae desidero, quae desideria seu volita inquiro et, cum possibile est et licet, acquiro volita, desiderata et appetita. Ego, inquam, una et indivisa manens per omnia haec, alio-quin nec scire, nec intelligere, nec ullo modorum cognoscere cuiuscumque virtutis quid esset, sicut evidenter declaratum est tibi in proxime praecedentibus" (*De anima*, chap. 3, part 10; as cited in Étienne Gilson, "Pourquoi Saint Thomas a cri-tiqué saint Augustin," *Archives d'histoire doctrinale et littéraire du moyen âge* 1 [1926–27], p. 54, n. 1).

might be in the soul: essentially, substantially, or accidentally. They exclude the first, an essential identity of the powers, *pace* William of Auvergne. Only in God are essence and power identical. Like William, however, they exclude an accidental inherence of the powers, showing the same concern that accidental means adventitious. They adopt a middle position: the powers of memory, intelligence, and will are *one substance* with the soul. In this they count themselves faithful followers of Augustine.[13]

Bonaventure's position resembles the position just described, though he makes some noteworthy precisions. Faithful to Augustine, he affirms that the *imago Dei* in man is found in the unity of the three powers in one essence, and that the three powers are *consubstantial* with the soul.[14] In the *Itinerarium*, Bonaventure expresses this unity of powers this way: these three powers are "consubstantial, co-equal, co-aeval, and circumincessive."[15] One can sense in this formulation how much the issue of the *imago Dei* in man forms his thinking about the unity of powers and essence.

When Bonaventure asks whether the three powers are one in essence with the soul, he agrees with his Franciscan forebears: the powers are one with the soul substantially, not essentially (which is too strong) or accidentally (which is too weak). But he introduces this important refinement: the powers "go out" (the verb is *egredior*) immediately from the soul.[16] "They go out and they do not recede, like splendor from light."[17] They go out so as to differ from essence, but not such as to pass into the genus of accident.[18] They are consubstantial with the soul.

The metaphors Bonaventure uses to describe the relation of soul and power are of interest as we prepare to turn to Aquinas. There is the

---

[13] In this paragraph I have relied on Lottin, "L'Identité de l'âme et de ses facultés," pp. 198–204.

[14] Among many places see Bonaventure, *Collationes in Hexaemeron*, II, 27 (ed. Quaracchi, vol. 5).

[15] Bonaventure, *Itinerarium mentis in Deum*, III, 5 (ed. Quaracchi, vol. 5).

[16] "Contingit iterum nominare potentias animae, ut immediate egrediuntur a substantia, ut per haec tria: memoriam, intelligentiam et voluntatem. Et hoc patet, quia omni accidente circumscripto, intellecto quod anima sit substantia spiritualis, hoc ipso quod est sibi praesens et sibi coniuncta, habet potentiam ad memorandum et intelligendum et diligendum se. Unde istae potentiae sunt animae consubstantiales et sunt in eodem genere per reductionem, in quo est anima. Attamen, quoniam egrediuntur ab anima—potentia enim se habet per modum egredientis—non sunt omnino idem per essentiam, nec tamen adeo differunt, ut sint alterius generis, sed sunt in eodem genere per reductionem" (Bonaventure, I *Sent.*, d. 3, p. 2, a. 1, q. 3 [ed. Quaracchi, vol. 1]).

[17] "Exit et non recedit, ut splendor a luce" (ibid.).

[18] "Quia enim egreditur, ideo differt, sed non transit in aliud genus" (ibid.).

metaphor of going out from the soul.[19] This conveys the dynamic unity of essence and power. Second is the metaphor of light: the powers are the soul's splendor, or outshining. In Bonaventure's light metaphysic, light propagates itself without transmutation, and with self-consonance.[20] We shall recall these images when we discuss Aquinas, to whom I now turn.[21]

III

Since Aquinas's discussion of the relation of the soul to its powers in his *Sentences*, book I, distinction 3, is the first place he grapples with the received teaching we have briefly discussed, I shall direct most of my attention there, with occasional reference to Aquinas's mature teaching in *ST* I, q. 77. Straight away in the *Sentences* Aquinas shows his desire to re-ask and re-order. Whereas Bonaventure, in the parallel location in his *Sentences* commentary (book I, distinction 3), first asks whether the *imago Dei* consists in memory, intelligence, and will, to which he responds affirmatively, Aquinas asks whether the mind is the subject of the *imago* (I *Sent.*, d. 3, q. 3, a. 1). Aquinas's answer is an early expression of a teaching that will take fuller shape in *ST* I, q. 93: man is made to the image of God inasmuch as he possesses an intellectual nature.[22] Here in the *Sentences* commentary emphasis is clearly shifted away from the triad of memory, intelligence, and will as the locus of the *imago* in man. Thus, when Aquinas asks soon afterward (I *Sent.*, d. 3, q. 4, a. 2), as does Bonaventure, whether the soul is its powers, he is, unlike Bonaventure, free to proceed without express concern to preserve the literal Augustinian formula when he defines the image of God in man.

[19] Cf. Bonaventure, II *Sent.*, d. 24, p. 1, a. 2, q. 1, ad 8 (ed. Quaracchi, vol. 2): "Prima enim agendi potentia, quae egressum dicitur habere ab ipsa substantia, ad idem genus reducitur. . . ."

[20] "Lux simul est et lucet et illuminat" (II *Sent.*, d. 13, a. 1, q. 2, ad 4); "cum lucis sit ex se ipsa se ipsam multiplicare . . . " (II *Sent.*, d. 13, a. 2, q. 1).

[21] I leave aside a discussion of the position of Albert the Great. According to Lottin, while Albert makes some precisions that approach Aquinas's position, he remains largely in the line of Franciscan thought on this issue; Lottin, "L'Identité de l'âme et de ses facultés," pp. 205–08.

[22] "Et ideo in illis tantum creaturis (i.e. the intellectual) dicitur esse imago Dei quae propter sui nobilitatem ipsum perfectius imitantur et repraesentant; et ideo in angelo et homine tantum dicitur imago divinitatis, et in homine secundum id quod est in ipso nobilius. Alia autem, que plus et minus participant de Dei bonitate, magis accedunt ad rationem imaginis" (Aquinas, I *Sent.*, d. 3, q. 3, a. 1). The stress is on the *imago's* perfection and nobility in being, not on a trinity of powers. Cf. *ST* I, q. 93, a. 1–7. "Sed quantum ad hoc non attenditur per se ratio divinae imaginis in homine, nisi praesupposita prima imitatione, quae est secundum intellectualem naturam . . ." (*ST* I, q. 93, a. 3).

To this question whether the powers of the soul are its essence, Aquinas answers that in God, and in Him alone, are substance and operation the same. In every creature operation is an accident, and therefore the power that is the proximate principle of operation is an accident. This means that *all* the soul's powers, including intellect and will, are in some sense accidents. On this point, then, Aquinas confronts an entire tradition, a small portion of which we surveyed above. He quickly shows, however, that he is not insensible to the concern of his predecessors that accidental might mean adventitious. He shows his sympathy with two critical precisions.

First, he says that the powers of the soul *flow* from the essence of the soul. Since the soul is a substance, he says, no operation goes forth (*egreditur*) from it except through the mediation of a power, and the soul's powers flow from the essence of the soul itself (*potentiae fluunt ab essentia ipsius animae*). That is, in action there is a causal stream that flows from the soul through the power into operation. I suggest that Aquinas's employment of the verb *fluere* shows that he wants us to envision the causality precisely *as a stream*, lest the distinction he has made between soul, power, and action should lead us to sunder the three from each other. The image of fluidity serves to unite what has been distinguished, and combats the tendency to make distinct powers discrete.

Second, he distinguishes proper accidents, which flow from the principles of the species, from common accidents, which flow from the principles of the individual. Intellect, will, and suchlike are proper accidents. These "follow upon" and "originate from" the principles of the species, he says. They are necessarily present wherever the species is.[23]

The way is thereby prepared for the question of the article that immediately follows: whether one power arises (*orior*) from another (I *Sent.*, d. 3, q. 4, a. 3). Aquinas answers: manyness that comes forth from some one thing must come forth according to an order, because from one thing, only

[23] "Similiter dico, quod ab anima, cum sit substantia, nulla operatio egreditur, nisi mediante potentia: nec etiam a potentia perfecta operatio, nisi mediante habitu. Hae autem potentiae fluunt ab essentia ipsius animae, quaedam ut perfectiones partium corporis, quarum operatio efficitur mediante corpore, ut sensus, imaginatio, et huiusmodi; et quaedam ut existentes in ipsa anima, quarum operatio non indiget corpore, quod sunt accidentia: non quod sint communia accidentia, quae non fluunt ex principiis speciei, sed consequuntur principia individui; sed sicut propria accidentia, quae consequuntur speciem, originata ex principiis ipsius: ipsius simul tamen sunt de integritate ipsius animae, inquantum est totum potentiale, habens quamdam perfectionem potentiae, quae conficitur ex diversis viribus" (Aquinas, I *Sent.*, d. 3, q. 4, a. 2. Cf. *ST* I, q. 77, a. 1, ad 5).

a unity can proceed (*ex uno non exit nisi unum*). Therefore, since many powers go out (*egredior*) from the soul, they must have a natural order; and since each flows from the soul, one must flow by the mediation of another.[24]

Notice that Aquinas first says that the powers "go out" (*egredior*), and then adds, they not only go out, but flow out. For Aquinas, I suggest, "flow" completes *egressus* by deepening the notion of the causal communication from soul to power. In the text at hand, Aquinas wants to show that there is an order among the powers precisely because there is a causal flow by which the soul *communicates its unity to the powers*—a unity that shows forth in the order among the powers. There is, then, not just going out, but serial, causal flow.

Elsewhere Aquinas says more about the dynamics of this causal flow. In one place he says: "As the efficacy (*virtus*) of the soul's essence is left (*relinquitur*) in a power, so the efficacy of prior powers is found in subsequent powers, such that in one power the efficacy of many powers can be collected."[25] There is, in other words, a real communication of a *virtus* from soul to power, and from power to power, so that the *virtus* of the prior is deposited or "left" in the posterior power.[26] Aquinas also speaks of a *redun-*

---

[24] "Omnis numerositas quae descendit naturaliter ab aliquo uno oportet quod descendat secundum ordinem, quia ab uno non exit nisi unum; et ideo cum multae potentiae egrediantur ab essentia animae, dicimus quod in potentiis animae est ordo naturalis; et cum omnes fluant ab essentia, una tamen fluit mediante alia" (Aquinas, I *Sent.*, d. 3, q. 4, a. 3).

[25] "Sic enim est in potentiis animae, quod cum omnes ab essentia animae oriantur, quasi proprietates ab essentialibus rei, est tamen quidam ordo huiusmodi originis, ut scilicet origo unius potentiae originem alterius praesupponat, qua mediante quodammodo ab essentia animae procedat: quod ex actibus considerari potest. Actus enim unius potentiae necessario actum alterius praesupponit: sicut actus appetitivae actum apprehensivae: et inde est quod sicut virtus essentiae animae in potentia relinquitur, ita etiam virtus unius potentiae praecedentis relinquitur in subsequenti; et inde est quod aliqua potentia virtutes plurium potentiarum in se colligit . . ." (Aquinas, II *Sent.*, d. 24, q. 1, a. 2). In this article Thomas seeks to correct Bonaventure's teaching that *liberum arbitrium* is a habit resulting from the conjunction, or cooperation, of intellect and will (see Bonaventure, II *Sent.*, d. 25, p. 1, a. 1, q. 4). He strives to correct Bonaventure's notion of cooperation among powers with an ordered flow among powers.

[26] A form's productive causality of its proper accidents is an intimate communication of its whatness or suchness to the accident. The language of flow conveys this. See, for example, *De Veritate*, q. 10, a. 1: "Sed anima humana pertingit ad altissimum gradum inter potentias animae et ex hoc denominatur, unde dicitur intellectiva et quandoque etiam intellectus, et similiter mens in quantum scilicet *ex ipsa nata est effluere talis potentia*, quod est sibi proprium prae aliis animabus (emphasis added). See also the end of the corpus of the same article.

dantia—a kind of reverberation—amongst the soul's powers, of the flow and reflow of communication among them.[27]

In *ST* I, q. 77, a. 6–7, the mature treatment of this causal flow, Aquinas makes it clear that the soul is the *productive cause* of its powers.[28] He says that the flow of the powers from the soul is not a transmutation but a natural *resultatio*, the way color naturally results from light.[29] By *resultatio* Aquinas means to signify something easeful, or for lack of a better word, automatic, so much so that he says the *resultatio* of the properties of the soul from the soul itself is *simul cum anima*.[30]

Let us return to I *Sent.*, d. 3, q. 4, a. 3, on whether one power arises from another. I would argue that since Aquinas has some version of Bonaventure's *Sentences* in front of him as he writes his own commentary,[31] Aquinas's use of Bonaventure's verb *egredior* is deliberate.[32] What Aquinas is seeking to do is to develop what Bonaventure and the other medieval thinkers, to varying degrees, either missed or left underdeveloped, namely, the full meaning and depth of the causality exercised by essence with respect to its proper accidents, in which essence begets the serial flow of these accidents. (Bonaventure's metaphors—going out, splendor—do not bespeak an ordered flow.) For Aquinas this causal flow explains the unity of the soul with its powers, and thus answers William of Auvergne's concern to preserve the unity of man. It also ensures that the powers not be adventitious: the flow of powers from the soul is a necessary *resultatio* that

---

[27] "Ex viribus superioribus fit redundantia in inferiores. . . . Et e converso ex viribus inferioribus fit redundantia in superiores" (*De Veritate*, q. 26, a. 10; cf. *ST* I–II, q. 38, a. 4, ad 3). It seems clear that for Aquinas, the causal flow within form is the condition for the intercommunication *redundantia* signifies. Notice the juxtaposing of *fluere* and *redundantia* in the following passage: "Quamvis potentiae sensitivae, secundum quorumdam opinionem, per suam essentiam non maneant post mortem, manent tamen in sua radice, scilicet in essentia animae, a qua potentiae fluunt: et sic manet peccatum sensualitas in anima, secundum quod peccatum unius potentiae in totum redundat" (Aquinas, I *Sent.*, d. 24, q. 3, a. 2, ad 6).

[28] For an instructive account of the soul's productive causality of its powers, and of the flow of powers from the soul, see Lawrence Dewan, O.P., "St. Thomas and the Integration of Knowledge into Being," *International Philosophical Quarterly* 24 (1984), pp. 383–93.

[29] "Emanatio proprium accidentium a subiecto non est per aliquam transmutationem, sed per aliquam naturalem resultationem, sicut ex uno naturaliter aliud resultat, ut ex luce color" (*ST* I, q. 77, a. 6, ad 3).

[30] "Sicut potentia animae ab essentia fluit, non per transmutationem, sed per naturalem quandam resultationem, et est simul cum anima; ita est etiam de una potentia respectu alterius" (*ST* I, q. 77, a. 7, ad 1).

[31] See Jacques Guy Bougerol, *Introduction à saint Bonaventure* (Paris: J. Vrin, 1988), p. 115.

[32] See notes 16 and 18 above.

is *simul cum anima*. Further, and what is very important, Aquinas pursues a properly metaphysical line of reasoning that is not directly beholden to a theological consideration of the image of God in man. He argues from the way that finite essence gives rise to its proper accidents. At the heart of Aquinas's attempt to redirect the tradition is a metaphysical insight into the nature of form and its proper fluidity.

IV

In concluding, I shall suggest a way in which these reflections on Aquinas's notion of form and fluidity might undergird Maritain's already rich psychology of creative intuition. In chapter 3 of *Creative Intuition* Maritain says that the spiritual unconscious could be called the musical unconscious, "for being one with the root activity of reason, it contains from the start a germ of melody."[33] Thus he speaks of the "music of intelligence." In chapter 8 of *Creative Intuition* Maritain furthers this notion by saying that in the "fluid and moving milieu" of the preconscious, "a kind of music is involved":[34] poetic intuition gives rise to intuitive pulsions—mental waves or vibrations charged with dynamic unity that constitute a musical stir. From this wordless, preconscious music springs artistic creativity.[35]

Aquinas would certainly agree that there is a music of intelligence. I believe, however, that his notion of form and fluidity bids us find music not only in intelligence, but a deepdown music in the very forms of things. When Aquinas uses the words *fluere, ordo, relinquere, resultatio, redundantia* in the manner we have seen, he is bidding us hearken to a music that is the internal life of form—any form. What is the ordered outwelling from essence to power to action but a kind of primeval music? While Maritain rightly speaks of a preconscious music of intelligence, Aquinas would stress, I suggest, that the music of intelligence is not first the music of the power of intellect, but the music of the immaterial essence that gives rise to intellect.[36] This is a music which the power of intellect can harness, and to which it can apply its creativity, though it does not fully grasp its origin.

---

[33] Maritain, *Creative Intuition in Art and Poetry*, p. 99.

[34] Ibid., p. 301.

[35] He cites Raïssa Maritain here: "Ce chant qui sans être encore formulé se compose au fond de l'âme—et qui demande à passer plus tard au dehors, à être chanté, voilà où se reconnaît l'expérience poétique proprement dite, dès l'origine orientée vers l'expression" (*Creative Intuition in Art and Poetry*, p. 301, n. 2).

[36] See Aquinas, *De Spiritualibus Creaturis*, q. 11, ad 12: "Ex hoc contingit quod ab essentia animae aliqua potentia fluat quae non est actus corporis, quia essentia animae excedit corporis proportionem, ut supra dictum est. . . . Ex immaterialitate essentiae sequitur immaterialitas potentiae." Cf. *ST* I, q. 79, a. 4, ad 5.

There is a beauty in Bonaventure's evocation of an egress and outshining of powers from essence, but there is not music. In the fluidity that is *simul cum anima* there is music: the music of form; the music of being. Maritain points to the spiritual preconscious and says, rightly, "there is a kind of music here"; Aquinas points to form and says "there is a kind of music *here*." Aquinas heard that music.

Scholastic Hylomorphism and Western Art: From the Gothic to the Baroque

Christopher M. Cullen, S.J.

The transition from Romanesque to Gothic is one of the significant changes in the history of Western art. It affected architecture, sculpture, and eventually painting. This transition was constituted by a realism and naturalism that transformed Western art and remained a constant element of its development through the many variations in style. One of the principal causes of this profound change is the rise of scholasticism. Erwin Panofsky argued this point with regard to architecture in his well-known book, *Gothic Architecture and Scholasticism*. He hints at the possibility that scholasticism also affected sculpture. Taking up this cue, this paper will argue that scholasticism also transformed Western sculpture and painting by introducing a new conception of man. This new conception of the human being can be seen in the way painting and sculpture portray the human body and use it to communicate spiritual truths.

The medieval scholastics appropriated two Aristotelian doctrines: (1) that form is immanent in sensible matter such that it enters into actual composition with matter, and (2) that the rational soul is the substantial form of the body. Man is thus a unified being, and this unity is so profound that one must speak of man as an embodied soul or a spiritualized body. It is this scholastic hylomorphism as a metaphysical position that makes possible a dramatic turn to naturalism and realism in Western art in general from the Gothic to the Baroque and Rococo.[1]

---

[1] Panofsky also sees scholasticism's influence ending in the fourteenth century. See Erwin Panofsky, *Gothic Architecture and Scholasticism* (1951; rpt. New York: The World Publishing Company, 1957), pp. 10ff. He speaks of scholasticism's

These two doctrines enter Western culture at the time of the Gothic cathedrals and reach the apex of their influence in the Baroque, when the body becomes the expression of the inner spiritual life in all its drama and eternal import. The dynamism and fluidity of the Baroque is the classic and clearest expression of the doctrine that the soul gives life to the body, and concomitantly, that the rational soul confers certain faculties that make man a spiritual being. This scholastic understanding of man is reflected in the Baroque fascination with the psychological or spiritual life. Baroque art is thus the culmination of scholastic hylomorphism.

While taking account of the differences within the scholastic tradition, this study will first outline the basic theses of scholastic hylomorphism. Then, it will examine certain artistic examples that manifest the influence of these doctrines and its expression in Gothic and Baroque art.

THE CAUSE: ARISTOTELIAN UNITIVE FORM AND HYLOMORPHISM

Anton Pegis has brilliantly chronicled in detail the development of the scholastic doctrine of the soul in the thirteenth century in his work, *St. Thomas and the Problem of the Soul in the Thirteenth Century*. But let me recall a basic outline of this position. First, the soul is the form of the living being. In the Aristotelian-Scholastic conception this means that the soul is both the principle of life and the principle of organization. The soul is what makes the thing to live and to carry out its other functions. It is also what confers that order that is so vital to the living organism.

Secondly, the soul forms a profound unity with the matter. It orders the matter and so makes it into an organic whole. It is important to understand that the soul's enlivening of the matter transforms the material cause. Soul as form is both dynamic and unitive. Thus, in the Aristotelian conception, the soul is neither a ghost in a machine nor one thing glued to another nor one thing juxtaposed with another. Rather, the animate being is a composite whole.

On a spectrum of theories about the soul, the Aristotelian position is a middle position. It is the mean between a reified understanding of the soul in which the soul is a substance in its own right—a position that renders the union of body and soul inexplicable and extrinsic, and a non-substantialist

---

decline and decadence at some length. While he is basically correct, this paper is addressing a fundamental thesis of scholasticism, namely hylomorphism, that remains a key thesis throughout the whole scholastic tradition, even though various scholastics disagree about the fine points of this hylomorphism.

view—a position that regards the soul as an epiphenomenon. Hence, in this doctrine the soul is not a substance in the sense of a separate thing or a certain stuff. In other words, in the Aristotelian view the soul is neither a property or attribute of the thing nor a thing or substance in the sense of a being complete in its own genus and species.[2] The soul, however, *is* a substance in the sense that it is a form and has an activity that transcends matter. This is a brief sketch of the underlying scholastic doctrine. It is the common scholastic doctrine that makes the artistic developments in question possible.

There are well-known areas of dispute within this Aristotelian-Scholastic doctrine. There are two major disputes that I should mention but from which I wish to prescind, since they do not affect my thesis: (1) the number of substantial forms within a composite and (2) the demonstrability of the immortality of the soul. (There are also different understandings of matter itself within the scholastic tradition. This conception of "matter" is closely connected with the number of substantial forms in a composite whole.)

The most important disputed issue is whether the rational soul is the unique substantial form of the body (the Thomistic position) or whether it is one substantial form among others (the Franciscan position). The Thomistic position argues that the unity of the substance requires a unicity of substantial form. It is by his one rational soul that Socrates is a substance and all that this entails for him, i.e., his corporeality, animality, and rationality. For the Franciscan tradition, the unity of the substance is found in the hierarchical ordering of a plurality of the substantial forms (corporeity, animality) under the one form that makes it to be a particular species, in the case of man, the rational soul. In the Franciscan view, as Anton Pegis puts it, "[T]he presence of these forms does not oppose the unity of the individual because such a unity is derived, not from the substantial form, but from the completing individual form."[3] Furthermore, the two traditions understand the metaphysical principle of matter differently. One relies primarily on Aristotle; the other upon Neoplatonic conceptions.

Bonaventure maintains, for example, that the rational soul is the form of the body, but that the soul is already a composite of form and matter. Hence, Bonaventure argues that the soul is closer to being a substance in its own right than would Thomas after him. Without going into details, let it suffice to say that the Franciscan and Augustinian position rests on the con-

---

[2] This is not to deny that some commentators have argued that Aristotle conceived the soul as an attribute, such as the well-known scholar, Jonathan Barnes.

[3] Anton Pegis, *St. Thomas and the Problem of the Soul in the Thirteenth Century* (Toronto: Pontifical Institute of Medieval Studies, 1978), p. 55.

viction that a created being must have a material principle within it in order that it may be capable of receiving forms. Matter is the universal principle of receptivity as well as of change.[4] And, of course, if this is the case, then it follows that there must be a plurality of substantial forms perfecting matter in different ways.[5]

A second major issue of dispute is the immortality of the soul. In the thirteenth century, the immortality of the soul becomes a vital issue after the Averroists deny that the soul is immortal with their monopsychism and after Scotus denies that the immortality of the soul could be demonstrated. The issue resurfaces again in the sixteenth century after Pomponazzi denies that the individual soul is immortal while also affirming the immortality of the general agent intellect. The second issue is closely bound up with the status of the agent intellect. Nevertheless, we can consider the more general and underlying unity of scholastic doctrine found in its doctrines of immanent form and hylomorphism.

ARTISTIC CHANGES

Gothic Sculpture

I want to look at three moments in the history of art in these centuries in order to illustrate the change that I am talking about. Two are from the early period of scholasticism when it was just beginning to make its influence felt, and one is from the height of scholasticism when it had become an integral part of Catholic thought.

The first of these moments is found at Chartres Cathedral. It is usual to turn to Chartres to study the transition from Romanesque to Gothic sculpture, because the only place where the transition began earlier, namely the Abbey of Saint Denis, is mostly lost to us, since its sculpture was heavily damaged by the French Revolution.[6]

There is a significant shift that takes place from the austerity of Cistercian art and the stylization, angularity, even rigidity, of Romanesque art to the Gothic. This is due to various factors, not the least of which is the twelfth-century Renaissance and the revival of humanism in various European centers. The very beginnings of this change in sculpture can be found

---

[4] Étienne Gilson, *The Philosophy of Saint Bonaventure* (New York: St. Anthony Guild Press, 1965), p. 287. Gilson points to the Boethian roots of this attitude.

[5] Boethius, "Forma vero quae est sine materia non poterit esse subjectum," quoted in Gilson, *The Philosophy of Saint Bonaventure*, p. 288.

[6] Charles M. Radding and William W. Clark, *Medieval Architecture, Medieval Learning: Builders and Masters in the Age of Romanesque and Gothic* (New Haven, Connecticut: Yale University Press, 1992), p. 109.

in the west façade, or Royal Portal (1145–1170) at Chartres Cathedral. Erwin Panofsky made this point in passing in *Gothic Architecture and Scholasticism*:

> It has justly been remarked that the gentle animation that distinguishes the early Gothic figures in the west façade of Chartres from their Romanesque predecessors reflects the renewal of an interest in psychology which had been dormant for several centuries; but this psychology was still based upon the Biblical—and Augustinian—dichotomy between the "breath of life" and the "dust of the ground."[7]

Sir Kenneth Clark also alludes to this change in his well-known work, *Civilization*, when speaking of the statues of kings and queens there: "Do not the kings and queens of Chartres show a new stage in the ascent of Western man? Indeed I believe that the refinement, the look of selfless detachment and the spirituality of these heads is something entirely new in art. Beside them the gods and heroes of ancient Greece look arrogant, soulless and even slightly brutal."[8]

But the change becomes even more pronounced as one moves from the sculpture of the west façade to the statues done just a generation later on the north and south porticoes. The statues of the north and south transepts become more natural and realistic. These statues seem to come alive. It is here that one can see even more clearly manifested the different understanding of human nature—an understanding that the Royal Portal only showed the first glimmerings of. William Fleming discusses the north and south porticoes in his work on the relation between art and ideas:

> The figures on both the north and south porches, in comparison with the earlier ones on the west façade, have bodies more naturally proportioned; their postures show greater variety and informality, and their facial expressions have far more mobility . . . and in comparison with the impersonality of those on the west front, many of the human figures are so individualized that they seem like portraits of living persons.[9]

Erwin Panofsky, although speaking of the High Gothic at Reims and Amiens, attributes this increasing lifelikeness to Aristotelianism, which saw the soul as the "organizing and unifying principle of the body rather than a substance independent thereof." Indeed, he says this quality proclaims the victory of Aristotelianism: "The infinitely more lifelike—though not, as yet

---

[7] Panofsky, *Gothic Architecture and Scholasticism*, p. 6.
[8] Kenneth Clark, *Civilization* (New York: Harper & Row, 1969), p. 56.
[9] William Fleming, *Art and Ideas*, 7th ed. (New York: Holt, Rinehart, and Winston, 1986), p. 157.

portraitlike—High Gothic statues of Reims and Amiens, Strasbourg and Naumburg and the natural—though not as yet, naturalistic—fauna and flora of High Gothic ornament proclaim the victory of Aristotelianism."[10]

The art historian, Adolf Katzenellenbogen, wrote an excellent work on the sculptural program at Chartres Cathedral. In it he provides a detailed and penetrating analysis of these porticoes. But what is of importance to this paper is that he identifies the philosophical source of this artistic change. He explicates this source in more detail than Panofsky. A new understanding of the human being changed the way the sculptures were executed, he says. He compares the differences between the sculpture of the Royal Portal, west façade, at Chartres and that of the north and south portals (1194–1264). As he explains, "Gone is the columnar shape, the architectural elongation, the harmonious unity of pure line and volume. The statues have gained bulk. Their proportions are less drawn out. Drapery folds are no longer bound as a dense linear pattern to bodily forms. . . . The human dignity of the figures is stressed by more natural shapes."[11] He characterizes the various differences as the "humanization" of the sculptures. He explicitly ties this "humanization" to the influence of Aristotelianism at the University of Paris. "Here [the University of Paris] the Aristotelian concepts—that universal ideas have reality within visible forms, that the soul is the form of the body—had taken firm roots. The ascendancy of these concepts may well be reflected in the sculptures of the transept wings at Chartres."[12]

Painting and Giotto

This new philosophical position took somewhat longer to work its way into painting. Nevertheless, one can see the influence of scholastic hylomorphism in the fresco paintings of the early Renaissance master, Giotto. Nearly all art historians recognize the extraordinary difference between Giotto's painting, with its realistic portrayals of the human being, and what went before. It is striking. Giotto moved away from the two-dimensional paintings in which the figures are set against a background of solid gold to amazingly naturalistic paintings in which human beings come alive in a three-dimensional world literally filled with drama and narrative. The art historian, Cesare Gnudi, describes this phenomenon in Giotto's work:

> In Giotto's art, reality was not constricted but was intensified by that metaphysical order in which the soul's impulses were represented *sub*

[10] Panofsky, *Gothic Architecture and Scholasticism*, pp. 6–7.
[11] Adolf Katzenellenbogen, *The Sculptural Programs of Chartres Cathedral* (New York: W. W. Norton & Company, 1959), p. 92.
[12] Ibid., p. 99.

specie aeternitatis. The inner reality of the passions and spirit generated new forms, created their architecture, and determined their spatial
articulation. . . . It is a powerful pictorial architecture that places each
individual manifestation of life within a context of related motifs, it
embodies the capacity to distinguish and individuate different human
situations, states of soul, and feelings.[13]

One can see this in Giotto's well-known masterpiece, the Arena Chapel in
Padua, especially, for example, in his *Pietà* or *Lamentation* (1305–06) over
the dead Christ.

There were many factors that influenced Giotto and that gave rise to the
changes in his style. Without minimizing the role of these influences, it is
important to recognize the philosophical source that makes the changes
possible. It is found in a different understanding of the human being and of
the relation between soul and body. In scholasticism's doctrine the body exists in such a unity with the soul that the body can express the highest aspirations and deepest religious beliefs of the soul.

Giotto's connection with this Aristotelianism is difficult to establish. But
I think it can be found in that he turned to sculpture as a model for his
painting. Sculpture was ahead of painting in his time, and so, he looked to
the best sculpture of his day for the model of the human form in his paintings—he looked to Nicola Pisano (c.1210/1220–c.1278/1284).

Nicola is generally regarded as the most important thirteenth-century
sculptor, along with his son Giovanni (c. 1245–1304). He introduced a new
classicism and thus a new realism into sculpture. Now what is significant
for this thesis is that Nicola was trained at the court of Frederick II, the
Holy Roman Emperor. The court of Frederick II in Palermo was a center of
Aristotelianism; indeed, remember that it was at the University of Naples,
which Frederick II founded in 1224 to train men for imperial service, that
Aquinas himself was first exposed to Aristotle by Peter of Ireland, who was
"part of an Aristotelian movement generally associated with the court of
Frederick II."[14] Torrell says in his biography of Aquinas, "Aristotelian sci-
ence, Arabic astronomy, and Greek medicine all were flourishing in
Palermo, Salerno, and Naples."[15] It was in Naples, for example, that

[13] Cesare Gnudi, "Giotto," in *Encyclopedia of World Art* (New York: McGraw-
Hill, 1968), vol. 6, p. 346.

[14] Thomas F. O'Meara, O.P., *Thomas Aquinas: Theologian* (Notre Dame, Indiana: University of Notre Dame, 1997), p. 4.

[15] Jean-Pierre Torrell, O.P., *Saint Thomas Aquinas*, trans. Robert Royal (Washington, D.C.: The Catholic University of America Press, 1993), vol. 1, p. 6. Torrell
points out that Thomas studied Aristotle's metaphysics and natural philosophy at
Naples, at a time when they were still officially forbidden at Paris (ibid., p. 7).

Michael Scot, who entered the emperor's service in 1220, was busy making translations of parts of Aristotle, as well as Arabic and Greek sources. Nicola was, in part, influenced by this Aristotelianism at the court of Frederick II.

Nicola may have also been influenced by the architectural sculpture of Northern cathedrals after he perhaps traveled to some of these centers of Gothic architecture.[16] For example, there is evidence of the influence of French iconography in his famous octagonal pulpit in the cathedral at Siena. Of course, he also looked to antique sarcophagi and the Tuscan pulpit tradition for models for his work.[17]

Another model for Giotto's painting may be Arnolfo di Cambio.[18] Arnolfo was trained by Nicola Pisano. He then worked in Tuscany, where Giotto could have visited his works. It is Giotto who is usually considered the first of the Renaissance painters.

The Aristotelian-Scholastic metaphysical doctrine, when combined with the Renaissance's return to classicism, made it possible for sculpture and painting to reach new heights. Much is usually made of the influence of classical humanism on the Renaissance artists. But this influence must be balanced with a recognition that both the artists and the patrons were believing Catholics, who were influenced by the more profound penetration into the nature of the human soul that is found in scholastic psychology. Classical naturalism is no doubt an important influence, but perhaps, it is not the whole story. After all, the examples of naturalism from classical antiquity had been around quite some time without being imitated, especially in areas where there were extensive Roman ruins, such as the Italian peninsula. One could list countless examples from this period that indicate the increased naturalism.

By way of contrast, consider the artistic path of Eastern Christianity,

[16] What is important first of all is that he [Frederick II] loved science. . . . A science which came from Aristotle, but also from other books, translated from Greek and Arabic at the emperor's expense. . . . At all events it was in the circles of Frederick II that a natural science distinct from divine science developed for the first time in the Christian world" (Georges Duby, *The Age of the Cathedrals: Art and Society 980–1420*, trans. Eleanor Levieux and Barbara Thompson [Chicago: The University of Chicago Press, 1981], pp. 179–80).

[17] M. M. Schaefer, "Pisano, Nicola and Giovanni," *New Catholic Encyclopedia*, vol. 11 (New York: McGraw-Hill Book Company, 1967).

[18] "Giotto," *New Catholic Encyclopedia*. "Giotto's most intimate source may be in the work of the less prominent Arnolfo di Cambio who was active in Florence in Giotto's youth and whose style reveals a greater emphasis on simple mass" (Creighton E. Gilbert, "Giotto," *The Dictionary of Art* [New York: Macmillan, 1996], vol. 12, p. 694).

which never moved away from the immovable and two-dimensional character of the icon. This development no doubt reflects various factors. It no doubt reflects a Neoplatonism, which regards the image as a window into reality. The icon is a sort of half-way house or a compromise between the realism embraced by the West and the abstract art that characterizes those religions that do not permit portrayals of the human being.[19]

In the period between the Gothic style and the Baroque, it is important to keep two points in mind. First, scholasticism continued to be influential even after other theological and philosophical developments occurred. One must remember that Renaissance Neoplatonism, for example, existed alongside scholasticism and that the Renaissance debates in psychology took place within a fundamentally Aristotelian framework. The basic scholastic position of immanent form and hylomorphism formed the general field for disputes in subsequent centuries.[20] Even the Renaissance, from the Trecento through the Cinquecento, remains within the framework of Aristotelian psychology. What one usually studies in intellectual history are the latest developments; but one can easily forget the continued parallel existence and developments in an older system. In the centuries after the thirteenth, scholastic hylomorphism continued to be influential; indeed, the debates within anthropology transpired within a fundamentally Aristotelian position.

Furthermore, certain ecclesiastical councils, while not making the scholastic position an official church teaching, did defend it from certain misinterpretations or from certain theological heresies. As is usually the

---

[19] Thanks to conversations with Fr. Brian Van Hove, S.J.

[20] In particular see "The Organic Soul," in *The Cambridge History of Renaissance Philosophy*, ed. Charles B. Schmitt (Cambridge: Cambridge University Press, 1988). William Wallace points to the continuity of the Aristotelian tradition from the thirteenth through the seventeenth centuries: "At one time it was fashionable to propose a sharp dichotomy between the philosophy of the Middle Ages and that of the Renaissance, as though their subjects of interest and methods of investigation were markedly different. . . . The development of thought in this area [natural philosophy] from the onset of the thirteenth century to the mid-seventeenth may be likened more to a continuum than to a series of discrete jumps. Beginning with Albertus Magnus at Paris and with Robert Grosseteste and Roger Bacon at Oxford, and continuing to the textbook syntheses of four centuries later, natural philosophy was concerned with much the same questions and yielded answers that were intelligible within a fairly constant framework. By and large the setting was that provided by Aristotle's *libri naturales*, i.e., the *Physics, De caelo, De generatione et corruptione, Meteriology, De anima, Parva naturalia*, and so on, with accretions from other sources" (William Wallace, "Traditional Natural Philosophy," in *The Cambridge History of Renaissance Philosophy*, p. 202).

case, these councils helped to draw the boundaries for positions harmonious with official church doctrine, even if they did not actually define any one position. For example, the General Council of Vienne in 1311–12 condemned an understanding of scholastic hylomorphism not in harmony with official church teaching.[21] The Fifth Lateran Council in 1512–17 denounced Pomponazzi who held to an Averroistic monopsychism.[22] It defended reason's ability to know the immortality of the soul. It was the Council of Trent that was a major impetus for Baroque art and most important for the purposes of this paper. In its twenty-fifty session, the Council issued a decree defending the use of images in the Catholic faith. The Council argued that the honor showed to them is referred to the original which they represent.[23] The Catholic Church, without actually making any theory of the soul an official doctrine of the soul, did condemn views that would be destructive of the scholastic position.

The Baroque

The Baroque vividly gives expression to the scholastic understanding of man.[24] There are countless examples that one could choose from the

---

[21] The position "that the rational or intellective soul is not the form of the human body in itself and essentially" ("quod anima rationalis seu intellectiva non sit forma corporis humani per se et essentialiter" Denzinger, 481, cf. 738, 1655). The decision was directed against the Franciscan theologian Peter John Olivi who taught that the rational soul was not of itself, immediately the essential form of the body, but only mediately through the sensitive and vegetative form, which is really distinct from it. The decision of the Council was not a dogmatic recognition of the Thomistic teaching on the uniqueness of the substantial form nor of Aristotelian-Scholastic hylomorphism, but it was a council that encouraged hylomorphism.

[22] They held that the rational soul in all men is numerically one unique principle. Obviously, this eliminates the possibility of conceiving of a true unity for the individual human being. Denzinger, 1440.

[23] Denzinger, 1823. This is not to deny that the Council did attempt to restrain the sensuality expressed in some Renaissance art (1825).

[24] "The baroque style originated in Rome between the pontificate of Sixtus V (1585–90) and Paul V (1605–21). . . . The Carracci brought an end to the scrappiness, the insubstantiality and the compositional vagueness which typify the art of their immediate predecessors; all the painters of the seventeenth century learned from them how to organize the figures in a picture according to one unifying principle based on a single action. The Carracci brought the painter back to a rational study of the masters, but also to a study of nature and principally of the human body; they restored its robustness, and did not hesitate to seek models among the common people. In his frescoes on the roof of the Gallery of Hercules in the Palazzo Farnese, Annibale Carracci recaptures the sense of monumental composition achieved by Michelangelo in the Sistine Chapel; he uses the same methods, drawing his rhythm from the power of the human body, usually nude" (Germain Bazin, *The Baroque: Principles, Styles, Modes, Themes* [New York: W. W. Norton, 1978], p. 103).

Baroque to illustrate the scholastic conception, but perhaps, none better than the artist that dominated the late sixteenth and early seventeenth century, Gian Lorenzo Bernini (1598–1680). He worked under the patronage of seven popes; indeed, he served the papal curia for more than half a century. It was Pope Urban VIII (1623–44) who gave him numerous commissions and made him chief architect of St. Peter's in 1627. More than any other man, he is responsible for the way St. Peter's looks today—he was its foremost architect and sculptor. He was a true genius and is often regarded as the greatest sculptor of the seventeenth century. Bernini was a devout Catholic.

One of his contemporaries said of him that "he wanted his spirit to issue forth to give life to the stone."[25] Or as one modern art historian has put it, "Stone was now completely emancipated from stoniness by open form and by an astonishing illusion of flesh, hair, cloth, and other textures, pictorial effects that had earlier been attempted only by painting."[26]

He is responsible for such classic examples of the Baroque, as his *Apollo and Daphne*. One art historian writes of this work, which is in the Borghese Gallery in Rome:

> In these Borghese marbles Bernini responded to and competed with the new naturalism of contemporary painting as seen in the work of Annibale Carracci and Caravaggio. He felt that one of his greatest achievements was to have made marble appear as malleable as wax and so in a certain sense to have combined painting and sculpture into a new medium, one in which the sculptor handles marble as freely as a painter handles oils or fresco.[27]
>
> Or his *St. Teresa in Ecstasy* in Santa Maria della Vittoria in Rome.[28]

These works exemplify the scholastic understanding of the unity of man. In his statues the body becomes a vehicle for expressing the human soul. Bernini gives expression in stone to the scholastic, and specifically, Thomistic view that the body exists for the sake of the soul and not vice

[25] Quoted in Rudolf Preimesberger and Michael P. Mezzatesta, "Bernini," *The Dictionary of Art*, vol. 3, p. 838.

[26] *Encyclopedia Britannica*, s.v., "Sculpture, The History of Western Art," vol. 27, p. 100.

[27] Preimesberger and Mezzatesta, "Bernini," *The Dictionary of World Art*, vol. 3, pp. 828–31.

[28] "*St. Teresa in Ecstasy* is at once Bernini's undoubted masterpiece and the work that most completely captures the Counter-Reformation baroque spirit" (William Fleming, *Art and Ideas*, p. 284). Bernini's work perfectly captures the notion of the soul discussed in this paper. Even the recumbent body seems to come alive, as one can see in his *Blessed Ludovica Albertoni*. Other examples from his work include the *Cathedra Petri* in St. Peter's.

versa. Consider for a moment a work from the last years of his life, *The Blessed Ludovica Albertoni* (1674). In this amazing sculpture Bernini portrays the dying agony of Blessed Ludovica; but this is a woman joyfully anticipating eternal life. The body gives expression to this hope. The dying woman is incredibly alive.

The reason that the Baroque seems to move beyond a general scholastic view of the soul to a specifically Thomist one is that the art of this movement gives expression to the view that complete human nature is not found in the soul alone and to the concomitant view that the soul is naturally joined to the body. Anton Pegis explains well the Thomistic insight:

> To consider the soul as the complete nature of man or to hold that it is composed of matter and form is really to leave unexplained the union of soul and body. In other words, if the completeness of human nature cannot be found in the soul alone, and if to explain human nature as implying both body and soul becomes impossible when the soul is considered to be complete even by those who defined the unity of soul and body, the solution must lie in viewing the soul as joined naturally to the body, as part to part for the completion of the nature of man. The intellectual soul must become the form of the body in one act of existence from which will be derived all the operations of life, from the lowest to the highest.[29]

Another important link between the Baroque and scholasticism may be the latter's detailed analysis of the faculties, or powers, of the soul. One of the leading historians of the Baroque considers a deep interest in psychology to be one of the Baroque's essential elements.[30] This too may have its source in scholasticism's facultative psychology. But this takes us too far afield from the argument being pursued here. It is also important to keep in mind the close proximity in time between the development of the Baroque and the revival of Thomism, which began in the late fifteenth century and continued through the seventeenth. (This revival is often referred to as a "second Thomism.")

One could cite countless other examples from the Baroque to illustrate this new conception of the human being. Consider Andrea Pozzo's *St. Ignatius in Glory* in the nave ceiling at Sant' Ignazio's in Rome. Or one could look north of the Alps in Zimmerman's famous *Die Wieskirche* or any of

---

[29] Pegis, *St. Thomas and the Problem of the Soul in the Thirteenth Century*, pp. 184–85.

[30] John Rupert Martin, "The Baroque," in *Readings in Art History*, ed. Harold Spencer, vol. 2 (New York: Charles Scribner's Sons, 1976). However, Martin attributes this to the growing scientific spirit of the time. I think it more likely that the sources are in the facultative psychology of scholasticism.

the countless Baroque-Rococo churches of German-speaking central Europe, such as the abbey of Ottobeuren, just to mention one of the larger and more famous examples.

Western art took a dramatic turn to realism and naturalism in the High Middle Ages. Hylomorphism is the underlying philosophical position that makes possible the dramatic change and explosive development of the art of this period. As a result of the appropriation of this Aristotelian doctrine, scholasticism developed a different view of the human being. The human being is not a soul using a body but is an embodied spirit. The body is thus spiritualized; the corporeal gives expression to the spirit. The rediscovery of Aristotle led to a profound transformation in philosophy and theology. It did no less in art.

On the Ontological Priority of Ends
And Its Relevance to the Narrative Arts

Francis Slade

Against the assimilation of *end* to *purpose* I underline the distinction between ends and purposes and the ontological priority of ends. In other words, and contrary to Heidegger, I argue that *actuality stands higher than possibility*. In what can be considered to be the fundamental sentence of *Sein und Zeit* Heidegger asserts that "possibility stands higher than actuality,"[1] which means that there are no ends, there are only purposes, or as Heidegger calls them, "projects" (*Entwurf*). This is why ethics disappears from the account of human existence in *Sein und Zeit* to be replaced by authenticity[2] (*Eigentlichkeit*) and resoluteness[3] (*Entschlossenheit*). I also point to the distinction between *end* and *consequence*. I conclude with the claim that the distinctions among *end*, *purpose*, and *consequence* make possible the narrative arts or what Aristotle called "poetry."

I

End as a translation of *telos* means what a thing will be that has become fully determined in its being, the defined, the complete, a condition of perfection, completion, fulfillment. End, as *telos*, signifies a continuing state of perfectedness; it is akin to the meaning of *finish* where we are speaking about what a cabinet maker does last in making a piece of furniture: when

---

[1] "Höher als die Wirklichkeit steht die Möglichkeit" (Martin Heidegger, *Sein und Zeit* [Tübingen: Max Niemeyer Verlag, 1967], p. 38).

[2] Heidegger, *Sein und Zeit*, pp. 42–43.

[3] Ibid., p. 297: "In resoluteness the most primordial truth of Dasein has been reached because it is *authentic*." P. 298: "[R]esoluteness as authentic disclosedness is, after all, nothing other than *authentically being-in-the-world*."

he puts the finish on it the piece is brought to completion in perfection; it is displayed as a completed whole. End means the completion, perfection, fulfillment of a thing as the kind of thing it is. End means "fullness of being."[4] It is in this sense of "completed whole" that *end-telos* means "termination."[5] "Ripeness is all."[6]

It is said that *end-telos* also means "purpose," but although the words are commonly used as synonyms, *telos* does not mean purpose. A perusal of the entry under *telos* in the *Liddel-Scott Greek Lexicon* is instructive in this regard. Purposes characterize agents and actors as they determine themselves to action. *Purposes* are motives, "motors" propelling actions of various sorts. The words *motive and purpose* are words that denote something possessing an exclusively "mental existence," whose being is in consciousness. *Ends*, on the other hand, are characteristic of all kinds of things. Aristotle is at some pains to indicate that doing what they do for the sake of an end is not exclusively characteristic of beings that do things "on purpose." In *Physics* II he says: "It is absurd to suppose that nothing comes into being for an end if we do not see the moving cause deliberating."[7] In constructing the honeycomb and gathering the nectar the bee is not the executor of a purpose. Things that exist by nature and which act neither by art nor after deliberation or inquiry, i.e. "on purpose," nevertheless do what they do for the sake of an end.[8] It is the assimilation of end to purpose that obscures our view of this. Ends are not executed by agents. Purposes require agents. Purposes belong to agents as they determine themselves to actions. "Man" has an end; individual men have intentions and purposes in executing their actions.

The end of the art of medicine, a body of knowledge and skills, is the restoration and maintenance of the condition called health. A man's purposes in practicing medicine can be various, from the making of money to the relief of suffering humanity out of a love of mankind, just as long as the purpose is congruent with the end for which medicine exists. The art of medicine does not exist in order to provide the people who practice it with

---

[4] Thomas Aquinas, *Summa Theologiae* I–II, q. 18, a. 1–2.

[5] "Where a series has a completion all the preceding steps are for the sake of that" (Aristotle, *Physics* II.8.199a8–9). And *Physics* II.2.194a32–33: "Not every stage that is last claims to be an *end-telos*, but only that which is best."

[6] *King Lear*, Act V, Scene 2, lines 10–12. Edgar to Gloucester: "Men must endure their going hence, even as their coming hither: Ripeness is all."

[7] *Physics* II.8.199b26–28.

[8] "Things that act for the sake of something include whatever may be done as a result of thought or of nature" (*Physics* II.5.196b22).

money;[9] nor does it exist in order to allow those who practice it to demonstrate their sympathy with and benevolence toward their fellow human beings. One may, of course, execute such purposes in the practice of the art of medicine. But suppose that the money-making physician finds that there is much more money to be made using his medical skills to kill people rather than to cure them; or, suppose again, that the philanthropic physician's sympathy for the suffering leads him to kill his patients "mercifully." These purposes, making money and demonstrating love for one's fellow men, are no longer congruent with the end of the art of medicine. Systematic execution of such purposes by most physicians would lead to the destruction of the art itself. For, if physicians acquired a reputation for killing rather than, or even as much as, for curing, no one would wish to consult them. Since everyone would do everything possible to avoid them, there would soon be no physicians, for without patients the art cannot be practiced and so cannot be learned.

This is why the Hippocratic Oath, which used to be taken by all physicians, forbids the use of the art of medicine to kill people. Killing those upon whom they attend is forbidden to physicians by the Hippocratic Oath, not because it is morally wrong to murder people—the wrongness of murder is something that applies to all men and it is forbidden by whatever laws they acknowledge themselves to be subject to—but because to use the art of medicine to kill people destroys the art. The Oath does not forbid murder by medicine to physicians on account of the patients, nor on account of the physician considered simply as a human being, but on account of the art of medicine. It is aimed at the preservation of the art. A physician does not violate the Oath by murdering a person in a manner that does not depend upon the art of medicine: a doctor taking a shotgun and killing someone—even someone who was his patient—does not thereby violate the Hippocratic Oath. What makes the physician is the end pursued, in the case of the medical art the health of human beings, their physical well-being. A doctor using medical knowledge to kill is executing a purpose, but he is not doing what physicians do; he is doing what assassins do.

"The idea is that you start out with certain ends—things you favor or want."[10] This sentence from Gilbert Harman's *The Nature of Morality* exemplifies the confusion of ends with purposes. "What we favor," or "what we want," describe purposes, not ends. The doctor *favors* wealth; or he

[9] "Nor would you say that medicine is the art of receiving pay because a man takes fees when he is engaged in healing?" (Plato, *Republic* I.346).

[10] Gilbert Harman, *The Nature of Morality* (New York: Oxford University Press, 1977), p. 31.

wants to help people in need. These are not the ends of medicine, *that-for-the-sake-of-which* medicine exists. Nor are they ends—meaning fulfillments—of man. The end for the doctor *qua* man is to be actually a complete human being, something that is there independently of what he *wants* or *favors*. Depending on circumstances "making money" or "helping human beings" may or may not be compatible with that. Ends exist independently of our willing them to be; they do not originate in our willing them to be. Purposes take their origin from our willing them; purposes would not be if agents did not give them being. The reality of purposes is in consciousness. Human beings act, whether or not they recognize it explicitly in their purposes, in order to be complete as human beings, and physicians in order to heal. Completeness as a human being—what Aristotle calls εὐδαιμονία and we translate *happiness*—is the end of human life not because it is projected as such, but because of what human beings are. Just as health is the end of the medical art, regardless of the purposes of individual physicians, so happiness is the end of human life whatever the purposes of human beings may be. Happiness is the end not because I choose happiness and make it my purpose, but because of what I am, the intrinsic character, or nature, of the human being itself. Happiness is the end and my purposes must be congruent with it, if I am to be a fully realized human being.

Favoring and *wanting* are words indicating what can loosely be described as some kind of "mental activity." Purposes presuppose such activity, ends do not. The reality of ends is not constituted by such activity. The reality of purposes is always something directly given in consciousness and therefore, in so far as they are my purposes, something I am always aware of. The purpose with which I act is never hidden from me, but the ends for which I act often are.[11] I do not have to be conscious of the end that an action has for the action to have that end. I can always recognize my purpose, since it is after all something experienced in consciousness, and yet be ignorant of the end that my action presupposes. The doctor who practices "euthanasia" is an instance of this. My ignorance of the end and its absence from my consciousness does not lessen its reality; it only makes the impact of its reality more forceful. *"You can throw nature out with a pitchfork, but it always comes back, and breaking in unexpectedly is victorious over your perverse contempt."* This remains the most succinct statement of the distinction between purposes and ends and of the ontological priority of

---

[11] As in St. Augustine, *Confessions*, X, 27: "Late have I loved Thee, O Beauty so ancient and so new; late have I loved Thee!"

ends.[12] The reduction of ends to purposes is the reduction of the ontological to the psychological. The psychologizing of ends as purposes is the true anthropomorphism.

Without presence in consciousness, there is no purpose. The being of purpose is in consciousness. The description of ends as *favored* or *wanted* things implies that *favoring* and *wanting* are what make "the thing" an end. This is to construe ends as things that have their being in consciousness, whose reality in so far as they are ends is entirely psychological. The criticism of teleology as "anthropomorphic" issues from this assumption that ends are a form of psychological reality. John Stuart Mill's statement is typical in this regard: "Phaenomena are accounted for by supposed tendencies and propensities of the abstraction Nature; which, though regarded as impersonal, is figured as acting on a sort of motives, and in a manner more or less analogous to that of a conscious being."[13] More accurately, the construal of teleology as anthropomorphic depends upon the reduction of end to purpose.

> For we are bringing forward a teleological ground where we endow a conception of an object—as if that conception were to be found in nature instead of in ourselves—with causality in respect of the object, or rather where we picture to ourselves the possibility of the object on the analogy of a causality of this kind—a causality such as we experience in ourselves—and so regard nature as possessed of a capacity of its own for acting *technically*; whereas if we did not ascribe such a mode of operation to nature its causality would have to be regarded as blind mechanism.[14]

It is this reduction of end to purpose that makes possible the argumentative strategy employed against teleological explanation. And here lies the ground for the explanation of how prudence comes to be construed, as in Kant,[15] as cleverness in contriving the production of effects, how to assure

[12] Horace, *Epistles* I, 10, 24–25. "Naturam expellas furca, tamen recurret; et mala prerrumpet furtim fastidia victrix." Though far removed from Horace's elegant succinctness, Rudyard Kipling's verses, *The Gods of the Copybook Headings*, make the same point with some force.

[13] John Stuart Mill, *Auguste Comte and Positivism* (Ann Arbor, Michigan: University of Michigan Press, 1961), p. 11.

[14] Immanuel Kant, *Critique of Judgement*, trans. James C. Meredith (Oxford: Oxford University Press, 1952), Part II, Introduction, p. 5. Contrast Kant's statement with the sentence quoted above (note 7) from Aristotle, *Physics* II.8.199b26–28: "It is absurd to suppose that nothing comes into being for an end if we do not see the moving cause deliberating."

[15] Prudence, for Kant, means skill in producing effects contributing to one's own greatest advantage. "Now skill in the choice of means to one's own greatest well-being can be called prudence" (*The Groundwork of the Metaphysic of Morals*, trans. H. J. Paton [New York: Harper & Row, 1964], p. 83).

the occurrence of consequences favorable to the execution of my purposes and to avoid those which hinder it. As an executor of purposes I must anticipate—hold before my consciousness—consequences, calculating their probabilities. Skillfulness in this comes to be called prudence. Being able to anticipate means being able to shape what is brought about or effected. Just to the extent that I am able to envisage the consequences, there is some chance of my being able to produce the consequences specified by my purposes. Being-able-to is power.[16] Prudence becomes the power to shape the future to conform to my purposes. The foregoing simply paraphrases *Leviathan*, chapter 8, where Hobbes says: "When the thoughts of a man, that has a design in hand, running over a multitude of things, observes how they conduce to that design; or what design they may conduce unto; if his observations be such as are not easy, or usual, this wit of his is called *prudence*. . . ."[17] "The thoughts of a man that has a design in hand" = purpose; "running over a multitude of things," observing "how they conduce to that design; or what design they may conduce unto" = calculation of consequences.[18] Prudence is "the knowledge, or opinion each one has, of the causes, which produce the effect desired."[19] Hobbes is a great critic of teleology. It is pride, of course, to think that what are your own designs are plans of nature. But if nature has plans, we had best be sure that our purposes conform to them. If nature has no plans, then it would appear that we are free to follow our own. Nature must be construed as *end-less* for modern freedom. Thus, determinism in nature guarantees human freedom. Ends are constituted by our choice. They are our "projects."

Prudence as the *techne*, or skill, of producing consequences is the prudence of an economic, not a moral, agent. In the perspective of such an agent *end* means a desirable consequence, a "favored or wanted thing."[20] Having been effected, a consequence which it was my purpose to effect is no longer an end, since it is no longer a "favored or wanted thing." Again, this does no more than paraphrase Hobbes, *Leviathan*, chapter 11: "Felicity is a continual progress of the desire from one object to another; the attaining of the former, being still but the way to the latter."[21] Ends, however, are

---

[16] "For the foresight of things to come, which is providence, belongs only to him by whose will they are to come" (Thomas Hobbes, *Leviathan*, I, 3, in *Blackwell's Political Texts*, ed. by Michael Oakeshott [Oxford: Blackwell, n.d.], p. 16. Hereafter cited as *BPT*).

[17] Hobbes, *Leviathan*, chap. 8, in *BPT*, p. 48.

[18] Ibid.

[19] Hobbes, *Leviathan*, chap. 11, in *BPT*, p. 63.

[20] See above, note 2.

[21] See note 19.

real whether they are our purposes or not, whether they are *favored or wanted things* or not, and *prudence, the knowledge of ends,* is not the calculation of consequences in terms of costs and benefits. Acts may have consequences which are high benefit plus low cost, but the act itself is destructive of the actuality of the actor as a fulfilled and completed human being. *Life is action (πρᾶξις), not production (ποίησις).*[22] *What does it profit a man to gain the whole world and suffer the loss of his soul?*

II

End as *telos* is to be distinguished from such notions as *consequence* or *result*, something that follows upon or happens after an act. It may be a consequence of attending college that after graduation I happen to find opportunities to make a substantial amount of money. But "making money" is not the end of the action "attending college." If it were the end of this action, the condition of having made a substantial amount of money would generally obtain among those who have attended college, which of course is not the case. The end of the action "attending college" is the acquisition of arts and sciences. This end will generally be realized if the action is not frustrated, i.e., the students do not study, the teachers do not teach, and the college awards degrees solely on the condition that the students' fees are paid. However, if the perception of a strong correlation between the occurrence of a consequence and a given action exists, this consequence may be confused with the end. Thus, there is a perception that economic advantage is strongly correlated with graduation from college, and hence the judgment is made that colleges and universities exist in order to promote economic and social advancement.[23] As the number of those attending colleges motivated by such purposes increases, many, if not most, of the things traditionally done by colleges and universities seem irrelevant. Consequence and purpose conspire to obscure end.

Though I intend them to occur, consequences may or may not occur. Other things may happen instead of, or as well as, the intended consequence. There is the unintended consequence: something that happens as a result of what I do that was not part of my purpose. "Every policy disaster of the last half-century started out as someone's sensible idea."[24] Even if

[22] Aristotle, *Politics* I.5.1254a6.

[23] The significance of the facts that until relatively recently scholars were "poor" and colleges and universities were regarded as eleemosynary institutions are lost sight of.

[24] James L. Payne comments on the role of the *Community Mental Health Centers Act of 1963* in creating the problem of "the Homeless." Payne, "Solutions That Made the Problem Worse," *The Wall Street Journal,* 9 March 1994.

we did not intend them to occur, we are held responsible for some of the consequences of what we do, because it is reasonable to expect us to foresee the possibility of their occurrence, and when they fail to occur we say we were "lucky." That many consequences can be foreseen does not mean that they will inevitably occur, only that there is "a chance" that they may. But some consequences could not have been foreseen and are not part of anyone's purpose; when they occur we speak of "accidents." We cannot be assigned responsibility for consequences, which cannot be foreseen, even if we believe that we intend them.

When I buy a lottery ticket I say that I intend to win. But since I cannot foresee this consequence, and it cannot be my purpose—buying a lottery ticket does not *cause* me to win, it is an *occasion* of my winning—what I mean is that I *hope* to win. Thus we call them "games of chance." The imputability of responsibility for the consequences of one's acts depends upon their being able to be foreseen, not solely on whether or not they are *intended*. With respect to my actions I am responsible for unintended foreseeable consequences just as much as for intended foreseeable consequences. It is not sufficient *not to intend* a consequence and to *hope* it will not happen, if it can be foreseen that it may happen as a consequence of what is going to be done and that, if not done, will not happen. "I didn't mean it" does not excuse when I should have taken care. Examples of this abound on every side. Take the action of the FBI in the instance of the Branch Davidians near Waco, Texas. It could have been foreseen that use of the chemical agent CS to force the Davidians out of their buildings might result in fire and cause the death of a large number of persons, but while it is not likely that it was the *intention* of the FBI directors to produce this state of affairs, nevertheless they must be assigned the responsibility for the deaths of these people as it was a foreseeable consequence. (It was a culpably irresponsible act.) Consequences insofar as they are unforeseeable are the realm of *chance*, or what in human affairs is known as *fortune*, what there is no reason to expect, the undeserved for good or ill.

> In the following days we could hardly understand that the operation [the evacuation of the German forces from Sicily in August 1943] had been such a complete success. There had been so many chances against us. An indication of the fact that the success could not be understood was the fact that otherwise sane people maintained that the Allies had intentionally allowed the German divisions to escape to the mainland, and they based this nonsense on fantastical political theories. Sober and clear-thinking comrades laughed at this of course, but the fact that such rumors were spread throws remarkable light on the

events of the preceding days and weeks, which seemed like a miracle.[25]

Thus, while we may reasonably anticipate many of the consequences of our actions, or those of others, we can never know consequences in all their complicated detail.[26] But it is always possible to know the ends for which we act, though their being ends is not dependent upon their being known as such. Ends are never accidental, never a matter of chance.

We are surprised when what comes to be does not correspond to our purposes. It is just because ends are real and I can be ignorant of them that mistakes are made about what we are doing with consequences that had not been calculated and our purposes revealed to be "purposes mistook fall'n upon the inventor's head."[27] The incongruity of purpose with end is revealed by the presence of the end in realization or frustration.

> Our indiscretion sometime serves us well
> When our deep plots do pall, and that should learn us
> There's a divinity shapes our ends,
> rough-hew them how we will.[28]

Ends are the nature, which cannot be tossed aside with the pitchfork of purpose. "Between the wish and the thing the world lies waiting."[29]

III

Narrative art attempts the presentation of what R. P. Blackmur called "the theoretic form of life itself."[30] It is *theoretic* form because something is offered to our gaze to be contemplated. Narrative, presenting the interplay between purpose and end, is the classic form that allows us to contemplate human life in its completeness and incompleteness. Theoretic form in this sense is what narrative art, however it is practiced, is "all about," for, as Aristotle indicates in the *Poetics*, "all human happiness or misery takes the form

[25] Colonel Bogeslaw von Bonin [Chief of Staff, XIV Panzer Corps], "Consideration of the Italian Campaign, 1943–44," quoted in Carlo D'Este, *Bitter Victory, The Battle for Sicily*, 1943 (New York: Harper Collins, 1988), p. 526. The differences between *end* and *consequence*, or *result* are brought out by Aristotle, *Nicomachean Ethics* I.10.

[26] Thus Francis Bacon's well-known saying that having children is "giving hostages to fortune."

[27] *Hamlet*, Act V, Scene 2, lines 385–86.

[28] *Hamlet*, Act V, Scene 2, lines 8–11.

[29] Dueña Alfonsa in *All the Pretty Horses* by Cormac McCarthy (New York: Vintage Books, 1992), p. 238.

[30] R. P. Blackmur, *The Lion and the Honeycomb* (New York: Harcourt, Brace and Co., 1955), p. 269.

of action,"[31] and whether in novels, on the stage, in film, or in painting, poetry imitates action. The story imitating an action complete in itself manifests an *end-telos* against which are profiled those images or representations of ends that are human purposes. The narrative arts presuppose the ontological priority of ends to purposes because without that priority there is nothing to be revealed about the adequacy or inadequacy of human purposes to the completeness of human life, for in action a human being "purposes" the realization of his life as a whole, complete in itself. Life as action is a whole, and it is the presence of an end that makes it a whole. Stories imitate actions by being themselves wholes that represent the manifestations of ends in action. In doing so they attempt to present "the underlying classic form in which things are held together in a living way, with the sense of life going on."[32]

What happens when end is reduced to purpose and consequence becomes visible in the films of Quentin Tarentino,[33] which picture a "world" in which there are only the purposes of human beings, a "world without ends." In such a world there cannot be any congruity or incongruity of purposes with ends. There being no ends by which purposes can be measured, all purposes are in themselves incommensurate and incongruous with one other. This is a world in which everything is violent, because there is no natural way for anything to move. But a world in which everything is violent means that violence becomes ordinary, the usual, the way things are. The violent displaces and becomes "the natural." Nietzsche observed that "[o]nce you know that there are no ends (*zweck*), you also know that there is no accident; for it is only beside a world of ends (*zweck*) that the word 'accident' has meaning."[34] The violence shocks because we are not nihilists, because we are still measuring what people do in these films by a world in which there are ends, not just human purposes. Tarentino says he doesn't take violence seriously and finds it funny. "To me, violence is a totally aesthetic subject."[35] Commenting on these films Michael Wood says:

[31] Aristotle, *Poetics* 6.1450a17–19.

[32] Blackmur, *The Lion and the Honeycomb*, p. 269.

[33] *Reservoir Dogs, True Romance, Pulp Fiction, Natural Born Killers.*

[34] Friedrich Nietzsche, *The Gay Science*, #109, trans. Walter Kaufmann (New York: Vintage Books, 1974).

[35] In an interview excerpted and printed in the published screenplays of both *Reservoir Dogs* (London: Faber, 1994) and *True Romance* (London: Faber, 1995), Tarentino goes on to observe that "saying you don't like violence in movies is like saying you don't like dance sequences in movies." Michael Wood thinks the violence in these films "an act of immature bravado" ("My Kind of Psychopath," *London Review of Books*, 17, no. 14 [20 July 1995], pp. 9–10.) According to Wood, what these films are really about is "evoking the ungovernable and . . . unspoiled energies of the world" (p. 9). In other words, Heidegger's words, "Possibility stands higher than actuality."

[T]he violence mainly suggests that everyone and everything is out of control, that no rules apply and chaos is come again. What interests Tarentino is not violence . . . but fiasco, the sense that life is a mess even in fiction. And then into this mess he introduces *not order but style* and a peculiar kind of innocence.[36]

A world of purposes only is a world of cross-purposes, the definition of fiasco. What is intended in the portrayal of such a world is not, of course, a "classic form," the manifestation of an order, "things held together in a living way with the sense of life going on," but the manifestation of an author. Style, then, not order. Where there are only the purposes of human beings, there are no actions to imitate; there are events to be strung together, not stories to be told. Life must be a string of events strung together "anyhow."[37] Just how must depend upon the postures assumed by the author. Works such as these films reveal—and are intended to reveal—the sensibility of their creators, in this instance "a peculiar kind of innocence." A "peculiar kind of innocence" for there is no place for dismay that what is done wrecks havoc. In such a world that is a "natural" result of anything anyone does. A world of fiasco is a world in which guilt is impossible, because guilt requires responsibility for actions, and there are actions only if purposes are measured by ends. Wood remarks that in Tarentino's films: "A desperate ordinariness might inhabit the most extreme of circumstances."[38] The *ordinariness* is human purpose *desperate* when detached from ends, because detached from ends there are no "reasons" other than our purposes for doing anything. Wood continues: "There is also the sense that if you can't get a plausible reason for behaving the way you want to, an implausible one will have to do."[39] Reason reduced to purpose produces *the most extreme of circumstances.*

Macbeth inhabits a world in which he acknowledges only human purposes, a world in which he must ceaselessly strive to become the master of consequences. When the achievements of great ambition fall apart, his life seems to him, as all lives seem to him, "a tale told by an idiot, full of sound and fury, signifying nothing."[40] Macbeth cannot tell the story of his own life. But Shakespeare could and we understand Macbeth's life because we see it within the context of the whole which human life is as apprehended by Shakespeare. The screenplays of Tarentino are and are intended pre-

---

[36] Wood, "My Kind of Psychopath," pp. 9–10.
[37] Actions, in contrast, are wholes manifesting ends.
[38] Wood, "My Kind of Psychopath," p. 9.
[39] Ibid., pp. 9–10.
[40] *Macbeth*, Act 5, Scene 5, lines 26–28.

cisely to be "tales full of sound and fury signifying nothing"—but without paying the price of having to regard himself as an idiot. *Pulp Fiction* and *True Romance*, the titles he chose for two of his films, suggest that Tarentino believes that he can maintain a distance between himself and the tales that he tells. "Pulp fiction" and "true romance" do not describe Tarentino's view of his own films, but the character and status he attributes to the stories human beings tell in the effort to understand and give substance to their lives, which these films expose (supposedly) as "pulp fiction" and "true romance." Tarentino, self-indulgently, ridicules all purposes except his own. But if there are no ends, what privileges the purposes of the artist?

In contrast to Tarentino's pop post-modernism Franz Kafka, an artist of high order, understood that there is a price to be paid for telling the tales of an idiot. In one of his letters Kafka described his understanding of his practice of the narrative art:

> Somewhat as if one were to hammer together a table with painful and methodical technical efficiency, and simultaneously do nothing at all, and not in such a way that people could say: "Hammering a table together is really nothing to him," but rather "Hammering a table together is really hammering a table together to him, but at the same time it is nothing," whereby certainly the hammering would have become still bolder, still surer, still more real and, if you will, still more senseless.[41]

Seldom have such tales been told with such perfection. In them Kafka achieved the anti-poetry appropriate to a world without ends.

> It was very early in the morning, the streets clean and deserted, I was on my way to the station. As I compared the tower clock with my watch I realized that it was much later than I had thought and that I had to hurry; the shock of this discovery made me feel uncertain of the way, I wasn't very well acquainted with the town as yet; fortunately, there was a policeman at hand, I ran to him and breathlessly asked him the way. He smiled and said: "You asking me the way?" "Yes," I said, "since I can't find it myself." "Give it up! Give it up!" said he, and turned with a sudden jerk, like someone who wants to be alone with his laughter.[42]

[41] Franz Kafka, *The Great Wall of China*, trans. Willa and Edwin Muir (New York: Shocken, 1946), p. 136. See Erich Heller, *The Disinherited Mind* (New York: Harcourt Brace Jovanovich, 1975), p. 219.

[42] Franz Kafka, *Give It Up!* in *The Basic Kafka* (New York: The Washington Square Press. 1979), pp. 157–58.

Beauty, Mind, and the Universe

Alice Ramos

Although there is revived interest in the transcendentals and especially in the transcendentality of the beautiful, insufficient emphasis has been placed, in my opinion, on the role of the transcendentals in the second perfection of the universe.[1] Normally, when we read about the transcendentals, we are told that they are convertible with being: that insofar as something possesses actuality, that is, being or the first perfection, it possesses the transcendentals; and that although the transcendentals and being are really identical, they differ conceptually.

Now a recent study of the transcendentals in St. Thomas tells us that the originality of Thomas's doctrine of the transcendentals is its anthropological motif: the correlation of *anima* and being.[2] Being under the *ratio* of knowability and being under the *ratio* of appetibility are the formal objects of the spiritual faculties of the human soul. The *anima*, which "is in a sense all things," is thus open to all being, to all that is true and good.[3] And because of this transcendental openness, man is not only *capax entis* but also *capax dei*. Thus, in addition to the anthropological motif of Thomas's doctrine, there is a theological motif and the two converge.[4] The same study further notes that the doctrine of the transcendentals provides the meta-

---

[1] Among the more recent studies on the transcendentals may be cited: Jan Aertsen, *Medieval Philosophy and the Transcendentals, The Case of Thomas Aquinas* (Leiden, The Netherlands: Brill, 1996). Jorge Gracia, ed. of the special issue of *Topoi* 11 (1992), devoted to "The Transcendentals in the Medieval Ages."

[2] Aertsen, *Medieval Philosophy and the Transcendentals*, p. 430.

[3] Thomas Aquinas, *Summa Contra Gentiles* II, chap. 47 and III, chap. 112 (hereafter cited as *SCG*), and *De Veritate*, q. 2, a. 2. See also Josef Pieper, "The Truth of All Things," in *Living the Truth* (San Francisco: Ignatius Press, 1989).

[4] Aertsen, *Medieval Philosophy and the Transcendentals*, p. 431.

physical foundation for a theory of knowledge and a theory of human action;[5] and that the connection between transcendentality and morality is certainly one of the most interesting aspects of Thomas's doctrine.[6] Now when attention is given to the difference between the transcendental and the moral good, between being good in a certain respect (*secundum quid*) and being good absolutely (*simpliciter*), the reason for the differentiation lies in the non-identity of a being's being and its activity. The absolute goodness of a thing is brought about by its activity, by its second act or perfection; only thus does a creature complete or perfect itself and thus attain to the fullness of its being.

When St. Thomas works out the fullness of being in terms of the fullness of perfection or the fullness of goodness with regard to both natural things and human actions, the relation to the end they depend upon is seen as essential. Since to know the end and the ordering of things and activities to the end pertains to intellect, intellectual creatures are necessary for the fullness of the perfection of the universe. The purpose of this paper will be first, to consider the order among the diverse things that compose the universe, which order is described as the "chief beauty in things,"[7] and how this order is due to divine wisdom, since the divine mind does not give being in a haphazardly way, but rather gives things being with order;[8] and second, given the differences in being of the creatures that compose the universe, of the parts that constitute the whole, which differences account for the various kinds of activity of beings, to consider the role of intellectual creatures in the second perfection of the universe and to see how the provident activity of men cooperates in giving the universe its final form and thus leads to a beautifying of being.

THE BEAUTY OF THE ORDER OF THE UNIVERSE AND ITS RELATION TO MIND

The order and intelligibility of the universe has been observed not only by medieval philosophers and theologians but also by contemporary scientists. In an article titled "So Finely Tuned a Universe," the physicist John Polkinghorne says: "When we look at the rational order and transparent beauty of the physical world, revealed through physical science, we see a

---

[5] Ibid.
[6] Ibid.
[7] *SCG*, III, chap. 71.
[8] *In De Divinis Nominibus*, chap. 7, lect. 4, n. 733 (hereafter cited as *In De Div. Nom.*).

world shot through with signs of mind. . . . [I]t is the mind of the Creator that is being discerned that way."[9] According to Polkinghorne, the rationality of our minds and the rational order of the physical world have as their common origin "that deeper rationality which is the reason of the Creator."[10] It is interesting to note that Polkinghorne should speak of the intelligible order and beauty of the universe in the same sentence. For Aquinas, the first actuality of things, their being, accounts for their intelligibility and their luminosity or radiance, the latter being a feature of the beautiful. Were it not for the radiance and intelligibility of being, things could not be known. There is, as it were, a "fit" which exists between the world and our minds. "Created things are [thus] resplendent with an intelligibility that is answered by the participated intellectual power of the created mind."[11] Within Aquinas's creationist framework, the beauty and intelligibility present in created beings is due to the creative mind of God, or simply, to the divine light, to the spiritual clarity of divine reason.[12]

Aquinas speaks of the divine mind as the mind of an artist; in fact, he sees the whole of nature as an artifact of the divine artistic mind. As the artist produces a determinate form in matter by reason of an idea, that is, the exemplar interiorly conceived in his mind, so also in God, whose nature is intellectual, does the likeness of His effects preexist in Him in an intelligible way. Since God is an intelligent and infinitely perfect agent, He conceives the plan of His work and there is thus in His intelligence the model or exemplar according to which He realizes His work. This exemplar, however, is nothing distinct from God: it is His very self, His essence; God knows all things by a sole form which is His very essence.[13] The exemplar,

[9] In *Commonweal*, 16 August 1996, p. 13. Concerning the beauty and the intelligibility of the universe, Polkinghorne notes: "Some of the most beautiful patterns thought up by the mathematicians are found actually to occur in the structure of the physical world. In other words, there is some deep-seated relationship between the reason within (the rationality of our minds—in this case mathematics) and the reason without (the rational order and structure of the physical world around us). The two fit together like a pair of gloves. That is a rather significant fact about the world, or so thought Einstein. Einstein once said: 'The only incomprehensible thing about the universe is that it is comprehensible.' Why, we should ask, are our minds so perfectly shaped to understand the deep patterns of the world around us?" (ibid., p. 12). In my opinion, a reading of Aquinas's *SCG* makes comprehensible what Einstein terms "incomprehensible."

[10] Ibid.

[11] Mark Jordan, "The Evidence of the Transcendentals and the Place of Beauty in Thomas Aquinas," *International Philosophical Quarterly* 29, no. 4 (December 1989), p. 402.

[12] See *Summa Theologiae* I, q. 36, a. 8, resp. (hereafter cited as *ST*).

[13] *SCG* I, chap. 55.

which is one, gives rise to the multiplicity that we see in creation; it is reproduced, so to say, in partial, distinct, and multiple imitations which constitute the diversity of created beings that make up the universe. The variety of creatures in the universe is thus due to the first exemplary cause, which is none other than divine wisdom. As Aquinas puts it: "It is manifest that things made by nature receive determinate forms. This determinateness of forms must be reduced to the divine wisdom as its first principle, for divine wisdom devised the order of the universe, which order consists in a variety of things."[14]

Since God is the most perfect agent, He induces the form of His art, that is, His wisdom, His likeness, into created things in a perfect way as far as the effect will admit it. Simplicity and unity characterize the first cause, whereas its effects are composed and multiple. If all created things were of one degree, then God's likeness and His goodness could not be adequately represented. As we have mentioned above, an agent that acts by intellect reproduces the species of his intellect in the thing made, just as the artist by the form of his art produces his like. God made creatures as an agent by intellect. But since His intellect understands many things, it is not sufficiently reproduced in one creature only. Therefore, the divine intellect reproduces itself more perfectly if it produces creatures of varying degrees of being.[15] Since no one creature could perfectly imitate divine goodness nor manifest divine wisdom, there was need for a variety of things in creation to thus better represent the divine goodness and wisdom from whence they originate. To further illustrate this point, St. Thomas compares the eminence of divine perfection present in God in a simple and unified way to a man's mental conception. Just as a man's thought is expressed adequately by various and multiple words, rather than by one spoken word only, God's perfect goodness is expressed in creatures through a plurality of things.[16] The diversity of forms in things, by which they participate to a greater or lesser degree in being, thus allows for the representation of divine goodness and for the manifestation in varying degrees of the conception of the divine mind.

St. Thomas does not, however, emphasize only the variety of forms; relying on Aristotle and on Dionysius, he also points to the order and the continuity which exist among the forms, since the perfection of the universe cannot simply consist in mere diversity. Things that are too unlike one an-

---

[14] *ST* I, q. 44, a. 3, resp.
[15] *SCG* II, chap. 45.
[16] *SCG* III, chap. 97.

other or too remote from one another do not tend to unite, and thus nature proceeds little by little from things that are lifeless to animal life, in a continuous, upward scale of ascent. And in this continuity of nature, what is impressive is the similarity that exists among neighboring kinds of beings: "The degrees of beings are continuous with one another according to some similitude: hence those things that are totally dissimilar follow one another in the order of things through some middle that has similitude with both of the extremes."[17] This continuity is seen by St. Thomas as a contact among beings, which is brought about through the influence of the First Being on the varying levels of beings: "Orders of this kind, since they proceed from the one first principle, have a certain continuity with one another in such a way that the order of bodies touches on (attingit) the order of souls and the order of souls touches on the order of intellects, which touches on the divine order."[18] The similarities which exist between like kinds of beings are due to the different orders of reality "touching on" one another. This contact allows something to pass from the higher order to the lower order, so that the lower has some part in what is only fully found in the higher. "Saint Thomas sees an indication of this in the fact that some animals, inferior to man, have something akin to reason, and some plants have something akin to a differentiation of sexes. Everything appears as if something 'rubbed off' on the inferior from the superior through this 'contact.'"[19]

For St. Thomas, the continuity in the order of the universe is due to God's wisdom, in the same way that order and diversity are due to His wisdom. Levels of beings are thus not independent of one another; they are not merely in sequence to one another, but there is a continuity and community among beings. Continuity is therefore inseparable from the very being of things, because things have being with order. If things in the universe were unconnected, without order, things would not be fittingly disposed. In the same way that disorder is not good for the individual, it is even worse for the universe as a whole. Aquinas states: "[B]eings do not wish to be badly disposed. The disposition of natural beings is such as to be the best possible. This we see in individuals, namely, that each is of the best disposition in its nature. Hence we should think that it is much more the case in the

---

[17] *In De Causis*, lect. 31, n. 456. Cited in Oliva Blanchette, *The Perfection of the Universe According to Aquinas* (University Park, Pennsylvania: The Pennsylvania State University Press, 1992), p. 193. According to Blanchette, similitude is a notion associated with formal causality and is a norm for order. See pp. 191–202, which are on the principle of continuity.

[18] *In De Causis*, lect. 19, n. 352.

[19] Blanchette, *The Perfection of the Universe According to Aquinas*, p. 194.

whole universe."[20] The order of the universe is such that one level cannot be independent of the other, since all beings which proceed from the one first intelligent principle have a certain continuity with one another. According to Aquinas, the ordering of the parts to each other, which is what is meant by disposition, is what pertains to divine art: "[F]or things are said to be disposed in as much as they are put on different levels by God, who is like an artist arranging the different parts of his work in different ways."[21] So, if the different degrees of being and of goodness were not present in creatures, then there would be no degrees of likeness to the first principle. And this would deprive things of their chief beauty.[22]

Now harmony, another essential feature of the beautiful in addition to radiance, "is present in things by virtue of their ordering among themselves."[23] Had this order, this harmony, been missing in God's work, it would have been unbecoming and unfitting to the work of a perfect agent: "Supreme perfection should not be wanting to a work made by the supremely good workman. . . . The good of order among diverse things is better than any one of those things that are ordered taken by itself: for it is formal in respect to each, as the perfection of the whole in respect of the parts."[24] In attributing perfection to the whole, to the order of the universe, Aquinas once again, in my opinion, points to the best disposition of things, to their interconnectedness and continuity, and also to the beauty of the order, for perfection or integrity is also a condition of the beautiful. Without the good of order, God's work would have been impaired; it would not have been well disposed, as we said above. And so, Aquinas argues that "[t]he order of the universe . . . is the ultimate and noblest perfection in things."[25]

It is evident that the unity of order in the universe is a unity in being, insofar as things come together due to a similitude in being; however, the unity of the universe may also be considered as "a unity of action between a diversity and a multiplicity of beings, a working together of all things toward their common final end."[26] One might therefore say that the order of being is for the sake of the order of activity. God produces being with

---

[20] *In XII Metaphysicorum*, lect. 12, n. 2662.

[21] *De Veritate,* q. 5, a. 1, ad 9.

[22] *SCG* III, chap. 71.

[23] *In De Div. Nom.*, chap. 4, p. 270. I am using here Vernon J. Bourke's translation of chap. 4, lect. 4–5 of the *Exposition of Dionysius on the Divine Names* found in *The Pocket Aquinas* (New York: Washington Square Press, 1960); page numbers are references to that translation.

[24] *SCG* II, chap. 45.

[25] Ibid.

[26] Blanchette, *The Perfection of the Universe According to Aquinas*, p. 198.

order so that beings may help each other in the order to the final end.[27] The continuity which exists between the parts of the universe is there for their harmonization under the Ruler of the universe. "And thus the beauty of the universe is worked out through 'one conspiration of all things,' i.e., through concord and 'harmony,' i.e., through the necessary order and proportion."[28] The beauty which Aquinas is emphasizing here is not a static beauty, a mere property, so to speak, of being, but rather a dynamic understanding of beauty: a beauty of the universe that is to be realized. It is for this reason that there is in beings a diversity of activities which results from the diversity of forms. The ordering that exists among the parts, which we might call the first perfection of the universe, is for the sake of the second perfection of the universe, that is, for the ordering to the end— that end which is arrived at through activity. There is thus an initial beauty of the order of the universe, which is for an ulterior beauty. And I believe that this is confirmed by what St. Thomas says regarding the twofold ordering which is found in things, an ordering which involves the divine disposition of things and also divine providence, which is the ordering of things to their end:

> First, there is that order according to which things come from their principles. Second, there is the order according to which they are directed to an end. Now, the divine disposing pertains to that order according to which things proceed from their principles; for things are said to be disposed inasmuch as they are put on different levels by God, who is like an artist arranging the different parts of his work in different ways. Consequently, disposition seems to pertain to art. Providence, however, implies the ordering which directs to an end; for this reason it differs from the divine art and disposition. For divine art is so called because of its relation to the production of things, but divine disposition is so called because of its relation to the order of what has already been produced. Providence, however, implies the ordination to an end. Now, we can gather from the end of an art product whatever exists in the thing itself. Moreover, the ordering of a thing to an end is more closely related to the end than is the ordering of its parts to each other. In fact, their ordering to an end is, in a sense, the cause of the ordering of the parts to each other. Consequently, divine providence is, in a sense, the cause of God's disposition of things, and for this reason an act of His disposition is sometimes attributed to His providence. Therefore, even if providence is not an art related to the production of things or a disposition related to the ordering of things one to another,

---

[27] *In De Div. Nom.*, chap. 7, lect. 4, n. 733.
[28] Ibid. See note 26.

it does not follow that providence does not belong to practical knowledge.[29]

In the same way in which the disposition of things in the universe is due to the art of the divine mind, providence also belongs to knowledge. The harmony and usefulness which are found in nature at all times or at least the majority of times is not simply the result of chance, but rather is due to an intended end. When natural things which have no knowledge direct themselves to an end, they do so because divine knowledge has established an end for them and thus directs them to that end. For this reason, it has been said that every work of nature is the work of intelligence, that is, of the divine mind.[30] Furthermore, "[T]he world is ruled by the providence of that intellect which gave this order to nature; and we may compare the providence by which God rules the world to the domestic foresight by which a man rules his family, or to the political foresight by which a ruler governs a city or a kingdom, and directs the acts of others to a definite end."[31] Were it not then for providence, for final causality, things in nature would not come together fittingly and well, that is, in a "good and orderly way."[32] They would in addition lack the "mutual fit" which we observe in the works of nature, since they would be without the order to the end.[33]

PROVIDENCE AND ORDER:
THE ROLE OF INTELLECTUAL CREATURES

Providence, like causality, is found not only in God but also in creatures; there are some creatures, some parts of the universe, which through their proper activities, contribute to the order of the universe to the end. Creatures which are more like God, which participate more in His likeness and goodness, can also act for the goodness of other creatures. "Therefore the creature approaches more perfectly to God's likeness if it is not only good, but can also act for the goodness of other things, than if it were merely good in itself. . . . Now a creature would be unable to act for the goodness of another creature, unless in creatures there were plurality and inequality: because the agent is distinct from *and more noble* than the patient."[34] To

---

[29] *De Veritate,* q. 5, a. 1, ad 9.

[30] *De Veritate,* q. 5, a. 2, resp. As Aquinas puts it in the reply to the same question, since providence has to do with the direction of things to their end, "whoever denies final causality should also deny providence."

[31] Ibid.

[32] Ibid.

[33] Ibid. See also Blanchette, *The Perfection of the Universe According to Aquinas,* p. 312.

[34] *SCG* II, chap. 45.

cause goodness as God does is one of the reasons why Aquinas insists that intellectual creatures are needed for the perfection of the universe. Intellectual creatures are like God in both nature and in activity. They can return to God by their very operation, by the act of the intellect and will. As Aquinas maintains: "The highest perfection of the universe requires that there should be some creatures in which the form of the divine intellect is reproduced according to an intelligible mode of being: and this means that there should be creatures of an intellectual nature."[35] Intellectual creatures are therefore necessary not only because in their goodness they represent the divine goodness, but because they can act in a way analogous to the way in which God acts, that is, for the goodness of others. They can, as a result, provide for others, care for them.

This is further explicated when Aquinas speaks of the relationship between order and providence and the manner through which divine providence is brought to perfection:

> Suitable order is a proof of perfect providence, for order is the proper effect of providence. Now suitable order implies that nothing should be allowed to be out of order. Consequently, the perfection of divine providence requires that it should reduce the excess of certain things over others, to a suitable order. And this is done by allowing those who have less to benefit from the superabundance of others. Since then the perfection of the universe requires that some share more abundantly in the divine goodness . . . , the perfection of divine providence demands that the execution of the divine government be fulfilled by those things which have the larger share of divine goodness.[36]

According to Aquinas, not only is order required for providence, but also the execution of order. The cognitive power is responsible for order: the greater the knowledge, the greater the capacity to order others; it is therefore proper to the wise man to order. On the other hand, the execution of order is the work of the operative power.[37] In executing the order, God acts by means of inferior powers, "as a universal and higher power through an inferior and particular power."[38] It is not unbecoming of God to execute His providence through the activities of secondary causes; on the contrary, it is in keeping with His dignity. "It belongs to the dignity of a ruler to have many ministers and various executors of his rule: because the greater the

[35] *SCG* II, chap. 46.

[36] *SCG* III, chap. 77.

[37] Ibid.

[38] Ibid. See also *ST* I, q. 22, a. 3, resp.: "Two things belong to providence— namely, the type of the order of things foreordained towards an end; and the execution of this order, which is called government."

number of his subordinates of various degrees, the more complete and extensive is his dominion shown to be."[39] It is fitting therefore that the execution of divine providence be delegated to intermediary causes. And since of all creatures the highest is the intellectual, lower creatures are subject to and governed by the higher creatures, that is, by rational creatures, just as the highest creatures are subject to God and governed by Him.[40]

Now rational creatures are able to execute the order of divine providence, because they share in the power of that providence: "While providence requires disposition of order which is effected by the cognitive faculty, and execution which is the work of the operative power, rational creatures have a share of both powers, whereas other creatures have only the latter."[41] Intellectual creatures can therefore exercise providence for the perfection of the universe; they can contribute to the order of the universe to the end through their own intellectual and free activity. Aquinas is then saying that although things in the universe have been created in being, the universe is not closed to further perfection, and that it is precisely the intellectual creature who can best contribute to the final formation of the universe. This openness of the universe to human providence is expressed in the following: "If . . . in the production of things there are some secondary causes, their ends and their actions have to be in view of the end of the first cause, who is the final end. . . . The end of the final cause, however, is the distinction and order of the parts of the universe, which is like the ultimate form. Therefore, it is not the distinction in things and the order which is in view of the actions of the secondary causes: but rather the actions of the secondary causes are in view of constituting the order and distinction in things."[42] As we stated before, the order of being is for the sake of the order of activity; it would seem, however, from the words just quoted of Aquinas, that a certain reversal has taken place, since Aquinas says that "the actions of the secondary causes are in view of constituting the order and the distinction in things."[43] The provident activity of intellectual creatures should therefore preserve and promote "the distinction and order of the parts of the universe, which is like the ultimate form."[44] If then "the ultimate form" of the universe is dependent to a certain extent on the providence exercised by intellectual creatures, we can then also say that the task of these secondary

---

[39] Ibid.
[40] *SCG* III, chap. 78.
[41] Ibid.
[42] *SCG* II, chap. 42.
[43] Ibid.
[44] Ibid.

causes is to beautify the universe, since form is said to be "a participation in the divine brilliance,"[45] and thus in divine beauty.

However, since man is free, he may or may not be a good provider; consequently, one might question how deficiency in human providence would bring about the final formation of the universe. Having created man free, however, God assumes, as it were, the risk of man's freedom, so that even from deficiency in human providence, he can and does bring about beauty and goodness.[46] Besides, to exclude from man the possibility of failing from goodness, would be to diminish his perfection; it would in fact be contrary to God's government if He did not allow man to act in accordance with his nature.[47] Aquinas expresses the difference between God's providence and the providence of creatures when he points to the relation between providence and the norm or end of the first provider:

> [S]ince providence is concerned with directing to an end, it must take place with the end as its norm; and since the first provider is Himself the end of His providence, He has the norm of providence within Himself. Consequently, it is impossible that any of the failures in those things for which He provides should be due to Him; the failures in these things can be due only to the objects of His providence. Now, creatures to whom His providence has been communicated are not the ends of their own providence. They are directed to another end, namely, God. Hence, it is necessary that they draw the rectitude of their own providence from God's norm. Consequently, in the providence exercised by creatures failures may take place that are due, not only to the objects of their providence, but also to the providers themselves.[48]

According to St. Thomas, the more a free creature adheres to the norm of the first provider, "the firmer will be the rectitude of his own providence."[49] Since the rational creature knows the reason of his action, laws were given by God to man so that he might be directed in his actions. A law is a reason or rule of action, and since the reason for an individual's action is his end, then the law guides man to his end, "even as the inferior craftsman is guided by the master-craftsman, and the soldier by the commander-in-chief."[50] And the end that God intends by His law, that is, "the chief in-

---

[45] *In De Div. Nom.*, chap. 4, p. 272. See note 23.
[46] *De Veritate*, q. 5, a. 5, ad 4.
[47] *SCG* III, chap. 71.
[48] *De Veritate*, q. 5, a. 5, resp.
[49] Ibid.
[50] *SCG* III, chap. 114.

tention of the divine law, is to lead men to God."[51] God's governing providence thus sets before the rational creature a law or a rule to direct him to his end. Since man's end consists in adherence to God, the divine law directs man to union with God. Now man adheres to God by his intellect and his will. Although man's end is a contemplative one, he does not arrive at this end solely by his intellect. And so Aquinas states: "The adhesion of the intellect is completed by the adhesion of the will, because by his will man, as it were, rests in that which the intellect apprehends."[52] And since the end of the law is to make men good, that is, more like God, "man is said to be good because he has a good will, whereby he brings into account whatever good is in him. Also, a will is good through willing the good, and above all the greatest good, which is the end. Therefore the more his will wills this good, so much the better is the man."[53]

In addition, it must be said that the rational creature's proper activities are not only the apprehension or understanding of the truth by the intellect and the loving of the good by the will, but also the work of justice. In speaking of justice, Aquinas points to a twofold understanding of this virtue:

> Since justice, by its nature, implies a certain rectitude of order, it may be taken in two ways: —First, inasmuch as it implies a right order in man's acts, and thus justice is placed amongst the virtues,—either as particular virtue, which directs a man's acts by regulating them in relation to his fellow-man,—or as legal justice, which directs a man's acts by regulating them in their relation to the common good of society. . . . Secondly, justice is so-called inasmuch as it implies a certain rectitude of order in the interior disposition of a man, in so far as what is highest in man is subject to God, and the inferior powers of the soul are subject to the superior, i.e., to reason. . . .[54]

Now since the good of order existing in created things belongs to providence, and since justice, as was noted above, implies a certain rectitude of order, man will exercise providence well (that is, execute the order established by God, bring things to their end, by governing), if he is just. For this reason, Aquinas equates providence with the observance of justice and right order:

> If [men] fail in their own providence they are called evil; but if they observe the demands of justice they are called good. . . . Now, men are

[51] *SCG* III, chap. 115.
[52] *SCG* III, chap. 116.
[53] Ibid.
[54] *ST* I–II, q. 113, a. 1, resp.

provided for in different ways according to the different ways they have of providing for themselves. For if they keep the right order in their own providence, God's providence in their regard will keep an ordering that is congruent with their human dignity; that is, nothing will happen to them that is not for their own good, and everything that happens to them will be to their own advantage. . . . However, if in their own providence men do not keep that order which is congruent with their dignity as rational creatures, but provide after the measure of brute animals, then God's providence will dispose of them according to the order that belongs to brutes, so that their good and evil acts will not be directed to their own profit but to the profit of others. . . . From this it is evident that God's providence governs the good in a higher way than it governs the evil. For, when the evil leave one order of providence, that is, by not doing the will of God, they fall into another order, an order in which the will of God is done to them.[55]

In accordance with Aquinas's thought, it is evident that when man, through the power of his will, subjects his acts to the order of divine providence, he observes due order. However, when he prefers his own will to God's, "by gratifying it against the divine ordinance,"[56] he is being unjust, since he does not acknowledge his relation to the order established. In this way, he makes it necessary that God mete out justice to him, thus setting aright, as it were, the good of order.[57]

It is important therefore that man be just, for it is precisely justice which rectifies man's deeds and his will. It is justice which enables man to do the good of reason, that is, to do the truth. For this reason, justice is likened to the truth; as Aquinas says: "Since the will is the rational appetite, when the rectitude of the reason which is called truth is imprinted on the will on account of its nighness to the reason, this imprint retains the name of truth; and hence it is that justice which sometimes goes by the name of truth."[58] Man is therefore just when his will realizes the good apprehended by the intellect, that is, the true good. "Among all the moral virtues it is justice

[55] *De Veritate*, q. 5, a. 7, resp.

[56] *SCG* III, chap. 140.

[57] "Since then human acts are subject to divine providence, even as natural things are: it follows that whatever evil occurs in human actions must be included in the order of some good. This is most fittingly done in the punishment of sins. For thus things that exceed in due quantity are included in the order of justice, which reduces them to equality. Now, man exceeds the mark of his quantity, when he prefers his own will to God's, by gratifying it against the divine ordinance. And this inequality is removed when against his will, man is compelled to suffer something according to the divine ordinance. Therefore, man's sins need to be punished by God; and for the same reason his good deeds will be rewarded" (*SCG* III, chap. 140).

[58] *ST* II–II, q. 58, a. 4, sed contra.

wherein the use of right reason appears chiefly . . . hence the undue use of reason appears chiefly in the vices opposed to justice."[59] Consequently, when the true human good is perverted, when order in things naturally human is disrupted, injustice reigns.[60] According to Aristotle, "Justice is the human good,"[61] and to this may be added: "Justice simply means 'doing one's own work' and 'fulfilling one's own task.'"[62]

Obviously, such a conception of justice is closely related to the secondary providence which is proper to rational creatures. When man exercises justice, both within himself, by ordering what is lowest in him to what is highest, to reason and to God, and also by ordering his relations with others, his just activity shapes the universe into its final form. When man is just by doing what he can, by fulfilling his own task, then he cooperates in and promotes divine providence. The intrinsic good, the final form or perfection, of the universe is thus brought about by the activity of rational creatures. St. Thomas affirms this of both angels and human beings: "Although the institution of nature, through which corporeal things are inclined to an end, is immediately by God, still their movement and action can be by the mediation of angels, just as the seminal ideas (*rationes seminales*) are in lower nature only from God but are helped along through the providence of the farmer so that they may come forth in act. Hence just as the farmer governs the sprouting of the field, so the administration of corporeal creation is done through angels."[63] Of course, we can imagine the farmer unjust, not doing his work, in the same way that we may know of politicians, professors, etc., who do not fulfill their own tasks. This is, however, the risk that God assumes in creating rational creatures; just as there is no necessity in God's creative activity, neither is there necessity in provident activity.

Thus, even though man can and does bring about disunity, falsehood, and evil when he does not adhere to the rectitude of order, it is consoling to think that the form of the universe, its order, its beauty will not be tarnished but heightened, just as a man's good will not be lessened by the evils in the world, "for his knowledge of the good is increased by comparison with evil, and through suffering evil his desire of doing good is kindled."[64] God

---

[59] *ST* II–II, q. 55, a. 8.

[60] Josef Pieper, *The Four Cardinal Virtues* (Notre Dame, Indiana: University of Notre Dame Press, 1966), p. 68.

[61] *In V Ethicorum*, lect. 15, n. 1077.

[62] Plotinus, *Enneads* I, 2, 6, quoted in Pieper, *The Four Cardinal Virtues*, p. 68.

[63] *De Veritate*, q. 5, a. 8, ad 4.

[64] *SCG* III, chap. 71.

does not therefore entirely exclude evil, since ultimately in the wisdom of divine providence, it too has a role in the beauty of the universe:

> The good of the whole is of more account than the good of the part. Therefore it belongs to a prudent governor to overlook a lack of goodness in a part, that there may be an increase of goodness in the whole: thus the builder hides the foundation of a house underground, that the whole house may stand firm. Now if evil were taken away from certain parts of the universe, the perfection of the universe would be much diminished; since its beauty results from the ordered unity of good and evil things, seeing that evil arises from the lack of good, and yet certain goods are occasioned from those very evils through the providence of the governor, even as the silent pause gives sweetness to the chant.[65]

Good and evil, like the lights and shadows of a painting, like the front and back of a tapestry, will therefore contribute to the final form of the universe, to its final beauty.

[65] Ibid.

Dante, Aquinas, and the Roots of the Modern Aesthetization of Reality

Patrick Downey

When a philosopher with the stature of Nietzsche can seriously ask: "Why couldn't the world *that concerns us*—be a fiction?"[1] we are dealing with what one might call the "aesthetization of reality." Whereas before the ancient philosophers were concerned with reality as a world of nature, a world that brought itself into existence and could be known through the highest human endeavor of a receptive *theoria*, the modern "aesthetization" of reality knows only what it has itself made, and the aesthetic contemplation of reality is more akin to a painter contemplating his painting than an astronomer contemplating the stars. Whereas in the ancients the relation to reality was that of the knower and the known, in the moderns it is the relation of the poet or audience to a poem. If we recall what was already in Plato's own day the "ancient quarrel between the poets and the philosophers," we might say that the poets have now won that quarrel; and that what goes along with that victory is the ascendancy of fiction over reality, lying over truth, and making over knowing. How was that quarrel decided? How did the poets, who since Plato's day seemed roundly defeated, finally end up victorious? Did they win all at once, with a sudden reversal? Or was this more a gradual affair where the battle was perhaps subtly lost early on, with victory becoming manifest only later as small losses accumulated into a final and wholesale rout? The latter, I believe, may well be what happened. Possibly, right after the highest flowering of philosophy in the Middle Ages, a poet came along who planted the seeds of its eventual defeat, seeds that would manifest their fruit only centuries later. The poet I am speaking of is Dante, and the philosopher he may

---

[1] Friedrich Nietzsche, *Beyond Good and Evil*, trans. Helen Zimmern, ed. Walter Kaufmann (Mineola, New York: Dover, 1997), #34, p. 26.

well have used as his Trojan Horse to bring down philosophical ascendancy was Thomas Aquinas. Nevertheless, what may well have made this defeat possible was that Aquinas was also a believer, a Christian believer, who believed that the one Poet and creator of everything that was, is, and will be, also became a man and dwelled among us. Perhaps ultimately the quarrel had been decided long before, and Dante merely pushed it along towards its conclusion and fundamental quarrel—who will be poet here, us or God?

But let us back up a bit. To begin this investigation we must remember what Aquinas claimed regarding Holy Scripture. In the last article of the first question in his *Summa Theologiae*, Aquinas takes up directly the distinctive nature of Holy Scripture. The heart of what he says is found in the following quotation from St. Gregory:

> St. Gregory declares that *Holy Scripture transcends all other sciences by its very style of expression, in that one and the same discourse, while narrating an event, transmits a mystery as well.*[2]

Unique among all ways of knowing, in Holy Scripture we find that "one and the same" discourse, by narrating an "event," opens us up to the possibility that it may also be transmitting a mystery. In other words, there is something about the very nature of biblical discourse that allows it to transcend all other sciences, both practical and theoretical, if and only if, God is its author. The "style" opens up this possibility; but as we shall see, it is not the style but rather its "Stylist" that moves it from being a possibility to an actuality that transcends all other sciences.

Aquinas bases this entire article on the belief in God as the author of Holy Scripture, and the effect that belief has on interpreting its meaning. As he puts it in his reply: "That God is the author of Holy Scripture should be acknowledged"; or again later: "Now because the literal sense is that which the author intends, and the author of Holy Scripture is God who comprehends everything all at once in his understanding, it comes not amiss, as St. Augustine observes, if many meanings are present even in the literal sense of one passage of Scripture."[3] In other words, the problem of interpreting the meaning of Scripture is a problem that can only be solved by attending to the role of its author; and yet this attention to its author, or poet, is nothing less than the attention to the poet required in all comedies.[4] The inter-

---

[2] Thomas Aquinas, *Summa Theologiae*, ed. Thomas Gilby, O.P., (Garden City, New York: Image Books, 1969), I, q.1, a. 10.

[3] *Summa Theologiae* I, a. 10, ad 1.

[4] The pre-eminent role of the "poet" in his reflexive relation to the audience is developed in my unpublished dissertation "Comedy and Tragedy and their Central Importance to Philosophy and Theology," Boston College, 1994.

pretative move to a transcendent author, then, does not overthrow or subvert the literal sense but is rather based upon and arises out of it. Scripture requires of any reader first and foremost a good reading; and it is that reading of its literal and comic sense that demands of us readers that we answer the question as to who its real poet is. For it is only in answering this question, even if we answer that it could not be God, that we can gain full access to its meaning. In typical comic reciprocity, the question as to the poet is equally a question as to the audience. It is only in this full circuit, then, this self-conscious-because-comic-circuit, that the full sense of a comic discourse's meaning can be found.

Yet, because of the historiographical intent of the Scriptures, the comic, literal sense must also be connected with what Aquinas calls the "historical" sense of Scripture. The way Aquinas explains the meaning of these juxtaposed terms is to set them off from what he calls the "spiritual senses" of Scripture. The literal and historical sense, he says, is the power of adapting words to convey meanings, a power that is no more nor less than the power of all human written and spoken discourse. Yet in addition to this power, there is the power of adapting "things themselves" to convey meanings, a power that is reserved to God alone. In speaking of Scripture, therefore, Aquinas says:

> In every branch of knowledge words have meaning, but what is *special* here is that the things meant by the words also themselves mean something. The first meaning whereby the words signify things belongs to the sense first-mentioned, namely the historical or literal. The meaning, however, whereby the things signified by the words in their turn also signify other things is called the spiritual sense; it is based on and presupposes the literal sense.[5]

The "specialness" of Scripture is thus the specific qualities of its poet, and those qualities are the unique qualities of the poetic maker of the world who alone can fit things-to-things together in the world to make meaning; just as any human poet can put words-to-things (and presumably words-to-words) together to make meaning in his own verbal world. The fact that Scripture has both a literal and spiritual sense is thus a result of the nature of its poet, and not a quality of the poem itself.

But what of the poem itself? Is Aquinas here espousing a crude sort of literalism, with a one-to-one correspondence between words and things, thereby making God the only poet who has written anything interesting or worth reading? Not at all, for if we turn to his reply to an objection on the

---

[5] *Summa Theologiae* I, a. 10, resp. (italics added).

parabolic sense, we will have a clear view of all that he includes under the literal sense. "The parabolic sense is contained in the literal sense, for words can signify something properly and something figuratively; in the last case the literal sense is not the figure of speech itself, but the object it figures."[6] Aquinas goes on to give an example of what he means by this in the following: "When Scripture speaks of the arm of God, the literal sense is not that he has a physical limb, but that he has what it signifies, namely the power of doing and making."[7] Now we have a better idea of what Aquinas could mean by the literal sense. For what this literal sense must include is the entire range of figurative meanings of the text (which would seem to include both the living and dead metaphors of language). This implies that the parabolic sense of Scripture is the norm rather than the exception, and that the literal sense includes the entire gamut of good readings with all their comic possibilities. On the other hand, it is only the spiritual sense that can include the actuality of meaning found in Aquinas's "Sacred Doctrine" and "articles of faith"; for this meaning can only flow from the reader's assent to the literal claim that God, rather than any man or men, is in fact the comic poet behind this comic narrative.

The equation between the historical and literal sense in Scripture is therefore what opens up the believing reader to the vertical dimension of Auerbach's "figural interpretation,"[8] for the trans-historical connection between "things and things" is at best only a literary conceit apart from faith. If that faith is presupposed, as it is in Aquinas's account of theology, then the grounding of Scripture in its initial historical and literal sense also allows for the three spiritual senses described in the following:

> Now this spiritual sense is divided into three. For, as St. Paul says, *The Old Law is the figure of the New*, and the New Law itself, as Dionysius says, *is the figure of the glory to come*. Then again, under the New Law the deeds wrought by our Head are signs also of what we ourselves ought to do.
>
> Well then, the allegorical sense is brought into play when the things

---

[6] *Summa Theologiae* I, q. 1, a. 10, ad 3.

[7] Ibid.

[8] "Figural interpretation . . . establishes a connection between two events or persons in such a way that the first signifies not only itself but also the second, while the second involves or fulfills the first. The two poles of a figure are separated in time, but both, being real events or persons, are within temporality. They are both contained in the flowing stream which is historical life, and only the comprehension, the *intellectus spiritualis*, of their interdependence is a spiritual act" (Erich Auerbach, *Mimesis. The Representation of Reality in Western Literature*, trans. Willard R. Trask [Princeton, New Jersey: Princeton University Press, 1953], p. 73).

of the Old Law signify the things of the New Law; the moral sense when the things done in Christ and in those who prefigured him are signs of what we should carry out; and the anagogical sense when the things that lie ahead in eternal glory are signified.[9]

What all three of these spiritual senses have in common is the presupposition of an historical continuity between the concrete situation of the believing reader (belief is what makes them "spiritual," for faith is a spiritual rather than natural possibility) and the historical world enunciated in Scripture. Another way of putting this would be to say that if the reader believes his own concretely historical world to be part of the comic world described as beginning with the creation *ex nihilo* in Genesis and ending in the future with the new creation seen in the vision of Revelation, then the spiritual senses are no more than what flows from assenting to the historical and literal sense of Scripture as true. Nothing is added to what is already potentially there, other than the transformation of the reader himself to an already existing, yet for the reader, an altogether "new" reality. The "newness" of the New Law in the allegorical sense is thus part and parcel of the morally new covenant brought about by Christ and the anagogical new creation that will bring this story to full closure. The centerpiece to this entire circuit, however, is the historical life, rather than a mere narrative of the "head," Jesus Christ of Nazareth, who in his unique historical particularity ties in the narrative of the Old Testament with both the literal and concretely historical position of any given reader.

Consider this in the light of Umberto Eco's own account of why the literal and historical are combined in Aquinas.

> But why should it be that the spiritual senses found in [S]cripture are not equally literal? The answer is that the biblical authors were not aware that their historical accounts possessed the senses in question. Scripture had these senses in the mind of God, and would have them later for those readers who sought in the Old Testament for a prefiguring of the New. But the authors themselves wrote under divine inspiration; they did not know what they were really saying. Poets, by contrast, know what they want to say and what they are saying. Poets therefore speak literally, even when they use rhetorical figures.[10]

Apart from the too historicized account of the historical meaning of Scripture, what Eco brings out well here is that the literal meaning of all other poetry besides the Bible, comic or tragic, is entirely literal even at the

---

[9] *Summa Theologiae* I, q. 1, a. 10, resp.

[10] Umberto Eco, *The Aesthetics of Thomas Aquinas*, trans. Hugh Bredin (Cambridge, Massachusetts: Harvard University Press, 1988), p. 154.

heights of its rhetorical and poetic force. Poets *as* poets do not, and cannot, write historically, and it is the Bible alone that makes the unique claim to be historical even while remaining poetic. Such a claim, of course, remains merely a "literal" claim, however unique or odd, if God is not in fact its poet and Jesus is not the Word of God that mediated all of creation.

There are thus two demands that must be distinguished in reading the Bible. The first is the demand to read it well and to discover the uniqueness of its comic narrative structure and the uniqueness of its literal claims to be also historical—a demand upon any reader, whatever his or her beliefs are. The second demand, dependent upon the first, is that the reader decide whether or not this poem's claim to be authored by God Himself is true; for it is only in the yes or no of that decision that the full circuit of meaning of this text can reach fruition, a fruition that fulfills the "historical" sense, so to speak, along with the spiritual sense.

If we turn to Dante at this point, what we find is a suspicious obscuring of these two distinctive demands. Initially, Dante lays out for us what he calls the "allegory of the poets" in contrast to what Aquinas has just described, which Dante calls the "allegory of the theologians." Not surprisingly, this description fits quite nicely into the way Aquinas describes the "parabolic sense":

> [O]ne should know that writing can be understood and must be ex-
> plained mainly in four senses. One is called the literal [and this is the
> sense that does not go beyond the letter of the fictive words, as are the
> fables of the poets. The other is called allegorical] and this is the sense
> that is hidden under the cloak of these fables, and it is a truth hidden
> under the beautiful lie, as when Ovid says that Orpheus tamed the wild
> beasts with his zither and caused the trees and stones to come to him;
> which signifies that the wise man with the instrument of his voice
> would make cruel hearts gentle and humble, and would make those
> who do not live in science and art do his will; and those who have no
> kind of life of reason in them are as stones. And the reason why this
> concealment was devised by wise men will be shown in the next to the
> last treatise. It is true that theologians understand this sense otherwise
> than do the poets; but since it is my intention here to follow after the
> manner of the poets, I take the allegorical sense as the poets are wont
> to take it.[11]

This quotation is from Dante's *Convivio*, written well before his *Commedia*. In it we can see that his description of the allegory of the poets fits in

---

[11] Dante Alighieri, *Convivio*, quoted in Charles Singleton, *Dante's Commedia: Elements of Structure* (Baltimore, Maryland: The John Hopkins University Press, 1954), p. 85.

well with the immanent possibilities of human authorship, insofar as the words of the poets that refer to the events of their fables can also refer not to other things, but to the other meanings or "truths" hidden under the beautiful lie of the poets. At this point, then, there is no problem. The "beautiful lie" of the poets is subordinated to the knowledge of the wise man, and the example Dante gives of poetry in Ovid is very little different from how one might read the poetry of Plato's dialogues in relation to the philosophical truth that is esoterically conveyed through them. If we turn to another argument of Dante we can see how the problem arises.

This writing is the "Letter to Can Grande," composed while Dante was in the midst of writing his *Commedia*, and seemingly an account of how to read his new poem. Many have accounted this writing spurious, most convincingly for the problem we will see it presents, but there is now a greater consensus as to its genuineness. To see the problem, as you read, ask yourself whether he is here describing what he has earlier called the "allegory of the poets" or "the allegory of the theologians."

> To elucidate, then, what we have to say, be it known that the sense of this work is not simple, but on the contrary it may be called polysemous, that is to say, "of more senses than one"; for it is one sense that we get through the letter, and another which we get through the thing the letter signifies; and the first is called literal, but the second allegorical or mystic. And this mode of treatment, for its better manifestation, may be considered in this verse: "When Israel came out of Egypt, and the house of Jacob from a people of strange speech, Judea became his sanctification, Israel his power." For if we inspect the letter alone, the departure of the children of Israel from Egypt in the time of Moses is presented to us; if the allegory, our redemption wrought by Christ; if the moral sense, the conversion of the soul from grief . . . if the anagogical, the departure of the holy soul from the slavery of corruption. . . . And although these mystic senses have each their special denominations, they may all in general be called allegorical, since they differ from the literal and historical. . . . [W]e must therefore consider the subject of this work [his *Commedia*] as literally understood, and then its subject as allegorically intended.[12]

What should leap out immediately from this account is its close modeling after the similar four senses of Scripture we have just seen in Aquinas. What should next be noted is the startling divergence from it. For in Dante's account we find no mention of what is all important in Aquinas— the complete dependence of the three spiritual senses upon the authorship of God. In Aquinas it is God alone who can connect "things to things" and

---

[12] Ibid., p. 87.

so make the allegorical, moral, and anagogical senses genuinely distinct from all the various figural meanings that could be included in the literal sense. Here, however, these spiritual senses are termed "mystic" or "allegorical" and then applied to the allegory intended in Dante's new poem. Is this, then, the old "allegory of the poets" of the *Convivio*, and not the "allegory of the theologians" found in Aquinas? If so, why would the example Dante uses to illustrate the various allegorical senses all be drawn from Scripture? His very choice of examples, drawing as they do from the possibility of connecting events to events, such as the departure of Israel from Egypt to the soul's redemption in Christ, would seem to apply to that possibility alone of connecting things disconnected in time and space that we find in an ever-present and omnipotent God of creation. Dante, you would think, should know better. What is he up to?

My contention is that Dante has, self-consciously or not, assimilated to himself the world-making powers of the Christian God. What we see here is Dante's radically new approach to poetry that gives to the poet divine powers unheard of in the pagan world. By taking up the prerogatives of Scripture, the poet assimilates himself to the world-making powers of the Christian God through a sleight of hand that simultaneously elevates the poet's creativity even while undermining the uniqueness of God's. Such a move is not at all surprising in light of the similar move made by the later Romantics, and the connection that Nietzsche draws between the murder of God and the transformation of reality into fiction would here find its primordial origin. But this sort of move is quite surprising in Dante, at the high-water mark of medieval piety and, seemingly, the poetic embodiment of Thomistic philosophy.

Nevertheless, something odd did seem to happen at this point. Erich Auerbach, in commenting on this and the following period, notes a significant transformation that he is nevertheless loath to blame on Dante. For even though "Dante's work remained almost without influence on the history of European thought; immediately after his death, and even during his lifetime, the structure of literary, cultured society underwent a complete change in which he had no part, the change from Scholastic to Humanistic thinking."[13] Drawing upon the example of Petrarch, Auerbach points out how even though a mere forty years younger than him,

> [H]e is distinguished from Dante above all by his new attitude toward
> his own person; it was no longer in looking upward . . . that Petrarch

---

[13] Erich Auerbach, "The Survival and Transformation of Dante's Vision of Reality," in *Dante: A Collection of Critical Essays*, ed. John Freccero (Englewood Cliffs, New Jersey: Prentice Hall, 1954), p. 10.

expected to find self-fulfillment, but in the conscious cultivation of his own nature. Although far inferior to Dante in personality and natural endowment, he was unwilling to acknowledge any superior order or authority. . . . The autonomous personality, of which Petrarch was to be the first fully typical modern European embodiment, has lived in a thousand forms and varieties; the conception takes in all the tendencies of the modern age, the business spirit, the religious subjectivism, the humanism, and the striving for physical and technological domination of the world. . . . From Christianity, whence it rose and which it ultimately defeated, this conception inherited unrest and immoderation. These qualities led it to discard the structure and limits of Dante's world, to which, however, it owed the power of its actuality.[14]

What Auerbach points out here is the uniquely Christian, and yet anti-Christian, inheritance following on closely after Dante. "Secularized Christianity," the deliberate transformation and defanging of Christian doctrines into an immanent historical process, begun by Rousseau and attaining its high-water mark in Hegel, would thus seem no more than the full working out of a possibility built into the first Christian poetic epic and its author's account of what he is doing.

For what we have neglected until now is that Dante, the poet, is facing off not exactly with a philosopher, à la Plato, but with a theologian. And the reason Aquinas is finally a theologian rather than a philosopher is that he believes in a poetizing, which is to say creating, God who has created what was once termed "nature" (that which was earlier conceived as bringing itself into being), and who has also appeared in this, His own poem, and made manifest its central plot. Aquinas, in other words, has reconciled in his own mind the quarrel between the poets and the philosophers, but this reconciliation is only possible if God is the sole poet of both the natural things of nature and the human things of history and politics. To quarrel with the theologian rather than the philosopher, can now only take the shape of quarreling for philosophy against poetry and theology, or of quarreling for one poet against another, which is to say, of quarreling for human poetry in general against the one Poet of nature and Scripture. When Dante therefore takes on the prerogatives of the author of Scripture in his own authorship, and when Dante is the central character in his own poem who along with Virgil, Statius, and the eternal maker of the gates of hell, raises the question of poetic making with all its rivalry and educational ascendancy, we cannot help but ask the question of whether or not Dante has himself opened up the gates to a serious poetic rivalry with God.

[14] Ibid., pp. 10–11.

At this point, however, you may have grown impatient with my argument, and responded with what is essentially the argument of both Charles Singleton and Erich Auerbach. For their response is embodied in the words with which Singleton ends his famous essay on Dante, "The Two Kinds of Allegory." "And if you say: 'I do not believe that Dante ever went to the other world,' then I say that with those who deny what a poem asks to be granted, there is no further disputing."[15] A poem, in other words, is meant to be "realistic," and so if it uses the realism of the Bible to graft on its own story, is not that itself a tribute to and continuation of the historical reality begun in the Biblical narrative? This, however, is exactly the problem. "Realism" is not reality. "Realism" and the "realistic" is something contrived to look like reality, but the contriver or poet is precisely he who stands between us and true reality. If the "as-if" quality of poetry is used to teach and illustrate historical reality, then history and reality will inevitably become no more than a species of human making wherein "realistic" will become the closest approximation to and finally one and the same with the real. Reality and history will become in their totality a fiction, and yet since there is no longer one poet responsible, this will be a fiction that, Nietzsche quite rightly proclaimed, has no author. But the reason this fiction we call "reality" has no author, the reason we now share in this common "aestheti-zation of reality," is that we no longer make the distinction between what a poet does when he makes a world, and the world that no one could make because it is made by the maker of creation and Scripture. Once we forget that making is not knowing, that we live in a world wherein all human making is a lie except God's own making in Scripture, then we have ourselves killed the God of Creation and Scripture through a violent act of usurpation. As Nietzsche says, "Lightning and thunder require time; the light of the stars requires time, deeds though done, still require time to be seen and heard."[16] We have killed God long ago, but only now are beginning to see its full effects through our glorification of human creativity that follows apace with our denigration and hostility to the creator of Scripture.

It is no surprise, then, that any well-educated student today, particularly a graduate of a Catholic liberal arts college, is more likely to know something about Dante and the poetic world of his making, than the biblical world found in the Bible. This is not to say such a student has not studied the Bible. On the contrary, he or she has probably taken a required course

---

[15] Singleton, *Dante's Commedia: Elements of Structure*, p. 94.
[16] Friedrich Nietzsche, *The Gay Science*, trans. Walter Kaufmann (New York: Vintage Books, 1974), #125, p. 181.

to both the Old and New Testaments. Yet what have they learned in those courses? The God who is their author? Or the "human, all too human" authors who poetically expressed their religious experience through their beautiful, but—admit it—not nearly as beautiful, poetry as Dante's. God is now, in fact, no longer the author of Scripture, and the graffiti of higher criticism that covers over his words are no less opaque than the blood that covers our own hands for the murder of that poet of all poets, the divine Logos through whom everything was made that has been made.

PART II

THE ARTS, THE ARTIST,
AND INTERPRETATIONS

Art's Invaluable Uselessness

Gregory J. Kerr

Every work of art reaches man in his inner powers. It reaches him more profoundly and insidiously than any rational proposition, either cogent demonstration or sophistry. For it strikes him with two terrible weapons, Intuition and Beauty, and at the single root in him of all his energies, Intellect and Will, Imagination, Emotion, Passions, Instincts and obscure Tendencies. Art and Poetry awaken the dreams of man, and his longings, and reveal to him some of the abysses he has in himself.[1]

When I was young, my father who was a drama critic, had me read twenty pages of fiction a day and, at the same time, would argue with me about art. "Art really had no 'use' and was in no way 'good' for us," he would say. If he thought that, why would he force me to read and experience so much of it? While I knew that there was something wrong with artists teaching or preaching, I wondered about this: If art was no "good" for us, why should we appreciate it? What benefits would we get?

Yes, of course there is pleasure and it is good. According to St. Thomas, no one can live without it.[2] Thomas goes so far as to say that if one does not enjoy spiritual pleasures one will turn towards carnal ones.[3] But to stop

---

[1] Jacques Maritain, *The Responsibility of the Artist* (New York: Charles Scribner's Sons, 1960), pp. 58–59.

[2] For references, see Jacques Maritain, *Creative Intuition in Art and Poetry* (Princeton, New Jersey: Princeton University Press, 1977), p. 190; *The Responsibility of the Artist*, p. 85; Thomas Aquinas, *Summa Theologiae* II–II, q. 35, a. 4, ad 2 (hereafter cited as *ST*). All separate references to the *Summa* will be to the Benziger Edition (New York: Benziger Brothers, 1947). See also Aristotle, *Nicomachean Ethics* VIII. 5 and 6.

[3] Jacques Maritain, *Art and Scholasticism and The Frontiers of Poetry*, trans. Joseph Evans (Notre Dame, Indiana: University of Notre Dame Press, 1974), p. 75; Aquinas, *ST* II–II, q. 35, a. 4, ad 2. The source of this notion is found in Aristotle,

the explanation at pleasure is not enough. To tell others that they should appreciate art, and then when they ask why, to tell them it is only a matter of pleasure might cause them to wonder why they are working so hard at getting it! Their bewilderment seems justified. Although it is true that the artist aims at the formally well-constructed object, and although it is true that the viewer views to receive pleasure, it is also true that all pleasures are not the same. There must be other reasons why teachers want their students to read, to go to museums, or to see movies rather than watch television. While my father would write in the book, *The Decline of Pleasure*, that "We must learn to live with the fact that nothing 'good' is going to come of pleasure," he would also write that pleasure makes him "certain that [he is] not a displaced person in a universe indifferent to [him]," and that it enables him "to move about in it." He even adds, "But if I have no direct, deep experience of how much the universe and I agree, I shall doubt the likelihood of our ever coming to a mutual understanding and so become immobilized or very angry."[4]

This brings us back to the question of the value in finding pleasure in great works of art. Maritain claims that art should not give us speculative truths nor practical moral advice. In addition, claims Maritain, it cannot add one drop of grace to the spiritual life. Why then should we value works of art? Why not claim as do Plato and Augustine that most art simply diverts us away from the truth and the real meaning of life? There was no more profound critic of the aesthetic experience than Plato. Plato's and Socrates's basic philosophical idea was that the "unexamined life is not worth living for a human being." Philosophers all tell us (with Socrates chief among them) that it is critical to human living that we critically examine how we are and how we "see" reality. Those who fail to do this to some degree are, in the words of E. F. Schumacher, "being lived" rather than living; they are living their lives according to a default program—the agendas of others. If we are to flourish as human beings, we must then examine ourselves and how we critically understand reality. Now the aesthetic experience, Plato would assert, does not help us to do either one. In fact, Plato would claim, the aesthetic experience makes its appeal to our passions and appetites, not to our reason where we could critically deal with it. Plato tells us in the *Republic* that "[r]hythm and harmony insin-

Nicomachean Ethics VIII.5 and 6, and X.6. Clearly one of the basic benefits of the aesthetic experience is pleasure.

4 Walter Kerr, *The Decline of Pleasure* (New York: Simon and Schuster, 1964), pp. 245, 311–12.

uate themselves into the innermost part of the soul and most vigorously lay hold of it."[5] He claims that art does not knock at the front door of our reason to ask permission to enter into our souls, but instead, invites itself right in and plays with us. He forbids the craftsman to practice his art so that our youths will not be reared on images of vice, as it were on bad grass, every day, grazing little by little from many places; and, while they are totally unaware of it, putting together a big bad thing in their souls.[6] Homer's lies are harmful to us, for if we are not careful, we will be sympathetic toward ourselves when we are bad.[7] Ultimately, Plato feels that human beings should be searching for the decisive and universal truths that lie beyond the vicissitudes of space and time, but art deals with none of this. Art is concerned with the contingent, the singular, the changing, and the sensual. The artist turns away from the metaphysical domain, from the forms, from logic, to the flesh of material reality. Plato thinks that art's lies are very powerful and penetrating, and may very likely wreck havoc on our souls.

Would Maritain come to the rescue here and claim that art does indeed intend to educate and improve us? Absolutely not! According to Maritain, to respond thus would be to miss the whole point about art and the aesthetic experience. Surprisingly, Maritain thinks that much of what Plato says is true! We must start with the fact that the artist does lie to us and that the work of art does in fact seduce us! Our purpose here is to show that art is most valuable to the human being when it is most useless. It is so because it does what no other dimension of human intelligence can do, and we will find out why by looking at Maritain's famous line: "Beauty is the splendor of all the transcendentals united."

In a way, Plato was right! Maritain argues along with St. Thomas Aquinas, himself no hater of art, that art is supposed to have a *defect in truth* and to seduce us. Thomas tells us that "reason is unable to grasp poetic knowledge on account of its *defect in truth*."[8] Aquinas tells us in another passage that through figures our reason is even seduced[9].

There are lies given in the aesthetic experience, but why? To understand

---

[5] *Republic* III.401d, trans. Allan Bloom (New York: Harper Collins, 1991).

[6] Ibid., 401c.

[7] Ibid., 391e.

[8] *ST* I–II, q. 101, a. 2, ad 2. "Poetica scientia est de his quae propter defectum veritatis non possunt a ratione capi; unde oportet quod quasi quibusdam similitudinibus ratio seducatur" (Aquinas, *In I Sententiarum*, prol., q. 1, a. 5, ad 3, cited by Jacques Maritain, "Concerning Poetic Knowledge," in *The Situation of Poetry* [New York: Kraus Reprint; Philosophical Library, 1968], n. 16).

[9] Ibid.

this we must examine the creative process and the nature of the creative intelligence.

II

According to Maritain, one of the definitive acquisitions made by philosophy is the distinction between the speculative and practical intellect.[10] Although strongly insisting with Thomas that the intellect is one power,[11] it has these distinct and often opposing functions. Maritain holds that the virtue of art, which is a virtue of the practical intellect, disposes the artist not to a knowledge of something, but rather to an object to be made.[12] While the speculative intellect wants only to know being, the practical wants only to use energies to perform some action or to make something. Art has its identity as a virtue of the practical intellect.[13]

While he cannot work without the speculative intellect, the artist nevertheless does not primarily rely on it in making a work of art. Thus, he does not import discursive, step by step, logical, factual "truths" found there into the work of art. For these can only be produced by the speculative intellect. The result is that there is little discursive meaning for the viewer to detect. Maritain maintains this dichotomy all throughout his work, insisting that the artist, insofar as he is in the act of creating, does not and should not consciously and intentionally import any pre-packaged "truths" into the work of art.

Not only does the virtue of art not directly concern discursive truths, but it also does not directly concern the good of man. The viewer will not receive anything resembling moral instruction through the artwork. The artist is not trying to serve men or make them better, he works for the work alone. While art, the capacity to make things well, and prudence, the capacity to

---

[10] Maritain, *Creative Intuition in Art and Poetry*, pp. 45–46, 168, 173, n. 22. According to St. Thomas, "[T]he speculative and practical intellects differ. . . . For it is the speculative intellect which directs what it apprehends, not to operation, but to the consideration of truth; while the practical intellect is that which directs what it apprehends to operation" (*ST* I, q. 79, a. 11, resp.).

[11] For an excellent analysis of the practical and speculative intellect and the unity of the intellect, according to St. Thomas, see Josef Pieper, "Reality and the Good," trans. Stella Lange, in *Living the Truth* (San Francisco: Ignatius Press, 1989).

[12] It might be said in this regard that the creative activity of the artist serves the viewer's ultimate end by helping his intellect in some obscure fashion to be adequated to the ultimate truth about things; but this is not the end of the artist *qua artist*, his end is to make a beautiful object.

[13] "The *practical* order is opposed to the speculative order because there man tends to something other than knowledge only. If he knows, it is no longer to rest in the truth, and to enjoy it (*frui*); it is to use (*uti*) his knowledge, with a view to some work or some action" (Maritain, *Art and Scholasticism*, p. 6).

act well, are both virtues of the practical intellect, they are nevertheless different. While prudence concerns the good of the human being, art is concerned with the good of the work alone.[14]

Even evil people can be great artists. Maritain writes that "Oscar Wilde was but a good Thomist when he wrote: 'The fact of a man being a poisoner is nothing against his prose.'"[15] In *The Responsibility of the Artist* he quotes St. Thomas as saying, "The kind of good which art pursues is not the good of the human will or appetite [or the good of man], but the good of the very works done or artifacts."[16]

Thus, the artist cannot edify the viewer in any way. Any attempt to do so results in polluting the work. Maritain writes in *Art and Scholasticism*, "In this sense every thesis, whether it claims to demonstrate some truth or to touch the heart, is for art a foreign importation, hence an impurity."[17] He rejects the utilitarian and social theory of art and he holds that to the degree that art is put to the purposes or interests of the moral or social order, it is to this "very extent . . . warped and bent to the service of a master who is not its only genuine master, namely the work." Such art, for Maritain, is inevitably "propaganda."[18]

III

Now, if art lies and seduces us, what can possibly be beneficial about all of this? A clue to the benefits of the aesthetic experience is found in a rather strange and elusive remark by Maritain: "Strictly speaking, beauty is the radiance of all the transcendentals united."[19]

---

[14] "But the practical order itself is divided into two entirely distinct spheres, which the ancients called the sphere of Doing (*agibile, prakton*) and the sphere of Making (*factibile, poietikon*). . . . Art, which rules Making and not Doing, stands therefore outside the human sphere; it has an end, rules, values, which are not those of man, but those of the work to be produced" (Maritain, *Art and Scholasticism*, pp. 7–9).

[15] Maritain, *The Responsibility of the Artist*, p. 24.

[16] Ibid.

[17] Maritain, *Art and Scholasticism*, pp. 62–63.

[18] Maritain, *The Responsibility of the Artist*, pp. 72–73. The artist or poet deals with that which lies beyond his purposes. On this activity and the ecstasy it brings to the artist see Deal W. Hudson, "The Ecstasy Which is Creation: The Shape of Maritain's Aesthetics" in *Understanding Maritain: Philosopher and Friend*, eds. Deal W. Hudson and Matthew Mancini (Macon, Georgia: Mercer University Press, 1987).

[19] Maritain, *Art and Scholasticism*, p. 173, n. 66; translation of "A vrai dire il est la splendeur de tous les transcendantaux réunis" (*Art et scolastique*, p. 225, n. 66). The phrase first appears in the footnotes of *Art et scolastique* in the second edition in 1927. May we suggest at this point the significance of the word *réunir*? According to Cassell's *French and English Dictionary*, the primary meaning is "to

We may see in this phrase either something so abstract that it doesn't seem to help us much, or nothing but a simple truism. If we know our perennial philosophy, we know that being is one, true, good, and beautiful and we might think that we can mix and match as we please, but this is not the case, according to Maritain. Unless one were God, the transcendentals do not appear united; the good is not necessarily the true, and vice versa.[20] While operating in the world, the different faculties of man grasp being differently. Our "will . . . does not of itself tend to the true, but solely and jealously to the good of man."[21] The intellect by itself desires the truth, which of itself does not inspire but "only illumines."[22] In fact, nothing with a drive toward the infinite—as is the human aspiration for truth or for goodness—is in accord with any other similar drive.[23] Maritain even tells us that they can be enemies. We see the resulting conflict being played out in those who, according to Maritain, in the "spirit of Luther, Rousseau, or Tolstoy defend the order of the moral good,"[24] while others like Aristotle[25] and Aquinas defend the order of truth. "Here are two families which hardly understand each other, here as elsewhere, the prudent one dreads the contemplative and distrusts him."[26] Often, even in ordinary life, we separate out

---

reunite." The beautiful brings the transcendentals back together. It is interesting to note that Cornelia N. Borgerhoff, who worked with Maritain on *Creative Intuition* and *The Responsibility of the Artist*, translates the same phrase as the "splendor of all the transcendentals gathered together" (*An Introduction to the Basic Problems of Moral Philosophy* [Albany, New York: Magi Books, 1990], p. 69; *Neuf leçons sur les notions premières de la philosophie morale* [Paris: Pierre Téqui, 1960], p. 63).

[20] "Wherefore beauty, truth, goodness (especially when it is no longer a question of metaphysical or transcendental good itself, but of moral good) command distinct spheres of human activity, of which it would be foolish to deny *a priori* the possible conflict, on the pretext that the transcendentals are indissolubly bound to one another" (Maritain, *Art and Scholasticism*, p. 174, n. 68). It must be clarified that while the "moral good" with which much of art is concerned, is not the ontological "good" of the transcendentals, nevertheless it, like the relationship of aesthetic beauty to transcendental beauty, is a particularized form of it and is based upon it. For references see *ST* I–II, q. 18, a. 1–2.

[21] Maritain, *Art and Scholasticism*, p. 7.

[22] Ibid., p. 26.

[23] "The fact is that all these energies, insofar as they pertain to the transcendental universe, aspire like poetry to surpass their nature and to infinitize themselves. . . . Art, poetry, metaphysics, prayer, contemplation, each one is wounded, struck traitorously in the best of itself, and that is the very condition of its living. Man unites them by force" (Maritain, "Concerning Poetic Knowledge," in *The Situation of Poetry*, p. 56).

[24] Maritain, "An Essay on Art," in *Art and Scholasticism*, p. 98.

[25] Maritain, *Art and Scholasticism*, p. 33.

[26] Maritain, "The Freedom of Song," in *Art and Poetry*, trans. Elva de Pue Matthews (New York: Philosophical Library, 1943), p. 103.

either the truth or the value of something and focus upon that. We look upon a thing and immediately categorize it as "good," that is, somehow beneficial to us or others, or "intelligible," and we try to figure out its meaning, but "beauty is the splendor of all the transcendentals united." This tells us that here, in the aesthetic experience, the different transcendental energies can and do unite. Knowing how they do so is crucial to understanding the effects upon the viewer. They do so by surrendering and consenting to the seduction of the aesthetic experience. The faculties of intelligence and will must lay down their arms. The viewer is neither taught nor moved to action. If he consents, if he is seduced, his intelligence becomes bound by the *magical sign*. This is a sign not for his logical reason but for his imagination and emotion only. Here, his ego is not in control.

To understand why the aesthetic experience is so powerful for Maritain, we need to examine his view of the soul's powers. Maritain claims that in every human soul there are the different speculative, practical, and creative aspirations mentioned above. When we are thinking in any of these modes, we are engaged in a specialized way of thinking. However, for Maritain, there is an extremely cognitive and common root of the soul where all of the different energies of man originate, develop, and evolve. It is like a common factory or laboratory where all of the theoretical concepts, the practical ideas, and creative germs are born and are first formed. It is into this molten core of his personhood that the artist's soul suffers and takes in reality, and that the viewer receives the effect of the aesthetic experience. This is illustrated by Joseph Conrad:

> Confronted by the same enigmatical spectacle, the artist descends within himself, and in that lonely region of stress and strife, if he be deserving and fortunate, he finds the terms of his appeal. His appeal is made to our less obvious capacities: to that part of our nature which, because of the warlike conditions of existence, is necessarily kept out of sight.[27]

According to Maritain, it is only by giving up any chance at benefitting or being "useful" to any single faculty of the human being that the work of art really enriches the viewer. Reality has to be completely digested by the artist, recollected, known through emotion, and encoded in *magical signs*. Signs in which all of the distinctions between viewer and viewed, subject and object, and all of the laws of contradiction and identity break down. It

---

[27] Joseph Conrad, Preface to "The Nigger of the Narcissus," in *Great Short Works of Joseph Conrad* (New York: Harper & Row, 1967).

is this revised reality that reaches the viewer beyond the faculties in an astonishing integrity.

In the aesthetic experience, we are given a reality more real than in its logically interpreted appearances.[28] According to St. Thomas, "[R]eality is more real when taken up by the intellect than it is in itself."[29] But here we go one step further, it is even more real when taken up not by the intellect alone but with the will and with the integral whole of man together in all his faculties.[30] When there is no separation of the faculties we receive an impression like none other. Maritain frequently quotes his wife Raïssa in this regard:

> Poetry asks to be expressed by life bearing signs, signs which conduct the one who receives them back to the ineffability of the original experience, since in this contact all the sources of our faculties have been touched, the echo of it ought itself to be total.[31]

If it is true that an artist cannot impart logical or scientific truths, then it is also true that the primary reception of art is non-discursive. We are neither instructed in propositional truths nor moved to action. We are hit behind the front lines and at the heart. We are touched at the area of ourselves where will and intellect are one.

If it is true that the work of art cannot simply be an intelligibility to be understood nor a good to be possessed, it is not because it lacks either, but because it has a superabundance of both. The work of art must be not only a good object, but also a good object full of signification; otherwise the work of art, according to Maritain, would have nothing to say.[32]

But, again, this "saying" cannot be purposively intended by the artist. It

[28] Maritain, *Creative Intuition in Art and Poetry*, p. 30, n. 254.

[29] Maritain, "Frontiers of Poetry," in *Art and Scholasticism*, p. 127, n. 182. See *ST* I, q. 19, a. 1, ad 3.

[30] Poetic knowledge uses the entire human self, with all of the body, will, emotions, instincts, senses, etc., as an instrument to catch and detect reality. Reality reverberates through all of this.

[31] Maritain, "Concerning Poetic Knowledge," in *The Situation of Poetry*, p. 61. "Née dans une expérience vitale, vie elle-même, la poésie veut s'exprimer par des signes porteurs de vie, et qui ramèneront celui qui les reçoit à l'ineffabilité de l'expérience originelle. Comme dans ce contact toutes les sources de nos facultés ont été touchées, l'écho en doit être total, lui aussi" (*Situation de la poésie*, pp. 122–23).

[32] "The greatest poets and the most disinterested ones, the most 'gratuitous' ones, had something to say to men" (Maritain, "An Essay on Art," in *Art and Scholasticism*, p. 95); Maritain also writes, "If he (the artist) unhappily has nothing to tell us, his work is valueless" (*The Range of Reason* [New York: Charles Scribner's Sons, 1952], p. 20); for further discussion see Maritain, *The Responsibility of the Artist*, p. 56.

cannot be a thesis.[33] This "saying" cannot even be apart from the artist's life, but must arise from within his bloodstream.[34] What is said must be the result of an expression of the artist's own self into words on paper or paint onto canvas. By bringing forth his own self, he also casts out, with himself, the world that he suffers (experiences) at his depths. It is, as Deal Hudson has highlighted well, "the ecstasy which is creation."[35] The resulting work of art then is a well-constructed object whose value and significance lies within itself and yet reverberates with meanings.

If what we have said is true, then there are going to be two conditions for an effective reception of art. The vision, ideas, and values that pass through the work of art have to be of the form that will organically flow through the artist and his brush and then permeate the viewer; and the viewer needs to have a posture that will allow that vision, embodied in the canvas, inside. The beauty of the work must be, as Plato said, "a soft smooth, slippery thing, and therefore of a nature which easily slips in and permeates our souls."[36]

From the viewer's perspective, all great art causes itself *to be perceived* at a subdiscursive level so that the ultimate impact of the work cannot be discovered in advance. It can only be discovered by *magical signs* that cast a spell on our intelligence causing it to operate at a deeper and more condensed level. As Maritain quotes Henri Bergson in the very first edition of *Art and Scholasticism*:

> *The aim of Art* is to lull the active or rather the resistant powers of our personality and so bring us to a state of perfect docility, in which we realize the idea suggested, or sympathize with the feeling expressed.[37]

Once there and through our consent, our intelligence is held joyful prisoner by the imagination, and the work reveals to us—viewers whose various human transcendental energies are always fighting—a reality that is both true and good simultaneously.

[33] Maritain, *Art and Scholasticism*, p. 62; *Art et scolastique*, p. 109.

[34] Maritain frequently uses the image of nutrients moving through a plant or tree. For references see *Art and Scholasticism*, p. 74; *The Responsibility of the Artist*, pp. 58, 72.

[35] See Hudson, "The Ecstasy Which is Creation," in *Understanding Maritain*, pp. 235–56.

[36] Plato, *Lysis*, 216b.

[37] Maritain, *Art and Scholasticism* 1923, p. 164; "*L'objet de l'art* est d'endormir les puissances actives ou plutôt résistantes de notre personnalité et de nous amener ainsi à un état de docilité parfaite où nous réalisons l'idée qu'on nous suggère, où nous sympathisons avec le sentiment exprimé" (*Art et scolastique* 1920, p. 166). While for Maritain this entrancement is not the object of the work of art, it nevertheless characterizes all great art.

In the aesthetic experience, we do not focus on one type of knowledge or concern, we do not experience the dichotomies that arise between theory and practice, the true and the good, knowing and loving, but have an experience of these transcendentals united. They are united in the creative sufferings of the artist, they are united in the work of art, and they are united in the receptive intuition of the viewer. This experience gives us a powerful sense of the simultaneous synthesis of different transcendental perspectives, hence enabling us to drop the restrictions of logic and form in the speculative sphere, the restrictions of preconceived purposes in the practical sphere, and to acquire a fresh and more holistic perspective on being.

Usually, in ordinary life, we need to make distinctions, to isolate and define the natures or structures of things or, in the practical sphere, to categorize things as good or useful, but the artist does not do this. No, the artist experiences or "suffers"[38] reality at a level within himself, where intellect and will are one.[39] He produces an object that displays some aspect of reality as well as his will's relationship to it.[40] Finally, his work will reach us at the place where our will and intellect are both active.

It is the combination of the faculties in the artist and the combination of transcendental properties in the work of art and the subsequent combination of faculties in the posture of the viewer that allows the viewer to penetrate reality, to see the insides of things and people. For the intellect alone seeks the transcendental of "truth." It wants only to possess abstract forms and equations. The will alone wants to seek—at the level of the moral good— the transcendental "good," that is, the perfection of its own being. It wants only to go out from the human to be in union or sympathy with the other. Thus, the intellect has clarity but little penetrative power by itself. The will,

---

[38] Cf. Pseudo-Dionysius, *Mystical Theology*, chap. I; see "The Experience of the Poet," in *The Situation of Poetry*, p. 80. For further discussion, also see Maritain, "The Freedom of Song," in *Art and Poetry*, pp. 90, 198–99.

[39] "Confronted by the same enigmatical spectacle, the artist descends within himself, and in that lonely region of stress and strife, if he be deserving and fortunate, he finds the terms of his appeal. His appeal is made to our less obvious capacities: to that part of our nature which, because of the warlike conditions of existence, is necessarily kept out of sight" (Preface to "The Nigger of the Narcissus," in *Great Short Works of Joseph Conrad*, pp. 57–58).

[40] One can examine what Maritain has said of Rouault and Chagall. In *Rouault*, Maritain writes, "Beauty is the form love gives to things" (*Rouault Retrospective Exhibition* [New York: The Museum of Modern Art, 1953], p. 28). He writes elsewhere that Rouault "makes (natural forms) his own through the love he bears them" (*Creative Intuition in Art and Poetry*, p. 78, n. 6). Concerning Chagall he writes, "[H]is clear eyes see all bodies in a happy light, he delivers them from physical laws, and makes them obey the hidden law of the heart" ("Marc Chagall," in *Art and Poetry*, p. 17).

on the other hand, can penetrate but cannot possess knowledge of this union or penetration immanently within itself. It is only in the synthesis of both faculties that we have an intellectual penetration *and* possession of reality. It is only with both that we can appropriate our continual discovery and penetration into things.[41] Because it is a knowledge by connaturality, it is a knowledge which involves both intellect and will, knowledge and love. Because love goes beyond the frontiers of our present knowledge,[42] we can go out of ourselves towards the good. Often we know that something is good before we know facts about its nature; and it is precisely because of beauty that we often know about the nature of a particular good, "for," as Aquinas writes, "beauty adds something to the good, namely an order which enables cognition to know that a thing is of such a kind."[43]

Now, according to general Aristotelian and Thomist philosophy, we learn about things and their natures by receiving the effects of their activity on us. Ordinarily, in the case of scientific knowledge we receive sense impressions and abstract or intuit an essence and judge it. We do likewise in practical knowledge where we have our ready-made categories. In either area, we straightjacket reality and grasp its contours; however, reality is "more than is dreamt of in our philosophies," and Aquinas wrote that we can never fully know the essence of a single fly.[44] It is the artist who em-

---

[41] Maritain, *Creative Intuition in Art and Poetry*, pp. 93–94, 237–38. It is also remarkable in this regard that two prominent philosophers of science see scientific discovery as aesthetic or poetic. According to Thomas S. Kuhn, in the acceptance of new scientific paradigms, "the importance of aesthetic considerations can sometimes be decisive," and "Something must make at least a few scientists feel that the new proposal is on the right track, and sometimes it is only personal and inarticulate aesthetic considerations that can do that" (Kuhn, *The Structure of Scientific Revolutions* [Chicago: The University of Chicago Press, 1970], pp. 156–58). According to Karl Popper, "In this way, theories are seen to be the free creations of our own minds, the result of an almost poetic intuition, of an attempt to understand intuitively the laws of nature," and "Among the real dangers to the progress of science is not the likelihood of its being completed, but such things as lack of imagination" (Popper, *Conjectures and Refutations: The Growth of Scientific Knowledge* [New York: Harper & Row, 1965], pp. 192, 216).

[42] Maritain, *The Situation of Poetry*, p. 48; *Situation de la poésie*, p. 100.

[43] Thomas Aquinas, *In De Divinis Nominibus*, IV, 5.

[44] According to St. Thomas, "Our knowledge is so weak that no philosopher was ever able to investigate perfectly the nature of a single fly. Hence we read that one philosopher passed thirty years in solitude in order that he might know the nature of the bee" (*Symbolum Apostolorum Expositio*, quoted by Norris Clarke, S.J., "Action as the Self-Revelation of Being," in *History of Philosophy in the Making: Essays in Honor of James Collins*, ed. Linus Thro [Lanham, Maryland: University Press of America, 1982], p. 73).

braces this knowledge and mystery and has penetrating knowledge of it. Instead of receiving the impressions of things in reality and then confining
them by definition or reducing them to objects of utility,[45] he loves them[46]
enough to continue to suffer the actions of these natures. If it is true, as
Norris Clarke claims, that we know by the activity of things and people
what kind of "actors" they are,[47] it is also true that by letting go of the contours and conceptual outlines of things and people, by continuing to love
and suffer them,[48] the artist learns about their insides, their hidden meanings, energies, inclinations, and motives. This can only be done through the
intellectual "sharpening" of the artist's senses and by letting the actions of
things and of men penetrate and echo in his interiority.[49] In a real sense he
is the keyboard the world is playing, he is the canvas the world is stroking
with its brush. Only by filling himself up with the things of the world can
he, the artist, come out of sleep together with reality.[50] And we, the viewers, are invited to his awakening. We in turn are penetrated,[51] played,
painted on the inside by both the artist's interior vision and the reality he
suffers.[52]

IV

If Beauty is the radiance of all the transcendentals united, that is, if it is
the radiance of being confronting the power of knowledge (the true), being
as confronting the power of desire (the good),[53] and being as undivided (the
one), then these three dimensions can be separated out for analysis.

As the beautiful is the radiance of being confronting the intelligence, it
gives the viewer a penetrating vision of reality. The work of art enables the

---

[45] Maritain, *Creative Intuition in Art and Poetry*, p. 335, n. 3.

[46] Ibid., p. 58.

[47] Clarke, "Action As the Self-Revelation of Being," in *History of Philosophy in the Making*, pp. 63–80.

[48] Maritain, *Creative Intuition in Art and Poetry*, pp. 93–94.

[49] Maritain, *Art and Poetry*, p. 90.

[50] Maritain, *Creative Intuition in Art and Poetry*, p. 114.

[51] "We feel penetrated by a deeper mystery, a transcendent poetry, an absolute-
ness in liberty and pictorial science which convey to us a kind of burning serenity"
(Maritain, "Georges Rouault," in *Rouault Retrospective Exhibition*, p. 4).

[52] "It is above all with the reverse sign that investigations are concerned wherein
the work of art is, for example, studied as a sign of the cultural backgrounds which
engross the psychic life of the artist and of his epoch, and as a sign of the forces
which clash in him without his even being aware of them" (Jacques Maritain, *Ransoming the Time* [London: G. Bles, The Century Press, 1943], p. 254). The work of
art reveals the life of social groups, most often those other than the viewer's own.

[53] Maritain, *Creative Intuition in Art and Poetry*, p. 162.

viewer through the instrumentality of intentional emotion, which in the fine arts binds the true and the valuable together, to have a glimpse of the depths of reality.[54] The emotion that is the form of the work of art unites our energies and our very selves with the work of art and with the reality it embodies. It draws us toward things and toward knowing more of being.[55] While there are always essences in the world, it is primarily *esse* or the existential aspects of reality that the viewer is drawn or led to grasp.[56] It is those aspects of reality that the existentialists have been trying to get us to appreciate.

The aesthetic experience through the knowledge by connaturality allows us to penetrate things, to go deeper than science and philosophy, and to discover the kind of "actors" natural things and men truly are. It enables the intellect to see in, around, and between the contours of the natures of things in reality. Ordinarily, we do not want to go deeper. We like our formulas and our comfortable consciences. Our knowledge in the speculative domain gives us security and stability, but we must be "seduced" out of ourselves. The receptive intuition does this. It draws us out into an ecstasy which is vision—an existential vision of *esse,* the inner life source of things and their actions.

As beauty is the radiance of being confronting the power of desire, we receive a vision of our own hearts[57] and of the various crags and cavities within its own caverns.[58] We see what it is that our heart wants, a heart hitherto obscured by the cages of science and the fog of practical concerns. We feel our hearts, our desires beating with the work, and if no other in-

---

[54] Ibid., p. 31.

[55] Ibid., p. 8. Emotion draws us to see new and different relationships in reality.

[56] Maritain, *Art and Scholasticism*, p. 195, n. 130 (added in 1935 version). Maritain for all his existentialism was careful never to abandon natural forms or essences. They, after all, are the matrices through which *existence* (*esse*) flows into action and freedom.

[57] "Poetry . . . forces every lock, lies in wait for you where you least expected it. You can receive a little shock by which it makes its presence known, which suddenly makes the distances recede and unfurls the horizon of the heart" (Maritain, "The Frontiers of Poetry," in *Art and Scholasticism*, p. 129). Also, Maritain writes, "For in the long run any deeper awareness of what is hidden in man turns to a greater enlightenment of moral conscience" (*The Responsibility of the Artist*, p. 88).

[58] John Updike, for example, insists that "Fiction is nothing else than the subtlest instrument for self-examination and self-display that mankind has invented yet. . . . For the full *parfum* and effluvia of being human, for feathery ambiguity and rank facticity, for the air and iron, fire and spit of our daily mortal adventures there is nothing like fiction" (*Writers on Writing*, ed. Jon Winokur [Philadelphia, Pennsylvania: Running Press, 1990], p. 126).

sight about the world occurs, still we know how we have felt. While we may not be able to identify completely the subject being viewed, we know that it probes us profoundly. The hole left in our heart is enough. At some point in the past, reality has left its trace or footprint. Experiencing the music of Bach or a tragedy like *Othello*, we know that we have the capacity to feel this way, and to some extent, our feeling grasps reality. To have a tiny glimpse of the inner mountains and glaciers of our inner world[59] is to know that some reality has left its imprint there.[60] Nothing comes from nothing, and the inner cravings of the heart are sublime as it thirsts to see the vistas it has been made for.[61] Thus, for Maritain, an artist may be a devout believer or an atheist; what matters is the depth of the heart he has reached. The artist or poet shows us reality in reverse, not in its positive material dimension, but in its negative imprint left on the heart by some reality through emotion and feeling.[62] There is truth in art and it is the conformity of reality with emotion. It is reality as suffered, reality as felt.[63]

This is especially helpful because man is a seriously *incommodated* spirit.[64] Following Augustine, Maritain holds that we don't know our own heart and its desires.[65] He quotes Pascal saying that man's heart is full of

---

[59] "The reality expressed by Music is the universe and the soul as fused together, the astounding oceans and glaciers and skies of the inner world of man, in which the world of created things is transfigured and mirrored" (Jacques Maritain, "The Drawings of Arthur Lourié," *Latitudes* 2, no. 2 [1968], p. 6). According to Franz Kafka, "A book ought to be an icepick to break up the frozen sea within us" (*Writers on Writing*, ed. Jon Winokur, p. 46).

[60] Maritain, *Creative Intuition in Art and Poetry*, p. 254. The work of art is a "by-product of the state, a trace, the footprint of the state."

[61] "Art . . . begins groping about for Heaven. It may take the wrong road, go astray in a false night that is but a counterfeit of the divine night: we recognize the hunger that is in it" (Maritain, *Art and Faith: Letters Between Jacques Maritain and Jean Cocteau*, trans. John Coleman [New York: Philosophical Library, 1943], p. 104).

[62] Perhaps we may suggest that the heart, or the root of the soul, is like emotional photographic paper and the work of art is like a playful combination of reverse images which suggest both the contours of the heart and the reality that has shone on it.

[63] In many ways Maritain is very close to the philosophy of Suzanne Langer. See "The Symbol of Feeling," in *Feeling and Form* (New York: Charles Scribner's Sons, 1953), especially pp. 27ff. Their views are similar except for the key fact that for Langer it is emotion that is known, as *medium quod*, and not, as it is for Maritain, a *medium quo*, that through which something else is known. We would argue that both the emotion plus the strange clues and signs of both the reality of the feeler (subject) and the world are given together.

[64] Maritain, *The Situation of Poetry*, p. 38.

[65] "Man does not know himself through his own essence. His substance is hidden from him" (Maritain, *Art and Poetry*, p. 89).

dirt.[66] Any knowledge that can be given concerning the invisible world which stirs within him is of utmost help,[67] for we act through notions and desires, the existence and nature of which we do not have the slightest clue. But because the intellectually appetitive *élan* toward the sign involved in a work of art is the same as the *élan* toward the actual object,[68] we can become dimly aware of our actual feeling and desire for things.[69] We can see what our soul's depths truly want—what is truly good.

But the aesthetic experience is not only about the "good," it also reveals to us the mysterious workings of evil. "He who does not know the regions of evil, does not know much about the world," writes Maritain.[70] But we cannot know evil except in the good that it wounds.[71] Although, as Augustine had discovered, evil has no intelligible nature of its own, in the aesthetic experience, it can have a life of its own. Through the various "defects in truth," deformations, distortions of logical and natural appearances of the forms of things and life, it can become a legitimate part of the universe of art,[72] and while not having to corrupt us (we do not need to eat from the tree), it becomes observable. It shows itself and its ways, so that we can see it! Having a knowledge of what Maritain calls a "geography of evil,"[73] we are better able to practically navigate through the deep waters of the soul and the world.

As the beautiful is the radiance of being as undivided or one, the work of art provides the viewer with a view of reality that includes and encom-

---

[66] Maritain, *Art and Faith*, p. 130.

[67] "For in the long run any deeper awareness of what is hidden in man turns to a greater enlightenment of moral conscience" (Maritain, *The Responsibility of the Artist*, p. 88). Our hearts become a sounding board for the work, for the novel especially. Maritain writes, "For the writer works with words, which convey ideas and stir the imagination and which act through intelligence on all the rational and emotional fabric of notions and beliefs, images, passions and instincts on which the moral life of man depends" (ibid., p. 68).

[68] Maritain, *Ransoming the Time*, p. 232. "Sic enim est unus et idem motus in imaginem cum illo qui est in rem" (*ST* III, q. 25, a. 3).

[69] Perhaps we can see in ourselves, as the artist does in his own heart, the various repressed tendencies and monsters of singularity. For further discussion, see Maritain, *The Responsibility of the Artist*, p. 105.

[70] Maritain, *Art and Faith*, pp. 94–95.

[71] Maritain, "Dialogues" and "The Freedom of Song," in *Art and Poetry*, pp. 55 and 83.

[72] Maritain, *Art and Faith*, p. 96. This in no way implies any evil on the part of the author or artist. He, like anyone else, needs only to look at his own repressed inner tendencies (*The Responsibility of the Artist*, pp. 111–12). He puts us in touch with ours.

[73] Maritain, *The Responsibility of the Artist*, p. 112.

passes him. It presents him with a view of reality that is not problematic, objective, cut-up, analyzed, but a reality of which he is a part; a reality that is mysterious, complete, and full of meaning. The resemblance to Gabriel Marcel's philosophy is striking. Marcel focused upon the encompassing nature of being and its ability to resist complete exhaustive analysis, such as would deprive it of value. Being has a mysterious nature of which we are an integral part, and from which we cannot be separated.[74] One might also consider here the world-views of the Native American Indian.

Maritain writes that it is in the presence of beauty that the soul makes contact with its own light, a light that is beyond it. We seek beauty as we seek our cause.[75] Beauty laden with emotion helps us to see the interpenetration of man and nature.[76] It helps us to see how our life breathes with nature and nature breathes with us. Beauty helps us to see how we fit or do not fit in with the world.[77] Look at Rodin's *La Main de Dieu* or *Le Baiser* and then look at a shriveled man of Giacometti. In the aesthetic experience, we perceive the hidden truth to which the work and our minds are subject.[78] In that experience, we sense our soul's attunement to the mathematical, musical, and spiritual laws of the cosmos.[79] It becomes clear why we cannot objectify this discursively! The truth we are concerned with is above and encompasses us. We and nature are the data.

[74] Maritain, "The Experience of the Poet," in *The Situation of Poetry*, p. 73; "L'Expérience du poète," in *Situation de la poésie*, p. 146; *Creative Intuition in Art and Poetry*, p. 382. See Gabriel Marcel, "On the Ontological Mystery," in *The Philosophy of Existentialism*, trans. Manya Harari (Secaucus, New York: Citadel Press, 1980), pp. 9–46, especially p. 14, "Being is what withstands—or what would withstand—an exhaustive analysis bearing on the data of experience and aiming to reduce them step by step to elements increasingly devoid of intrinsic or significant value." While Maritain's philosophy is very different from Marcel's, still this is close to his aesthetic grasp of being.

[75] Maritain, *Art and Scholasticism*, p. 173, n. 66.

[76] Maritain, *Creative Intuition in Art and Poetry*, p. 5.

[77] Ibid., pp. 9ff.

[78] Maritain, "On Artistic Judgment," in *The Range of Reason*, p. 19. The selection is from the 1943 issue of *Liturgical Arts*.

[79] See Maritain, *Art and Faith*, p. 100. The work of art presents us with a reversal of what C. S. Lewis called transposition. See "Transposition" in *The Weight of Glory and Other Addresses*, ed. Walter Hooper (New York: Macmillan, 1980), pp. 54–73. According to Lewis, the higher reality can and often is made known through a lower one with some elements of the lower being repeated due to the lower's relative capacity. Thus both joy and grief, two very deep emotions, may be displayed through one facial expression. According to Maritain, art does the reverse. It uses paradoxes, transfigurations, "defects in truth," and "departures from form" (John O'Connor's translation of *déformations* in the first edition of *Art et Scolastique*) to reveal a higher reality through emotion. Through the aesthetic experience, the viewer experiences a "kinship with eternal things" (*Creative Intuition in Art and Poetry*, p. 87).

Just as the child learns his first things through imitation and through play, so we, too, through the aesthetic experience learn, not what can be formulated and taught, but how to navigate through life. Or, as Maritain reminds us, "It is for beauty that wisdom is loved."[80] We may not see the rocks under the waters of our hearts, but art provides us with bell-bearing buoys that warn us in the dark. If art provides us with an echo of reality, it is because we are bats[81] and depend on our soundings in the aesthetic experience to know our position.

Watching the movie, *Sterile Cuckoo*, we sense the grey arbitrariness of a world that lacks the mountains and valleys of any objective values. Through seeing the ending of Chaplin's *City Lights*, we resonate with Chaplin's depiction of charity's invisible face. Through reading Dostoyevsky's *Brothers Karamazov*, we sense the "rightness" of child-like trust in the face of a mad world. The storm of Bach's *Passacaglia and Fugue in C minor* drowns all of the listener's interests and affirms the power and greatness of creation in motion. Through Rouault's canvases we sympathize with and see the beauty in men and women trapped in the cages of society. Eliot's "Love Song of Alfred J. Pufrock" reveals modern man's suffocation of the spirit. Frank Capra's *It's a Wonderful Life* reveals the value of an ordinary single existent man and the powerful impact of his freedom on the social fabric of society. But these works of art do not teach us anything new; rather they reveal some mystery of our world through what we already connaturally know or feel in our depths. The "heart has its reasons" and the receptive intuition reveals these.

And when the work is truly a masterpiece, the viewer experiences an unexpected synchronocity of his various transcendental aspirations to desire truth, to desire goodness, and to desire unity. This synchronocity brings into play a teleological sense that permeates the entire human being and shows him that he is made for more than himself. It makes him aware that his concepts capture only a small portion of the mystery of life. He finds out that his thoughts and desires are not blind but conspire secretly along different lines of being, and speak softly about a distant source from which they all

---

[80] Maritain, *Art and Scholasticism*, p. 26.

[81] Mark D. Jordan writes: "We require human arts in order to simplify and reduce the natural beauty of the world for our bat-like eyes" ("The Evidence of the Transcendentals and the Place of Beauty in Thomas Aquinas," *International Philosophical Quarterly* 29, no. 4 [December 1989], p. 407). While there is a reduction of natural beauty, that is not all that is happening. There is the interaction of the "free" artist with creation. We do introduce something new into works of art. Dante was right in saying that art is the grandchild of God.

flow. Maritain writes, "Poetry is spiritual nourishment, but it does not sati-
ate, it only makes man more hungry and that is its grandeur."[82]

In sum, the aesthetic experience allows us to appropriate our "emotional" perceptions of reality.[83] Just as we feel that one of the values in
studying philosophy is the self-appropriation of our minds via the understanding of concepts and ideas and frameworks through which we do and
should think, so too the aesthetic experience does the same for the heart and
emotions. To reap this benefit, we must forego the ordinary, the predictable,
and the philosophical. In order for the Son of God to be known, He had to
speak in parables, so that those listening would not understand (Recall that
in the Gospels the Son of God has to *explain* the parables.), and attain no
more than the worth of a crucified thief—He Who called Himself the Way,
the Truth, and the Life! How else would we have known God's love and the
paradoxical nature of the Christian life?

The reconciliation of opposites now becomes clear as we see the separate lines of the transcendentals uniting ever more closely in the distance.
The saints tell us that the only place where one's appetites are completely
in accord and are satisfied is in the beatific vision. Meanwhile, on earth, the
best of the fine works of art draw everyone, the Thomists and the Augus-
tinians, the intellectualists and the voluntarists, the theorists and practical
people, to the greatest receptive intuition of all.

---

[82] Maritain, *Creative Intuition in Art and Poetry*, p. 235. This is similar to C. S.
Lewis's notion of joy, a desire which is itself wonderful. See "The Weight of
Glory," in *The Weight of Glory and Other Addresses*, pp. 3–19.

[83] Lloyd J. Aultman-Moore writes of Aristotle's *Politics* VIII.5.1340a23f, that
the "confirmation of feeling appropriately through tragic catharsis will educate the
viewer of the play to understand what it means to feel and act appropriately in actual life situations." Aultman-Moore adds that, according to Cicero, emotions or
passions can be useful: "If one were to remove fear, all carefulness in life, which is
greatest among those who fear the laws, would be eliminated" (*Tusculan Disputa-
tions*, IV, 19–20). See L. J. Aultman-Moore, "Aristotle and Sophocles on the Elements of Moral Virtue" (Diss. Loyola University, Chicago, 1991), pp. 239–40.

Portraits of the Artist:
Joyce, Nietzsche, and Aquinas

Thomas S. Hibbs

Kettle . . . pleased Joyce with the remark that "The difficulty about
Aquinas is that what he says is so much like what the man in the street
says." In Paris, as Joyce was discussing Aquinas, someone objected,
"that has nothing to do with us," and Joyce replied . . . , "It has everything to do with us."[1]

Drawing widely upon work in the Neo-Scholastic revival of Aquinas,
William T. Noon's *Joyce and Aquinas* makes a compelling case for the importance of Aquinas in the entirety of Joyce's literary corpus. The book,
published forty years ago,[2] is still regularly cited in studies of Joyce, even
if its suggestions of Joyce's affinities with pre-modern philosophy have
been less well received in the trendy attempts to deploy Joyce as an authority for a host of "post-modernisms." The recent study by Weldon Thornton,
entitled *The Antimodernism of Joyce's Portrait*, puts into serious question
these recent trends and reasserts the link between Joyce and pre-modern
philosophy.[3] Thornton does not, however, consider the possibility of a Nietzschean reading of the *Portrait*. Given what I just said about the implausi-
bility of current post-modern interpretations of Joyce, the suggestion of
parallels between Joyce and Nietzsche might seem surprising. But even on

---

[1] Richard Ellmann, *James Joyce* (Oxford: Oxford University Press, 1982), p. 63.
[2] William T. Noon, *Joyce and Aquinas* (New Haven, Connecticut: Yale University Press, 1957).
[3] Weldon Thornton, *The Antimodernism of Joyce's Portrait* (Syracuse, New
York: Syracuse University Press, 1994).

Thornton's understanding of the *Portrait*, there are striking similarities between it and Nietzsche's *Birth of Tragedy*. Indeed, recent work on Nietzsche puts into question the deconstructive appropriation of his writings.[4] What I will pursue in this essay is a reading of the *Portrait* that takes seriously the possibility of a Nietzschean interpretation. In light of the strengths and weaknesses of that approach, I will consider the viability of a pre-modern, specifically Aristotelian-Thomist, interpretation of the *Portrait*.

In *The Birth of Tragedy*, Nietzsche depicts the history of the West as a struggle between two gods, two models of art, and two experiences of the relationship of the individual to the whole of society and nature.[5] The hidden source of Greek society and hence of the West is Dionysius, the primordial will, the surging force of chaos at the root of all human activity and thought. Dionysius is prior to the distinctions between good and evil and among objects. Dionysius, who is the primal suffering and source of wisdom and creativity of all things, is the spirit of music and is prior to language. Since it eliminates the possibility of individuation, it is void of conscious awareness and hence cannot know its own wisdom. By contrast, Apollo, as the *principium individuationis*, is responsible for the introduction of distinctions between good and evil and among objects. It is embodied in the plastic arts. It thus makes rational comprehension and articulation possible.

Given its dependence on Dionysius, the triumph of Apollo is always tenuous and unstable. If Apollo seeks to dominate Dionysius, it becomes effete, rationalistic, and static. The "entire existence" of Apollo depends "on a hidden substratum of suffering and knowledge revealed to him by Dionysius."[6] Nietzsche writes,

> And now let us imagine how into this world, built on mere appearance and moderation and artificially damned up, there penetrated, in tones ever more bewitching and alluring, the ecstatic sound of the Dionysian festival; how in these strains all of nature's excess in pleasure, grief, and knowledge became audible, even in piercing shrieks; and let us ask ourselves what the psalmodizing artist of Apollo, with his phantom harp-sound, could mean in the face of this demonic folk-song.[7]

[4] See, for example, Stanley Rosen, *The Question of Being* (New Haven, Connecticut: Yale University Press, 1993) and Peter Berkowitz, *Nietzsche: The Ethics of an Immoralist* (Cambridge, Massachusetts: Harvard University Press, 1995).

[5] Friedrich Nietzsche, *The Birth of Tragedy*, trans. Walter Kaufmann (New York: Random House, 1967).

[6] Ibid., p. 46.

[7] Ibid.

For a brief but remarkably fertile period, the period of Greek tragedy, the Dionsyian and the Apollonian existed in a kind of harmony. The Apollonian elements in tragedy, the role of speech and individual characters, make possible our indirect apprehension of the primal will, whose confrontation we cannot endure directly. Apollo, who is the source of the maxims "know thyself" and "nothing in excess," individuates and allows for conscious apprehension and expression.

The history of the West is the story of the increasing dominance of Apollo, the crucial stage of which is the Socratic turning away from poetry and music toward the good, the true, and the beautiful. Socratic rationalism is developed further in Christianity and especially in modern science. The following out of the trajectory of rationalism undermines itself: "Science, spurred by its powerful illusion, speeds irresistibly toward its limits where its optimism, concealed in the essence of logic, suffers shipwreck."[8] The "limits of theory" engender a "turn to art";[9] logic "bites its own tail" and gives rise to a "tragic insight."[10] Socratic culture suffers from "the delusion of limitless power."[11] Another way to express science's undermining of itself is in terms of the search for truth, which Judaism and Christianity introduced into the world and which is carried forward most forcefully by science. That very pursuit leads inevitably to the acknowledgment that all these systems are but lies, concealing the chaotic abyss at the root of all things.

By contrast, tragic culture exalts "wisdom over science," seeks a "comprehensive view," and embraces "with sympathetic feelings of love, the eternal suffering."[12] Tragic art serves life and restores health and wisdom to the human soul. Nietzsche urges that we consider science in light of art and art in light of life.[13] This does not entail the rejection of reason but rather its relocation. It can no longer stand apart from the rest of nature as its tribunal; instead, it is but a part, subordinate to, and nourished by, an extra-rational order of instinct. Its ideal is the Socrates who practices music. Where does this view leave the artist?

In some ways, Nietzsche's theory is compatible with a romantic understanding of the artist. He exalts art over science, instinctive wisdom over discursive reason, and myth over inquiry. In other and more important ways, his theory is surprisingly critical of the standard romantic view of the

[8] Ibid., p. 97.
[9] Ibid., p. 96.
[10] Ibid., p. 98.
[11] Ibid., p. 111.
[12] Ibid., p. 112.
[13] Ibid., p. 19.

artist. As Peter Berkowitz observes, it deprives the artist of self-consciousness, autonomy, and creativity.[14] As a participant in the Dionysian primordial unity, he is "no longer an artist"; instead, he has "become a work of art."[15] Nietzsche goes so far as to say that the "individual with egoistic ends" is the "antagonist of art."[16] He also repudiates the romantic, and for Nietzsche residually Christian, view of nature. He comments that "this harmony . . . this oneness of man with nature . . . is by no means a simple condition that comes into being naturally. . . . It is not a condition that, like a terrestrial paradise, must necessarily be found at the gate of every culture. Only a romantic age could believe this."[17] This view of nature, which is an Apollonian myth, culminates with the thoroughly modern image of the "sentimental, flute-playing, tender shepherd."[18]

How would a Nietzschean reading of the *Portrait* proceed? The very structure of the *Portrait* mirrors that of the progression toward a recovery of pagan art in *The Birth of Tragedy*. The Christian religion occupies the third and middle chapter in the *Portrait*; it has the same intermediate status in the novel that it does in Nietzsche's history. The description of the religious life is reminiscent of the dominant themes in Nietzsche's own account. It is founded in fear; the entire focus of the third chapter is the part of the Ignation retreat that treats of the last things: death, judgment, heaven, and hell. Yet heaven is not touched upon at all. Fear of the unknown or of the certainty of eternal punishment for the unrepentant drives a wedge between the rational system of final judgment and the passions and instincts. Indeed, the notion of the self is atomistic, isolated into discrete moments, and to be subject to the control of isolated acts of will. The narrator describes Stephen's life immediately after his conversion as being "laid out in devotional areas."[19] As he begins to be tempted again by the "insistent voices of the flesh," he experiences an "intense sense of power to know that he could by a single act of consent, in a moment of thought, undo all that he had done."[20] But then "almost at the verge of sinful consent," he would be "saved by a sudden act of will."[21]

[14] Berkowitz, *Nietzsche: The Ethics of an Immoralist*, p. 45.

[15] Nietzsche, *The Birth of Tragedy*, p. 37.

[16] Ibid., p. 52.

[17] Ibid., p. 43.

[18] Ibid., p. 61.

[19] James Joyce, *A Portrait of the Artist as a Young Man*, eds. Hans Walter Gabler and Walter Hettche (New York: Garland Publishing, Inc., 1993), p. 172. Hereafter cited as *Portrait*.

[20] Ibid., p. 177.

[21] Ibid., p. 178.

To emphasize exclusively the negative elements in the Christian religion is to obscure Nietzsche's view of it; for, he detects in the religious impulse an inchoate and unconscious artistic impulse. We are awed by the interplay of opposites in the saint, by his project of self-overcoming, of transforming the self into a work of art.[22] Similarly, Stephen Dedalus inclines toward an aesthetic view of the religious life. He speaks of how "beautiful" it would be to love God. To the mortification of the senses, especially touch, "he brought the most assiduous ingenuity of inventiveness."[23] The kinship between art and grace is clear from its power to create an entirely new world, "The world for all its solid substance and complexity no longer existed for his soul save as a theorem of divine power and love and universality."[24] In fact, certain elements of the purported life of grace as Stephen experiences them resemble the vices of the romantic artist. Stephen's scrupulous vanity is akin to artistic self-absorption.[25] Both grace and art sever his ties with the ordinary lives of others. He was unable to "merge his life in the common tide of other lives."[26]

As in *The Birth of Tragedy* so too in the *Portrait*, the opposition of the pagan and the Christian is prominent. The contrast is present in the name of the novel's protagonist, Stephen Dedalus, who has both the name of the first Christian martyr and that of the famous artificer of Greek myth. At the crucial transitional section of the novel, Stephen rejects the possibility of a vocation to the priesthood and proceeds to realize his artistic call. In his meeting with the Jesuit who suggests that he pursue the path of a religious calling, he is counseled: "And let you, Stephen, make a novena to your holy patron saint, the first martyr."[27] Later in that chapter, precisely when Stephen realizes his artistic vocation, he is called Stephanos by his friends. The Hellenization of the Christian part of his name signifies the transition from the modern, Christian world to the pre-modern, pagan world. It thus reflects Nietzsche's rebirth of tragedy, wherein the limits to the Christian world-view open up the possibility of a recovery of the primacy of pagan culture.

In spite of these similarities between the development of Stephen's real-

---

[22] See Friedrich Nietzsche, *Beyond Good and Evil*, trans. Walter Kaufmann (New York: Viking Press, 1968), sections 47 and 58 of the chapter entitled, "What is Religious?"

[23] Joyce, *Portrait*, p. 176.

[24] Ibid., p. 175.

[25] Ibid., p. 179.

[26] Ibid., p. 177.

[27] Ibid., p. 185.

ization of his artistic vocation and Nietzsche's history, there are crucial differences, differences that might lead us to appraise Stephen's character as
falling short of the Nietzschean vision of the artist. As we noted above,
Nietzsche does not celebrate the crude romantic depiction of the artist as an
isolated individual, cut off from others, who creates from autonomous
sources. Precisely this vision of the artist entraps Stephen. Many commentators have expressed a sense of disappointment at the final chapter of the
Portrait. Instead of a further development of Stephen's character, we find a
kind of stasis and an inability to create anything substantial. His lone piece
of writing is a short villanelle that critics have described as narcissistic and
as Joyce's parody of symbolism. Stephen thinks it crucial to his artistic
achievement that he "fly" past the nets of nation, language, and religion.
His goal is "to discover the mode of life or art whereby" his "spirit could
express itself in unfettered freedom."[28] Stephen's assertions of independence are undermined throughout the novel, but nowhere more explicitly
than in his growing awareness of and identification with the myth of
Dedalus. The primacy of that myth is evident in the epigraph to the entire
work from Ovid's *Metamorphoses*: "Et ignotas animum dimittit in artes."[29]
The primacy of myth indicates that, although there is a gap between Nietzsche and Stephen's self-understanding, that gap may be bridged by the
perspective of the narrator.

Stephen is repeatedly described as yearning for and answering a call:
first in his desire to sate his lust with the prostitute, then in his repentance
of his lust and his flirtation with a religious vocation, and finally in his realization of his artistic mission. In all these cases, he is moved by things
outside him or by passions that are within him yet beyond his control. In
fact, the entire work begins with Stephen's father telling the children's
story of the meeting between a moocow and baby tuckoo, in which Stephen
is identified with the "nicens little boy named baby tuckoo."[30] The location
of an individual within a myth, story, or tradition can be given various interpretations. One plausible interpretation is that of Nietzsche.[31] Consider,
for example, Stephen's earliest non-religious experience of self-transforma-
tion which occurs as he performs his part in a school play, where he sheds
his normal timidity and self-consciousness: "Another nature seemed to

[28] Ibid., p. 274.

[29] *Metamorphoses*, VIII, 188, quoted in Joyce, *Portrait*, p. 23.

[30] Joyce, *Portrait*, p. 25.

[31] For an alternative, Thomistic account of myth, see Frederick Wilhelmsen,
"The Philosopher and the Myth," in *The Paradoxical Structure of Existence* (Irving,
Texas: University of Dallas Press, 1970), pp. 129–47.

have been lent him. . . . It surprised him to see that the play which he had known at rehearsal for a disjointed lifeless thing had suddenly assumed a life of its own. It seemed now to play itself, he and his fellow actors aiding it with their parts."[32] The passage is strikingly reminiscent of Nietzsche's description of the tragic chorus: "[T]he tragic chorus is the dramatic proto-phenomenon: to see oneself transformed before one's own eyes and to begin to act as if one had actually entered into another, another character. . . . Here we have a surrender of individuality and a way of entering into another character."[33]

Consider, furthermore, that the rebirth of tragedy arises, as Nietzsche's subtitle indicates, out of the spirit of music. Stephen is frequently described as hearing and being moved by music. "The vast cycle of starry life bore his weary mind outward to its verge and inward to its center, a distant music accompanying him outward and inward."[34] Music breaks the artificial divisions, characteristic of Apollo, between inner and outer. As he begins to escape from family into the university, he anticipates a "new adventure." He hears "notes of fitful music leaping upwards a tone and downwards a diminished fourth. . . . It was an elfin prelude, endless and formless; and as it grew wilder and faster, the flames leaping out of time, he seemed to hear from under the boughs and grasses wild creatures racing, their feet pattering like rain upon the leaves."[35] The passage comes remarkably close to Nietzsche's depiction of the Dionysian.

For all the apparent approaches toward the Dionysian, Stephen falls short of the achievement Nietzsche lauds. Stephen's lack of creativity mirrors his moral and psychological solipsism. He is detached from and indifferent to all others and thus suffers from an inability to communicate or to love. In a telling exchange with Cranly, he is asked whether he loves his mother and responds that he doesn't know what the words mean. Cranly persists, "Have you ever felt love toward anyone or anything"? "Staring gloomily at the footpath," he responds, "I tried to love God. . . . It seems to me now I failed. It is very difficult. I tried to unite my will with the will of God instant by instant. In that I did not always fail. I could perhaps do that still . . . ."[36] The most persistent themes in the final fragmentary sections of the novel have to do with women. He is troubled by his inability to love or even remember in any detail his mother and confused and angered over his

[32] Joyce, *Portrait*, p. 107.
[33] Nietzsche, *The Birth of Tragedy*, p. 64.
[34] Ibid., p. 126.
[35] Ibid., p. 191.
[36] Joyce, *Portrait*, p. 269.

complicated feelings toward the woman he cannot love and yet cannot free himself from. His adolescent self-consciousness is evident in one meeting with her: "Talked rapidly of myself and my plans. In the midst of it unluckily I made a sudden gesture of a revolutionary nature. I must have looked like a fellow throwing a handful of peas into the air."[37] Stephen's pathologies and vices are summed up in his repeated use of the phrase "*non serviam*." His life is a kind of comic *imitatio diaboli*. How are we to appraise Stephen's multiform lack of fecundity?

Given what I have argued above about the parallels between the novel and Nietzsche's theories, it might make sense to understand Stephen's impotence as a failure to break through the Apollonian to the Dionysian. Does not Stephen embody precisely that antagonism to art that Nietzsche detects in the individual with egoistic ends? Stephen's romanticism is the antithesis of, and an enduring impediment to, true art. For the Nietzsche of *The Birth of Tragedy* and *The Advantage and Disadvantage of History for Life*, creation is possible only through a kind of historical rootedness and, at least in *The Birth*, through a radical subordination of the individual self to the primordial will, by becoming its instrument. The modern notion of progress with its abandonment of tradition and memory eliminates the conditions for the possibility of creativity. Yet Nietzsche himself often depicts creation as an act of violence and destruction, as an evisceration of the past and present for the sake of an unknown future. Perhaps on account of his growing realization that Germany would not provide creative, cultural soil, Nietzsche moves in the direction of the life-affirming individual who sets himself against a decadent culture to become a creator of values. This is but one of the many unresolved tensions in Nietzsche's thought.

In the *Portrait*, Stephen embodies this tension in Nietzsche's account of creativity. In Stephen's mind, the contrast is embodied in the distinction between the feminine cultivation of memory and the voluntarist, masculine orientation toward the future. One pertinent passage runs thus, "Certainly she remembers the past. Lynch says all women do. Then she remembers the time of her childhood—and mine if I was ever a child. The past is consumed in the present and the present is living only because it brings forth the future."[38] The emphasis on creativity and novelty entails not only overcoming the past but also emptying the present—the only moment of time we actually experience—of any except instrumental significance. Stephen's conscious attempt to repudiate the past is rooted in his voluntarist concep-

---

[37] Ibid., p. 281.
[38] Ibid., p. 280.

tion of Christian conversion, evident in his momentary belief that the past was now behind him. The project of gaining an autonomous, conscious control over all of one's powers alienates one from the past and from the penumbral elements of one's conscious awareness. Such a project is doomed to failure. As Stephen attempts to forget the object of his affection, "on all sides distorted reflections of her image started from his memory. . . . She was a figure of the womanhood of her country, a batlike soul waking to the consciousness of itself in darkness and secrecy and loneliness."[39]

One difficulty in aligning the Nietzsche of *The Birth of Tragedy* with the narrator's appraisal of Stephen is the former's emphasis on, and understanding of, the tragic. The *Portrait* might be read as a kind of tragedy of an exceptional human being's failure to realize his potential. The ending of the work anticipates a tragic fall. Stephen's calling upon Dedalus in the words, "Old father, old artificer, stand me now and ever in good stead,"[40] clearly portends Stephen's own failure, as it identifies Stephen with Icarus whose ambitious flight ended in a fall. Yet whatever elements of tragedy there may be at the end, they arise not by our hero facing the Dionysian and thereby undergoing a kind of destruction but precisely by avoiding the darker sources of the human race.

The deeper incongruity between Joyce and Nietzsche has to do with the latter's celebration of aristocratic tragedy, which is virulently anti-democratic, perhaps even anti-political. Joyce's approach, by contrast, is democratic and more comic than tragic. The only passages wherein Stephen seems heroic he also appears foolish. In the penultimate fragment, Stephen writes of his mother, "She prays now, she says, that I may learn in my own life and away from home and friends what the heart is and what it feels."[41] Her answer to Stephen's dilemma is that he should identify himself more fully with ordinary folk. This seems to be the attitude the narrator wishes to induce in the reader as well. Stephen is young; we feel a sympathy for him that we feel for a precocious but inexperienced child. We also pity his foolishness; we want to laugh gently at his silly ambitions.

Such a perspective presupposes that the narrator's point of view is not simply to be identified with that of Stephen. If this is right, then the simplistic account of Joyce's style as first person stream of consciousness must be abandoned. The individual consciousness gives way to a more comprehensive third person point of view. As Thornton persuasively argues, the

---

[39] Ibid., p. 248.
[40] Ibid., p. 282.
[41] Ibid.

narrator does not seek to reflect the flow of conscious activity in the protagonist but to capture the more complex flow of his entire psychic environment, much of which Stephen is unaware.[42] The narrator does, as Stephen suggests he should, disappear behind or beyond his work, but it is not at all clear that he adopts a position of neutrality or indifference toward his main character. As both Thornton and Sultan show, Joyce's use of irony frequently serves to enrich rather than merely subvert a character's self-understanding.[43] Irony does not undermine the individual quest for meaning, but rather locates it within a more comprehensive account; it urges compassion toward human weakness; and its laughter presupposes some measure of identification with ordinary human beings. Ellmann nicely captures this: "The initial and determining act of judgment in his work is the justification of the commonplace. . . . Joyce's discovery . . . was that the ordinary is the extraordinary."[44] This locates Joyce's project more in the lineage of Aquinas, at least as that is adumbrated in our opening quotation linking Aquinas and the common man, than in that of Nietzsche.

The prominence of the common man calls to mind Aristotelian comedy, wherein there is a certain proportion between characters in a drama and the audience. Comedy contains persons at our own level or slightly lower. The narrator in Joyce's novels treats these ordinary folks as objects neither of romantic celebration nor of cynical dismissal. He may share some of Nietzsche's reservations about the deleterious effects of religion on the human psyche, but he shares none of his virulent criticisms of slave morality or his devotion to noble ethics. The references to Zarathustra are thoroughly comic and mocking; indeed, in *Ulysses* they are spoken by the cruelly mocking Buck Mulligan, the least admirable character in the novel.[45] One can of course find comic elements in the later Nietzsche. In contrast to *The Birth of Tragedy*'s dismissal of comedy as the realm of the absurd, later works assert a correspondence between the rank of character and a scale of laughter. Nietzsche urges us to mock the spirit of gravity, found in religion, morality, and all too often in philosophy itself. But when he associates his laughter with the project of making himself into a god, a result of which would be superhuman laughter, he is at variance with Joyce, whose laughter is closer to that appropriate to Aristotelian comedy.

---

[42] Thornton, *The Antimodernism of Joyce's Portrait*, pp. 71–76, 109–36.

[43] Ibid., p. 79. See Stanley Sultan, *Eliot, Joyce, and Company* (Oxford: Oxford University Press, 1981), pp. 63, 76.

[44] Ellmann, *James Joyce*, p. 5.

[45] James Joyce, *Ullyses*, ed. Hans Walter Gabler (New York: Garland Publishing, Inc., 1986), chap. I, p. 19, lines 727–28.

If this interpretation is correct, then there is a disparity between Stephen's account of the relationship between author and work and that operative in the novel. At the end of his development of his aesthetic theory in chapter V, Stephen traces the transition from the lyrical through the epical to the dramatic, wherein the author progressively distances himself from his work. "The personality of the artist . . . finally refines itself out of existence, impersonalizes itself. . . . The mystery of esthetic like that of material creation is accomplished. The artist, like the God of the creation, remains within or behind or beyond or above his handiwork, invisible, refined out of existence, indifferent, paring his fingernails." Lynch's retort, "Trying to refine them also out of existence"[46] is aptly sardonic and indicates that the creator's indifference is actually an antipathy. Aquinas, to whom Stephen has been appealing as his authority in things aesthetic, pervasively deploys analogies between human and divine artistry, but he does not take them as literally as Stephen does, nor does he depict the creator of the universe as indifferent to his creation. The author of the *Portrait* does not cynically mock the all-too-human foibles of his characters, nor does the narrator imply that he is indifferent or that the reader should be.

The ambivalence we feel toward Stephen at the end of the book allows for multiple interpretations. As some critics have argued, the vices that impede Stephen's growth as a human being and an artist are precisely those decried in the sermon on Hell that stands at the center of the story. Consider, for example, the echoes of Satan's "*non serviam*" in Stephen's proud refusal to identify himself with the lot of others and his self-absorbed attempt to create *ex nihilo*. The painful isolation of Stephen at the end recalls St. Thomas's teaching—cited by the priest—that the greatest spiritual punishment of Hell is the pain of loss, the isolation from the greatest good and hence from all other goods.

As critics have remarked, Joyce may have lost his faith but he retains many of its philosophical categories. In part what the novel seems to retain is a Thomistic moral and philosophical critique of the exaltation of the creative will. The final section of the *Portrait* draws out the untoward consequences of radical voluntarism, a voluntarism that emerges in the sermon on Hell, a sermon replete with a thoroughly modern and typically Jesuit conception of the Christian life. As Stephen's pagan roots begin to eclipse his Jesuit education, the voluntarism continues to surface. The echoes of the Satanic refusal to serve reveal the envy and pride at the root of Stephen's willfulness. The self thus supplants the divine and becomes a sort

---

[46] Joyce, *Portrait*, p. 242.

of self-creating divinity. For all of the positive reflections of Nietzsche in the novel, there is in the critique of voluntarism a crucial departure from certain tendencies in his thought. According to the perceptive analysis of Berkowitz, the fundamental tension in Nietzsche is this: Although he wished to base right making on right knowing, to ground a proper evaluation of levels of creative power on a rank order of character, his complete repudiation of any sort of natural, civil, or religious standard puts his entire project into question. As Berkowitz puts it, Nietzsche "pursues the antagonism between knowing and making to its breaking point."[47] The primacy of the will stultifies the understanding and ends up paralyzing the will itself, since there is nothing in light of which the will might deliberate and act. The project of absolute self-mastery, of unconstrained independence, engenders a self without action and void of freedom. Nietzsche's project of incessant self-overcoming would seem to lead to precisely the sort of nihilism that he detests.

To see this more clearly, we need but advert to the structure of the *Portrait*, which exhibits the problem of individual creativity by juxtaposing and thus putting into question diametrically opposed conceptions of the relationship between the individual and the community.[48] The first four chapters alternate between corresponding sets of opposites: the social vs. the individual, outer vs. inner, and male vs. female. The family and the cliques at school dominate the first chapter; in these social contexts, where men are dominant, Stephen struggles to decode the language and to find his place within the community. The discovery of the interior impulses to sensuality pervades the second chapter; these impulses set Stephen apart from others and lead up to his encounter with the prostitute. The third chapter focuses upon the Jesuit teaching of religious doctrine, in light of which he strives to interpret his own experience. Finally, in the fourth chapter, Stephen, in isolation from all others, experiences the vision of the girl on the beach and the accent is on his internal sense of ecstasy. The alternation between these opposites is not so neat as it might appear. Two examples will suffice. Stephen supposes that his lust is somehow peculiar to him, yet he comes to see it as common to all men. Conversely, he thinks that he can willfully separate himself from the institutional church, yet its teachings are deeply constitutive of who he is. These superficially clear oppositions, upon which the novel plays and which are endemic to modern thought, are characteris-

---

[47] Berkowitz, *Nietzsche: The Ethics of an Immoralist*, p. 269.

[48] See the masterful explication by Thornton in *The Antimodernism of Joyce's Portrait*, pp. 85–107.

tics of the immature Stephen, of the sorts of conflicts he must overcome to reach maturity. The novel works toward, without ever reaching, their reconciliation. In fact, Stephen's retreat into quasi-solipsism in the last chapter serves to re-entrench the dichotomies. What has thwarted the progress is precisely the exaltation of the creative, individual will in Stephen's self-understanding.

Another way to bring out the problem of aesthetic self-creation is to attend to the novel's persistent contrast between art and life and the way the former can be used as a refuge from and falsification of the latter. At the very end of chapter IV, Stephen experiences his aesthetic ecstasy, which is described variously as a "profane joy," as an ecstasy and a rapture.[49] At the very beginning of the next chapter he is at home with his family the following morning: "He drained his third cup of watery tea to the dregs and set to chewing the crusts of fried bread that were scattered near him, staring into the dark pool of the jar."[50] As he leaves the house and walks through the squalid neighborhood, his mind takes refuge in books. The "splendor" of his thoughts allows the world to "perish about his feet as if it had been fireconsumed."[51] Art is ambivalent; it provides for a transforming experience of the world, even as it tempts the artist to an evasion of life. Of course, the artistry of the narrator of the novel captures all of this and so his art is not subject to the same criticisms as is that of Stephen. How are we to understand the art of the narrator?

A Nietzschean interpretation is possible, since for him art affirms all things, both good and evil.[52] Indeed, Nietzsche's insistence that art be appraised in light of life rather than the reverse offers a corrective to Stephen's understanding. Yet Nietzsche's typology of tragedy and comedy does not fit neatly with Joyce's writing. Nietzsche contrasts the universal typology of the tragic hero with the treatment of the individual as an individual in the comic.[53] He attributes the decline of tragedy to the "victory of the phenomenon over the universal, and the delight in a unique, almost anatomical preparation." In place of tragedy's "eternal type," we find the "prevalence of character representation and psychological refinement."[54] Joyce's novel might be described as treating Stephen as a type of the artist, but the peculiarities of his history and character are also prominent. In spite

[49] Joyce, *Portrait*, p. 198.
[50] Ibid., p. 200.
[51] Ibid., p. 203.
[52] Nietzsche, *The Birth of Tragedy*, p. 41.
[53] Ibid., p. 73.
[54] Ibid., p. 108.

of Nietzsche's claim to comprehensive affirmation, his own tendency toward the portrayal of universal types in tragedy could be the basis of Joycean counter-accusation that he has failed to embrace the petty, ugly details of life. Joyce's narratives have no place for ideal, aristocratic types, either of the tragic sort or of the laughable *übermensch* variety.

Another interpretation, derived from Aristotle and Aquinas, of the comedy of the *Portrait* is possible. A congruence can be seen in the *Portrait's* conception of art and life. On Aristotle's view, art partly imitates and partly completes nature, by aiding in the realization of possibilities to which nature points but rarely achieves. Do not the first four chapters point to an overcoming of a set of peculiarly modern oppositions? Given the parallel and related failures of Stephen as artist and human being, would not this anticipated reconciliation mark the way toward a healthy human life and a fecund artistry? If Stephen thwarts the realization of this *telos*, the art of the narrator gives us more than a glimmer of it. Such a reading of the *Portrait*[55] presupposes something like the Aristotelian teaching on potency and act, which Hugh Kenner has identified as the "sharpest exegetical instrument we can bring to the work of Joyce."[56] Although Kenner does not draw out this line of reasoning, an important role of the doctrine of potency may be to suggest unrealized possibilities toward which the action of the novel points but which remain frustrated by particular defects in the characters.

The prominence of Aquinas and Aristotle in the final section of the book lends further support to this interpretation. Aquinas appears as an authority late in the book, after Stephen has acknowledged his artistic vocation, when Stephen elucidates his aesthetic theory. But this is precisely the point at which we begin to realize that Stephen's progress as an artist and a human being is far from complete. If art is sometimes conceived as an inappropriate escape from life, then Stephen's taking refuge in aesthetic theory rather than immersing himself in the artistic process might be seen as a further retreat from life. Stephen would thus embody an antithesis to Nietzsche's subordination of science or theory to art and of both of these to life. Furthermore, Stephen's emphasis on the stages in the rational apprehension of objects in aesthetic perception lies clearly on the side of the Apollonian, not the Dionysian. All this is true but it fails to capture the complexity of Stephen's character as revealed in his theory. One of the problems with ap-

---

[55] Thornton develops this interpretation in *The Antimodernism of Joyce's Portrait*, pp. 39–63.

[56] Hugh Kenner, "The Cubist Portrait," in *Approaches to Joyce's "Portrait,"* eds. Thomas F. Staley and Bernard Benstock (Pittsburgh, Pennsylvania: University of Pittsburgh Press, 1976), p. 179.

praising the use of Aquinas is that there are so many errors of interpretation interspersed with the insights that it is difficult to know what to attribute to whom.

That we should take the theory somewhat seriously is, I think, evident from its usefulness in accounting for Stephen's ecstatic, aesthetic vision of the girl on the beach, a vision that marks the realization of Stephen's call and the highpoint of the novel. The vision illustrates not only the stages of apprehension, but also the claim that aesthetic perception is void of desire and loathing, indeed of kinesis itself. The vision is an example of static, aesthetic experience.

The theory, which Stephen explicitly claims to have borrowed from Aquinas, explicates the famous statement that "the beautiful is that which pleases when seen" in light of the three marks of the beautiful: wholeness, harmony, and radiance. The first stage is the observation of an object as distinct from all others, as "selfbounded and selfcontained."[57] So, on the beach, Stephen first sees a "girl . . . before him in midstream, alone and still."[58] In the second stage, there is an apprehension of the fitting relationships among the parts of the object and of each part to the whole. So, he proceeds to observe her bodily parts, her legs, her thighs, her waist, her bosom, her hair, and finally her face. Stephen compares the first stage to the second as the "synthesis of immediate perception" to the "analysis of apprehension." The third stage is also described as a synthesis, in which the "supreme quality of beauty, the clear radiance of the esthetic image, is apprehended luminously by the mind which has been arrested by its wholeness and fascinated by its harmony."[59] So Stephen sees in the girl's face, to which her bodily parts have gradually led his gaze, the "wonder of mortal beauty."[60]

There are a number of problems with Stephen's purported fidelity to Aquinas, not the least of which is his couching the theory in epistemological terms. What is more important, the theory embodies a set of dualisms alien to Aquinas. The split between soul and body, intellect and sensation, reason and desire runs through the entire discussion. True art, according to Stephen, is static rather than kinetic because the latter is associated with passions that are nothing "more than physical."[61] At one point, Stephen revealingly comments to Cranly that, although we are animals we are just

---

[57] Joyce, *Portrait*, p. 239.
[58] Ibid., p. 197.
[59] Ibid., p. 240.
[60] Ibid., p. 197.
[61] Ibid., p. 233.

now in a mental world. While in his examples of aesthetic perception he focuses on the concrete apprehension of sensible objects, he also speaks of the senses as "prison gates of the soul." None of these oppositions is characteristic of Aquinas. Might these dichotomies point us in the direction of a more unified and more adequate account of aesthetic experience, the rudiments of which can be found in Aquinas?

If there is a compatibility between the narrator's description of Stephen's aesthetic vision of the girl on the beach and Stephen's own aesthetic theory, then perhaps the weaknesses of the latter can also be seen in the former. In the exultant, "Yes. Yes. Yes. He would create . . . as the great artificer,"[62] there is an important affirmation of the beauty of the girl, of his place in the cosmos and of his own vocation. Yet the affirmation may be constrained by the limits of Stephen's own character. It does mark a progress over his previous interactions with women; he is no longer the son in need of coddling, nor the immature devotee of Mary, nor the adolescent succumbing to a woman merely as an object to satisfy his lust. Between him and the girl on the beach there is a sort of communion, even a kind of reverent acknowledgment of one another. And yet in the detached vision, "no word had broken the holy silence of his ecstasy."[63] Is it wrong to see in this an anticipation of the multiple failures of speech in the final chapter, failures that both illustrate Stephen's defective character, his isolation from others, and that have a mysterious connection to his inability to create? Language is the vehicle of communication between persons. It is the instrument through which we have access to the traditions and myths in light of which we understand ourselves in relationship to others. By contrast, Stephen's aesthetic vision, to which we have access only because of the language of the narrator, is a sort of Rousseauean attempt to bypass language in the attempt to establish a pre-linguistic harmony.

Immediately preceding the vision, Stephen speaks softly to himself: "A day of dappled seaborne clouds." The narrator comments, "The phrase and the day and the scene harmonized in a chord."[64] As Stephen begins to contemplate the words, he seems to retreat from the harmony of word and world into language itself. The question is then asked, "Was it that . . . he drew less pleasure from the reflection of the glowing sensible world through the prism of language manycoloured and richly storied than from the contemplation of an inner world of individual emotions mirrored per-

---

[62] Ibid., p. 196.
[63] Ibid., p. 198.
[64] Ibid., p. 192.

fectly in a lucid supple periodic prose?"[65] The collapse of language upon itself is symptomatic of Stephen's artistic failure. He fails to mediate his ideal, timeless vision of beauty to others through language.

Further support for this interpretation can be found in the "Nausika" chapter in *Ulysses*, wherein Bloom's contemplation from afar of the young Gerty culminates with his act of auto-eroticism. Only vision links them, yet Bloom comments that there was a kind of language between them. The irony of the assertion is lost on Bloom but not on the reader. The absence of speech, the safe distance of sight, enables Bloom and Gerty to idealize one another in their imagination. When Bloom realizes that Gerty is lame, the falsity of his idealized vision is revealed and he is disappointed. Conversely, the masturbatory culmination of Bloom's watching of Gerty underscores his own isolation and impotence.

Aquinas's emphasis on the unity of understanding, speech, and will in communication and on friendship as essential to the human community provide Stephen with the theoretical and implicitly practical material to overcome the voluntarism and atomism endemic to modern philosophy. In order to see this, we must leave the *Portrait* and turn to *Ulysses*.

In the opening chapter, Buck Mulligan, Stephen's nemesis, jokes to another fellow that Stephen has a theory about Hamlet: "He proves by algebra that Hamlet's grandson is Shakespeare's grandfather and that he himself is the ghost of his own father."[66] Later in the same chapter Stephen reflects to himself about the earlier Trinitarian heresies, among which the error of Sabellius, who held that the "Father was Himself His own Son,"[67] figures prominently. The same pairing of Stephen's Hamlet theory and Trinitarian doctrine is central to Stephen's lengthy theoretical diatribe later in the book. He refers to the "bulldog of Aquin, with whom no word shall be impossible," as refuting Sabellius.[68] Yet Stephen's theory of artistic creation is itself a version of the Sabellian heresy. He asserts not only a special relationship between Shakespeare and Hamlet, but also an identity of Shakespeare with every character in the play. "He is the ghost and the prince. He is all in all. . . . In *Cymbeline*, in *Othello* he is bawd and cuckold. He acts and is acted on."[69] Stephen then generalizes from art to life: "He found in the world without as actual what was in his world within as possible. . . . Every life is many days, day after day. We walk through ourselves, meeting

[65] Ibid., pp. 192–93.
[66] Joyce, *Ulysses*, p. 15.
[67] Ibid., p. 18.
[68] Ibid., p. 171.
[69] Ibid., p. 174.

robbers, ghosts, giants, old men, young men, wives, widows, brothers-in-love, but always meeting ourselves."[70] It is not surprising that this theory, which entirely denies the reality of otherness and is thus a variant on Sabellianism, leads Stephen to conclude by echoing Hamlet's prohibition of future marriages. There are no independent others left to be united in matrimony and no new beings to be brought forth into the world. Both procreation and artistic creation have been rendered otiose.

Three Thomistic teachings are mentioned during the discourse. First, there is Thomas's refutation of the heresy of Sabellius, to which we have referred. Thomas's orthodox position depicts the divine life as a union of thought, speech, and love among three distinct persons, a social harmony of personal differences. Second, Stephen quotes Aquinas on the necessity for society of there being friendship among many: "In societate humana hoc est in maxime necessarium ut sit amicitia inter multos."[71] Friendship presupposes distinction between the persons united through common activities and traits of character. The friend may be described as another self, but he is a distinct self, whose association with me expands and enlarges my experience and my knowledge. What distinguishes true friendship from its simulacra is that only in the former is the friend loved as an end in himself, not as a means to my achievement of some extrinsic good. For Aristotle and Aquinas, friendship is the centerpiece of their view of human nature as inherently social. The unity of civil society presupposes distinct individuals who complement one another in the pursuit and enjoyment of common goods, chief among which is the good of friendship itself. By contrast to the Aristotelian-Thomist understanding of friendship, Stephen's account of the unity of characters and persons negates all difference.

It is no coincidence that in the midst of Stephen's diatribe, reference is made to both incest and masturbation. In the discussion of incest, we find the third use of Aquinas. In his "gorbellied works," Aquinas writes of "incest from a standpoint different from that of the new Viennese school" and "likens it to an avarice of the emotions. He means that the love so given to one near in blood is covetously withheld from some stranger who, it may be, hungers for it."[72] Incest thus shortcuts an affection whose natural *telos* is to communicate with an-other. Thus, experience and creation utterly lack novelty or difference; they are but redundant expressions of the self. In the order of sexual sins, the logical term of this failure to open oneself to the offer and reception of love is auto-eroticism. Stephen's theory, which he

---

[70] Ibid., p. 175.
[71] Ibid., p. 169.
[72] Ibid., p. 170.

concedes even he does not believe, involves a similar sin on the level of intellect. After the speech, Mulligan mockingly announces a play. The title, "Everyman his own Wife or a Honeymoon in the Hand," captures the upshot of Stephen's theory. We are invited to compare Stephen's form of intellectual masturbation with Bloom's physical act of auto-eroticism in chapter XIII. In both cases, impotence or sterility is the theme. As he departs the library, he senses with apprehension the presence of Mulligan behind him and stands aside to let him pass. "Part. The moment is now. . . . My will: his will that fronts me. Seas between."[73] In life, if not in theory, Stephen confronts otherness. He thus alternates between indulging in a theory that consumes otherness in the self and living a life of evasion of others, whom he sees as threats to his autonomous will. Creation itself lacks difference or novelty; it is but the redundant expression of the self.

Implicit in Stephen's theory of artistic creation is a series of oppositions, which pervade the whole of *Ulysses*. Perhaps the most important oppositions are those between the same and the other, and between newness and repetition. Both can be found in Bloom's reflections in the Nausika chapter. Just as his idealized view of Gerty is corrected by her movement, so too he comes to see that what he had at dusk taken as clouds on the horizon were actually trees. Gaining a new perspective thus allows one to correct the limitations of one's previous point of view. Bloom observes to himself in this context that it is good "to see oneself as others do."[74] He proceeds to ponder over the fact that "history repeats itself" and that "there is nothing new under the sun." The conclusion is that you "think you're escaping and run into yourself."[75] A short time later, Bloom wonders to himself what it is women love in men and responds hypothetically "another themselves?"[76] Yet at the end of the same paragraph, he recalls posing the question to Molly of why she chose him. Her answer: "Because you were so foreign from the others." These oppositions are, I think, related to the sets of contraries that Thornton has identified in the *Portrait* and they may well perform similar functions. Neither of the mutually exclusive alternatives is adequate and the story points toward but never exhibits their reconciliation. In Thomistic language, the reconciliation would involve seeing the self-other relation as neither univocal nor equivocal but analogical. How might we determine the validity of such an interpretation?

Since the scope of this paper precludes the possibility of making a final

[73] Ibid., p. 178.
[74] Ibid., pp. 307–08.
[75] Ibid., p. 309.
[76] Ibid., p. 311.

judgment, it will suffice to indicate precisely what would need to be done to reach a judgment. The principal alternative to the quasi-Thomistic exegesis we have been developing is the so-called deconstructive reading, which celebrates the "drama of the alternatives." On this view, the oppositions we have described perdure. There is no sense of potentiality, realized or unrealized, but only the dynamic interplay of opposites without hope of resolution. The sense of sameness and continuity is exploded by the jarring encounter with otherness and with utterly unanticipated novelty. The question, then, is how to decide between these two views?

At least three issues are at stake. First, there is the question of the self-other relationship, especially of friendship. Stanley Sultan has argued that the overlappings of, and resemblances between, the life-stories of the various characters in *Ulysses* represent more than mere coincidence. They hint at the substantive likenesses between characters and at subtle interconnections in their destinies. He develops a compelling case for seeing Buck Mulligan and Bloom as representing the fundamental options for Stephen. The latter's movement from Mulligan to Bloom would thus be a sign of progress in the development of his character.[77] Given the way we have framed the issue, the key question is whether we can see the Stephen-Bloom relationship as a kind of friendship? If we can, then it would be necessary to provide a detailed comparsion of Aristotle's friendship among those of complete virtue, Aquinas's conception of friendship as charity, and Joyce's view.[78]

A second and related issue concerns the question of teleology in the novel, of whether there is a potency, a direction to the action it describes. Many critics adopt the view that the characters of *Ulysses* are incapable of growth, insight, or development. A Nietzschean interpretation of the lack of development suggests itself: eternal return. The circular shape of Bloom's travels, which dimly mirror those of Odysseus, fails to reconcile opposites or to reveal any progress. There is instead only the affirmation of the interplay of differences, the resounding "Yes" of Molly's soliloquy. If, on the other hand, Molly's affirmation indicates a kind of progress in her domestic relationship with Bloom, then it may be seen as a sign of development in the action of the novel.[79]

[77] Sultan, *Eliot, Joyce, and Company*, pp. 49–87.

[78] Marilyn French, *The Book as World* (Cambridge, Massachusetts: Harvard University Press, 1976), p. 85. French argues that Bloom embodies *caritas*.

[79] For a summary of recent interpretations and a reading of the soliloquy as an "auto-debate" in which Molly resolves her attitude to Bloom and reaffirms her fidelity, see Sultan, *Joyce, Eliot, and Company*, pp. 289–98.

In his depiction of Molly, Joyce seems simultaneously to identify her as the life source, the earth-goddess so many feminist critics celebrate, and to undercut the seriousness with which we are to take that association. Upon a careful reading, her celebrated sexual freedom seems more imaginary than real and more conventional than disruptive. In the midst of her musings, she pauses to slight the atheists, who "might as well try to stop the sun from rising" as to uproot belief in God from the human heart.[80] Her conception of God as a just judge is blandly traditional. The question of the divine is intimately connected to the question of directedness. The link between the two is, as Sultan has noted, providence. Ample use of coincidence by an author leads inevitably to the question of who is orchestrating events and thus to the question of providence, the third relevant issue. Defending an alternative to the deconstructive reading of Joyce, then, would involve an articulation of the explicit and implicit theology of his works.

Even if the theological element in Joyce can be resurrected in this way, it will remain the case that his theism is far from that of Aquinas. It might seem to occupy an uneasy middle position between the orthodoxy of Aquinas and the blatant secularism of the self-proclaimed post-modernists. Such an approach is popular among those who wish to fend off nihilism without embracing revealed religion.[81] Of course, the Nietzschean rejoinder is that such an approach is an unwarranted and incoherent attempt to retain the rudiments of Christian morality and certain of its symbolic elements while disregarding their peculiar historical origins. In their pessimism regarding the prospects for the success of such a theism, Nietzsche and Aquinas are closer to one another than either is to Joyce.

As is true of many of the issues we have touched upon, Joyce's dramatic reckoning with theism and the threat of nihilism merits further literary and philosophical analysis.

[80] Joyce, *Ulysses*, chap. XVIII, lines 1561–70.
[81] See James Edwards, *The Plain Sense of Things: The Fate of Religion in an Age of Normal Nihilism* (University Park, Pennsylvania: The University of Pennsylvania Press, 1997).

The Novel as Practical Wisdom

Daniel McInerny

"Christian morality," the French Imperial Attorney, Ernest Pinard averred to a royal court in 1857, "stigmatizes realistic literature, not because it paints the passions—hatred, vengeance, love (the world only lives by these, and art must paint them)—but because it paints them without restraint, without bounds. Art without rules is no longer art. It is like a woman who throws off all garments."

The Imperial Attorney's analogy between "realistic literature" and a disclad female was aptly chosen; for the particular novel which served as the object of his indictment was *Madame Bovary*, the so-called heroine of which was a badly married provincial girl with a penchant for throwing off all garments. The stigma of Christian morality upon the alter-ego of Emma Bovary, Gustave Flaubert, was evident despite the mercy shown to him by his judge. Though he was censured only for "forgetting that literature, like art, if it is to achieve the good work that is its mission to produce, must be chaste and pure in its form as in its expression"—it remained clear that "Christian morality" would henceforth brook no forays, in the name of "realistic literature," into the wayward hearts of lonely provincial housewives.[1]

The trial of *Madame Bovary* casts a particularly harsh light on the claim that the novel must be a form, or at least a reflection of, practical wisdom. Twenty-five years after Flaubert's public chastisement, a more oblique light was cast on the claim by an American novelist, late of Beacon Hill but now living as an ex-patriot in London, who wrote an essay for *Longman's Mag-*

---

[1] My source for this account of Flaubert's trial is Hugh Kenner's illuminating study of the novel's transition from naturalism to modernism: *Joyce's Voices* (Los Angeles: University of California Press, 1978), pp. 10–11.

azine entitled "The Art of Fiction." The essay serves as nothing less than a manifesto for naturalism, and solidified its author, Henry James, in the ranks of the great naturalists, Flaubert, Zola, Turgenev.[2] The essay, published in 1884, was a response to a pamphlet by a bestseller of the day, Walter Besant, who took the occasion to proclaim a "conscious moral purpose" for the novel (or at least the *English* novel, the object of Besant's immediate concern). James did not so much dispute Besant's claim as accuse him of ambiguity. "Will you not define your terms and explain how (a novel being a picture) a picture can be either moral or immoral?" Questions of art, James went on to add, are questions of "execution," while questions of morality "are quite another affair." But James, it must be said, did not himself attempt to clear up all ambiguity on the question. Instead, he offered two modest distinctions. The first was that the English novel's moral purpose was blunted by its timidity, that is, by its desire to maintain a "difference" between what can be talked of in conversation and what can be talked of in print. "The essence of moral energy," James insisted on behalf of the novel, "is to survey the whole field" of human interaction and response, a task the English novel had been, in James's view, resolute in not pursuing. "That is very well," he concluded, "but the absence of discussion is not a symptom of the moral passion."[3]

The second distinction was a more positive contribution to the question. Here James sought to identify one point at which the moral sense and the artistic sense lie very near together, "that is in the light of the very obvious truth that the deepest quality of a work of art will always be the quality of the mind of the producer. In proportion as that intelligence is fine will the novel, the picture, the statue partake of the substance of beauty and truth." To avoid superficiality, that was the principle which for James covered "all needful moral ground."[4]

Novels are like pictures: they depict, they record, with integrity and honesty, and the fineness in this act of depiction is itself the moral content of the writing. Picking up on this Jamesian point Iris Murdoch credits Tolstoy with the same "unsentimental, detached, unselfish, objective attention"

---

[2] For the purposes of this paper I see no reason to make any hard and fast distinctions between "naturalism" and "realism," and so will use these terms interchangeably. For a discussion of "The Art of Fiction" as naturalist manifesto, see Lyall H. Powers, *Henry James and the Naturalist Movement* (East Lansing, Michigan: Michigan State University Press, 1971), chapter 3.

[3] The quotations in this paragraph are drawn from Henry James, "Art of Fiction," reprinted in *The Portable Henry James*, ed. Morton Dauwen Zabel, revised by Lyall H. P. Powers (New York: Viking Press, 1968), pp. 410–12.

[4] Ibid., p. 412.

which characterizes the moral vision of those who have emerged from Plato's cave.[5] Fine works of art in general, Murdoch declares, are a kind of "goodness by proxy." In the same spirit Martha Nussbaum has written the following of James's late masterpiece, *The Golden Bowl*:

> [T]he adventure of the reader of this novel, like the adventure of the in-
> telligent characters inside it, involves valuable aspects of human moral
> experience that are not tapped by traditional books of moral philoso-
> phy. . . . To work through these sentences and these chapters is to be-
> come involved in an activity of exploration and unraveling that uses
> abilities, especially abilities of emotion and imagination, rarely tapped
> by philosophical texts. But these abilities have, at the very least, a
> good claim to be regarded as important parts of the moral assessment
> process.[6]

The fine awareness embodied by the central character in *The Golden Bowl*, Maggie Verver, is for Nussbaum exactly the sort of moral *aisthēsis* Aristotle encourages us to imitate in the *Nicomachean Ethics*. Pericles has been replaced.

Perhaps it is not so strange that the long naturalistic novel should be found worthy of the company of Plato and Aristotle. For is not the shared purpose of the *Republic* and the *Nicomachean Ethics* to teach us how to move, as characters in novels do, from appearance to reality? Doesn't Aristotle, no matter your interpretation of *katharsis*, affirm the role that tragedy's imitation of men in action can play in that transition? Aristotle would seem to have anticipated the naturalist credo by over two millennia. The poet, he says in the *Poetics*, "should, in fact, speak as little as possible in his own person, since in what he himself says he is not an imitator."[7] Compare that to Flaubert's advice to be show-ers and not tellers of stories. Elsewhere in the *Poetics* Aristotle produces the following practical hint: "The poet, as he constructs his plots and is working them out complete with language, should as far as possible place the action before his eyes; for in this way, seeing the events with the utmost vividness, as if they were taking place in his very presence, he will discern what is appropriate and will be

---

[5] Iris Murdoch, *The Sovereignty of Good* (New York: Shocken Books, 1971), pp. 64ff.

[6] Martha Nussbaum, "Flawed Crystals: James's *The Golden Bowl* and Literature as Moral Philosophy," in *Love's Knowledge* (New York: Oxford University Press, 1990), p. 143. See also in this same volume, "The Discernment of Perception: An Aristotelian Conception of Private and Public Rationality."

[7] *Poetics* 24.1460a9–10, trans. James Hutton (New York: W. W. Norton & Co., 1982).

least likely to overlook discrepancies."[8] In hearing this one can only think of Conrad's view that his task was to make the reader *see*.

Still, the question remains of what exactly we see when we look at the reality of the human condition. What is the ethical viewpoint of the finely-tuned awareness? If Martha Nussbaum's reading of James—at least that of the later James—is correct, the reality we see just *is* the clash of appearances, the clash of what seems good and right from one perspective, with what seems good and right from another. What we learn is not what some reality is like behind the appearances, but the ineluctability of tragic conflict between those appearances. Nussbaum's observation is echoed by Graham Greene, who in one of his essays on James wrote, "He had always been strictly just to the truth as he saw it, and all that his deepening experience had done for him was to alter a murder to an adultery, but while in *The American* he had not pitied the murderer, in *The Golden Bowl* he had certainly learned to pity the adulterers. There was no victory for human beings, that was his conclusion; you were punished in your own way, whether you were of God's or the Devil's party."[9] In the preface to *The Princess Casamassima*, James describes his ideal character as being "finely aware and richly responsible." Yet that responsibility, as Nussbaum has written, follows upon the perception of a world "where values and loves are so pervasively in tension with one another that there is no safe human expectation of a perfect fidelity to all throughout a life."[10] But yet—and this is the wisdom Nussbaum would have us glean from *The Golden Bowl*—the native hue of resolution is to affirm one's love in spite of tragedy; or better, to see that love *is* tragedy: the fulfillment of one desire, the crushing of another.

Such a view of human action suggests analogies to material necessity, one of which James provides in the preface to *What Maisie Knew*: "No themes are so human as those that reflect for us, out of the confusion of life, the close connexion of bliss and bale, of the things that help with the things that hurt, so dangling before us ever that bright hard metal, of so strange an alloy, one face of which is somebody's right and ease and the other somebody's pain and wrong."[11] The human condition, then, is "bright hard metal," its necessary properties the elements of tragedy.

---

[8] Ibid., 17.1455a30–34.

[9] Graham Greene, "Henry James: The Religious Aspect," in *The Lost Childhood and Other Essays* (New York: Viking Press, 1952), p. 30.

[10] Nussbaum, "Flawed Crystals: James's *The Golden Bowl* and Literature as Moral Philosophy," p. 133.

[11] Henry James, *The Art of the Novel*, ed. Richard P. Blackmur (New York: Charles Scribner's Sons, 1962), p. 143.

Grossly apparent here is the fact that reality for the realistic novelist is somehow inhospitable to our ethical concerns. C. S. Lewis, in a famous cautionary essay, explained a large part of the reason for this by way of his own material analogy. With the modern world's abandonment of a conception of human nature as naturally ordered to certain ends, we have left ourselves with a morality that is an imposture of beneficence and in reality consists in the most tyrannical executions of force. "The ultimate springs of human action are no longer . . . something given. They have surrendered—like electricity. . . ."[12] So we now find it our business to control human nature just as we control electricity, which further suggests that what we are as human beings are bundles of impulses, of forces. Obedience to impulse, Lewis writes, is the only guideline left for human action.[13]

Such impulsiveness often takes the form of a romantic individualism, as for example in the fiction of Ernest Hemingway. In reacting to the upcoming publication of yet another batch of fiction Hemingway did not see fit to publish in his lifetime, Joan Didion has written: "The very grammar of a Hemingway sentence dictated, or was dictated by, a certain way of looking at the world, a way of looking but not joining, a way of moving through but not attaching, a kind of romantic individualism distinctly adapted to its time and source." She then goes on to relate this observation to the opening of *A Farewell to Arms*: "If we bought into those sentences, we would see the troops marching along the road, but we would not necessarily march with them. We would report, but not join."[14] In this light we are then able to draw a straight line from the opening sentences of *A Farewell to Arms* to the famous animadversions of its "hero," Frederic Henry, to whom the ancient virtues can only be so many "shouted words":

[12] C. S. Lewis, *The Abolition of Man* (New York: The Macmillan Company, 1969), p. 74.

[13] "If you will not obey the *Tao* [Lewis's rhetorical term for the natural law], or else commit suicide, obedience to impulse (and therefore, in the long run, to mere 'nature') is the only course left open" (ibid., p. 79). Compare this remark with Alasdair MacIntyre's comments, gleaned from William Gass, on the significance of James's *A Portrait of a Lady*: "*The Portrait of a Lady* has a key place within a long tradition of moral commentary, earlier members of which are Diderot's *Le Neveu de Rameau* and Kierkegaard's *Enten-Eller*. The unifying preoccupation of that tradition is the condition of those who see in the social world nothing but a meeting place for individual wills, each with its own set of attitudes and preferences and who understand that world solely as an arena for the achievement of their own satisfaction, who interpret reality solely as a series of opportunities for their enjoyment and for whom the last enemy is boredom" (*After Virtue* [Notre Dame, Indiana: University of Notre Dame Press, 1984], p. 25).

[14] Joan Didion, "Last Words," *The New Yorker*, 9 November 1998.

> I was always embarrassed by the words sacred, glorious, and sacrifice and the expression in vain. We had heard them, sometimes standing in the rain almost out of earshot, so that only the shouted words came through. . . . There were many words that you could not stand to hear and finally only the names of the places had dignity. Certain numbers were the same way and certain dates and these with the names of places were all you could say and have them mean anything. Abstract words such as glory, honor, courage, or hallow were obscene beside the concrete names of villages, the numbers of roads, the names of rivers, the numbers of regiments and the dates.[15]

A world drained of meaning. This is the world one finds when one looks at it with the cold, journalistic eye which Ernest Hemingway made famous. The "facts" of this world—"the concrete names of villages"—precisely because they can be detached from the values Frederic Henry finds so embarrassing, retain a certain dignity, as does Henry's love for his girl. And in this new world, for a time and with a measure of style, one can successfully shore such fragments against the ruins of the ancient order. But what is also well illustrated by Hemingway's fiction is the fleetingness of this success. What James refers to as "the close connexion of bliss and bale" becomes an even more menacing conflict. In Hemingway, the bale finally swallows up the bliss:

> What did he fear? It was not fear or dread. It was a nothing that he knew too well. It was all a nothing and a man was nothing too. It was only that and light was all it needed and a certain cleanness and order. Some lived in it and never felt it but he knew it was all *nada y pues nada y nada y pues nada*.[16]

The best then one can do about the bliss, if one lives to tell about it, is to write about it, trying to recapture something of the moment that will never come again.[17]

In contrasting Nietzschean style, however, the clash of necessities is celebrated in the latter episodes of James Joyce's *Ulysses*. For Joyce, like Nietzsche, learned to regard the standards of his inherited culture as masks and to find joy in that discovery. The literary implication of this discovery is that all is perspective, all is the rhetoric of impulse. What is left for the

[15] Ernest Hemingway, *A Farewell to Arms* (New York: Charles Scribner's Sons, 1957), pp. 177–78.

[16] Ernest Hemingway, "A Clean, Well-Lighted Place," reprinted in *The Collected Short Stories of Ernest Hemingway* (New York: Charles Scribner's Sons, 1987), p. 291.

[17] For these thoughts on Hemingway I have benefited greatly from Hugh Kenner's *A Homemade World: The American Modernist Writers* (Baltimore, Maryland: The Johns Hopkins University Press, 1975), especially chapter 5.

writer to depict is the voices, all the voices that fill the hundreds of pages of *Ulysses* long after Joyce had left the canons of naturalism behind. If these voices have anything to say, perhaps it is what Hugh Kenner has summarized, namely that

> [s]crupulous homespun prose, the plain style of narrative fidelity, was a late and temporary invention, affirming the temporary illusion that fact and perception, event and voice are separable. Far from delivering a final truth about things, as it seemed to do in the days when it was new, far from replacing the excrescences of rhetoric with "so many things, almost in an equal number of words," it corresponded . . . to a specialized way of perceiving for specialized purposes. . . . Rhetoric in all of its play is a human norm, the denotative style one of its departments merely.[18]

Thus in the final episode of *Ulysses*, where we hear for page after page the frivolous inertia of Molly Bloom's thoughts, we find ourselves ultimately delivered from "a final truth about things" unto a world of voices crackling like electricity in the air.

"[W]ith the death of James," Graham Greene wrote in his essay on François Mauriac,

> the religious sense was lost to the English novel, and with the religious sense went the importance of the human act. . . . Even in one of the most materialistic of our great novelists—in Trollope—we are aware of another world against which the actions of the characters are thrown into relief. The ungainly clergyman picking his black-booted way through the mud, handling so awkwardly his umbrella, speaking of his miserable income and stumbling through a proposal of marriage, exists in a way that Mrs. Woolf's Mr. Ramsay never does, because we are aware that he exists not only to the woman he is addressing but in a God's eye. His unimportance in the world of the senses is only matched by his enormous importance in another world.[19]

Trollope's ungainly clergyman exists in *a God's eye*. The significance of his action is thus taken not from himself alone, but as his action is measured by something beyond himself. James, according to Greene, was the last of England's great "religious" novelists in the sense that he was the last to manifest a larger context of good and evil against which his characters moved. (Alas, if Greene is right, James's religious sense was also tragic; the power of evil was, for him, always something stronger than the power of good.) Here we might mark the privation which typifies the modern novel's peculiar understanding of itself as practical wisdom. What it

[18] Kenner, *Joyce's Voices*, pp. 94–95.

[19] Graham Greene, "François Mauriac," in *The Lost Childhood and Other Essays*, p. 69.

lacks—indeed what it abjures—is a sense of human nature as a measured measure. At the end of his famous essay "Tradition in the Individual Talent," T. S. Eliot distinguishes between the *significant* emotion and the emotion which is merely a moment in the psychology of the poet. To adapt this distinction: what the modern novel tends to reject is the expression of *significant* action, of action which puts one's soul in the balance, as opposed to the action which is merely impulsive, without resonance in any life existing beyond the psychology of the character.[20] Whether, contra Greene, James's own novels fail to portray significant action is a question worthy of consideration. In any event, it is significant action, revealing man as a measured measure, which separates in Greene's mind, for example, the writing of a Mauriac from that of a Woolf. "It is true to say," Greene quotes Eliot's essay on Baudelaire, "that the glory of man is his capacity for salvation; it is also true to say that his glory is his capacity for damnation. The worst that can be said of our malefactors, from statesmen to thieves, is that they are not men enough to be saved."[21]

To close with a few qualifications on this notion of significant action. First, to call attention to this notion is not to condemn whole-cloth either the techniques of naturalism or the techniques of high modernism. It is rather to call attention to the way in which these novels reveal a different understanding of human action. The rigors of maintaining point of view, or the disruption of linear time, can produce effects extremely moving in themselves. What is missing is the "backdrop" of time and point of view against which "characters have the solidity and importance of men with souls to save or lose."[22]

Second, this is not a call for devotional or baldly didactic fiction. Graham Greene's use of the word "religion" is quite broad, referring to a transcendent principle but not necessarily to any particular dogma or institution. Moreover, the claim is not that such "religious" fiction was not written by nineteenth and early twentieth-century authors. What the notion of significant action does entail, however, are traditions built on the virtues. Homer's warriors take significant action, not because Zeus is watching

---

[20] Compare this with Jacques Maritain's statement, "Any man who, in a primary act of freedom deep enough to engage his whole personality, chooses to do the good for the sake of the good, chooses God, knowingly or unknowingly, as his supreme good; he loves God more than himself, even if he has no conceptual knowledge of God" (*The Responsibility of the Artist* [New York: Charles Scribner's Sons, 1960], p. 31).

[21] *Selected Prose of T. S. Eliot*, ed. Frank Kermode (Orlando, Florida: Harcourt Brace Jovanovich, 1975), p. 236.

[22] Greene, "François Mauriac," p. 70.

them but because of their honor, the Homeric principle of transcendence. This principle has an analogous relationship to what compels Fanny Price's rejection of Mr. Crawford's offer of marriage in Jane Austen's *Mansfield Park*. We can see the analogy breaking down, two centuries later, in *A Farewell to Arms*.

Finally, while the notion of significant action no more collapses the distinction between art and prudence as docs James in "The Art of Fiction," it does imply that a nuanced version of that distinction must be developed. The good of the novelist remains the good of the work, but now we must ask: What does the good of the work consist in? Aristotle calls for the imitation of men in action, which is to say *significant* action, and this situates us squarely in an ethical world which Hemingway's Frederic Henry does not inhabit.

The judge who condemned *Madame Bovary* but acquitted its author called for a fiction that was as "chaste and pure in its form as in its expression." He was right in this: the novelist who aspires to portray significant action must possess the virtues of chastity and purity. He must be respectful of the dignity of human action, not simply for the sake of "Christian morality" *qua* religious authority, but because he sees that human action is directed to an order that no novelist can make.

The Agony and the Ecstasy of the Annunciation in Anne Sexton's "The Fierceness of Female"

Carrie Rehak

Anne Sexton's poem "The Fierceness of Female" describes an erotic encounter with God which both resembles and deviates from historical portrayals of the Annunciation. As images of Mary evolve according to the contexts in which they appear, recognizing and engaging contemporary depictions of Mary may require from us a greater intuitive and creative receptivity than would more traditional portrayals of her.

In this paper, I read Sexton's poem in concert with selected relevant past and contemporary theologies. I then discuss the religious dimensions of this poem in particular, and of art and poetry in general, based for the most part on Jacques Maritain's theories of beauty, art, poetry, and creative intuition. I conclude with some final reflections on poetic and revelatory experience.

Let us begin by turning to the poem itself, in its entirety:

THE FIERCENESS OF FEMALE[1]

I am spinning,
I am spinning on the lips,
they remove my shadow,
my phantom from my past,
they invented a timetable of tongues,
that take up all my attention.
Wherein there is no room
No bed.

[1] Anne Sexton, "The Fierceness of Female," in *The Complete Poems*, foreword Maxine Kumin (Boston: Houghton Mifflin Company, 1981), p. 547. Originally published in *45 Mercy Street* (1976).

The clock does not tick
except where it vibrates my 4000 pulses,
and where all was absent,
all is two,
touching like a choir of butterflies,
and like the ocean,
pushing toward land
and receding
and pushing
with a need that gallops
all over my skin,
yelling at the reefs.

I unknit.
Words fly out of place
and I, long into the desert,
drink and drink
and bow my head to that meadow
the breast, the melon in it,
and then the intoxicating flower of it.
Our hands that stroke each other
the nipples like baby starfish—
to make our lips sucking into lunatic rings
until they are bubbles,
our fingers naked as petals
and the world pulses on a swing.
I raise my pelvis to God
so that it may know the truth of how
flowers smash through the long winter.

"The Fierceness of Female" begins with a physical description of spinning: "I am spinning, / I am spinning on the lips." Through the repetition of the word "spinning," the speaker draws the reader into the vortical form of the poem, like a finger guiding the gaze of another as it traces the inward convolutions of a rose.

The lulling, hypnotic tone of the poem invites the reader deep within the experience of the speaker, wherein her shadow, her "phantom of the past" is removed, and "a timetable of tongues" take up all her attention. The interior world is sparse, empty: "Wherein there is no room. / No bed. / The clock does not tick." Half-way through this stanza, however, the poem shifts; where there was nothing, now appears an other: "where all was absent, / all is two." An erotic tension builds: "touching like a choir of butterflies, / and like the ocean, / pushing toward land / and receding / and pushing / with a need that gallops / all over my skin, / yelling at the reefs."

The mounting tension reaches its climax in the first short line of the second stanza: "I unknit." A torrent of images follow: "Words fly out of place / and I, long into the desert, / drink and drink / and bow my head to that meadow / the breast, the melon in it, / and then the intoxicating flower of it." The desert has been transformed into a feminine and fertile landscape.

Still deeper inside, in a dreamy womb-like paradise, the speaker in the poem becomes immersed in a mystical yet physical relationship with the other: "Our hands that stroke each other / the nipples like baby starfish— / to make our lips sucking into lunatic rings / until they are bubbles, / our fingers naked as petals / and the world pulses on a swing." This complete immersion, resembling baptism, is followed by a resurfacing of the speaker, indicated by the change in tone and reknitting of the syntax: "I raise my pelvis to God / so that it may know the truth of how / flowers smash through the long winter."

It is difficult to discern whether or not in this poem Sexton is intentionally conjuring up or alluding to images of Mary's union with God at the time of the conception of Christ, or if depictions of the Annunciation informed Sexton's poetic vision. While in some earlier poems Sexton explicitly identifies Mary, in "The Fierceness of Female" she reveals neither the identity of the speaker nor that of the "other."

Drawing a comparison between the encounter in this poem and Mary's union with the Holy Spirit at the moment of Christ's conception is further complicated by the vagueness of the description of the latter event as recorded in Scripture, in two of the canonical gospels, Matthew's and Luke's. If we were to take the time to compare the imagery in Sexton's poem with these two Scriptural passages we would probably agree that, even if this poem is an allusion to the virginal conception, the primary influential source is not likely Scriptural, since neither Matthew nor Luke describes the encounter between Mary and the Holy Spirit as explicitly sexual.

Sifting through the wealth of historical references to the Annunciation would probably not help us to discern if historical depictions did or did not influence Sexton's poem, since there is no single or correct way that the Annunciation has been portrayed. For example, unlike the erotic pleasure expressed in Sexton's poem, many traditionally depicted bridal images of Mary are associated with the purity and holiness of virginity, and hence, connected with the sacred and undefiled body of the Church. In the fourth century, St. Ambrose said, in opposition to Arianism, "The Holy Church, immaculate where coitus is concerned and fertile where birth is concerned, is virgin through chastity and mother through issue. She gives us birth in a virginal way, made pregnant not by man but by the Holy Spirit."[2] The sentiments of St. Ambrose are echoed in the words of St. Augustine's reflection on Mary's virginity: "Born by the power of the Holy Spirit and from the Virgin Mary: that's how he came, and to whom he came: from the Virgin Mary in whom the Holy Spirit, and not a human husband, acted; he made the chaste one fecund, conserving her intact."[3]

However, other historical reflections concerning the conception of Christ seem to indicate a rather erotic union between Mary and the Holy Spirit. As a matter of fact, the imagery in Sexton's poem is especially reminiscent of some twelfth-century sermons. In the twelfth century, Marian devotion was sensuous and fervent. Anthropomorphic allusions to God, especially in relation to Mary, were common during this period.

The descriptive language in a twelfth-century sermon by Amadeus of Lausanne, a former novice of St. Bernard, sounds particularly similar to the imagery in Sexton's poem:

> Your Creator has become your Spouse, he has loved your beauty. . . .
> He has coveted your loveliness and desires to be united to you. Impatient of delay, he hastens to come to you. . . . Hurry to meet him, that you may be kissed with the kiss of the mouth of God and be drawn into his most blessed embraces. . . . Go out, for the nuptial chamber is already prepared, and your Spouse is coming, the Holy Spirit comes to you . . . suddenly he will come to you, that you may enjoy happiness. . . . The Holy Spirit will come upon you, that at his touch your womb may tremble and swell, your spirit rejoice and your womb flower. . . .[4]

Although Amadeus of Lausanne does not state explicitly that the union between Mary and the Holy Spirit was sexually pleasurable, the tone in the sermon is certainly erotic. God is in love with Mary's beauty, and desires to be united with her. Furthermore, the last line quoted from the sermon, which sounds very similar to Sexton's closing lines ("I raise my pelvis to God / so that it may know the truth of how / flowers smash through the long winter"), suggests erotic pleasure: "At his touch your womb may tremble and swell, your spirit rejoice and your womb flower."

---

[2] St. Ambrose, *Commentary on the Gospel of Luke* II, 7 (*CSEL* 32, 4, p. 45), quoted in Raniero Cantalamessa, *Mary: Mirror of the Church*, trans. Frances Lonergan Villa (Collegeville, Minnesota: The Liturgical Press, 1992), p. 179.

[3] St. Augustine, *Sermons*, 213, 3 and 7 (*PL* 38, 1961, 1064), quoted in Cantalamessa, *Mary: Mirror of the Church*, p. 179.

[4] Amadeus of Lausanne, from his eight Marian homilies, *Sources Chrétiennes*, eds. G. Bavaud, J. Deshusses and A. Dumas (Paris, 1960), quoted in Hilda Graef, *Mary: A History of Doctrine and Devotion* (New York: Sheed and Ward, 1963), vol. 1, p. 245.

However, Amadeus of Lausanne continues this sermon by rendering the image of God as the bearer of male seed: "For you, most beautiful Virgin, have been joined in close embraces to the Creator of beauty, and, having been made more a virgin, indeed, more than a virgin, because mother and virgin, have received the most holy seed by divine infusion."[5] Unlike the gender-specificity of this description and others of its kind, in "The Fierceness of Female" the gender of the other remains ambiguous, and the speaker in the poem is not portrayed as an open field passively receiving an infusion of holy seed. Although Sexton does not forsake the relational or complementary aspects of the union, she renders neither the lover nor the beloved as recipients or agents of fertilization and procreation. The flowering in Sexton's poem appears, rather, to be an end beyond the end, and not the object, of the speaker's supplication for union with God. In other words, the desired object of the union is first and foremost the union itself.[6]

The shift in focus reflected in Sexton's poem, from the biological or procreative functions of sex to loving union, echoes areas of debate and reevaluation in feminist discourse and Christian ethics. Although Sexton neither identified herself as a Christian nor as a feminist, she has, like many Christian feminists, emphasized the loving aspect of sexual union in "The Fierceness of Female" as well as in other works. However, Sexton's language is, for the most part, devoid of technical theological as well as feminist terminology.

Perhaps the two most troubling areas for many critics of Sexton's poetry are her religious views and her identity as a woman in relation to feminist discourse. The problem here, I believe, is that Sexton defies most ideologies. While some of her poems may bolster religious or feminist causes, others can just as easily deflate them. Perhaps this is because Sexton's investment, like that of all good artists, is to tell the truth. By truth I mean that she does not seem to soften or ameliorate her poetic vision, nor does she attempt to taper it, in order to reach any end beyond the good of the poem itself. And in this way it is an honest, unadulterated, and chaste relationship between artist and artwork.[7] As a matter of fact, Sexton considered her poetry closer to the truth than her own self. She said in one interview,

---

[5] Ibid.

[6] This notion echoes Maritain's theory of the engendering of art as a result of the superabundant overflowing of poetic knowledge into an object made.

[7] On the operation of art for the good of the work, see Maritain, *Art and Scholasticism, With Other Essays by Jacques Maritain*, trans. J. F. Scanlan (London: Sheed and Ward, 1930), p. 14.

"In some ways, as you see me now, I am a lie. The crystal truth is in my poetry."[8]

Rodin said, "The ugly in art is the fake, whatever grins at you without cause, senseless affectations, pirouettes and capers, mere travesties of beauty and grace, whatever tells a lie."[9] Jacques Maritain reiterates this idea when he says that "every work of art must be logical. Therein lies the truth. It must be steeped in logic; not in the pseudo-logic of clear ideas, not in the logic of knowledge and demonstration, but in the working logic of every day, eternally mysterious and disturbing. . . ."[10]

Part of my fascination with Sexton's poetry is that it cannot be easily defined; it cannot be captured; that is, it cannot be contained in any category, religious or political. Instead, it moves freely between opposite poles, between belief and unbelief, between comedy and tragedy, between life and death. Sexton's poetry, prose, and personal history are full of reconciled and unreconciled contradictions. For example, in her poem "Words" she recognizes that words can be "both daisies and bruises."[11] At times, Sexton synthesizes the dualities. At other times, she appears to sit comfortably with them. And then there are periods where the contradictions seem to torment her. However, she never seems to undermine the complexity, "mysterious and disturbing," by denying or simplifying it.

Take, for example, Sexton's "religious" poetry. It has been rejected by many as "junk," a product of "self-indulgence" or "madness." Sexton herself described her series of poems *The Jesus Papers* in *The Book of Folly* as "either 'blasphemous' or 'devout'—it's probably blasphemous."[12] One critic, James Wright, wrote the following in the margins of the manuscript of *The Awful Rowing Toward God*: "Leave God his own poems, and cut these lines out. . . . [S]top trying to be a saint. Be a poet, and get rid of that junk."[13] Another critic calls her religious poems "verbal comic

---

[8] Anne Sexton, interview by Bridgett Weeks, in *No Evil Star: Selected Essays, Interviews, and Prose*, ed. Steven E. Colburn (Ann Arbor: University of Michigan Press, 1986), p. 115. Originally published in *Boston Magazine*, August 1968.

[9] Maritain, *Art and Scholasticism*, p. 52.

[10] Ibid.

[11] Anne Sexton, "Words," in *The Complete Poems*, p. 464. Originally published in *The Awful Rowing Toward God* (Boston: Houghton Mifflin Co., 1975).

[12] Anne Sexton, interview with William Heyen and Al Poulin, in *No Evil Star*, pp. 154–55. Originally published in *American Poets* in 1976, ed. William Heyen (Indianapolis, Indiana: Bobbs-Merrill, 1976).

[13] Diane Wood Middlebrook, *Anne Sexton: A Biography*, with a foreword by Martin T. Orne (Boston: Houghton Mifflin, 1991), p. 367.

strips."[14] However, Sexton believed irreligious people had a more difficult time with her "religious" poetry than with her "confessional" kind. Regarding the critics, she once said, "I think they tackle the obvious things, without delving deeper. They are more shocked by the other, whereas I think in time to come people will be more shocked by my mystical poetry than by my so-called confessional poetry."[15] On the other hand, she remarked that the Jesuits "find my work very religious, and take my book on retreats, and teach my poems in classes."[16]

Discerning the value of art for theological reflection is visibly difficult, as reflected by the criticisms of Sexton's work. Two main areas of debate surround questions of content, and issues of morality and authority. Let us first consider the question of content.

Sexton's poetry is not solely or simply explicitly religious, although many of her poems incorporate religious themes. In an essay by Frances Bixler, "The Religious Pilgrimage of Anne Sexton," the following observation is made:

> Anne Sexton's religious poetry presents different problems to different readers. For those who no longer accept the Christian God as a reality, her search seems dated and inexplicable. Those who empathize with her need to make God a reality may feel at a loss to comprehend the twistings, contradictions, and confusions displayed by a large body of her work. Sexton's poetry is also a puzzlement for believers because of her frequent disregard for orthodox theology. Thus, no reader comes away from her religious poetry feeling fully at ease.[17]

I consider the sense of discomfort produced in the reader by Sexton's poetry an achievement rather than a weakness of the work. The disturbing character of Sexton's poetry is not entirely unlike many Biblical narratives themselves, which are also largely unsettling and complex. Furthermore, for a work of art to be religious, or even Christian, does not require that its content be identifiably "religious." In the words of Jacques Maritain, "Christianity does not make art *easy*. It deprives it of its facile means, it stops its progress in many directions, but in order to raise its level."[18] In

---

[14] William H. Shurr, "Mysticism and Suicide: Anne Sexton's Last Poetry," in *Soundings: An Interdisciplinary Journal* 68 (Fall 1985), pp. 335-56. Reprinted in *Critical Essays on Anne Sexton*, ed. Linda Wagner-Martin (Boston: G. K. Hall & Co., 1989), p. 204.

[15] Anne Sexton, interview with Barbara Kevles, in *No Evil Star*, p. 107.

[16] Ibid.

[17] Frances Bixler, "Journey into the Sun: The Religious Pilgrimage of Anne Sexton," in *Original Essays on the Poetry of Anne Sexton*, ed. Frances Bixler (Conway, Arkansas: University of Central Arkansas Press, 1988), p. 203.

[18] Maritain, *Art and Scholasticism*, p. 73.

this way, I find Sexton's poetry raised beyond the level of much intentionally illustrated liturgical art and devotional depictions.

One reason that contemporary fine arts may be more valuable for theological inquiry and reflection than intentionally religious illustration is that contemporary fine art is often imbued with infinite layers of meaning, whereas illustrative art often lacks depth and dimension. In his essay entitled "Absurdity in Sacred Decoration," Thomas Merton distinguishes between symbol and illustration:

> Symbolism fortifies and concentrates the spirit of prayer, but illustration tends rather to weaken and to dissipate our attention. Symbolism acts as a very efficacious spiritual medium. It opens the way to an intuitive understanding of mystery—it places us in the presence of the invisible. Illustration tends rather to become an obstacle, to divert and to amuse rather than to elevate and direct. It tends to *take the place of* the invisible and obscure it.[19]

Similarly, Maritain distinguishes between Christian art and art which intends to be, among other things, religious. This distinction made by Maritain is related to what he considers to be the "thesis" as opposed to the "habit" of art.

> The term *thesis* will be applied to any intention extrinsic to the work itself, when the thought inspired by such an intention does not act upon the work by means of the artistic habit moved instrumentally, but puts itself in juxtaposition to the habit so as itself to act directly upon the work. In such a case the work is not wholly produced by the artistic habit or wholly by the thought inspired, but partly by one and partly by the other, like a boat pulled by two men. In this sense any thesis, whether it profess to demonstrate or to move, is an alien importation in art and as such an impurity. It imposes upon art, in its own sphere, that is to say in the actual production of the work, an alien rule and end; it prevents the work of art issuing from the heart of the artist with the spontaneity of a perfect fruit; it betrays calculation, a dualism between the intelligence of the artist and his sensibility, which the object of art is to have united.[20]

In this way, "religious" illustration which intends to demonstrate or move may have a thesis; it may be "an art specified by an object, an end, and definite rules."[21] Christian art, on the other hand, is free. However, according to Maritain, it is only Christian insofar as it "overflows from a

---

[19] Thomas Merton, "Absurdity in Sacred Decoration," in *Disputed Questions* (New York: Farrar, Straus and Cudahy, 1960), p. 265.

[20] Maritain, *Art and Scholasticism*, p. 66.

[21] Ibid., p. 68.

heart possessed by grace."[22] That is, "the work will be Christian in proportion as the love is alive."[23]

Can contemporary art, such as "The Fierceness of Female," which is not necessarily intentionally sacred or explicitly Christian be a valuable, valid, and revelatory source for theological interpretation? Art and theology, according to Maritain's classically influenced categories, are two distinct disciplines governed by their own sets of rules, goals, and objectives.[24] Theology is a habit of the speculative order, and art of the practical.[25] Art, like wisdom, is a virtue, valuable in itself, but the virtue of art tends to the good of the work to be made, and not to knowledge for its own sake.

The practical order is further divided into two distinct spheres, Action and Making. It is with this distinction that Maritain defends *art's complete freedom from external rules and moral judgments*. Moral judgment, or prudence, is distinguished from artistic judgment, although both are concerned with the means to an end. Prudence, however, is the intellectual determination of *actions to be done*, while art is the intellectual determination of *works to be made*. Making, as opposed to Action, is ordered not to the common end of all human life, but to the object made.

Maritain also distinguishes between poetry and art, a distinction which he describes at length in *Creative Intuition in Art and Poetry*. Although art and poetry are interconnected, they are also vastly different according to the terms which Maritain assigns them. Art, defined by Maritain, is "the creative or producing, work-making activity of the human mind." Poetry, on the other hand, is "not the particular art which consists in writing verses, but a process more general and more primary: that intercommunication between the inner being of things and the inner being of the human Self. . . ."[26] It is "the free creativity of the spirit, and the intuitive knowledge through emotion, which transcend and permeate all arts, inasmuch as they tend toward beauty as an end beyond the end."[27]

Poetry, according to Maritain, has no external object but tends to the infinite, through a "release and actuation of the free creativity of the spirit."[28]

---

[22] Ibid., p. 70.

[23] Ibid., p. 71.

[24] Ibid., p. 9.

[25] For a further discussion on the practical and speculative orders, see Maritain, *Art and Scholasticism*, pp. 1-8, and *Creative Intuition in Art and Poetry*, The A. W. Mellon Lectures in the Fine Arts, National Gallery of Art, Washington, D.C., Bollingen Series, 35 (New York: Pantheon Books, 1953), pp. 44–51.

[26] Maritain, *Creative Intuition in Art and Poetry*, p. 3.

[27] Ibid., p. 393.

[28] Ibid., p. 236.

It is "free," unlike art, insofar as it is not oriented toward making; it is not bound to an object. In this way, poetry transcends art since it is the "secret life of all the arts."[29] Therefore, although poetry is knowledge oriented toward expression, it is not practical knowledge, as is art. Poetry is not limited to the practical knowledge of making, but is instead bound up with being.

Creative intuition has both objective and subjective elements which are finally revealed in the object made. In poetic intuition, objectivity and subjectivity, the world and the whole of the soul, coexist inseparably.[30] Poetic intuition is "filled with the subjectivity of the poet as well as with the thing grasped, since the thing grasped and the subjectivity are known together in the same obscure experience, and since the thing grasped is grasped only through its affective resonance in and in union with the subjectivity."[31]

By way of knowledge through connaturality, the objective reality of the world is grasped through the subjectivity of the poet, "according to any direction whatever in which an act of spiritual communication with the things of the world can be brought about," and which can be expressed only by recasting these things into an object.[32] Poetry is thus made concrete.

The work of art brings poetic intuition into objectification. "And it must always preserve its own consistence and value as an *object*."[33] However, it is a "sign"—"both a direct sign of the secrets perceived in things, of some irrecusable truth of nature or adventure caught in the great universe, and a *reversed sign* of the subjective universe of the poet, of his substantial Self obscurely revealed."[34] It is "both a revelation of the subjectivity of the poet and of the reality that poetic knowledge has caused him to perceive."[35] The process of creative production is mirrored in the creative reception by the beholder of the work made. In both creative production and reception, the spiritual is revealed intuitively and affectively in and through the physical.

According to this design, we can see that art is not in line with doing but with making. Therefore, moral judgments are generally inapplicable to what concerns the good of the work, that is, the process of the creative production of the work of art. We can also see that objects of contemporary

[29] Ibid., p. 3.
[30] Ibid., p. 124.
[31] Ibid., p. 127.
[32] Ibid., p. 130.
[33] Ibid., p. 128.
[34] Ibid.
[35] Ibid.

fine art, even those considered as "secular," are or may be valid and valuable sources for theological inquiry, because they are revelatory.

I consider Sexton's poetry religious poetry, or better yet, revelatory, and not only those poems which incorporate "religious" themes. Sexton's poetry is like a glass, darkly, through which an obscure yet deep encounter takes place between created and creator, between herself, her readers, the world, and ultimate mystery.

Sexton intentionally gives her poems to her readers. For her there is no single or correct answer when it comes to responding to the question of meaning in her poems. The poem, according to Sexton, "should be what it means to its *readers*. They can grow with it. If some reader likes a poem, he might read it five years later and see in it something very different, because he's lived a little longer and suddenly sees something very startlingly new."[36]

Sexton's "confessional" mode of poetry is one of the techniques by which she invites her readers into the poem, and through which her readers may find a voice for their own experiences. Confessional poetry, which was introduced as a genre by W. D. Snodgrass and Robert Lowell in the mid-1950s, begins with the autobiographical experience of the poet and is usually expressed in the first person. In this way, the reader may feel an intimate relationship, or an identification, with the voice in the poem. Furthermore, Sexton as a "confessional" poet becomes the authority of her own experience. It is through the form of the poem that Sexton penetrates the truth of her life—reaching universal proportions through the concrete and particular.

As I read and reread the "The Fierceness of Female," I witness a joyful mystery, which is the mystery and miracle of recognizing a loving union between self and other, between the physical and spiritual. However, I also experience the painful lack, the yearning for complete and eternal fulfillment. The poem ends with the speaker raising her pelvis to God in supplication, before or without God's response. We are left with an image of desire—to be wedded to God, to know fully. But for now, "we know only in part" (I Cor. 13:12).

This thirst for complete union with God is temporarily quenched in the union with beauty. If beauty belongs to the order of the transcendentals—that is, to the order of properties, such as the one, the true, and the good, "which surpass all limits of kind or category and will not suffer themselves to be confined in any class, because they absorb everything and are to be

---

[36] Anne Sexton, interview by Gregory Fitzgerald, in *No Evil Star*, p. 186. Originally published in *Massachusetts Review* 19 (1978).

everywhere"[37]—then we, when we experience beauty, also experience God; or, as stated by Maritain: "Once we touch a transcendental, we touch being itself, a likeness of God."[38]

Quoting St. Thomas, Maritain says that beauty, *per effectum*, is what gives pleasure on sight, *id quod visum placet*. It is "a vision," an "*intuitive knowledge*, and a *joy*."[39] He continues, "The beautiful is what gives joy, not all joy, but joy in knowledge; not the joy peculiar to the act of knowing, but a joy superabounding and overflowing from such an act because of the object known."[40] Beauty "has the savor of the terrestrial paradise, because it restores for a brief moment the simultaneous peace and delight of the mind and the senses."[41] It is "essentially delightful. Therefore by its very nature, by its very beauty, it stirs desire and produces love. . . ."[42]

Furthermore, Maritain suggests, it is love that ultimately produces ecstasy: "Love in its turn produces ecstasy, that is to say, makes the lover beside himself: an ec-stasy of which the soul experiences a lesser form when it is gripped by the beauty of a work of art, and the fullness when it is absorbed, like dew, by the beauty of God."[43]

Edgar Allan Poe describes the ecstasy and the sorrow of temporarily experiencing union with God through beauty:

> Inspired by an ecstatic prescience of the glories beyond the grave, we struggle by multiform combinations among the things and thoughts of Time to attain a portion of that Loveliness whose very elements perhaps appertain to eternity alone. And thus when by Poetry, or when by Music, the most entrancing of the Poetic moods, we find ourselves melted into tears, we weep them not, as the Abbate Gravina supposes, through excess of pleasure, but through a certain petulant, impatient sorrow at our inability to grasp *now*, wholly here on earth, at once and for ever, those divine and rapturous joys of which *through* the poem, or *through* the music, we attain to but brief and indeterminate glimpses.[44]

---

[37] Maritain, *Art and Scholasticism*, p. 30.

[38] Ibid., pp. 32-33.

[39] Ibid., p. 23. See *Summa Theologiae* I, q. 5, a. 4.

[40] Ibid., p. 23.

[41] Ibid., p. 24.

[42] Ibid., p. 26.

[43] Ibid., p. 27.

[44] Edgar Allan Poe, *Tales and Poems*, vol. 4 (London: J. C. Nimmo, 1884), quoted in Maritain, *Art and Scholasticism*, p. 174, n. 70. Maritain writes, "Baudelaire is here reproducing an extract from the preface to his own translation, *Nouvelles Histoires Extraordinaires*, an extract inspired by and almost a translation of a passage in a lecture by Poe, *The Poetic Principle*."

"The Fierceness of Female" describes a longing for God similar to that expressed by Poe in his reflection on beauty. The speaker in this poem has experienced a glimpse into the life of the divine, into the transcendent, albeit briefly and indeterminately. At the end of the poem, it appears that the speaker is trying to grasp, "at once and forever, those divine and rapturous joys" which she has encountered in love. Similarly, in an earlier poem entitled "When Man Enters Woman" (1975), which also depicts an erotic encounter, Sexton expresses the frustration of having touched, without having fully reached, wholly and eternally, God. This poem ends with the following passage: "This man, / this woman / with their double hunger, / have tried to reach through / the curtain of God / and briefly they have, / though God / in His perversity / unties the knot."[45] It appears that the speaker in the "The Fierceness of Female" has also experienced an untying of the knot, and so attempts to reconnect by raising her pelvis to God. According to my interpretation, the final physical image in the poem is a personal and theological testament to the Incarnation; the speaker desires God to reveal the truth in and through her body.

Whether Sexton intentionally alluded to the conception of Christ in this poem, it is for me an icon of hope for the holy union of self and other, of self and God, and for the fruit of that union. The fruit of that union lies in the final supplication for the truth to smash through the long winter like flowers. What is the "fierceness of female"? For me it is the fierceness of the activities of the Spirit, which create and sustain love and new life—that which is best expressed by Sexton in the final fierce image of faith, hope, and love.[46]

The "fierceness of female" is also revealed in and through the image of Mary, who comes to communicate with the physical universe spiritual things. In order to communicate, her image evolves according to the needs, languages, and symbols recognizable to the people of particular historical and socio-cultural contexts. The ambiguity of contemporary images of Mary requires from us an even greater intuitive, a deeper, or more alert, receptivity to the persons and things revealed therein, and likewise, a more active participation on our behalf than would more easily recognizable portrayals. In other words, we must, through our creative receptivity penetrate the depths of these images so that their spirit may be revealed.

---

[45] Anne Sexton, "When Man Enters Woman," in *The Complete Poems*, p. 428. Originally published in *The Awful Rowing Toward God*.

[46] For a discussion on female imagery of Spirit, see Elizabeth A. Johnson, *She Who Is: The Mystery of God in Feminist Theological Discourse* (New York: Crossroad, 1994), p. 83.

Music and Religion in Gilson's Philosophy of Art

Ralph Nelson

It surely would be difficult to find two metaphysicians as different as Georg Hegel and Étienne Gilson. Nowhere is this more evident than in Gilson's important study *L'Être et l'essence*,[1] or in the later version, *Being and Some Philosophers*.[2] What a difference between the concrete or absolute idealist, on the one hand, and the Thomist noteworthy for the emphasis given to *esse* or *actus essendi*, on the other. For Gilson often remarked that the notion of *esse* was a central feature of Aquinas's philosophy which many so-called Thomists had managed to ignore. Of Hegel's thought, he said, "This doctrine which recognizes nothing more lowly than being, unless this be existence itself, seems to announce the most extreme devaluation of the act of existing that is conceivable."[3]

And yet there is a similarity in the way in which they both approach the philosophy of art, even though that truth that is in the details reveals that behind a somewhat similar terminology, there are vast differences related to incompatible metaphysical orientations. What I refer to as a similarity or, perhaps better, an analogy is the fact that Hegel begins his *Lectures on Aes-*

---

[1] Étienne Gilson, *L'Être et l'essence* (Paris: Jules Vrin, 1948).

[2] Étienne Gilson, *Being and Some Philosophers* (Toronto: Pontifical Institute of Mediaeval Studies, 1949).

[3] Gilson, *L'Être et l'essence*, p. 210. "It is probably not by chance that Germany is the country of both idealistic metaphysics and of music. Hegel, Schelling, Fichte can assume a metaphysical theme and weave it into a world with no less freedom than Bach can write a fugue. Such metaphysical fabrics are far from lacking beauty, but Bach was right because, as an artist, his end was to achieve beauty, whereas Hegel was wrong because, as a philosopher, his end should have been to achieve truth" (*Being and Some Philosophers*, p. 213).

thetics[4] by distinguishing between the philosophy of art and aesthetics, and Gilson does that as well.

Although Hegel finally decides to use the popular term aesthetics to describe his course, he wants to distinguish between the philosophy of art or the philosophy of fine art and aesthetics. The former term "denotes more accurately the sciences of the senses or emotions."[5] The latter has as its object "to unfold the essential nature of the beautiful, and—apart from any intention to propound rules for the executant—how it is illustrated in actual work, that is, works of art."[6] This study "must combine metaphysical universality [the idea] with the determinate content of real particularity,"[7] the famous concrete universal.

The problem in Hegelian aesthetics is that art within the system is a moment in the development of absolute spirit, that is, art in some sense is seen as a form of consciousness and knowledge, albeit inferior to religion and philosophy. Such an acute observer as Benedetto Croce maintained that the autonomy of art was lost in the dialectical series.

> The artistic activity is distinct from the philosophical only through its imperfection, only because it apprehends The Absolute in a sensible and immediate form, whereas philosophy apprehends it in the pure medium of thought. . . . Art is practically reduced (whether he like it or not) to a philosophical error, or an illusory philosophy.[8]

Attempts have been made to show that the validity of Hegelian aesthetics holds up even if one rejects the ontology, but it is hard to see how this is so.[9] If the ontology is the basis of Hegel's philosophy of art, then a rejection of that ontology entails a rejection of that philosophy of art as well. What might remain of value would be his insights and observations on art and its history, but not the philosophical science he aspired to construct. I have mentioned Hegel at some length because he represents an interpretation of art vehemently criticized by Gilson, the position that art consists in a kind of knowledge.

---

[4] Georg Hegel, *Lectures on Aesthetics: The Philosophy of Fine Art*, vol. 1, trans. F. P. B. Osmaston (New York: Hacker Art Books, 1975).

[5] Ibid., p. 1.

[6] Ibid., p. 23.

[7] Ibid., p. 28.

[8] Benedetto Croce, *What is Living and What is Dead of the Philosophy of Hegel*, trans. Douglas Ainslie (New York: Russell and Russell, 1969), p. 129.

[9] Jack Kaminsky, *Hegel on Art: An Interpretation of Hegel's Aesthetics* (New York: State University of New York, 1962), pp. 3, 27. See also Andrew Bowie, *Aesthetics and Subjectivity from Kant to Nietzsche* (Manchester: Manchester University Press, 1990), pp. 9–10.

And now to Gilson. The issue of defining and understanding the philosophy of art is considered in the three volumes—*Painting and Reality* (1958), *The Arts of the Beautiful* (1963), and *Forms and Substances in the Arts* (1966)—dedicated to the arts of the beautiful.[10] He raises doubts as to whether aesthetics is a science, and proceeds to distinguish between the philosophy of art and aesthetics. The former "considers the work in its relation to the artist who produces it, the latter considers it in its relation to the spectator, the listener or the reader who perceives it."[11] It is evident that Gilson's focus is primarily on the former consideration. Like Maritain, Gilson was a pioneer in developing a Thomist-inspired philosophy of art. They ventured into a "zone of free exchange,"[12] for no such philosophy of art existed; there is no precedent to be extracted from the works of Thomas Aquinas, so we may happily avoid that perspective in which a doctrine is judged as to whether or not it conforms to Thomas's thought (*ad mentem divi Thomae.*) In short, Thomistic metaphysics provides the means for the development of a philosophy of art, not a matter of recovery, but of discovery.

There are several important negations at the heart of Gilson's approach: the refusal to identify art as a particular mode of knowing—and Kant and other philosophers are singled out for criticism on this point[13]—and, secondly, the rejection of art as imitation. There are other negations, such as the critique of expressivist or expressionist theories, but these two seem to be salient. The contention that art is a kind of cognition is characterized as the "'sophism of misplaced knowledge,' for which idealism is but another name; for indeed idealism ultimately consists in saying that everything is knowledge, even reality itself."[14] This negation means that, contrary to Keats's famous lines: "'Beauty is truth, truth beauty,'—that is all ye know on earth, and all ye need to know,"[15] the concept of truth is not really relevant to art.

---

[10] Étienne Gilson, *Painting and Reality* (New York: Meridian Books, 1959); *The Arts of the Beautiful* (New York: Charles Scribner's Sons, 1965); *Forms and Substances in the Arts*, trans. Salvator Attanaseo (New York: Charles Scribner's Sons, 1966).

[11] Gilson, *Forms and Substances in the Arts*, p. 25.

[12] Henry Bars et al., *Jacques Maritain et ses contemporains* (Paris: Desclée, 1991), p. 304. The phrase is Bars's. He compares Gilson and Maritain briefly, pp. 304–07.

[13] Locke and Leibniz are mentioned. *The Arts of the Beautiful*, pp. 142, 149–50.

[14] Gilson, *The Arts of the Beautiful*, p. 13.

[15] John Keats, "Ode on a Grecian Urn." The example is mine. Gilson refers to Boileau, the famous critic, as having made this identification, in *The Arts of the Beautiful*, pp. 25–26.

The relation of the arts of the beautiful to the good is another matter. At the end of the nineteenth century two opposing positions about art were developed. Tolstoy the stern moralist had excised beauty from the realm of art and replaced it by the notion of the moral good, so that the older Tolstoy, as moral scold, condemned the great novels of his earlier self. Effectively good art serves moral and religious truth.[16] Nietzsche, in contrast, must be taken at his word when he speaks about going beyond moral and ethical categories, elaborating an aesthetic view of life in which the self is both potter and clay, the self envisaged as a work of art, self-making.[17]

What Gilson wants to do is recognize that the beautiful, while not a species of knowledge, "is the good of sense knowledge for the sensibility of an intelligent being."[18] He wants to recognize the autonomy of the arts of the beautiful without denying that there are other tribunals to which they may be subject, since art is not the one thing needful.

> This does not mean that works of art are not subject to other tribunals judging them on the strength of other rules, such as those of religion or of morality; but it does mean that, if it is a question of judging a painting precisely *qua* work of art, the principles to be followed in judging it should be borrowed from the notion of art understood as the creative activity that has just been defined.[19]

What he objects to is the substitution of "knowledge for art,"[20] the tendency to "discuss art from a viewpoint other than that of its essence."[21] Hence, the importance of the definition of the philosophy of art as "a meta-

---

[16] "The best works of our time transmit religious feelings urging towards the union and the brotherhood of man" (Leo Tolstoy, *What is Art?*, trans. Aylmer Maude [London: Walter Scott, Ltd., 1899], p. 189). Both Beethoven and Wagner are criticized, the former surprisingly for the *Ninth Symphony*, whose "Ode to Joy" is often used today as an anthem of brotherhood, the latter for the *Ring Cycle*. His summary of the plot of the *Cycle* is satirically exact. It was a similar reading, no doubt, which encouraged the popular takeoff by Anna Russell, a routine which held her in good stead in concert halls for a number of years.

[17] To cite just two of Nietzsche's works relevant to aesthetics: *Twilight of the Idols*, trans. Walter Kaufmann in *The Portable Nietzsche* (New York: The Viking Press, 1954) and *The Case of Wagner*, trans. Walter Kaufmann (New York: Random House, 1967). For a very interesting examination of Nietzschean aesthetics by an important contemporary French philosopher, see Luc Ferry, *Homo Aestheticus: the Invention of Taste in the Democratic Age*, trans. Robert DeLoaiza (Chicago: The University of Chicago Press, 1993), pp. 148–91.

[18] Gilson, *The Arts of the Beautiful*, p. 28.

[19] Gilson, *Painting and Reality*, p. 134.

[20] Gilson, *Forms and Substances in the Arts*, p. 130.

[21] Ibid., p. 312.

physics of Art, that is to say, an ontology which considers the works in their substantial structure and in their relation to their cause."[22]

The second important negation in Gilson's philosophy of art concerns the classical conception of art as the imitation of nature. He is categorical: "Art's essential purpose is not the imitation of nature."[23] Greatly influenced by French commentators on the arts such as Delacroix, Baudelaire, Focillon, and Valéry, Gilson stresses the goal of the artist as creating beauty. For "the specific distinction of art lies in its *proper end*, which is to make things of beauty."[24] The contrast is made in *Painting and Reality* between "an art of imitation" and the creation of "a new world of forms."[25]

There is a third negation, no doubt of lesser importance than the other two, which bears on the idea of art as expression, or the expressionist theory, not referring to a school of painting. This would construe art as expressing "the affective states by which man is ordinarily moved"; Gilson seems to dispose of the expressionist theory when he says of music, for instance, that while it "may not express these feelings, it causes them."[26] So, by implication at least, he would oppose this kind of theory.

Having now indicated certain general characteristics of Gilson's philosophy of art, I turn to his discussion of music. Even though his most notable work in the philosophy of art was the Mellon lectures on painting, we find an abundance of material, even in *Painting and Reality*, on music. The method followed here will be first to note some of Gilson's principal comments on music and then, subsequently, to note what he has to say about church music, sacred music, concluding with some personal observations about the current state of sacred music.

In modern philosophy there are a number of significant figures who have had a good deal to say about music. The list would include Schopenhauer and Nietzsche, of course; Theodor Adorno of the Frankfurt School, Vladimir Jankélévitch, and, most recently, Roger Scruton, whose essay on

[22] Ibid., p. 28.

[23] Ibid., p. 110.

[24] Gilson, *The Arts of the Beautiful*, p. 133. In *Forms and Substances in the Arts* Gilson says, "For in contrast to knowledge which takes cognizance of its object, the function of art is to create its own object in freedom and for beauty's sake" (p. 278).

[25] Gilson, *Painting and Reality*, p. 226.

[26] Gilson, *Forms and Substances in the Arts*, p. 174. For a valuable résumé of Croce's expressionist aesthetics and its underlying dualism, see H. Wildon Carr, *The Philosophy of Benedetto Croce: The Problem of Art and History* (New York: Russell and Russell, 1917), pp. 162–72. Charles Taylor interprets Hegel's philosophy as expressivism, a term he thinks avoids the ambiguity of expressionism, in *Hegel* (Cambridge: Cambridge University Press, 1975), p. 13, n. 1.

the aesthetics of music is due to be published this year.[27] With the notable exception of Jankélévitch, who was mainly interested in Bergson and existentialism in philosophy, and modern French music—Ravel and others—the other philosophers may all be situated in the German philosophical and musical tradition; Scruton, for instance, has been greatly interested in Hegelian philosophy, and is a fervent Wagnerite.[28]

Unlike Maritain who only speaks of music in asides, in passing as it were, Gilson from his youth was passionately interested in music.[29] His good friend and successor in the chair of the French Academy, Henri Gouhier, in the traditional *discours de réception*, in which the new member eulogizes his predecessor, said that music had played a great part in Gilson's life, but not as a pastime or distraction.[30] For him it was a form of expression of the ineffable *par excellence*. What cannot be expressed otherwise is expressed by music. Recalling Gilson's predilection for music, Gouhier recounts that Gilson was present for all the performances of *Pelléas et Mélisande* when a student at the Sorbonne. What Bizet's *Carmen* was for Nietzsche, *Pelléas* was for the young Gilson.[31] *Pelléas*, I suppose, is what is often referred to as an acquired taste, meaning in common parlance that one will be relatively alone in its appreciation.[32] We know that

[27] See Arthur Schopenhauer on the metaphysics of music in *The World as Will and Representation*, trans. E. F. J. Payne (New York: Dover Publications, 1958), vol. 2, pp. 447–57. For an overview of Nietzsche's views on art and music, see Julian Young, *Nietzsche's Philosophy of Art* (Cambridge: Cambridge University Press, 1992). Adorno wrote on Wagner and Mahler in addition to *Philosophy of Modern Music*, trans. Anne G. Mitchell and Wesley V. Blomster (New York: Seabury Press, 1973). On Jankélévitch, see Guy Suarès, *Vladimir Jankélévitch, Qui suis-je?* (Lyon: La Manufacture, 1986). Roger Scruton discusses music in *Art and Imagination: A Study in the Philosophy of Mind* (London: Methuen, 1974) and *Modern Philosophy: An Introduction and Survey* (New York: Allen Lane, The Penguin Press, 1994).

[28] Roger Scruton, "On the Way to Extinction," a review of Michael Tanner, *Wagner* in the *Times Literary Supplement*, 7 March 1997, pp. 18–19.

[29] For some of Jacques Maritain's remarks on music, see *Art and Scholasticism*, trans. Joseph W. Evans (New York: Charles Scribner's Sons, 1962), p. 17n., pp. 45, 57; and *Creative Intuition in Art and Poetry* (Princeton, New Jersey: Princeton University Press, 1977), p. 293.

[30] Henri Gouhier, "Discours," in Marie-Thérèse d'Alverney et al., *Étienne Gilson et nous: La Philosophie et son histoire* (Paris: Jules Vrin, 1980), pp. 156–57. Cf. Henri Gouhier, *Étienne Gilson: trois essais* (Paris: Jules Vrin, 1993).

[31] On Nietzsche's passion for *Carmen*, see Dietrich Fischer-Dieskau, *Wagner and Nietzsche*, trans. Joachim Neugroschel (New York: The Seabury Press, 1974), p. 179.

[32] Cf. Karl Haas, *Inside Music: How to Understand, Listen to, and Enjoy Good Music* (New York: Doubleday, 1948), p. 338, and A. L. Bacharach and J. R. Pearce, eds., *The Musical Companion: A Modern Guide to Classical Music* (New York & London: Harcourt Brace Jovanovich, 1978), p. 415.

the passion was not exclusive, for Gilson might also be called a Wagnerite.[33] This is not to ignore numerous references to other composers.

The influence of Bergson on Maritain has often been mentioned, some seeing it in the inclusion of intuition, whether intellectual or creative, in Maritain's philosophy. Gilson has told us in memorable terms what Bergson meant to him, as well as the reasons why he lost interest in the former's philosophy.[34] In what, I believe, is Gilson's earliest venture in the philosophy of art, "Art et métaphysique," which appeared in 1916,[35] one finds pervasive references to intuitions, be they metaphysical or aesthetic, terminology completely foreign to what we may call the later or definitive Gilson. No doubt some of what he has to say anticipates themes to be developed in the important treatises appearing half a century later. Significantly, he stresses that it is in music, more than in painting, that we find an independence from the given physical world. This suggests that music is a higher, more spiritual art.

The relevance of musical experience to his evaluation of Bergson is perhaps best illustrated in a postface he contributed to a Gilson *Festschrift*. Bergson in his metaphysics maintains that the intellect following its natural slope or tendency is adequate to deal with matter analytically by a process of decomposition: "It is made to utilize matter."[36] Metaphysics, on the contrary, involves "a reversal of the habitual work of the intellect," it is "an effort to re-ascend the slope natural to the work of thought, to place oneself immediately, through a dilation of the mind, in the thing that one is studying."[37] Metaphysics, then, consists in going against the natural grain of the intellect itself.

Now Gilson objects that such a contortion was not required and significantly it is through music that he opposes Bergson, even while recognizing him as a metaphysician of genius. He refers to Bergson's disciples as "brothers of Jean-Christophe [the composer-protagonist of Romain Rol-

[33] Comments on Wagner are found in "Art et métaphysique," *Revue de Métaphysique et de Morale* 23, no. 1 bis (1916), pp. 257, 264; *Painting and Reality*, p. 347; *The Arts of the Beautiful*, pp. 45, 57, 90, 97, 99, 121, and 124; *Forms and Substances in the Arts*, pp. 156, 175, 180n., 183, 244, 245n., 247n., and 269. There is also Gilson's chapter on Wagner and Matilda in *Choir of Muses*, trans. Maisie Ward (London: Sheed and Ward, 1953), chap. IV.

[34] Étienne Gilson, *The Philosopher and Theology*, trans. Cécile Gilson (New York: Random House, 1962), pp. 107–31, 133–52, and 156–73.

[35] Gilson, "Art et métaphysique," pp. 243–67.

[36] Henri Bergson, *La Pensée et le mouvant*, 47th ed. (Paris: Presses Universitaires de France, 1962), p. 35.

[37] Henri Bergson, "Introduction to Metaphysics," in *The Creative Mind*, trans. Mabelle L. Andison (New York: Philosophical Library, 1946), p. 216.

land's *roman fleuve*], their life carried on under a musical enchantment of which they were the passionately consenting and happy victims."[38] He goes on to say for "those of us who knew from daily experience how a theme contained its development, no twisting on ourselves was necessary in order to attain a mobile continuity, free from any spatial morcellation. Through music we were in becoming as fish in the sea."[39] To say the least, it is an unusual refutation, or correction, of Bergsonian metaphysics.

In *Forms and Substances in the Arts*, the analysis of music reminds us of the Bergsonian enhancement of memory. It is commonplace to say that music is a temporal art, while painting obviously is not. Gilson says: "The fluid and successive being of musical substance entails its intellectuality since the work, inasmuch as it forms a whole, requires that it be structured in the memory by the mind."[40] Hence it is "an art of the moment" for "music, being essentially ephemeral, is the art of that which is to die."[41] He goes on to say that "what is inconceivable is a music without form, because this would be a music without being, and one which has reverted to the status of noise."[42] The keynote of the analysis, which recalls his general comments on art, is to emphasize "that music's function is not to signify or express anything any more than its function is to imitate something in nature."[43] He admits that any kind of music may make us think of something, but "musical sounds do not have a signifying function."[44] This is the case as long as the focus is on pure music as opposed to musical drama.[45] Once you bring in a text, of course, you have apparently significant sounds. Gilson quotes the famous critic Edouard Hanslick as having been right about the essence of music, though he does not by any means accept his well-known polemic against Wagner. Pure music having no signifying function is bound to be depreciated by those, like Kant, who judge art by knowledge. For them music has "the lowest place among the fine arts,"[46] while for Beethoven, music, because of its transcendence, might well be awarded the highest place. The denial that pure music has a signifying

[38] Étienne Gilson, *Étienne Gilson: Philosophe de la Chrétienté* (Paris: Les Éditions du Cerf, 1949), p. 282.

[39] Ibid., p. 283.

[40] Gilson, *Forms and Substances in the Arts*, p. 145.

[41] Ibid., p. 146.

[42] Ibid., p. 167.

[43] Ibid., p. 169.

[44] Ibid., p. 170.

[45] "Music is pure to the degree in which, existing only for its own sake, it is at one and the same time, its own cause and its own end" (ibid., p. 177).

[46] Ibid., p. 182, n. 17.

function is accompanied by the denial, once again, of the expressionist conception of art.[47]

Secondly, Gilson objects to the idea that musical art is an imitation of nature. First of all, one has to distinguish between music and natural sounds or noise. Musicians do introduce natural sounds into their works, and *The Pastoral Symphony* is mentioned in this regard as is *La Mer*, yet "the attempts of musicians to insert natural noises, or their imitation, in the web of a musical dialogue merely ends up as anecdotal and picturesque curiosities."[48] After examining the concept of imitation in music, Gilson concludes that actually music succeeds only in imitating itself (use of French horns, bands, dances, etc.).

However, the situation is quite different if it is a matter of musical drama, rather than pure music, in which "the song [is] wed to spectacle in which case it becomes theatre, free to organize itself according to the system of leitmotif."[49] In this way it becomes a kind of language and makes possible a musical "lexicon in which sonorous forms *signify* personnages, situations, objects and even intelligible notions such as the curse of gold."[50] The reference is obviously to Wagner's *Ring Cycle*. (It would also be true of the popular *Peter and the Wolf*.) Roger Scruton makes the same point.[51] Moreover, Gilson recognizes that there are those who enjoy a referential aspect to music, and that "those [who] would like a musical composition to suggest precise images to them and, if possible to recount an intelligible story, are entirely within their rights and no objections can be raised."[52] Indeed, the symphonic poem and all kinds of program music "are there to grant them satisfaction."[53] In regard to Debussy's *La Mer*, if one concen-

[47] Ibid., p. 174.

[48] Ibid., p. 168.

[49] Ibid., pp. 171–72.

[50] Ibid., p. 172. In *Webster's New World Dictionary*, leitmotif is defined as "a short musical phrase representing and recurring with a given character, situation, or emotion in an opera: first developed by Richard Wagner."

[51] "We certainly speak of music as though it had representational powers: indeed the whole theory of the *leitmotif* is based on this supposition. The woodbird's music in *Siegfried* can certainly be heard as the song of a bird, just as passages in *La Mer* can be heard as the sound of waves or the call of seagulls. But if this were all musical representation amounted to then it would be of little interest" (Scruton, *Art and Imagination*, p. 208).

[52] Gilson, *Forms and Substances in the Arts*, p. 224.

[53] Ibid. The *Dictionary* defines program music "as instrumental music that depicts or suggests a particular scene, story, etc." and the symphonic poem as "an extended musical composition for full symphony orchestra, usually in one movement, programmatic in nature, and freer in form than the symphony; also called *tone poem*." Of imitative music, Gilson says it contains "A more or less remote analogy

trates on this kind of picturing, one misses the point about music taken in itself. The lesson is that the essence of music is to be found in pure music, not in these other forms.

Let us now summarize Gilson's points: (1) What he centers on is the musical work itself, its form, structure, and duration. He rejects the idea that music is essentially significant, expressive, or imitative. (2) He identifies contexts in which music is integrated in drama and when it is used for other purposes as, for instance, therapy or religion.[54] In such instances it is not the rule of beauty that is primary but another end to which music is subordinate. Music is no longer an end in itself, but a means.

So when he reflects on sacred music, Gilson recognizes another tribunal, as he said earlier, for this kind of music is "subservient to the ends of Christian worship."[55] More specifically, sacred music is there "to teach, to remind, and to affect worshippers with religious emotion."[56] Of the *Lauda Sion* of Thomas Aquinas, he says that it "has an austere beauty of its own. It is the beauty of didactic poetry in the service of Christian worship. It is poetry absorbed by religion."[57] To which if suitable music is added, we may rightly say that "he who sings prays twice."[58] Speaking of liturgies for the common people, he observes:

> The liturgy which consists in ceremonies and prayers regulated according to a certain order is the religious art par excellence. For there is no art that may not make a contribution . . . everything is mobilized or can be mobilized for the ends of the religious cult.[59]

But the church is not interested in literature or philosophy as such, but in view of its proper ends.

The main lesson one draws from these remarks is that sacred music is not defined by its source, nor simply by its content, but on whether or not it

---

of which the listener would not even be aware if the composer and program did not tell him by a literary title or an explanatory note what he was being invited to imagine" (*Forms and Substances in the Arts*, pp. 168–169).

54 Katherine Le Mée, *Chant: The Origins, Forms, Practice, and Healing Power of Gregorian Chant* (New York: Bell Tower, 1994), pp. 8–9, 139–42.

55 Gilson, *The Arts of the Beautiful*, p. 163.

56 Ibid., p. 171.

57 Ibid., p. 179. Compare with the comments of F. J. E. Raby, *A History of Christian-Latin Poetry from the Beginnings to the Close of the Middle Ages*, 2nd ed. (Oxford: Clarendon Press, 1953), pp. 402–09.

58 *Catechism of the Catholic Church* (Liguori, Missouri: Liguori Publications, 1994), p. 299.

59 Étienne Gilson, *La Société de masse et sa culture* (Paris: Jules Vrin, 1967), p. 108.

serves religious purposes. It may be the case that some who have composed excellent church music have not themselves been believers. In regard to content Gilson points out that it is not enough for a composer to produce an arrangement for the Ordinary of the Mass, for the aim of the artist is beauty and the aim of the liturgy is worship; so an antinomy may arise between these two aims. For

> a Mass written by Haydn or Mozart is the product of an art conceived by musicians anxious to create beautiful sound structures willed for the sake of their own beauty, whereas plain-song is an art willed for the sake of the religious end which is its function to serve. Mozart submits religious worship to the end of his own art; plain-song submits its art to the ends of religious worship.[60]

Gilson refers to those "liturgical monstrosities" produced by great composers which "are badly suited to the religious purpose of a priest bravely attempting to say [M]ass during the performance."[61] It is thus his contention that properly sacred music is such by the purpose it fulfills, a purpose different from beauty alone. However, having said that, is it not also true that beauty serves better than its opposite?

To illustrate Gilson's point, I use three instances of Masses in which the music either detracted from worship, was considered apart from its religious function, or was successfully in tune with the liturgy. I recall a military Mass in which we were treated to as many brass instruments as are found in those famous marches in the first part of Verdi's *Aida*. The effect was just to overwhelm the celebration of the Mass. In a second instance—Gilson's point about the possible opposition between musical beauty as an end and music in church worship—I was invited by a musician friend to sit in the choir loft of an Episcoplian church to hear a performance of Haydn's *Nelson Mass*. Whether that particular composition was chosen because of the British connection, I know not, but as a non-participant in the service, my focus was almost completely aesthetic, which presumably would not have been right had I been a parishioner. One would then have to determine through one or more of the parishioners whether the music served religious purposes, or whether they had the feeling of being at a concert.

The third instance involved a Schubert Mass—I forget which one; he wrote six—on the feast of the Epiphany in the Franziskaner Kirche in Salzburg when the participant had the feeling that far from a competition between the celebrant and the choir, there was a harmonious relationship.

---

[60] Gilson, *The Arts of the Beautiful*, p. 175.

[61] Ibid. As a case in point, there is the syncretism of Paul Winter's *Gaia/Earth Mass*.

While Gilson does not opt for a return to plain-song as a remedy for what ails the liturgy, he does note that "its main quality is precisely to be *plain*, that is to say not to indulge in musical beauty willed for its own, but rather to put itself entirely at the service of the liturgy and of its properly religious meaning."[62] In the Eastern Orthodox Church the use of chant remains extremely important and the deacon has a special place in the liturgy. "In the Orthodox Church today, as in the early Church all services are sung or chanted."[63] With some rare exceptions singing is unaccompanied and the organ has been viewed askance, a fact highlighted in Sergei Eisenstein's *Alexander Nevsky*, whose score is a cantata by Sergei Prokofiev; the organ-supported chant of the Teutonic Knights is mocked by the use of harsh dissonance. Plain-chant is also widely used in the Church of England which has a rich choral tradition.

Gilson's main theme is quite simple, though its actualization is far from being so. The music used in the liturgy should be suitable to, appropriate for Christian worship. Appropriateness is a concept easily recognized in other musical spheres. It has often been remarked that "The Star Spangled Banner" is easier to abuse than to sing, and some have suggested the pacific and pastoral "America the Beautiful" as more suitable because more singable. On the occasion of the bicentenary of the French Revolution, many queasy republicans in France thought it was time to eliminate the more sanguinary lines of the eminently singable "La Marseillaise," such as "let an impure blood water our furrows." In Canada we are blessed with a national anthem singable and available in a bilingual version.

In martial music it is recognized, at least in the United States, that John Philip Sousa's works are more appropriate for marching than, say, the "Radetsky March" by Johann Strauss, Sr. In academic processions, intended to be slow and stately, dignified if you will, Elgar's "Pomp and Circumstance" ("Land of Hope and Glory") and the "Trumpet Voluntary" are deemed more appropriate than Dmitry Kabalevsky's entrance of the "Comedians." And the point is that what is true in these spheres is also true of sacred music.

In closing this summary account of Gilson's reflections on music, pure, mixed, and sacred, the reader of Gilson's impressions on what was happening in the church in the 60s is struck by his pessimism. The essay entitled

---

[62] Ibid.

[63] Paul Verghese, *The Joy of Freedom: Eastern Worship and Modern Man* (Richmond, Virginia: John Knox Press, 1967), p. 274. Cf. Katherine Le Mée, *Chant*, p. 38.

"Ramblings in the Ruins" says it all.[64] In it he looks askance at what is happening in the church. Furthermore, in a book based on a series of lectures he gave on mass society and culture, he is apprehensive about mass-culture where "the only universal form of taste is bad taste."[65] He decries bad religious art. He leaves the impression that the coincidence of art for the sake of beauty and art for the propagation of the faith is only accidental and that it is unlikely to occur in the present situation. That pessimism was not Gilson's alone.

Adopting Gilson's leading ideas, I now propose to extrapolate with some comments on the contemporary use of music for religious purposes. Two interesting studies on church music in America provide points of comparison in the attempt to understand the current situation: Paul Hume, *Catholic Church Music* (1956) and Thomas Day, *Why Catholics Can't Sing* (1990).[66] The latter work may be supplemented by reading the journal, *Sacred Music*. Paul Hume, a distinguished music critic, based his reflections on studies of church music—and in parentheses, such studies would be welcome today—and examines "the principles regulating sacred music in the functions of public worship"[67] for "music in the church exists only for the purpose of serving the liturgy, a circumstance which puts its position in a very clear light indeed."[68] Hume was particularly concerned about those pastors who allow "atrocities to run rampant in the choir loft." When I read what Hume next said, I felt the shock of recognition.

> What do you do with dear old Miss Tessy Tara who has been singing in the choir for fifteen years and whose piercing soprano now assaults the ear like the song of a steel gimlet? What do you tell Mr. Cassidy, your favorite insurance salesman, whose basso profundo, penetrating as the foghorn off Sandy Hook, dominates the ensemble?[69]

For in my adolescence I was well acquainted with Tessy and Cassidy, whose performances convinced me that church music was part of the cross to be borne, that just in case you did not have a Pauline thorn in the flesh, one would be provided for you at the High Mass. I suppose there is something to be said for the solidarity of suffering, to discover that many others

[64] Étienne Gilson, *Les Tribulations de Sophie* (Paris: Jules Vrin, 1967), pp. 139–69.

[65] Gilson, *La Société de masse et sa culture*, p. 115.

[66] Paul Hume, *Catholic Church Music* (New York: Dodd, Mead, and Company, 1956); Thomas Day, *Why Catholics Can't Sing: The Culture of Catholicism and the Triumph of Bad Taste* (New York: Crossroad, 1990).

[67] Hume, *Catholic Church Music*, p. 7.

[68] Ibid., p. 3.

[69] Ibid., p. 23. See Gilson, *Painting and Reality*, p. 272.

had also suffered, and that was a kind of consolation, for one was not alone. But it was some time before I discovered that liturgical music need not be painful. One also discovered why silence can sometimes be golden.

Hume, alluding to papal norms on sacred music, indicates the influence of the Victorian sentimental ballad on church music and finds a typical example "Bring Flowers of the Fairest"—still flourishing today—as among the objectionable hymns.[70] He articulates the conviction—we also find it in Gilson—that only the beautiful will serve religious purposes well. He recalls the use of the chant in the Church, and observes that "once its primary rules have been mastered, it is the easiest of music to sing . . . the supreme model of Church music."[71] However, "the quaint old custom of singing the 'Tantum Ergo' to the music of the Sextet from *Lucia*" we can do without.[72] He has a good deal to say about weddings and the use of the old chestnuts. He recounts the mistake made by the bride who wanted "Liebestod" (love-death)—she meant "Liebestraum" (love's dream)—which "seemed a bit on the morbid side for a wedding."[73] Hume should be writing today when so many couples apparently believe that matrimony is indeed *Liebestod*.

Hume's was but one of many voices in the fifties who were attempting to identify appropriate sacred music, mindful of papal encyclicals on the subject, to eliminate music with clearly secular connotations, and to return to practices that had served the Church so well.

However, in the sixties something rather different occurred in the Church, the introduction of the guitar or folk Mass. For roughly beginning in the fifties, there was a folk music craze with an international flavor as witnessed by the performers who made their reputation at that time. Furthermore, folk music had always provided a reservoir for sacred music, a fact illustrated by the hymns of Ralph Vaughan Williams. Initially the guitar accompaniment had the merit of simplicity, the kind of simplicity we find in Franz Gruber's "Silent Night." Granted the limits of the performers—put down by professional musicians as three-chord guitarists—or strummers, if you prefer, it seemed a good means to insure participation, a liturgical singalong. However, the pieces composed for the folk Mass were often insipid, uninspiring, and some of dubious orthodoxy (one I always thought of as a hymn for agnostics), and it turned out that the guitar was not enough, so you had combinations that began to sound like McNamara's

[70] Ibid., p. 73.
[71] Ibid., p. 48.
[72] Ibid., p. 54.
[73] Ibid., p. 94.

Band. The greatest objection, however, was that the older tradition was seemingly forgotten in many places. Where were the snows of yesteryear?

In some fortunate instances, the parishioner had a choice between the folk group and more traditional church music, but the impression one had as one travelled was of considerable disarray. That is why Thomas Day's book coming after decades of experimentation is salutary, for it should raise the issue once again of the role of music in the liturgy for the choir and the congregation.[74]

I shall conclude by indicating a tendency that I think runs contrary to the whole notion of appropriate sacred music as understood by Gilson, Hume, and Day. This tendency is not completely novel, though it has a peculiar contemporary flavor. I refer to the contention that in order to attract the youth, the Church should adapt to their tastes and customs, rather than expecting young and old alike to recognize significant musical differences. Once the introduction of operatic numbers was used for the purpose of raising the tone. In my parish, for example, they indulge in de-Masonizing Mozart by giving a new text to his aria which originally invoked Isis and Osiris. I think it still does. Music has contexts and connotations and is not easily transferred from one setting to another. So much of what is now called Christian music, as sung by Amy Grant and others, is simply popular music with a more or less explicit reference in the lyrics to religion. Christian rock, like rock in general, reinforces the conviction that lyrics really don't matter, even if you could make them out. Whether sentimental or hard, there is no guarantee that such sounds might cause an attention to religious ceremonies rather than summon up memories of last night's secular gig. Again it is not content alone that determines liturgical suitability. Remember the liturgical monstrosities.

Another sample is taken from the musical theater. A recent comparison of diocesan life in America, using two instances, said this of the music used in Saginaw, Michigan: "The music is modern and attractive with the Andrew Lloyd Webber/Stephen Sondheim sound that characterizes much of the newer Catholic church music."[75] You may agree depending on how you feel about Webber's *Jesus Christ Superstar*. On the contrary, you may find choral renditions of the title song vulgar and the idea of the Savior as per-

---

[74] Catherine Dower, "Why Catholics Don't Sing," a review of Thomas Day's book in *Sacred Music* 118, no. 4 (Winter 1991), pp. 23–25.

[75] Charles Morris, "A Tale of Two Dioceses: From Lincoln to Saginaw," *Commonweal* 124, no. 11 (6 June 1997), p. 16.

former even sacrilegious. But in our world in which being a star was not enough, so there were superstars, and that still was not enough, so there are now megastars, Jesus of Nazareth at least deserves some upgrading. If this kind of music is seen as attractive, the latest development in church music would only inspire dismay. It is as if we have learned nothing and have forgotten a great deal. There is a rich treasury of sacred music that includes plain-chant, polyphony, great classical compositions by Bach, Schubert, César Franck, Gabriel Fauré, and Ralph Vaughan Williams, to mention but a few; there is the fund of folk songs adapted for religious purposes, and there are the spirituals. A variety of kinds of music have indeed been reckoned suitable for the liturgy. The point I believe Gilson was trying to make, and that I have been elaborating, is a simple one: sacred music should be different, it should be appropriate, and happily, it should be beautiful, for beauty too serves in a way that ugliness cannot.

Maritain on Music:
His Debt to Cocteau

Stephen Schloesser, S.J.

Imagine for a moment the musically informed reader of 1927 consulting Jacques Maritain's *Art et scolastique* for aesthetic guidance. The index for proper names lists the following numbers of entries: for Bach, three; for Beethoven, two; for Chopin, one. So much for the "canon"! Now, note the entries for the "moderns": for Igor Stravinsky, four entries; for Erik Satie, five; for Richard Wagner, six. Surely, the reader would be astonished! Why, in a book about the perennial scholastic aesthetic, do the moderns get such a large piece of an admittedly small pie while Bach, Beethoven, and Chopin go away begging? The answer, I suggest, lies in Maritain's appropriation of Jean Cocteau's musical rhetoric for his principal project: namely, the reconstruction of anti-modernist Catholicism as the ultra-modernist movement of the Jazz Age.

MARITAIN ON SATIE, STRAVINSKY, AND WAGNER

Let me begin with a passage from the original 1920 version of *Art et scolastique*:

> The essential is not that the representation be exactly conformed with a given reality; it is rather that, through the material elements the beauty of the work, the clarity of a form should clearly shine, supreme and whole—of a form, and thus of *some truth*. . . . But if the joy of the beautiful work comes from *some truth*, it does not come from the truth *of the imitation as reproduction of things*; it comes rather from the perfection with which the work expresses or manifests the form, in the metaphysical sense of this word; it comes from the truth *of the imitation as manifestation of a form*. This is what is meant by the "formal" aspect of imitation in art: the expression or the manifestation, in a work harmoniously proportioned, of some principle of intelligibility

which shines forth. It is this act of expression which gives art its *joy of imitation*. This is also that which gives art its value of *universality*.[1]

In this context Maritain wants to distinguish between "imitation" in art as the "manifestation of a [metaphysical] form" and "imitation as a reproduction of things." Apart from philosophical concerns, the cultural historian wants to note that Maritain's entire cultural project—i.e., redefining Thomistic Catholicism as embracing the "ultramodern"—depends on this distinction. For if "imitation" is the "reproduction of things" in some realist or naturalist sense, then Maritain's aesthetic theory is not going to be "universal"—not going to be able to account for 1920s artistic practice and its many forms of abstraction. This would be to reduce Neo-Thomism to a merely antiquarian system, and Maritain states his clear opposition to such reactionary irrelevance:

> We love the art of the cathedrals, of Giotto and Angelico. But we detest the neo-Gothic and the pre-Raphaelism. We know that the course of time is irreversible; as much as we admire the century of Saint Louis, we do not want *to return to the Middle Ages* on that account, along an absurd path which certain penetrating critics generously accuse us of. We hope to see the spiritual principles and the eternal norms which medieval civilization has given us reproduced [*restituer*] in a new world, informing a new matter. [Medieval civilization gave us these eternal norms] in its best epochs, in a particular historical realization, superior in quality despite their enormous deficiencies, but definitely in the past.[2]

However, the originality of Maritain's approach lies in making Thomism not an antiquarian system (as it was in Rome, for example, according to the complaint of young Giovanni Battista Montini, the future Paul VI[3]), but rather a "universal" system, capable of relevance in every historical epoch. By its very universality, he writes, Thomistic doctrine

> infinitely overflows, into the past as well as into the future, the tightness of the present moment. It is not opposed to the modern systems as the past is related to the given present; but rather as the eternal is re-

---

[1] Jacques Maritain, *Art et scolastique* (Paris: Librarie de l'Art Catholique, 1920), hereafter cited as *AS 1920 Fr*, pp. 81–82 (emphases in original); Jacques Maritain, *The Philosophy of Art*, trans. John O'Connor (Ditchling, England: St. Dominic's Press, 1923), hereafter *AS 1920 En*, pp. 86–87 (translation altered).

[2] Jacques Maritain, *Antimoderne* (1922), in *Jacques et Raïssa Maritain: Oeuvres Complètes*, eds. Jean-Marie Allion, Maurice Hany, Dominique and René Mougel, Michel Nurdin, and Heinz R. Schmitz (Paris: Éditions Saint-Paul, 1987), vol. 2, pp. 933–34 (translation mine; emphases in original).

[3] Philippe Chenaux, *Paul VI et Maritain: Les rapports du "Montinianisme" et du "Maritainisme"* (Brescia: Istituto Paolo VI, 1994), pp. 11–32, 97–100.

lated to the momentary. *Anti-modern* against the errors of the present time, it is *ultra-modern* for all the truths which are wrapped up in the time to come.[4]

In sum, for the sake of universality, Maritain *does not want* "imitation" as "reproduction of things."

On the other hand, he *does want* "imitation" as the "manifestation of a form," and "thus, of some truth." For Maritain cannot maintain his position that art provides privileged access to reality unless it concern itself with something outside the subject—and it is precisely this claim of access to reality outside the self which made him so appealing to the youth who had survived the Great War. As Jean-Jacques Becker and Serge Bernstein have observed, the youth of the 1920s accused their positivistic and historicist elders not merely of having "obsolete ideas"—an accusation perhaps common to every classical generational conflict—but rather of having permitted an unjustifiable massacre by means of their attachment to "outmoded myths" [*des mythes dépassés*]. Thus, "realism" became the key word for this generation which set out to discard all the "outmoded ideologies" [*des idéologies dépassées*] by searching for the "real" prior to and underlying all social constructions. Surrealism became the dominant intellectual innovation of the 1920s, and the success of Maritain's "critical realism" was due in large part to its attraction for those disillusioned by surrealism's failure. Maritain himself appeals quite directly to this felt disappointment over "outmoded ideologies" when he writes acerbically,

> It is well known, in fact, that Catholicism is as *anti-modern* by reason of its unshakeable attachment to the tradition as it is *ultra-modern* by reason of its boldness in adapting itself to the new conditions suddenly erupting in the life of the world. Is it necessary to remark, moreover, that today everything except Catholicism itself—even and perhaps above all those ideologies specifically modern (look at the Futurists, for example)—immediately appears to be old-fashioned and, as it were, a moon waxing full?[5]

---

[4] Maritain, *Antimoderne*, p. 929 (translation mine; emphases in original).

[5] On the youth of the 1920s as *"une génération réaliste"* see Becker and Bernstein, *Victoire et frustrations*, 1914–1929 (Paris: Éditions du Seuil, 1990), pp. 390–95. On the attraction of Maritain for those disillusioned by surrealism, see Jean-Luc Barré, *Jacques et Raïssa Maritain: Les Mendiants du ciel* (Paris: Stock, 1996), pp. 272ff.; *Correspondance Jean Cocteau-Jacques Maritain 1923–1963*, eds. Michel Bressolette and Pierre Glaudes (Paris: Gallimard, 1993), pp. 16ff; and Michel Bressolette, "Jacques Maritain et Jean Cocteau," in *Jacques Maritain et ses contemporains*, eds. Bernard Hubert and Yves Floucat (Paris: Desclée, 1991), pp. 103–04. The Maritain quotation is from *Antimoderne*, p. 928 (translation mine; emphases in original).

Maritain's appeal to a disillusioned "realist generation" depended heavily on the promise he made of privileged access to a reality underlying mere surface appearances. An older generation of positivists and historicists had been satisfied with facts; a new generation desired truth. Thus, for philosophical as well as cultural reasons, Maritain's "form" being "imitated" must be an interior metaphysical one offering privileged intellectual access to the real, and not merely an epiphenomenal "shape" perceived only by the senses.

This philosophical move gains him entry into the heady air of 1920s neo-classicism, spearheaded by Cocteau's avant-garde, among others, which retrieves "classical" forms and ideals. As Maritain writes:

> What makes the purity of the true classic is such a subordination of the matter to the light of the form . . . as admits into the work no material element except what is absolutely necessary to transmit this light [of the form] and which would otherwise dull or "debauch" the eye, the ear or the mind.[6]

Classical art expresses a "form"—not, as Maritain says, as a "reproduction of shape"—but rather "form" in the metaphysical sense, access to which gives art its "universal" value. Thus, the "classical" allows nothing "extraneous" or superfluous, nothing (as he says) except that "necessary to support or transmit this light" of the form. As examples of works which manifest and those which obfuscate such forms Maritain suggests the following:

> Compare, from this point of view, in the order of thought, Aristotle and Saint Thomas Aquinas to Luther or to Jean-Jacques Rousseau, in the order of art the Gregorian melody or the music of Bach to the music of Wagner and Stravinsky.[7]

In Aristotle and St. Thomas as in Gregorian Chant and Bach, nothing obfuscates the form. On the other hand, Wagner is to Luther as Stravinsky is to Rousseau—all of them are confused and "debauch" the senses. Their bombast obfuscates the form; its intelligibility can neither shine through nor manifest itself. Those acquainted with Maritain's *Three Reformers* (1925) know that his invocation of Luther and Rousseau (the third "reformer" is Descartes) signals that extreme reaction for which he became known to his contemporaries as a "visceral antimodernist."[8] Richard Wagner, made popular in France through the *Revue Wagnérienne* as a focal

---

[6] *AS 1920 Fr*, pp. 82–83; *AS 1920 En*, p. 87 (translation altered).

[7] *AS 1920 Fr*, p. 83; *AS 1920 En*, p. 87.

[8] See Chenaux, *Paul VI et Maritain*, pp. 26–27.

point for symbolism of every kind, became an object of contempt for those wanting to overcome what they perceived as *fin-de-siècle* decadence. As for Stravinsky, the Parisian première of his *Rite of Spring* provoked a riot at the Théâtre des Champs-Élysées on May 29, 1913; whether or not Maritain attended this performance, he was most certainly aware of its "scandal."[9] Given Maritain's idea of the "classic," then, such a reactionary broadside against the overblown Wagner and Stravinsky makes sense. For him, plainchant and Bach convey something eternal and "universal" while Wagner and Stravinsky are hopelessly contingent and particular.

Well then, given the interior logic of the passage, how can we possibly account for two astonishing alterations in the 1927 edition of *Art et scolastique*? First, all reference to Aristotle, Aquinas, Luther, and Rousseau is erased and reads simply, "Compare, from this point of view, the Gregorian melody or the music of Bach to the music of Wagner and Stravinsky."[10] The "visceral antimodernism" is suppressed.

Secondly, to what remains of this passage, Maritain appends the following note—not at the end as with the other one hundred-and-sixty endnotes, but rather as a retraction statement prominently displayed at the bottom of the page:

> I regret having thus spoken of Stravinsky. All I had heard [when I wrote the first edition] was *The Rite of Spring*, and I should have perceived then that Stravinsky was turning his back on everything we find distasteful in Wagner. Since then [Stravinsky] has shown that genius conserves and increases its strength by renewing it in light. Exuberant with truth, his admirably disciplined work teaches the best lesson of any today of grandeur and creative energy, and best answers the strict classical "austerity" here in question. His purity, his authenticity, his glorious spiritual strength, are to the gigantism of [Wagner's] "Parsifal" and the ["Ring" Cycle] as a miracle of Moses to the enchantments of the Egyptians.[11]

How can we explain this abrupt reversal from the 1920 text painting Stravinsky as the Wagnerian villain to this 1927 script: Stravinsky as the

---

[9] For Stravinsky and Wagner see Jay Scott Messing's *Neoclassicism in Music: From the Genesis of the Concept through the Schoenberg/Stravinsky Polemic* (Ann Arbor, Michigan: University of Michigan Research Press, 1988). For the *Rite of Spring* see the first chapter of Modris Eksteins' *Rites of Spring: the Great War and the Birth of the Modern Age* (Boston: Houghton Mifflin, 1989).

[10] Jacques Maritain, *Art et scolastique* (Paris: Louis Rouart et fils, 1927), hereafter cited as *AS 1927 Fr*, pp. 97–98; Jacques Maritain, *Art and Scholasticism*: with other essays, trans. J. F. Scanlan (New York: Scribner's, 1939), hereafter *AS 1927 En*, p. 60 (translation altered).

[11] *AS 1927 Fr*, p. 98; *AS 1927 En*, p. 60 (translation altered).

miracle-making Moses leading the Chosen [French] People out of their musical enslavement to the Teutons? Even bracketing the melodrama, consider that during the Great War Stravinsky's music did indeed change: he began to incorporate elements like imported American ragtime rhythms! How then can we possibly account for Maritain's use of Stravinsky as the paradigm of "strict classical 'austerity'"? As the purveyor of "purity"? Of "authenticity" and "truth" and of "glorious spiritual strength"? All in all, Maritain could not have chosen a better representative of the cacophonous avant-garde unless he had chosen Erik Satie—which, of course, he does.

In the 1927 edition Maritain writes that, after an epoch of decadence, 1920s music is evolving to a "respect for genuine subordination" to the truth, to "obedience, to sacrifice." The villainous Wagner, continues Maritain, had led music astray. But "the example of Satie is teaching it once more a chaste honesty" while Stravinsky is teaching it "grandeur." Appealing to a realist generation, Maritain writes that "after so much sentimentality," the evolution of art now wants *hard contact with stripped and naked reality* [*le réel dépouillé, dénudé*]."[12] In support of this appeal to "sacrifice" Maritain quotes Jean Cocteau, surely one of the most notorious figures of the postwar avant-garde (and hardly known for his "chastity"): "St. Thérèse of Lisieux says: *I prefer sacrifice to any ecstasy.* A poet ought to have these words tattooed upon his heart."[13]

Now, the musically informed 1920s reader, seeing Satie's name evoked along with Cocteau's, would immediately have remembered Satie's infamous collaboration with Cocteau and Picasso on the ballet *Parade*. Cocteau premiered *Parade*—with its sets by Picasso and music by Satie—as a benefit for the soldiers mutilated in war [*mutilés de guerre*] on May 18, 1917. Satie had scored *Parade* for an orchestra including, among other instruments, sirens, pistol shots, a lottery wheel, and a typewriter. After twenty minutes the audience jeered, hooted, and took to fist-fighting while shouting, "Krauts!," "Traitors!," and "Munich art!"[14] In a cacophony of this magnitude, what kind of obedience, sacrifice, subordination, chastity, and classical simplicity could Maritain possibly have been thinking about?

In short, how can we explain this astonishing paradox: that the artists

---

[12] *AS 1927 Fr*, pp. 185–86; *AS 1927 En*, pp. 120–21 (emphases added; translation altered).

[13] Jean Cocteau, *Letter to Jacques Maritain* (1926), in *AS 1927 Fr*, p. 338, n. 191; *AS 1927 En*, p. 231 (emphases in originals).

[14] See Kenneth Silver, *Esprit de Corps: The Art of the Parisian Avant-Garde and the First World War, 1914–1925* (Princeton, New Jersey: Princeton University Press, 1989), pp. 115–26.

chosen by the "visceral anti-modernist" Thomist to represent best his vision of the scholastic aesthetic spirit would be Erik Satie and Igor Stravinsky?

COCTEAU ON SATIE, STRAVINSKY, AND WAGNER

If we want to know the source of Maritain's rhetorical uses of Wagner, Stravinsky, and Satie, I suggest we must look at Jean Cocteau's own aesthetic work, *Le Coq et l'Arlequin*, which Fr. Charles Henrion brought to the Maritains.[15] Written in 1918 as an attempt to reaffirm Cocteau's patriotism after the debacle of *Parade*, this book served as a manifesto for the post-War "neo-classical" movement in music. The rhetoric of classicism had been deployed by both the political Right and Left during the Great War both as a vehicle for mourning the unexpectedly large numbers of casualties as well as legitimation of France as a "Latin" culture. After the War, *néoclassicisme*—formerly a pejorative term in French musical circles—was reconstructed as the new authentically "Latin" aesthetic movement for a resurrected France. Specifically, it eventually came to mean (for French commentators) the music of Stravinsky as opposed to that of Berlin's Arnold Schoenberg. Thus, the extreme jingoistic call in Cocteau's *Le Coq et l'Arlequin* for "a French music for the French" purged of all "foreign influences" served the post-War purpose of inscribing neo-classicism within a larger nationalistic project—namely, a resurrected French culture.[16]

In the dedication to *Le Coq*, Cocteau sets up an opposition between the French cockerel (i.e., *le coq gaulois*, traditional emblem of the "French fighting spirit") who reawakens with the morning sun and lives proudly in the full light of day. The cockerel, writes Cocteau, shuns the colossal because "he has *escaped from Germany [évadé d'Allemagne]*."[17] On the other hand, the Harlequin, a stock buffoon character in Italian opera, is constructed to represent German artists masquerading as Frenchmen. Cocteau writes: the Harlequin only comes out at night, prefers darkness and its dissimulating possibilities, hides his face behind a black mask, and wears a

[15] See *Jean Cocteau-Jacques Maritain Correspondance 1923–1963*, p. 63, n. 3.

[16] For classicism during the War see Martha Hanna's chapter "The Classicist Revival" in *The Mobilization of Intellect: French Scholars and Writers During the War* (Cambridge, Massachusetts: Harvard University Press, 1996), pp. 142–66. For musical "neoclassicism" both before and after the Great War see Jay Scott Messing's *Neoclassicism in Music*.

[17] Jean Cocteau, *Le Rappel à l'ordre*, in *Oeuvres Complètes de Jean Cocteau*, vol. 9 (Paris: Éd. Marguerat, 1950), hereafter cited as *Coq Arl Fr*, p. 13; Jean Cocteau, *A Call to Order: written between the years 1918 and 1926 and including "Cock and Harlequin," "Professional secrets," and other critical essays*, trans. Rollo H. Myers (New York: Henry Holt, 1926), hereafter *Coq Arl En*, p. 3. This phrase is italicized in the original.

"hodge-podge" costume made up of French and German scraps. As Cocteau observes acerbically in a footnote, the *Dictionnaire Larousse* gives as one connotation of Harlequin "a dish composed of various scraps" [*mets composé de restes divers*].[18] Like the Impressionist painters, the Harlequin for Cocteau is a German masquerading as a Frenchman! Hence, he is also a wartime traitor. Cocteau overlays this treason with biblical tones: "After denying the cock's crow, [Harlequin] goes away to hide." The allusion is plain: like St. Peter who denied Christ, the German Harlequin hears the French cockerel's crow at dawn and runs off to hide.

Given this primary opposition between pure French music and German music masquerading as French music, Cocteau goes on to consider three figures: Wagner, Satie, and Stravinsky.

First, Richard Wagner. For Wagner—pure unadulterated Teutonic colossalism—Cocteau has nothing but contempt. One of several vicious aphorisms dedicated to excoriating Wagner will suffice here:

> There are certain long works which are short.
> Wagner's works are long works which are long, and *long-drawn-out*, because this old sorcerer looked upon boredom as a useful drug for the stupefaction of the faithful.[19]

In short, Cocteau deployed Wagner as the symbol for all that was decadent and "anti-classical."

Second, Erik Satie. If Wagner is the melodramatic villain, Satie plays the rescuing hero. Cocteau establishes Satie's purity indirectly by painting the Impressionism of poor Claude Debussy in a vicious light. In a wonderfully illuminating passage Cocteau cites Satie's three *Gymnopédies*, those famous little sketches for piano meant to evoke the simple gracefulness of classical Greek gymnasts. Cocteau contrasts Satie's simple piano arrangements of these *Gymnopédies* with Debussy's impressionistic orchestral arrangements of them and then offers this critique:

> Debussy has deviated: on account of the German ambush, he fell into the Russian trap. Once again, the [piano] pedal grounds the rhythm, creates a kind of fuzzy atmosphere favorable to short-sighted ears. Satie remains intact. Hear his 'Gymnopédies' so clear in their form and melancholy feeling. Debussy orchestrates them, confuses them, and wraps their exquisite architecture in a cloud. . . . The thick lightning-pierced fog of Bayreuth becomes a thin snowy mist flecked with impressionist sunshine. Satie speaks of Ingres; Debussy transposes Claude Monet "in the Russian style."

---

[18] Ibid.
[19] *Coq Arl Fr*, p. 22. *Coq Arl En*, p. 14.

You can't get lost in a Debussy mist as you can in a Wagner fog, but you can still catch cold.[20]

We see Cocteau's opposition clearly: Satie's piano arrangements, like the work of Ingres, are marked by extraordinary simplicity in composition and clarity in line. But when Debussy orchestrates Satie, he blurs the simple lines with lavish Romantic textures and transforms the classical into the impressionist—a Wagnerian fog flecked with a snowy Valhalla mist. Worse yet, it is Monet inflected *à la Russe*—"i.e., in the Russian style." Put pithily, "Debussy played [the piano] in French, but he used the Russian pedal."[21]

Cocteau's post-World War jingoism reserves special venom for such cross-breeding: "Russian music is admirable because it is Russian music," he says. "Russian-French music or German-French music is necessarily bastard [*forcément bâtarde*], even if it be inspired by a Stravinsky, a Wagner. . . . The music I want must be French, of France."[22] This harsh use of the word "bastard" is echoed by Maritain in a passage astonishingly similar to Cocteau's:

> By reason of its subject and of its roots, [art] is of a particular age and of a particular country. . . . That is why *in the history of free peoples the eras of cosmopolitanism are times of intellectual bastardization [d'abâtardissement intellectuel]*.[23]

Since both Cocteau and Maritain were large intellectual figures during a period of astonishing cosmopolitanism—Maritain himself marrying a Russian Jewish *émigrée*—this self-indicting passage about "bastardy" seems difficult to explain. The irrationality of Maritain's statement is compounded when one considers that Thomas Aquinas's great accomplishment was precisely the synthesis of ancient Greek, Biblical Christian, and medieval Islamic authors during an extraordinarily "cosmopolitan" epoch of thirteenth-century Paris. Perhaps following recent cultural history we should follow the connection between *irrational fantasies* and *unsettled identities*.[24] In this case, then, attention to uncertain *paternité* points to trauma: a postwar anxiety, perhaps, over both illegitimate wartime births as well as over an uncertain *patrie*.

---

[20] *Coq Arl Fr*, pp. 24, 39; *Coq Arl En*, pp. 16–17, 33 (altered).

[21] *Coq Arl Fr*, p. 38; *Coq Arl En*, p. 33.

[22] *Coq Arl Fr*, p. 24; *Coq Arl En*, p. 17.

[23] The italicized words indicate that portion of the 1920 text which Maritain completely suppressed in the 1927 edition. *AS 1920 Fr*, p. 106; *AS 1920 En*, p. 112 (altered); *AS 1927 Fr*, p. 128; *AS 1927 En*, p. 79.

[24] See for example Gavin I. Langmuir, *History, Religion, and Antisemitism* (Berkeley, California: University of California Press, 1990), pp. 253–55, 291–305.

In any event, Cocteau's particularly ungracious aphorism directed against Debussy's Russian-French pedigree brings us to a genuinely Russian composer, Igor Stravinsky. In this 1918 edition, Cocteau was especially vicious to Stravinsky who only five years earlier had financially rescued him. Alluding to the Odysseus tale in which the singing of the Sirens lured ships to wreck themselves on the rocks, Cocteau writes:

> The theatre corrupts everything, even a Stravinsky. . . . I should not like this paragraph to affect our faithful friendship [*sic!*], but it is useful to put our young compatriots on their guard against . . . these stout golden sirens who caused even so formidable a ship [i.e., Stravinsky] to change its course. . . . Stravinsky gets at us by other means than Wagner; he does not try to hypnotize us or plunge us in a semi-darkness; he hits us deliberately over the head. . . .[25]

Despite Cocteau's fond hopes that these remarks would not "affect our faithful friendship," Stravinsky took them very personally indeed and their friendship foundered. These remarks are from the 1918 edition—the edition Maritain had read when he wrote the first edition of *Art et scolastique*.

In 1924, however, Cocteau issued a new edition of *Le Coq* collected with several other essays and entitled it, significantly, *The Call to Order* [*Le Rappel à l'ordre*]. In this revision, he appended a note positioned at the bottom of the page, retracted his "unjust remark," and then directed the reader to his appendix entitled "Stravinsky: Stop the Press!": "This unjust phrase is obviously annulled by *A Soldier's Tale* which I did not know at the time [1918] and by all the present work of Stravinsky."[26]

As seen above, Maritain's retraction three years later, inserted in exactly the same manner at the bottom of the page, read:

> I regret having thus spoken of Stravinsky [in 1920]. All I had heard was *The Rite of Spring*, and I should have perceived then that Stravinsky was turning his back on everything we find distasteful in Wagner.[27]

Maritain cites as his "turning point" the 1913 *Rite of Spring* ballet, clearly written during Stravinsky's "Russian" period. In citing the wartime *Soldier's Tale*, more ambiguously located on the cusp of Stravinsky's turn away from his Russian period to neo-classicism, Cocteau quite deliberately denies that *The Rite of Spring* carried the cultural meaning that Maritain gives it. Whatever this incongruity means, it seems unlikely that any al-

[25] *Coq Arl Fr*, p. 39; *Coq Arl En*, pp. 33–34.
[26] See "Stravinsky-Stop-Press!" (Appendix 1924).
[27] *Coq Arl Fr*, p. 40; *Coq Arl En*, p. 35; *AS 1927 Fr*, p. 98; *AS 1927 En*, p. 60 (translation altered).

leged change in Stravinsky's musical aesthetic provoked such a sea-change in this criticism on the part of Cocteau and Maritain. For this sea-change we must look to another kind of explanation.

In Cocteau's 1924 appendix, "Stravinsky—Stop the Press!" one line stands out in glaring relief. Recalling an incident in which Stravinsky translated a conversation from Russian to French, Cocteau writes:

> For it is the first time I have ever observed this miracle . . . A case of oriental romanticism (with its uneasiness and savage upheavals) submitting to the discipline of Latin order.[28]

Once again the universal French mission civilizes the oriental savages! Stravinsky himself, the exotic Russian primitivist composer of *The Rite of Spring*, is saved by submission to "Latin order." Recent scholarship suggests that Cocteau is here engaging in a discourse common to early twentieth-century French imperialism: the "wrapping" of native cultures within the "high culture" of France provided a way of retaining the exoticism of primitivism for consumption while at the same time subordinating those cultures to the Empire's.[29] Thus "wrapped" and packaged, redeemed by Latin order, Stravinsky is welcomed back into the fold.

As Cocteau concludes, "Genius cannot be analyzed any more than electricity. You either have it or you don't. Stravinsky has it. . . ." [30] Or as Maritain echoes in his own rehabilitating note, "Stravinsky has shown that genius conserves and increases its strength by renewing it in light."[31] This mutual assessment of Stravinsky's "genius" after his turn from a "particular" nationalism to a "universal" neo-classicism—the precise timing over which Cocteau and Maritain mutually contradict one another—has less to do with aesthetic theory than it does with a French rhetoric of musical cultural meanings.

REINVENTING THE ANTIMODERN
AS THE ULTRAMODERN

Maritain's position as the "ultra-modernist" Thomist owed Cocteau at least a twofold debt: first, for his nationalist rhetoric of musical cultural meanings; secondly, for wider cultural legitimation.

---

[28] *Coq Arl Fr*, p. 56; *Coq Arl En*, p. 60.

[29] See Frederic Jameson, *Postmodernism or the Cultural Logic of Late Capitalism* (Durham, North Carolina: Duke University Press, 1991), pp. 101–29; and Herman Lebovics, *True France: The Wars over Cultural Identity, 1900–1945* (Ithaca, New York: Cornell University Press, 1992), pp. 51–97.

[30] *Coq Arl Fr*, p. 56; *Coq Arl En*, p. 60 (translation altered).

[31] *AS 1927 Fr*, p. 98; *AS 1927 En*, p. 60 (translation altered).

A nationalist rhetoric carved out a meeting place where the French right and left could find common ground in the early twentieth century. Guillaume Apollinaire (the symbolist poet who coined the phrase "sur-réel"), André Gide (co-founder of the literary left's *La Nouvelle Revue Française*), and Marcel Proust all read and admired Charles Maurras's ultra-nationalist *Action Française* during the War.[32] Maritain consciously drew on this paradox: even after the 1926 papal condemnation of *Action Française*, Maritain appealed to both André Gide's *Reflections on Germany* and Charles Maurras's *Anthinéa* in order to legitimate his claim that the most "universal" is in fact what is most "national."[33] As Maritain argued,

> The most universal and most humane works are those which bear most openly the distinguishing mark of their country [*la marque de leur patrie*]. The age of Pascal and Bossuet was an age of vigorous nationalism. When France, at the time of Cluny's amazingly peaceful victories, and in St. Louis's reign, spread over Christendom an intellectual radiance most authentically French, then it was that the world knew the purest and freest International [Movement] of the mind, and the most universal culture.
>
> Thus it would appear that a certain kind of nationalism—*political and territorial* nationalism—is the natural safeguard of . . . the very universality of intelligence and art.[34]

After the papal condemnation of Maurras in 1926, Maritain retained this powerful note but substituted the words "a vigorous political and territorial *attachment to the nation*" for "*a certain nationalism*—a political and territorial nationalism."[35] One must wonder: why would he retain such a provocative note?

Nationalism, I suggest, provided the site where the "anti-modernist" Thomist and the "ultra-modernist" aesthetician could find a sacred union. On this nationalist ground, Cocteau's musical aesthetic—a "particularist" French aesthetic which was, simultaneously, a call for a "universalist" Latin neo-classicism—nicely accommodated Maritain's own seemingly contradictory appeals. This nationalist rhetoric of musical cultural meanings was the first debt that Maritain owed Cocteau.

---

[32] See Eugen Weber, *Action Française: Royalism and Reaction in Twentieth-Century France* (Stanford, California: Stanford University Press, 1962), p. 111. For Maritain's collaboration with Maurras and Massis on the *Revue Universelle*, see Martha Hanna's "Intellectuals and the Action Française: The Appeal of an Adversative Idiom for Jacques Maritain, André Gide, and Georges Bernanos" (Diss. Georgetown University, 1989).

[33] See notes 142 and 143 in all editions of *Art et scolastique*.

[34] *AS 1920 Fr*, pp. 106–07; *As 1920 En*, pp. 112–13.

[35] *AS 1927 Fr*, p. 129; *AS 1927 En*, p. 79.

As for cultural legitimation, Cocteau's ambiguous version of the "avant-garde" provided an avenue by which Maritain's rhetoric of eternal universals might sound just as hip as jazz. As early as 1914, Cocteau's hesitation between a self-conscious modernism and anti-modernist reaction had revealed itself.[36] If Cocteau's avant-garde could sound a "call to order" for "Latin forms," this made it eminently malleable for Maritain's purpose of reconstructing the "antimodern" as the "ultramodern." For Cocteau as for Maritain, art does not "imitate" forms in the sense of reproducing shapes; that would condemn art to repetition of the past. Rather, the avant-garde dresses up eternal forms in the latest fashions. (One might even say that eternal forms are the precondition for the very possibility of inexhaustible novelty.) However, only the avant-garde artist can perceive the eternal; the masses hold ignorantly onto past representations. As Cocteau put it in bold capital letters:

TRADITION APPEARS AT EVERY EPOCH UNDER A DIFFERENT DISGUISE, BUT THE PUBLIC DOES NOT RECOGNIZE IT EASILY AND NEVER DISCOVERS IT UNDERNEATH ITS MASKS.[37]

This peculiar mix of avant-garde gnosticism with a neo-classical twist made Cocteau the ideal precursor for Maritain's project. Cocteau's avant-garde credentials offered ultra-modernist legitimation to what might otherwise have seemed yet another episode in reactionary Catholic literature stretching back to the 1880s.[38] With Cocteau's assistance, however, Maritain's project surprised expectations and created something quite radically new.

That project, to conclude, was the re-invention of pre-War marginal antimodern Catholicism as the culturally central ultra-modernism—all this in service of a universal civilizing mission both embracing and expanding the traditional vocation of France. As Maritain wrote:

> Speaking of the Athenian people, Charles Maurras wrote: "The philosophical spirit, quickness to conceive the Universal, permeated all their arts. . . . Once it yielded to this tendency, it put itself in perpetual communion with the human race. . . . The classical, the Attic, is the more universal in proportion as it is more austerely Athenian—Athenian of an epoch and a taste better purged of all foreign influence. In the high moment when it was itself alone, Attica was the human race." *It*

[36] See Kenneth Silver, *Esprit de Corps: The Art of the Parisian Avant-garde and the First World War, 1914–1925*, pp. 74–145.

[37] *Coq Arl Fr*, p. 32; *Coq Arl En*, p. 26.

[38] See Richard M. Griffiths, *The Reactionary Revolution. The Catholic Revival in French Literature, 1870–1914* (New York: F. Ungar Pub. Co., 1965).

would appear that at the present time the French genius has a similar mission, but one compelling it to serve a more exalted universality than that of pure reason—the full catholicity of natural and supernatural truth.[39]

Eternal Latin order dressed up as the Jazz Age: this, I suggest, is anti-modern ultra-modernism.

---

[39] *AS 1927 Fr*, pp. 324–25; *AS 1927 En*, pp. 220–21. The italicized words indicate the text which Maritain added after the papal condemnation to lessen the Maurrasian tone. The 1920 final line, with the indicative "has" and not the subjunctive "would seem to have," read: "French genius has, in modern times, analogous characteristics" (*AS 1920 Fr*, p. 177; *AS 1920 En*, p. 113).

Maritain and Gilson on Painting[1]

Desmond J. FitzGerald

The two French philosophers, Jacques Maritain and Étienne Gilson, were not only contemporaries and friends, but both were eminent Thomists. This being the case, they took the same side in various scholastic disputes (e.g., "Christian philosophy," "act of existing in Thomistic metaphysics"). Maritain was a metaphysician, epistemologist, philosopher of science, moralist, political philosopher, and philosopher of art. He was also a great personal friend of Rouault, Chagall, and Gino Severini. He was the author of *Art and Scholasticism, Art and Poetry, Art and Faith,* and *Situation in Poetry,* and is noted in aesthetic circles for his book *Creative Intuition in Art and Poetry* (the A. W. Mellon Lectures in the Fine Arts, 1952).[2] Gilson was primarily a historian of philosophy, concerning himself with Descartes and the medieval sources of Descartes. He wrote works on Augustine, Abelard, Bernard, Bonaventure, Aquinas, Dante, and Scotus, as well as general histories of medieval thought. His most famous lectures were: *The Spirit of Medieval Philosophy*[3] and *The Unity of Philosophical Experi-*

[1] The first version of this paper was presented in 1958 at a meeting of the California Aesthetics Society in Santa Barbara. Later in 1981 at a meeting of the American Maritain Association in St. Louis, Professor Robert McLaughlin of St. John Fisher College, Rochester, and I presented papers studying the same issue: whether or not Gilson's Mellon lectures were in part a criticism of Maritain's lectures three years before. Laurence Shook, C.S.B., Gilson's biographer, who was the commentator for our session, confirmed that we were correct. Professor McLaughlin's paper "Nature in Art: Maritain versus Gilson" was published in Marquette University's *Renascence* 34, no. 4 (Summer 1982). Here I am returning to the topic but this time with more attention to *abstract expressionism* which as a movement was peaking in the mid-1950s in the work of Jackson Pollack and Mark Rothke, for example.

[2] Jacques Maritain, *Creative Intuition in Art and Poetry*, Bollingen Series 35.1 (New York: Pantheon Books, 1953).

[3] Étienne Gilson, *The Spirit of Medieval Philosophy*, The Gifford Lectures, University of Aberdeen, 1930–31 (New York: Charles Scribner's Sons, 1936).

ence.[4] In 1955 Gilson gave the A. W. Mellon Lectures in Fine Arts, and these lectures were published as *Painting and Reality*.[5] In addition to this work, *The Arts of the Beautiful*[6] presented some of his further reflections on art and beauty.

While Maritain's writings on art go back to the early 1920s, it is the work of his mature years, *Creative Intuition in Art and Poetry*, to which I shall refer in this essay. Let's look first at Maritain's reflections on painting and representation in the chapter "Beauty and Modern Painting." Maritain begins by suggesting that the painter is less likely than the poet or writer to be deceived by "the myth of the artist as a hero."[7] He justifies his remark by saying that the painter is less able to shift toward the glorification of the ego, because he is bound, without choice, to the world of visible matter and corporeal being. Maritain speaks of difficulties for modern painters in this respect, and of the "obligation to recast the visible fabric of things in order to make them an expression of creative subjectivity"[8]—an obligation which entails drawbacks, failures, and produces victims.

Maritain illustrates his thought by referring to the human figure, and then to the human face, indicating that in his judgement the development of painting from the nineteenth century into the twentieth century has had the effect of deforming the human shape of both the face and the body:

> The impotency of modern art to engender in beauty at the expense of the human figure. . . , [an impotency] which can be found, to one degree or another, in all great contemporary painters, cannot be considered a slight defect. The fact was, no doubt, inevitable: precisely because the human figure carries the intrinsic exigencies of natural beauty to a supreme degree of integration, it is particularly difficult to

[4] Étienne Gilson, *The Unity of Philosophical Experience*, The William James Lectures, Harvard University, 1936–37 (New York: Charles Scribner's Sons, 1937). It takes a philosopher to be a successful historian of philosophy, but in the epistemological controversies within Thomism in the 1930s Gilson emerged as a metaphysician/epistemologist in his own right; this culminated in the historical, metaphysical analysis one finds in *Being and Some Philosophers* (Toronto: Pontifical Institute of Medieval Studies, 1952). Cf. Desmond J. FitzGerald, "Étienne Gilson: From Historian to Philosopher," in *Thomistic Studies* II (Houston, Texas: Center for Thomistic Studies, 1986).

[5] Étienne Gilson, *Painting and Reality*, Bollingen Series 36.4 (New York: Pantheon, 1957).

[6] Étienne Gilson, *The Arts of the Beautiful* (New York: Charles Scribner's Sons, 1965).

[7] Maritain, *Creative Intuition in Art and Poetry*, p. 209.

[8] Ibid.

recast its visible fabric except in deforming it. Will this difficulty be overcome someday?[9]

In commenting on this question, Maritain indicates his approval of the recasting of the human figure accomplished by El Greco, but shows a disapproval for those whom he considers to be the illegitimate progeny of the great contemporary artist Picasso: "They have found in his lesson a means of releasing the resentments of a boorish soul and of getting at little cost the admiration of an idiot public."[10]

The context shows that Maritain had in mind cubism, and in particular, the work of Marcel Duchamp. His comments here are not unfavorable, but neither are they approving: "Such an attempt was logically conceivable. It had an exceptional theoretical interest. It was indeed an attempt at the impossible. For the entire process runs against the nature of our spiritual faculties."[11]

Thus, Maritain's epistemological approach to art is indicated. The artist is a knower who is receptive to the being of things; a knower who is passive in the first stage; a knower who is informed by the forms of things, but who, in expressing this information, recasts it according to the creative intuition of his artistry. He takes in "intelligibility"; what he puts forth should reflect, in his own way, according to his vision, something of the intelligibility he took in. This is not the case, however, with recent painting, and because it is contrary to the natural process of knowing—the intellect being informed by sense perception—there is something unnatural about it. According to Maritain,

> Creative intuition and imagination do not proceed in an angelic or demonic manner. They are human, bound to the alertness of sense perception. They grasp a certain transapparent reality through the instrumentality of the eye and of certain natural appearances, recreated, recast, transposed of course, not cast aside and totally replaced by other appearances proper to another realm of Things in the world of visible Being. . . . The Thing within which creative intuition has caught its diamond is not illuminated, it is killed. The other Thing which has been conjured up does not suggest it, it absorbs it, and expresses it only in secret cipher. The process cuts off in human art the intellect from its inescapable connection with sense perception. It is unnatural in itself.[12]

---

[9] Ibid., p. 210.
[10] Ibid., pp. 210–11.
[11] Ibid., p. 214.
[12] Ibid.

In a section titled "Nonrepresentative Beauty," Maritain presents his reflections on abstract painting. He recognizes that it is the intention of the abstract artist to "renounce the existential world of Nature," but not to repudiate beauty, and so he says:

> If it divorces itself from the things of Nature, it is with a view of being more fully true to the free creativity of the spirit, that is, to poetry, in a manner more faithful to the infinite amplitude of beauty. That's why I would say in this connection nonrepresentative or nonfigurative beauty as well as nonrepresentative or nonfigurative art.[13]

Maritain appreciates certain features of what he calls nonfigurative art, and he judges that by getting clear of the human figure, there has been a deliverance from ugliness and stupidity in representing the form of man. He says that he is grateful to Mondrian and Kandinsky for providing perfect and restful balance, and he sees in abstract art an element of contemplation which gives repose to the soul, like the contemplation of a Platonic ideal.[14]

There is, however, a certain ambivalence in Maritain's attitude toward abstract painting. He does not want to be too systematic, for he sees the possibility that poetry may penetrate anything and anywhere. Maritain insists that the painter's experience with things remains unconsciously in his soul and appears in his work as the product of the spiritual *élan* of poetic intuition. Yet he adds: ". . . such possibilities remain exceptional—and in the last analysis, very limited; . . . one cannot try to develop therefore a specific form of art without pushing painting farther and farther away from the very source of poetic intuition and creative emotion."[15]

Although Maritain reacts negatively to abstract art, he recognizes that many of its practitioners are technically skillful in what they do and that something has been gained from the movement. He acknowledges that the practice of abstract art has contributed to the development of modern painting and that it represents "a necessary moment in the individual painter's self-education [and that] with regard to the general evolution of painting, it was an unavoidable moment."[16] Yet on reflection, Maritain suggests that it represents a period of stagnation or regression.

However, Maritain's belief is that the abstract painter cannot really escape from his life experience. Try as he may, there appears in his paintings some echo of what he has seen transformed by his creative intuition, and this bears some likeness to the reality he had experienced. "Condensed and

---

[13] Ibid., p. 216.
[14] Ibid., p. 217.
[15] Ibid., pp. 219–20.
[16] Ibid., p. 221.

simplified as they may be, natural appearances are there. Through them the existential world of Nature is there. . . . Such painting, which is, it seems to me, characteristic of the effort of some contemporary painters still designated as abstract painters, is in reality no more purely abstract art than cubism was."[17]

As was said before, Maritain's approach to the philosophy of painting is that of an epistemologist or psychologist. He views the artist as a knower, who has taken in the intelligibility of things and who is reflecting this intuited intelligibility in his work; this reflected intelligibility will not be an imitation-copy of reality for it will be transformed in the light of the artist's creative intuition, but it will still have in it something of the shining splendor of the original form.

Unlike Maritain, Gilson's approach to the philosophy of painting is that of a metaphysician. His interest lies in the being of the painting—the painting as an existing thing—rather than in the cognitive processes of the artist. He studies these too, but where Maritain eulogizes a certain passivity before the object, the significant element in Gilson's analysis is the free creative activity of the artist who brings about new forms in the colors of the painting he chooses to make. If one might be permitted an over-simplification here, Maritain's philosophy of painting centers around "intellect," whereas Gilson's centers around "will and appetite." The resulting contrast is to be seen in Maritain's consideration of abstract painting as a legitimate experiment, but one which is a "blind alley," whereas Gilson regards this recent and contemporary movement as one wherein painting has achieved its emancipation from the obligation of imitation. By freeing itself of this burden, painting has come into its own. Gilson says:

> Paintings are physical beings—more precisely, solid bodies—endowed with an individuality of their own. . . . [E]ach painting . . . is a completely self-sufficient system of internal relations regulated by its own laws. In this sense, paintings are mutually irreducible beings, each of which needs to be understood and judged from the point of view of its own structure. . . . [T]o the extent that it succeeds in achieving its own mode of artistic existence, a painting is justified in being exactly what it actually is.[18]

Against Maritain's point that the painter starts with the experience of reality, Gilson counters: "[A] true painter does not borrow his subject from reality; he does not even content himself with arranging the material pro-

---

[17] Ibid., p. 222.
[18] Gilson, *Painting and Reality*, pp. 132–33.

vided by reality so as to make it acceptable to the eye. His starting point is fantasy, imagination, fiction, and all the elements of reality that do not agree with the creature imagined by the painter have to be ruthlessly eliminated."[19] According to Gilson, the painter through his art gives rise to a new being. Gilson is thus captivated by the reality of a painting as a being; it does not have to say anything; it just exists. Of course, it can be judged as a beautiful thing, or a less beautiful thing, or an ugly thing, but it is not evaluated in terms of some truth content. A painting involves knowledge, but it is not judged as knowledge is judged or criticized.

Where Maritain worried about the progressive deformation of faces and figures which has characterized recent painting, Gilson welcomed the trend which he regarded as the emancipation of the artist from the burden of imitation. "Reduced to its simplest expression, the function of modern art has been to restore painting to its primitive and true function, which is to continue through man the creative activity of nature."[20]

But what of the dominant trend of painting from the fifteenth to the late nineteenth century to be representative? What of its illustrations of myths, landscapes, religious scenes, its portraits and its records of historical events? Gilson classifies these works as "pictures" rather than "paintings."

> In virtue of its own nature, painting is inextricably enmeshed in another art, for which there is no name, and for which it is hard to find a name because, so far, it has called itself "picturing"—that is, the art of doing pictures. Why, and how, should it be distinguished from the art of painting?
>
> If there is such an art, its very essence is to represent, or imitate, and whatever can make imitation more nearly perfect can be considered as serving the very end and purpose of this art. Deception is not necessarily its most perfect expression, but there is no ground on which it could be rejected as foreign to the essence of picturing.[21]

In the section "Imitation and Creation" in his *Painting and Reality*, Gilson speaks of those who live under the spell of the doctrine stemming from the Italian Renaissance, according to which painting is an essentially representational art. While rejecting this view, Gilson says that he is by no means criticizing or belittling the art of the Renaissance, but he claims that the Renaissance conceived painting as a sort of language in which it told stories: "They say, by means of images, what a writer could say by means of words . . . in short, even if it were true to say that painting and represen-

---

[19] Ibid., pp. 130–31.
[20] Ibid., p. 285.
[21] Ibid., p. 260.

tation are always given together, it would be likewise true to say that representationality is not the essence of painting."[22]

Gilson presents some reflections on the use of the laws of perspective in traditional art, and these lead him to consider the question of deception in imitational or representative painting:

> All painters feel insulted if they are told that deception is the end of their art. Yet, if its end is imitation, why should it not be deception, which, after all, is the perfection of imitation? At any rate since there is no clearly defined boundary between imitation and deception, one should recognize at least the possibility of an art of painting that, in order completely to eliminate deception, would completely eliminate imitation.[23]

Against the suggestion that the object of their painting was imitation, Gilson quotes da Vinci and Reynolds to the effect that their painting was a poetry not copying nature in a servile way, but creating "it anew in a state of higher perfection." Here Gilson goes on to say:

> Now, creation is the very reverse of imitation, and since art cannot be both, at one and the same time, painting is bound to follow this new road to its very end, once it enters it for any reason whatsoever. Just as *trompe-l'oeil* is the logical term for representative art, so abstraction, or nonrepresentation, is the logical term for that notion of the art of painting that identifies it with poetry.[24]

As soon as they became aware of the true nature of the problem, modern painters discovered the principle that commanded its solution—namely, to eliminate from paintings all the merely representational elements and to exclusively preserve the poetic elements. This rule, more or less clearly conceived by a succession of great artists, became the driving force behind the evolution of modern painting. "Obviously, the intensity of the effect produced by a painting should increase in proportion to the plastic purity of its structure. Why not, then, eliminate all that, being merely representational, has no plastic value, and constitute a new type of painting containing nothing else than pure plastic elements?"[25]

Gilson reviews the history of the development of modern painting from Delacroix up to the recent past. It is a development out of representational painting, rather than a deformation. He says: "Far from resulting from an unexplainable aberration of the human mind, nonrepresentational art offers

---

[22] Ibid., p. 244.
[23] Ibid., p. 247.
[24] Ibid., p. 250.
[25] Ibid., p. 252.

itself to our study as rooted in the very nature of representational art."[26] His point is that the representational artist felt obliged "to make sacrifices," to omit creatively in order to change the nature he was portraying. Hence, this process of "abstracting," in the sense of "leaving out," entails the consequence of further and further "abstractions" until one has nonrepresentational painting. How far can this go?

It surprised me that Gilson, at the apex of abstract expressionism in 1955, goes no further in mentioning names than to refer in this connection to Mondrian's *Victory Boogie-Woogie* (1944):

> Where should one stop in making sacrifices? The answer is now known. Piet Mondrian seems to have gone the whole way, in this sense, that, if everything must be sacrificed to the pure plastic form, the sacrifice at least has now been made. By the same token, since to sacrifice the rest to preserve a certain element in its purity is to abstract this element from the rest, the art of Mondrian marks the *terminus ad quem* of the long pilgrimage of painting on the road to total abstraction.[27]

Without mentioning names, he does refer to others who seek "absolute formlessness." But I continue to be puzzled that Pollack and Rothko, for example, are not mentioned, given that these lectures date from the 1950s.

Interestingly enough, Gilson's remarks in this context seem to indicate that he may be closer to Maritain in his personal evaluation of abstract expressionism than his statement of the principles of painting would lead one to believe. He seems to find such painting "monotonous"; and after commenting on the freedom of nonrepresentational art, he speaks of the problem of contemporary painting as: "Where to go from here?"

> Countless paintings . . . look like so many plastic symbolizations of what the philosophers used to call "prime matter": something that is ceaselessly striving to be but never quite makes the grade; a "near nothingness," or, in Augustine's own words, an "It is and it isn't." The only objection to prime matter is that it is rather monotonous. . . . The victory of abstractionism has been so complete that it now takes much more courage and independence for a painter to be more or less representational than to follow the crowd of those who find it more profitable to exploit, at their own profit, the facilities of shapelessness. There is no denying the fact: painting is now free. There no longer remains any career to be made by fighting for its complete liberation.
>
> To the question, what use should painters make of their liberty? The

---

[26] Ibid., p. 256.
[27] Ibid., p. 257.

painters themselves must find an answer. A philosopher can contribute nothing to the debate beyond the clarification of notions whose obscurity adds to the natural difficulty of the problem.[28]

Whereas Maritain is concerned with the psychological sources of artistic production, as indicated by the title of his book *Creative Intuition in Art and Poetry*, Gilson's concern is with the metaphysics—the being—of the painting. The interests, of course, overlap, as we have noted in constructing a debate over representative elements in painting. They overlap again insofar as Gilson must treat the processes of "making sacrifices," of "eliminating" or "abstracting." Here Gilson's analysis is not unlike Maritain's, and while there are differences of emphasis, something of the "intelligibility" with which Maritain was concerned reappears in Gilson's language as "the germinal form" in the mind of the painter:

> All true painters have always agreed on the necessity of making sacrifices, but they seem also to have been in the dark as to the precise nature of what they had to sacrifice. . . . [A]bstraction essentially consists in the elimination of whatever is not required for the actual realization, under the form of painting, of the germinal form present in the mind of the painter.[29]

This "germinal form" reminds one of the reality which, according to Maritain, the painter takes in and refashions in his work of art. For Gilson the activity of the artist is comparable to solving a problem, which is the very painting he is working on. He says: "Painting is not good because it is representational, but not to be representational does not suffice to make it good. . . . Representational or not, a painting is a true work of art to the extent that it 'abstracts' from all the elements that are not compatible with, or required for the embodiment of the germinal form conceived by the painter. . . . [A]bstraction is creation."[30]

However, despite this apparent agreement concerning the form known by the artist, the basic differences between Maritain and Gilson still exist. Something of this difference is expressed in Gilson's working distinction between a "picture" and a "painting." "A painting has its own rule, its own justification within itself. A picture has its criterion outside itself, in the ex-

---

[28] Ibid., pp. 257–58. In conversation with Armand Maurer in 1997, he recalled that Gilson did not have much to say to him on abstract expressionism but he did remember that Gilson showed little enthusiasm for Andy Warhol's pop art. Maurer's *About Beauty* (Houston, Texas: Center for Thomistic Studies, 1983) is a valuable source for insights contrasting the aesthetics of Maritain and Gilson.

[29] Ibid., p. 258.

[30] Ibid.

ternal reality it imitates."[31] Gilson takes note that some critics of nonrepresentational art have argued that since this type of art is unrelated to any external reality, it has no criterion by which it can be judged. Gilson concedes that the objection would be valid if the art of painting were the art of picturing. "As it is, all judgements and appreciations of painting founded upon their relation to an external model are irrelevant to painting."[32]

While Maritain and Gilson affirm the same Thomistic philosophical principles, they can obviously differ widely in their evaluation of the trend of recent painting. The fundamental difference seems to lie in their view of the artist. Maritain tends to regard the painter as a knower who expresses his knowledge in painting. Gilson regards the painter as a maker who expresses his freedom through the creation of form in painting. With Gilson it is a matter of liberty rather than truth.

> An artist somewhat resembles a man who, before making a decision of vital importance, collects all the facts relevant to the case, weighs the various decisions that are possible, calculates their probable consequences, and still does not know how he will ultimately decide. These are the classical moments of the philosophical description of a free act. Just as previsibility attends determination, imprevisibility attends liberty. The true meaning of the word "creation" in the writings of painters is practically the same as that of the word "liberty" when it is understood in this sense. As Eric Gill once said, the artist does not create *de nihilo*, but he does create *de novo*.[33]

I believe it is evident that Gilson was criticizing Maritain, or correcting him, lest Maritain's views be taken as some doctrinal statement of Thomistic philosophy of art.

One further interesting point is the paradox that Maritain—despite his negative statements on abstract art—seems to be in practice, according to the illustrations he chose for his book, more open and receptive to what was being done by the abstract expressionists; whereas Gilson, despite his principles, fails at a crucial moment to document his analysis with illustrations of the work of such individuals, as might appear in Seuphor's *Dictionary of Abstract Painting*. Is this an indication of how fundamental are the conflicts and disagreements which characterize aesthetics?

---

[31] Ibid., p. 265. Edward A. Synan in an article "Gilson Remembered" in *The Catholic Writer* (San Francisco: Ignatius Press, 1991), p. 56, confirms this analysis. I did not come across this reference until this paper was being edited for publication.

[32] Ibid.

[33] Ibid., p. 288.

Incarnate Beauty:
Maritain and the Aesthetic Experience
of Contemporary Icons*

Katherine Anne Osenga

Maritain defines Christian art according to "the one in whom it exists and . . . the spirit from which it issues. . . . It is the art of redeemed human-ity. It is planted in the Christian soul, by the side of the running waters, under the sky of the theological virtues, amidst the breezes of the seven gifts of the Spirit."[1] My approach to Christian art, specifically to the art of icon making, is influenced by Maritain's aesthetic reflections and is an at-tempt to apply these to the iconographer and his work. In this paper I will briefly consider three aspects of Maritain's aesthetics: first, the epistemo-logical foundation of art; second, the relationship between art and beauty; and third, the role of contemplation in art.

I

Maritain's aesthetics is grounded in epistemology: in order to create the artist must necessarily see and know things as other than himself. "The re-ality with which the painter is confronted," states Maritain, "is the universe of visible matter, of Corporeal Being, through which alone the ocean of Being in its infinity comes to show through for him. The world of the painter is the world of the eye before being and while being the world of the intellect."[2] The essence of the artistic process consists in this visual

---

*This article is dedicated to my mentor and friend, Michael D. Torre.

[1] Jacques Maritain, *Art and Scholasticism and The Frontiers of Poetry*, trans. Joseph W. Evans (New York: Charles Scribner's Sons, 1962), p. 65.

[2] Jacques Maritain, *Creative Intuition in Art and Poetry* (New York: Pantheon Books, 1953), p. 129.

200

knowing, and through it the artist enters into a unique transrational relationship with the object known. This intimate connection or relationship with the object gives the artist the knowledge and the capacity to create. However, this is only a part of the artistic epistemology, for in the creation of a work of art knowledge of what is other than the self and of the artist himself is obtained through the very creative process. This knowledge becomes part of the life of the art work, and is signified therein. According to Maritain,

> Art is both a *direct sign* of the secrets perceived in things, of some irrecusable truth of nature or adventure caught in the great universe, and a *reversed sign* of the subjective universe of the poet, of his substantial Self obscurely revealed. Just as things grasped by poetic intuition abound in significance, just as being swarms with signs, so the work also will swarm with meanings, and will say more than it is, and will deliver to the mind, at one stroke, the universe in a human countenance.[3]

But how does this apply to the making of icons? Does Maritain's principle of aesthetic epistemology also hold true for this style of Christian painting? Are icons produced through the same knowledge and experience of the created world? To answer these questions, we must consider what an icon painting is.

This is not an easy question. There have been and still are many disputes on the nature of icon painting. St. John of Damascus, the great defender of icons during the iconoclastic period of the Eastern Church, said: "I make an image of the God whom I see. I do not worship matter; I worship the Creator of matter who became matter for my sake, who willed to take His abode in matter; who worked out my salvation in matter."[4] And more recently, Egon Sendler has said: "The icon points to a dimension which goes beyond the natural; it pushes out toward the ineffable. . . . According to St. Paul, Christ is the visible 'image of the invisible God.' (Col. 1:15); as Greek theologians say, on the other hand, the icon is . . . the reflection of God's reality."[5] What then is icon painting? It is making visible that which is not visible. What is the subject of the icon? Christ and Salvation History.

---

[3] Ibid., p. 128.

[4] St. John of Damascus, *On the Divine Images*, trans. David Anderson (Crestwood, New York: St. Vladimir's Seminary Press, 1980), p. 23.

[5] "The icon is a 'deuterotypos of the prototypos': the reflection of God's reality." Egon Sendler, S.J., *The Icon: Image of the Invisible Elements of Theology, Aesthetics and Technique,* trans. Steven Bigham (Redondo Beach, California: Oakwood Publications, 1988), p. 39.

Icons are not created to represent the world and nature; rather, they are made to represent the eternal truths revealed to us by God through Christ.

The painter of an icon, therefore, does not seek to imitate nature or produce worldly things; on the contrary, his work is meant to render an "image of the invisible and even the presence of the Invisible One."[6] The objects to be known by the painter are not corporeal being; rather they are the Divinity, Salvation, and Sanctified Humanity. These are not objects that may be simply known through human imagination and understanding. They are known primarily through faith. The authentic icon painter must be a believer, for only through supernatural faith will he truly know his subject matter. The reality with which he is confronted, therefore, is not visible matter, but revealed truth; it is not corporeal being, but spiritual being. The world of the icon artist is not the world of the eye before being, but the world of the soul before God.

This world of the artist is only known and experienced through faith, in faith, and with faith. It is not that the icon artist never experiences or relates to the created world; rather, he must see that world through faith in order to authentically produce his art, for without belief he cannot know nor interact with his subject matter.

II

The connection between knowledge and beauty is clear for Maritain: "The beautiful is what gives delight—not just any delight, but delight in knowing; not the delight particular to the act of knowing, but a delight which superabounds and overflows from this act because of the object known."[7] Beauty pleases the intellect, but our senses also take delight in the beautiful.[8] The beauty of art is a beauty "seized *in the sensible and through the sensible*."[9] And this beauty which delights our intellect through the senses is connatural to us.

Moreover, Maritain notes: "[A]lthough the beautiful borders on the metaphysical true, . . . [it] is not a kind of truth, but a kind of good."[10] Beauty is in its essence delightful; it not only illumines as does the true, but it also arouses desire and produces love. And beauty delights because of its essential characteristics of integrity, proportion, and radiance.[11]

---

[6] Ibid., p. 39.

[7] Maritain, *Art and Scholasticism and The Frontiers of Poetry*, p. 23.

[8] Ibid.

[9] Ibid., p. 25.

[10] Ibid., p. 26.

[11] Ibid., p. 27.

The beauty inherent in perfection, harmony, and splendor, and the beauty "seized in the sensible and through the sensible" are certainly present within the icon. Indeed, the aim of the iconographer is precisely to bring his subject matter to the viewer through the sensible, and thereby allow the viewer to delight in the beauty of the object portrayed. Yet there is more, for the icon painter is also presenting in and through matter the theological truths of the Christian faith. He is also, therefore, presenting the beauty of faith. In this sense, the icon depicts both supernatural truth and beauty.

The icon is not secular art with a religious content. The artist is not interested in himself nor in self-expression, but rather in God and in Salvation. Therefore, we may even go so far as to say that the icon, because of its object, is the apex of beauty in art. Maritain says: "God is beautiful. He is the most beautiful of beings. . . . He is beautiful to the extreme (*superpulcher*), because in the perfect simple unity of His nature there pre-exists in a super-excellent manner the fountain of all beauty." And, "In the Trinity, Saint Thomas adds, the name of Beauty is attributed most fittingly to the Son."[12]

It is through the beautiful that art reaches into the spiritual and that true communication and connection between persons takes place. In art, there are the useful arts, which are "ordered to the service of man, and [are] therefore a simple means." There are, in addition, the fine arts which tend to make beautiful works: "The work to which the fine arts tend is ordered to beauty; as beautiful, it is an end, an absolute, it suffices of itself. . . ."[13] And still, within the fine arts, there is the icon, which is at the service of Christ and His Church. The end of the icon, however, is not simply usefulness, even though icons are used for prayer; nor is their end beauty, although icons certainly depict the Beautiful; rather, icons are for the use of the Beautiful One. The end of the fine art of icon painting is to glorify God and to unite persons: to establish an intimate bond between the person of Christ and the people of the Church. Icons are for the sake of prayer, which raises the human person's mind and heart to God, and more specifically, for the liturgy. They are in effect for the service of the Mystical Body of Christ.

"The Annunciation" (figure 1), an icon by Michael Schrauzer, certainly combines theological beauty with artistic beauty. Here it is undeniable that the artist comes to know his object, the Incarnation, which is beautiful,

---

[12] Ibid., p. 31.
[13] Ibid., p. 33.

1. "The Annunciation," 1994.
Oil on panel, maple, 12 × 11 inches.
Courtesy of the Lazardi/Harp Gallery. Michael Schrauzer.

through faith. He enters into the beauty of the truth which he portrays and also into the sensible beauty that he perceives. The icon artist knows that it is the Beauty of God Himself that makes his art transcendent. The artist desires the Beauty that is God; he enters into a relationship with Beauty, and then embodies it by transforming matter into a work of art. The viewer sees matter that has been transformed into an image of Beauty, an image which speaks of the transcendence of God and of humanity. Indeed, this work "swarm[s] with meanings, and . . . say[s] more than it is."[14] The icon is art wed to faith, matter wed to spirit, it is beauty and faith purposefully enfleshed in matter, it is Beauty Incarnate. Yet, if the art work participates in

[14] Maritain, *Creative Intuition in Art and Poetry*, p. 128.

the Beautiful, so too must the artist. The artist participates in Beauty through contemplation.

III

The mode of being of the fine arts is contemplative.[15] The fine arts aim, as does wisdom, at intellectual delight; they also "presuppose in the artist a kind of contemplation, from which the beauty of the work must overflow."[16] What is it that the fine artist contemplates? Things. The artist contemplates material things, finds in them beauty, enters into their beauty and creates from the abundance of intellectual delight that is caused by seeing and knowing the object.

The icon painter, however, is not primarily interested in the contemplation of things, but in the contemplation of God and the supernatural. Because the painter meditates on God, his primary object, he finds in God beauty and truth, he enters into a deep relationship with God and creates from the overflow of intellectual delight and love that are caused by knowing his subject matter. For the icon painter, the contemplation of things is linked to the contemplation of God. The Transcendent enters, so to speak, into the painter's work, for the artist is a mediator, a priest for beauty and truth.

This contemplation of God allows for the creation of the icon. Indeed, the work made partly expresses the interior, contemplative life of the artist. It is the contemplative life of the painter which enables his creative intuition to become embodied in matter; it is his contemplation which illumines, as it were, his activity. The act of contemplating both God and the things of God is inseparable from his creative work. The icon makes of painting a good act, and can therefore make the painter good, and become a means to his salvation. The good of the work made and the good of the artist are fundamentally united in iconography.

For Maritain, however, the realm of art and the realm of morality are autonomous. He says: "Art and poetry tend to an absolute which is the Beauty to be attained in a work, but which is not God Himself, or Beauty subsisting by itself."[17] And he continues: "What the artist . . . insofar as he is artist, loves over and above all is Beauty in which to engender a work, not God as supreme ruler of human life nor as diffusing His own charity in

---

[15] Ibid., p. 34.

[16] Ibid.

[17] Jacques Maritain, *The Responsibility of the Artist* (New York: Charles Scribner's Sons, 1960), p. 32.

us."[18] Even though these boundaries between God, Beauty, and Art generally exist in secular art, they do not and should not exist in icon painting. The icon painter is primarily concerned with God, not with himself or his art work. He loves God as God and Beauty as an attribute of God. The icon artist serves God and paints in order to make Him loved and known. From beginning to end, grace fills the work of the painter; from the outset of the work the painter must have the gift of faith, and throughout the process he must have the gift of love of God, which spills over into the work made. The work is done through faith, with charity, and in hope. In the icon, the tension or conflict between art and morality is resolved, for when the work of art is authentically produced, it transfigures both the painter and the painting, as both are filled with the grace of the Holy Spirit and are made holy.

Furthermore, the icon is not simply a means to make the painter good, but should also make the viewer good. The work of art is the place where the fruit of the contemplation of the artist is seen, it is the place where the faith of the artist meets with the viewer. The icon is what may be called the meeting of two minds. The viewer, who sees a matter that has been transformed into an image of beauty, and intuits that it speaks of the transcendence of God and of human destiny, may be led to his own good. Here let us look at "The Madonna of the Holy See" (figure 2), a painting by the author. This painting shows the Madonna as representative of the Church, and as such she holds up the Christ Child for us to contemplate. The Christ Child in turn offers us the "pearl of great price": faith. The pearl is the focal point of the work, for through faith we are given knowledge of God and of our salvation. The icon invites us to embrace the faith.

In summary, icons are of the supernatural. The objects of the icon are Christ and Salvation History. These objects, which are beautiful, are known through faith. Icons themselves represent Beauty, Christ Himself, and the truth found in the account of salvation. In knowing his objects, the painter desires them, enters into their beauty, and embodies them in the icon. In this act of painting, whose object is Christ and His works, the artist may find his way to God and become holy. Icons are beautiful, but they do not primarily serve beauty; they are for the good of the artist, but they are not meant to serve the artist. They are for God, and because they are for God, all the goods of painting are found in this form of Christian art: for even the power of art is within the icon, a power that can mysteriously and

---

[18] Ibid., pp. 32–33

2. "The Madonna of the Holy See," 1997.
Oil on wood in mixed media. 23 × 31 inches.
Collection of the artist Katherine A. Osenga.

profoundly affect the viewer and move him more passionately than any rational argument. The icon artist knows this power, and knows that art, with beauty, can wound the viewer with love and move him to fall in love as the painter has. It is precisely this power of art that the icon artist uses for the glory of God.

PART III

ART, MORALITY,
AND THE POLIS

Dangerous Music

Wayne H. Harter

The ancient maxim concerning human excellence is *one man, one pursuit*. "Each one must practice one of the functions in the city, that for which his nature made him naturally most fit. And . . . justice is the minding of one's own business and not being a busybody. . . ."[1] Nowhere is the wisdom of this rule more evident than in attempts by philosophers (as philosophers) to judge the artistic merits of art or, likewise, in attempts by artists (as artists) to defend their work according to philosophical principles. For, the virtue of speculative knowing is not convertible with the virtue of making good things; the very temperaments proper to each are at odds; so much so, that one may say that the pursuit of the one excellence tends to make one unfit for the other. Unfortunately, this division of labor and all it implies makes little impression upon the imprudent. Unlike the admirable philosopher, Jacques Maritain, who once admitted, "I do not believe that a philosopher would dare speak of poetry if he could not rely on the direct experience of a poet,"[2] less humble souls rush to cash in their particular expertise for license to stray into realms of which they have not even the vaguest grasp of the landmarks.

Witness the case of more than ten years ago, when Allan Bloom in *The Closing of the American Mind*[3] attempted to apply principles of classical political philosophy to the question of rock music. The superficiality of his analysis is all too apparent even to those who are its ostensible concern, today's youth. Despite, thanks to a typically abysmal education, their inability to grasp his argument at the level of political principles, they never-

---

[1] Plato, *Republic* IV.433a, trans. Allan Bloom (New York: Harper Collins, 1991).

[2] Jacques Maritain, *Creative Intuition in Art and Poetry*, Bollingen Series 35.1 (Princeton, New Jersey: Princeton University Press, 1981), p. xxx.

[3] Allan Bloom, *The Closing of the American Mind* (New York: Simon and Schuster, 1987).

theless are able to see the excessiveness of sweeping generalizations such as "rock music has one appeal only, a barbaric appeal, to sexual desire—not love, not *eros*, but sexual desire undeveloped and untutored."[4] They themselves would never take it into their heads to defend "rock music" as a whole, a term they know is incredibly vague and covering an immense amount of musical territory. So nor can they take seriously any attempt by Bloom or others to discredit it.

It is too bad they are not equally reticent, again thanks to their education, to accept as wise the response to Bloom offered by the late musician Frank Zappa.[5] In essence, and in his own words, Zappa's musical criticism states the *"Ultimate Rule* ought to be: 'If it sounds good to you, it's bitchen; and if it sounds bad to you, it's shitty.'"[6] This is, of course, only a less elevated formulation of that tired relativism wherein everything (except those matters which inconvenience the holder) is simply a matter of shifting perspective (and therefore none of your damn business). But for those not inclined to musical solipsism, Zappa's rule appears as nothing more than aesthetic vulgarity.

In fact it is doubtful that Zappa, who is an accomplished musician, actually intended the statement in the witlessness it seems to convey. It is also possible that Bloom, had he been familiar with the work of Zappa and certain others, would not have written his chapter on music—at least not in the extreme form that it took. But in any event, the purpose of this writing is neither to defend Zappa as a thinker nor Bloom as a music critic. It is, rather, first to argue support for the work of these two men, at least in the respective realms to which they have legitimate claims; and secondly, to then ask what ought to be done when one accepts in principle the right of political censorship of the arts, but realizes that such practice is likely to target some very good, if questionable, works.

In order to achieve our goal what is needed is a hybrid wisdom, "the confluence of two independent streams of intellect, that of the philosopher and the artist."[7] This is not to say we must have in the concrete sense "a Socrates who plays the flute," or forego the ancient maxim on justice. Musical virtue is not to be confused with the ability to play an instrument; the

---

[4] Ibid., p. 73.

[5] Frank Zappa, "On Junk Food for the Soul. In Defense of Rock and Roll," *New Progressive Quarterly* 4 (Winter 1988), pp. 26–29.

[6] Frank Zappa with Peter Occhiogrosso, *The Real Frank Zappa Book* (New York: Poseidon Press, 1989), p. 188, emphasis original.

[7] John A. Oesterle, "Towards a Critique of Music," *The Thomist* 14 (1951), pp. 323–34.

musician in the proper sense of the term is the composer, not those who subsequently perform the work. As Maritain argued, "The oral or instrumental expression, which in the fluid successions of resonant matter transmits compositions thus completed in the spirit, is an extrinsic consequence and a simple means for such arts, and nothing more."[8] The virtue of art is an *intellectual* virtue, rooted in the ability to perceive intelligible relations between, in this case, sound and the good of the soul. And while, strictly speaking, the art of music refers to the rendering of such relations in concrete objects, and not to the cognitive basis for that work, still the excellence of a work of art as work of art can be discerned by one who sees *ex post facto* the intelligible relations between the structure of the work and the end it serves.

The pressing character for now finding such hybrid wisdom comes largely from the marketing success of the contemporary music industry. Although music has always had a place in human societies, the relative size of that place has certainly varied and it would be incredible to argue that any previous society could match the sheer quantitative presence of music in our own. An obvious indication of this new status for music comes from the hitherto unimaginable proliferation of retail markets and communication networks dedicated to its "consumption." Just thirty years ago the normal place to find music recordings—that is outside of radio—was in the relatively rare "music store" dealing in everything from accordions to private lessons. Today, on the other hand, every suburban mall has at least one and sometimes two retail outlets feeding the sustained demand for more and more music. And outside these rather expensive venues the expanding market has led to the advent of musical "superstores," as well as to mail-order houses (now conveniently accessed through the world-wide internet)—all of which are dominated overwhelmingly by what some would see as various categories of suspect music. Therefore, whatever inherent power for good or bad is possessed by music in its relation to the soul, such power has been increased, if not in direct proportion to, at least significantly by its cultural ubiquity. Even primary school children, wired into the musical video channels, have become mysteriously immersed in the fashionable world of pop music and delight in playground debates over the proper content of the category of "cool."

The problem is that music is potentially dangerous. About 2500 years ago the Greek philosophers discerned the important role of music for the

---

[8] Jacques Maritain, "Art an Intellectual Virtue," in *Art and Scholasticism* (London: Sheed & Ward, 1947), p. 17.

education of youth.[9] Youth, they argued, must come to feel happiness in those things a virtuous person finds happiness in, and pain in those things that to the latter bring pain. With the exception, however, of those rare souls who by nature are inclined toward the noble life, most children are driven by their desire for sensual gratification toward an adult life that will be a source of suffering not only to themselves but to the polity as well. What then must we do? We must lead them, the philosophers answered, by the only road they will accept, the road of sensual pleasure; but instead, thereby we must lead them toward a life of noble leisure and political virtue.

Enter the role of music. Pleasant melodies and rhythms act as vehicles for seducing youth into those principles necessary for the common good. Much more attractive are the difficult virtues of courage, temperance, and justice when presented in beautiful songs of heroes and famous citizens. Even the naturally disordered souls of children resonate to the good of difficult character, when the latter is presented within the seductive pleasures of tonality and measure.

Powerful tools, of course, always possess an ambiguous relation to the good. Thus the most effective tool for the education of youth, music, can be used as well as the instrument of their destruction. Through musical inculturation youth can become attuned to disorder and unbridled passions just as easily—perhaps more easily given their native bent— as they can to the tunes of moral virtue. Consequently, in jealousy for the souls of the city's youth, Socrates admonishes the good legislator to impose regulations upon musicians, forbidding the performing of dangerous music. They must avoid producing art in which the ignoble is portrayed in a good or pleasing light; they must avoid the sorts of sensual rhythms subversive of virtue; and they must accept the guidance of the legislator (who is the person rightly concerned with the common good) on this point or face banishment—or worse.

Lest in our modern prejudices we jump to the hasty opinion that the devious Socrates and his philosophical cronies advocated an early form of mind-control, aimed at sacrificing the freedom and happiness of the individual in deference to the interests of an ordered but joyless society, it is important to keep in mind that they were convinced (and it is impossible to imagine any educator not likewise convinced) that there is a *particular kind* of life deserving of the name "the good life." What Socrates was interested in, in the case of youth, was not indoctrinating them so as to render them incapable of choosing the good life, but rather in directing their passions so

---

[9] Cf. Aristotle, *Politics* VIII; Plato, *Republic* III.395–417b.

that when they attained the age whereat they might choose that life in freedom and in truth, they would not be hindered by disorder in their loves and hates. Given that human passions tend not to be in harmony with right reason and that reason right or wrong nonetheless must direct the passions in their blind search for happiness, and given that reason seldom attains any degree of rectitude without extensive training, then it becomes impossible to argue against the necessity for censorship in the education of youth.

Any society, but especially a democratic society, depends upon the education of its citizens. If they are the products of a misspent youth, degraded in their likes and dislikes by the seductive powers of decadent music, what hope can be held out against the demise of political life? And furthermore, given that there are philosophical and historical reasons for thinking that a democracy when it degenerates is liable to find itself metamorphosed into a tyranny, who can gainsay the seriousness of this consideration?[10] A healthy democracy is not one that can afford the luxury of decadent music. Quite the opposite.

Armed with this classical understanding of the role of music in the education of youth for the common good Allan Bloom waded into the ongoing fight against rock'n'roll, although his professed primary concern in *The Closing of the American Mind* "is not with the moral effects of this music— whether it leads to sex, violence or drugs. [His] issue," rather, "is its effect on education, and [how] it ruins the imagination of young people and makes it very difficult to have a passionate relationship to the art and thought that are the substance of liberal education."[11]

In short, the problem with rock music in Bloom's estimation is that it fails miserably in the educative function. Not only does it not express the highest reaches of human excellence, instead it panders to the crude, infantile passions of pubescent youth. It offers up to them as a good, even the greatest good, the immediate gratification of their vulgar, unswerving desires. "Rock music has one appeal only, a barbaric appeal, to sexual desire—not love, not *eros*, but sexual desire undeveloped and untutored." Rock music aims at the pleasures proper to barbaric youth, and contains "nothing noble, sublime, profound, delicate, tasteful or even decent" in its repertoire. "There is room only for the intense, changing, crude and immediate." Rather than offer a vision of what they could and ought to be, rock music confirms youth in their feckless pleasures. It is a sad irony, thinks

---

[10] For a philosophical consideration of the causes of change of government see Aristotle, *Politics* V.

[11] Bloom, *The Closing of the American Mind*, p. 79.

Bloom, that one of the greatest achievements in the history of political life has culminated in the person of a thirteen-year-old sitting rapt before MTV, a

> pubescent child whose body throbs with orgasmic rhythms; whose feelings are made articulate in hymns to the joys of onanism or the killing of parents; whose ambition is to win fame and wealth in imitating the drag-queen who makes the music. In short, life is made into a nonstop, commercially prepackaged masturbational fantasy.[12]

Rock music offers nothing transcendent to the savage soul of this developing youth. It thereby also corrupts his cultivation in that higher life which is his birthright.

Nothing here will be gainsaid of Bloom's estimation of songs straightforwardly glorifying parricide and self-abuse. If such melodic tributes truly exist, they certainly are degraded forms of human expression originating in disordered souls and appealing only to the most vicious or puerile, that is to say, to those in need of extensive therapy and/or prolonged incarceration. Nor will "rock music" find its defense here; the category is about as wide and therefore useless as is "religion." Most of what passes under its banner is certainly trite, crude, and thus unrelievedly boring, and it would be a great service if it were to disappear immediately from the already cluttered airwaves. But on that score it is not only rock music that is dangerous. Tasteless and cheaply manufactured goods, network television, much of what passes for primary education and almost all of what passes for higher education, not to mention insipid Sunday liturgies: these things are threatening to destroy our spirits with their noise, garishness, their bland and unmitigated stupidity. But that, of course, is a somewhat larger topic than the subject of this writing.

Returning to the more modest matter at hand, we can pass over quickly what Frank Zappa has to *say* in defense of his art. It is hard to take seriously Zappa's refutation of Bloom's claim—Bloom's claim that, unlike rock music, the music of Bach and Beethoven represents the product of an artistic unity born from a cultivation of the soul. It is hard to take seriously Zappa's counterclaim that sometime in the distant future similar estimations will be made of Michael Jackson's *Thriller* album; that the classics are no more than the surviving "hits" from an era wherein popes and kings, instead of music moguls, chose what would survive; that, in matters of aesthetics, the primary rule is personal taste. In fact, outside of some pointed references to the market forces behind the current level of popular music,

[12] Ibid., pp. 74–75.

the overall impression Zappa attempts to give of his art—of all art—is that it has no relation to any elevation or lowering of the soul. It is merely a pleasant pastime, more satisfying at least to himself than beer and television, but even then appealing only to his sense of gentle amusement:

> Beer and television bore me, so what am I going to do? I am going to be alive for X number of years. I have to do something with my time besides sleep and eat. So, I devise little things to amuse myself. If I can amuse somebody else, great. And if I can amuse somebody else and earn a living while doing it, that is a true miracle in the twentieth century![13]

In fairness, it is necessary to note that one should seldom presume Mr. Zappa to be speaking in all seriousness. But even if this were the rare occasion, we are not, as already admitted, interested in defending his stature as a critic. Artistic genius and political wisdom seldom cohabitate in one soul. Still, despite the nonsense Zappa is prone to utter, he provides us the perfect foil for Bloom, and this for two closely connected reasons. First, if in debate Zappa were to refrain from addressing Bloom on philosophical grounds and simply play his music, then Bloom would stand confounded (at least in his sweeping generalizations). But secondly, it is certainly questionable whether Bloom in that scenario would have ears to hear the goodness of Zappa's artistry, and thus it points in any case to the limits of the philosopher to discern the good in matters of the fine arts.

Beginning with the first point, the claim that Zappa's music is a refutation of the charge that all rock music appeals to degenerate tastes must seem strange to many who are only passingly familiar with his work. Certainly two fellow travelers of Bloom, both of whom exhibit much more familiarity with contemporary music than does Bloom himself, agree on at least one thing. Frank Zappa's music, despite whatever technical merits it possesses, is a prime example of what is wrong with contemporary culture. Robert Pattison, in *The Triumph of Vulgarity*,[14] and Martha Bayles, in *Hole in Our Soul*,[15] characterize Zappa's music as tasteless and perverse. But with them as well we might refer to the second point: only those with ears for certain forms of music can hear that music. The giveaway, particularly with Pattison, is these critics' reliance upon lyrics (or titles) to analyze a song. And certainly, if one restricts the analysis of Zappa's music to the

---

[13] Zappa, "On Junk Food for the Soul," p. 26.

[14] Robert Pattison, *The Triumph of Vulgarity: Rock Music in the Mirror of Romanticism* (New York: Oxford University Press, 1987).

[15] Martha Bayles, *Hole in Our Soul: The Loss of Beauty and Meaning in American Popular Music* (New York: The Free Press, 1994).

recitation of lyrics, it would be impossible in particular compositions to defend him against the charge of mindless vulgarity. For example, in the chorus to the song "Broken Hearts," on an album[16] that, incidentally, also contains the subject of protest to the Federal Communications Commission by the Jewish Anti-Defamation League, the listener is treated to a musical rendition of forced sodomy.

But unless one thinks that certain words or references to particular subjects is in itself decadent, it hardly makes sense to pass judgement upon "Broken Hearts" on this basis alone. Zappa, among other things, is a great satirist. Only humorless adults and the hopelessly puerile (and to the consideration of this latter class we must return) would assume that he is offering a straightforward encomium to rape. The lyrics, just like the words of a Swift or Voltaire, are intended to be humorous and operative on two distinct levels. Unlike such literary examples, however, Zappa's lyrics cannot be understood apart from the musical context they serve. Anyone posing as a music critic should have known this. Final judgement of the artistic and ethical merits of a work have to account for the conjunction of all elements present.

An essay, for obvious reasons, cannot demonstrate the very point upon which the truth of the present argument devolves. It must be satisfied with entertaining abstract possibilities. Therefore consider this. Simply in terms of artistic excellence, it is generally recognized by those who are familiar with his music, including those whose interests lie predominantly in "serious" music, that Frank Zappa is an accomplished composer. If it lends credence to this claim, then let it be added that among an impressive, lengthy list of achievements Zappa has been commissioned to conduct his orchestral works by numerous orchestras including the Residentie Orchestra (the Hague) and the Oslo Philharmonic; he has recorded with the London Symphony Orchestra, collaborated with Pierre Boulez on "Perfect Stranger," and was appointed special ambassador to the West on trade, culture, and tourism by Václav Havel, the President of Czechoslovakia. This author would argue that these facts alone prove very little, but very little is required here. All that must be admitted is that they indicate the *probable* merits of Zappa's "Broken Hearts." For, despite the all-too-real unevenness in the work of even the greatest of artists, such unevenness remains within elevated parameters. The recognition of excellence in the above mentioned endeavors thus gives basis for the supposition of excellence in Zappa's work in rock music.

---

[16] *Sheik Yerbouti* (Barking Pumpkin Records, 1990).

We therefore are left with the problem of reconciling compositional excellence with questionable lyrics. As a beginning, I think it is obvious that any attempt to see them, as some do, as forgivable distractions from otherwise well-crafted scores, caused by concessions to capitalist production in a vulgar market, would be in effect to abandon the defense of these works. It is not the business of the critic to pardon the artist from no doubt formidable forces aimed at diverting his art into more profitable avenues. It is certainly understandable when the merely human composer capitulates to market forces in the interests of eating and sleeping indoors and one must hope that such surrender finds mercy in the next life, but still the result is always a flawed work. So too any quirky impulses on the part of Zappa to add gratuitous "humor" must be judged as destructive of the artistic unity of the work—presuming, that is, that no greater unity was achieved by a resolution of disunity at a higher level. Only if the vulgar lyrics can be defended as an integral part of a beautiful whole would it be possible to spare "Broken Hearts" from the charge of defectiveness.

In fact, it is precisely in the dissonance created between the subject of the lyrics to this song and their musical treatment that makes the work not only artistically excellent, but highly moral and therefore, for reasons to be taken up shortly, important for consideration in the task of educating youth. Zappa's "Broken Hearts" has its most profound appeal to the sense of abstract pattern; it is music pleasing to the intellect in its delight of form, and what one cannot know from a simple reading of the lyrics is that the chorus "I'm gonna ram it, ram it, ram it, etc." comes packaged in a tightly harmonized vocal staccato. These lyrics, in relation to the form of their presentation, provide the song with an element of dissonance. They are a concrete reference to the vulgarity of contemporary life that constantly threatens to overcome beauty and from which music seeks to liberate us. In other words, these lyrics contrast to and thereby accentuate the elevating force of Zappa's music. They heighten our appreciation for how important and at the same time precarious is the place of music and all art in the modern world. They are vulgar because they signify the vulgar. But when heard within the context of Zappa's beautiful music, they are transformed through tonal and rhythmic exaggeration into sounds no longer commensurate with their everyday meaning; their vulgarity becomes defused. In consequence, they and the world they signify are rendered ridiculous, of value only insofar as they provide matter for the musical score. They take on a character subversive to their normal meanings, they become moralized in the same way that Swift's suggestion of serving up Irish children on the table of English gentlefolk is subversive to the contemporary meaning of the "Irish problem." Who can take seriously that familiar world wherein ramming it up another's "poop chute" is precisely what those words convey, once they have heard the same transformed by the most exacting of harmony and rhythm and humor?

Is it possible, then, to reverse the judgement of Bloom on "rock"? At least in Zappa's "Broken Hearts," do we have a clear example of music that, which for obvious reasons would appeal to a disordered youthful sensuality, would work to elevate the listener beyond his leering aesthetic ignorance and towards an appreciation of the good of virtue? Again, no essay could hope to establish this particular point. But consider for the sake of argument that such is the case. Even then, this alone would not allow us to conclude the question of whether "Broken Hearts" is a valuable tool for the education of the virtuous society or whether it ought to be suppressed, at least in regard to youth. Just because the ideal listener would discover a moral ally in Mr. Zappa, there is little reason to believe that outside of carefully directed instruction the typical thirteen-year-old of Professor Bloom's nightmare would be that listener. Indeed, we have Zappa's own testimony on this point. According to the lyrics of another song,[17] the fact that his work is musically accomplished is totally irrelevant to his listeners, because they like it only for one reason, because it's "stupid."

So, what comes now? Ought we to press for governmental censorship, as is periodically suggested by political interest groups, in concern for the sensibilities of the chronologically and constitutionally incapable?

Ultimately, the correct answer to this question lies in the realm of political prudence, not in the simple consideration of abstract principles. And governing all such decisions must be the realization that freedom is rightfully curtailed, both within education and without, only in the interests of greater freedom.[18] Furthermore, by virtue of the interdependence of all civic good, it must always be kept in mind that the sacrifice of one good is liable to impact in ways completely unforeseen in the good of related matters. One has only to think of Prohibition legislation to recognize this truth. "Because social freedoms interlock so tightly, it is not possible to know antecedently what the multiple effects of a regulation will be. At best, the effect you want can only be foreseen with probability, not certainty. And unforeseen effects may follow, with the result that a regulation, in itself

---

[17] "A Little Green Rosetta," from the *Joe's Garage* album (Barking Pumpkin Records, 1979, 1987).

[18] Cf. John Courtney Murray, S. J., "Should There be a Law?: The Question of Censorship," in *We Hold These Truths: Catholic Reflections on the American Proposition* (New York: Sheed and Ward, 1960), pp. 155–74.

sensible, may in the end do more harm than good."[19] But even while keeping these guidelines for prudent governing in mind, we nevertheless must
push on; for what matter is of greater concern than the formation of youth?
"No *politicus* should dare meddle with the laws of beauty," warns Maritain,
"but [the fine arts] still remain, by their generic nature, arts, 'practical sciences,' and on that score all the intellectual and moral values the work ab-
sorbs normally come under the control of whoever has the duty of taking
care of the common good of human life."[20] The correct policy here certainly depends upon political prudence. But prudence that is truly prudent
is ruled by reason, not fortune; so we must seek to establish guiding principles.

First, one might invoke the principle that "in a discussion of moral actions, although general statements have a wider range of application, statements on particular points have more truth in them."[21] We could thereby
sidestep the question of government intervention by appealing to the right-
ful claim that only one familiar with the particular needs of a person's education is in an adequate position to judge what material would benefit or
harm him or her. Following upon the principle of subsidiarity, censorship
thus would rightfully belong in the first instance to parents, and secondly to
educators commissioned by them. In a society of virtuous citizens/educa-
tors, this would be not only the easy and most prudent solution, but the just
decision as well.

Yes, in virtuous societies legislative decisions are easy to make, and
even largely unnecessary. But given the current state of cultural affairs, is
there any reason to suspect we live in such a society? Zappa's music delights in parodying the overwhelming stupidity of contemporary culture. It
therefore seems right to argue that it is impossible to proceed simply upon
the principle of what is right for a right society. When citizens have abdi-
cated or are no longer capable of discerning and regulating moral influences in the education of youth, the principle of subsidiarity no longer can
be invoked and it becomes right for government to intervene.

The hitch, of course, is that those then called upon to legislate these matters are generally, as we see in the example of Bloom himself, in no position to discern well in matters of artistic excellence. Consequently, in re-
sorting to governmental censorship many works of merit and even great

---

[19] Ibid., p. 162.
[20] Jacques Maritain, "Art and Morality," in *Art and Scholasticism*, n. 139.
[21] Aristotle, *Nicomachean Ethics* II.7.1107a30, trans. Martin Ostwald (New
York: Macmillan Publishing Company, 1962).

merit would be mistakenly censored and the cultural deposit proportionately impoverished. The seasonal efforts of civic-minded groups to ban reading of *Huckleberry Finn* in public schools is a case in point.

But it is important to keep in mind a causal relation set forward by the Greek philosophers. The life of virtue, including the ability to discern the good in matters of art, is secondary to a good character. In other words, whereas one can learn something *about* musical composition or market analysis and be at the same time a complete scoundrel, one cannot learn good government or how one ought to *apply* composition or market analysis without having first become good. One cannot learn what works of art are products of an elevated vision until one has learned to see from a height somewhere above the level of a barnyard animal. One thus could argue that the very attempt to regulate the moral climate for youth, even when undertaken by those whose sole credentials often are nothing more than good will united to the recognition of contemporary decadence, is a necessary first step away from the current state of affairs.

More importantly we must keep in mind the duty, the nobility of the lawmaker in relation to the common good. Political duty, especially as it is expressed in a modern democracy, lies heavily upon us, for it is weighed down by its order to the common good manifested in the most common life, in the life of those without adequate leisure or adequate education, of those who, living in a society driven by the incessant desire for matter, also have become insulated, in the interests of economics, from any profound critique of their passions. When the artist rightfully claims a certain moral autonomy in the line of his art, he has no such claim upon the life of man. Art, aiming at Beauty is speculative in character, and is, as Maritain reminds us, "metaphysically superior to Prudence." However, in relation to our final end, to our perfection as men and women, prudence is superior to art.

In the sometimes ensuing struggle between the good of the artist and the good of the prudent man, it is, as Maritain observes, difficult for the merely prudent man even to understand the artist:

> In finding fault with a work of art, the Prudent Man, firmly established upon his moral virtue, has the certitude that he is defending against the Artist a sacred good, the good of Man, and he looks upon the Artist as a child or a madman.[22]

In his relation to the artist the lawmaker is bound to sometimes fail in preserving the legitimate good of the artist, and thereby in a certain sense he is to be counted *imprudent* through lack of wisdom. But even so, he does not

---

[22] Jacques Maritain, "Art and Morality," in *Art and Scholasticism*, pp. 65–66.

fail by cause of his legislating. Indeed, to abdicate his responsibility by reason of some incapacity to judge adequately the value of art, would be a far greater failure in prudence. For, the right to legislate belongs to no other and the subject of education is not of slight importance, and the signs of contemporary education failing our youth are too patent to ignore. The practical man has not always the luxury of waiting upon wisdom; he must act; he must act now, and he must act by what lights he possesses.

One should never demand more certainty in inquiry than is warranted by the subject. Considering all the relevant factors any answer to the question at hand therefore will be probable at best. Nevertheless, the present writer concludes thus. There is no reason to characterize the music of certain contemporary artists as anything other than a delight to the senses of the virtuous person habituated to the modes of their composition. There is, however, no reason to suspect that said person exists in great numbers, certainly not among youths themselves, and not among those guiding the education of youth. There is, on the other hand, much reason to think that "dangerous music" will be misperceived by those most likely to be enticed by it. There is, in conclusion, sufficient reason to warrant its censoring. The damnable business of this is that such censoring could only be undertaken by those folk, the civic leaders, whose credentials are less than inspiring in these matters. But so be it. For, the final consideration and consolation in all political matters must be that if history depended upon the merits of its actors, it would have ended long ago.

Epiphany and Authenticity:
The Aesthetic Vision of Charles Taylor

Brian J. Braman

The language of self-fulfillment, self-actualization, and self-realization have become common currency in contemporary culture. In fact, these ideas can be subsumed under the inclusive term of authenticity. Cultural critics such as the late Allan Bloom and Christopher Lasch see this desire for individual self-fulfillment, for being authentic, as a form of narcissism that closes off concern for the greater issues that transcend the self, be they political or religious. For Charles Taylor, however, although a certain moral relativism can be associated with the desire for self-fulfillment, this position is in the last analysis a profound mistake. What the critics of authenticity fail to see is the moral ideal underlining this desire for authentic self-realization. This ideal is the intense desire to live one's life by a higher standard. In short, the question of the constitution of authentic human existence is a question of a moral ideal that ought to be taken seriously because the meaning of authenticity has shaped, and continues to shape, our understanding of what it means to be human.

For Taylor the idea of authenticity is a rich, vibrant, and vitally important addition to any conversation concerning what it means to be human. Authenticity, properly understood, is "a picture of what a better or higher mode of life would be, where better and higher are defined not in terms of what we happen to desire or need, but offer a standard of what we ought to desire."[1] Taylor's view of authenticity expresses the conviction that terms such as self-fulfillment and self-realization are not just cover stories for narcissism, nor are they terms that justify a stance that is labeled the "liber-

---

[1] Charles Taylor, *The Ethics of Authenticity* (Cambridge, Massachusetts: Harvard University Press, 1991), p. 16.

alism of neutrality." Authenticity is a moral ideal that ultimately answers the question: What is the good life?

Yet, with the rise of modernity and the dissolution of the medieval synthesis, there is no longer a publicly established order of references to articulate a normative vision of authentic human existence. Given the lack of publicly agreed upon references, the question then becomes the following: How are we to determine or discover that which is most important in shaping our identity, in articulating what our ideal of authenticity is to be? Is there a source other than the self? To answer these questions, Taylor turns to aesthetics, more specifically to the notion of epiphany. An epiphany is a manifestation which brings us into the presence of something which is otherwise inaccessible, and which is of the highest moral or spiritual significance. It is in modern art and poetry that Taylor finds the clearest expression of epiphanic events. Modern art and poetry respect modernity's concern for the subject, without falling into a disordered subjectivism. Modern art is at once inward, yet it involves the de-centering of the subject. Because we now live in an age where a "publicly accessible cosmic order of meaning" is no longer possible, the idea of epiphanic art bridges the gap that has been left by this disintegration of public order. In short, the idea of epiphanic art anchors Taylor's concern with the search "for moral sources *outside* the subject through languages which resonate *within* him or her, the grasping of an order which is inseparably indexed to a personal vision."[2]

The purpose of this paper, then, will be to first draw out Taylor's understanding of authenticity by focusing on the themes of identity and epistemology. Secondly, I will show how epiphanic art anchors Taylor's concern with the search for normative moral sources *outside* the subject.

For Taylor, to have an identity is not something that is optional. Deep within ourselves is a desire to have a sense of orientation within the world. We need to have a sense of who and what we are, and where our lives are leading us. From Taylor's perspective, our identity is ultimately determined by what we consider to be of utmost value, by a hypergood[3] that not only structures our choices but shapes the fundamental orientation of our lives. When we speak about who we are and what it means for us to be human, the touchstone is whatever hypergood we have chosen by which to structure our lives. Taylor defines authenticity as an ideal we choose and

[2] Charles Taylor, *Sources of the Self* (Cambridge, Massachusetts: Harvard University Press, 1989), p. 510.

[3] For Taylor, a hypergood is an architectonic good that structures all of our moral choices. It is the ideal that helps to shape our self-constituting choices.

whereby we do what we ought to do, and not what we merely wish to do. Authenticity and identity go hand in hand, since we always see ourselves in terms of whatever ideal we have chosen in order to give structure to ourselves as persons. Of course, Taylor recognizes that there exists, more often than not, a gap between the full realization of this vision, and what we claim as our chosen ideal of authenticity. There is one thing, however, that Taylor wants to be very clear about: while we choose this authentic ideal that shapes our identity, this choice is not made within a vacuum, nor can it be. Taylor reformulates Heidegger's notion of thrownness in terms of engaged agency to show that our being-in-the-world is a matrix of already constituted meanings and values.

Why is Taylor so insistent on showing that one's identity is always already contextualized? It is in large part because of modernity's changed understanding of the nature of reason. In working out his understanding of authenticity, Taylor has concomitantly rehabilitated an understanding of human reason that goes beyond what he sees as a current debasement. The modern understanding of reason for Taylor militates against any hope of moving beyond either procedural approaches or cost-benefit analysis in order to determine what authentic human existence is.

Modernity's diminished understanding of the nature and power of reason obviously begins with Descartes's understanding of reason in terms of clarity. We now are concerned with what the thinking subject generates. We are concerned that our thoughts be ordered properly so that certainty of knowledge may follow. "Now certainty is something that the mind has to generate for itself. It requires a reflexive turn, where instead of simply trusting the opinions one has acquired through one's upbringing, one examines their foundation, which is ultimately to be found in one's own mind."[4] According to Taylor, this shift in how reason is conceived occurs simultaneously with the rise of modern science. With the ascendancy of science, the whole of the cosmos is now understood as neutral. This neutrality suggests that nature waits to have its purposes imposed on it.[5] When science neutralizes the world, and the ordered sense of being disappears, the paradigm we use to guide our life is no longer given to us in nature or society. The paradigms are found within our reasoning powers. In short, "reason is no longer de-

[4] Charles Taylor, "Overcoming Epistemology," in *After Philosophy: End or Transformation*, eds. Kenneth Baynes, James Bohman, and Thomas McCarthy (Cambridge, Massachusetts: MIT Press, 1994), p. 468.

[5] Charles Taylor, "Justice After Virtue," in *After MacIntyre*, eds. John Horton and Susan Mendus (Notre Dame, Indiana: University of Notre Dame Press, 1994), p. 20.

fined substantively, in terms of a vision of cosmic order, but formally in terms of procedures that thought ought to follow and especially those involved in fitting means to ends, instrumental reason. The hegemony of reason is consequently redefined, and now means not ordering our lives according to the vision of order, but rather controlling desires by the canons of instrumental reason."[6] Because reason is no longer understood as substantive, that is, ordered to something other than itself, human reason becomes understood as an activity of making or *techne*. This new notion of reason gives rise to a view of the subject as autonomous. His or her freedom is rooted in a self-direction made by the person. To repeat, because reason has been disengaged from any order outside of itself, and the cosmos has no intrinsic meaning and simply stands at the disposition of the purposes imposed upon it by the person, human reason and existence are entirely self-directed according to orders constructed by the subject, "as against those which he is supposed to find in nature."[7]

This new notion of reason eventually gives rise to skepticism which leads to naturalism, utilitarianism, and formalism. For Taylor, naturalism seeks to define the human person according to the scientific canons that emerged in the seventeenth century. Behaviorism and computer theories of human knowing are such examples. But when it comes to the question of the ethical life, or what it means to be authentic, naturalism holds that goods or values are mere personal projections onto a world which in essence is neutral. Projection, then, is strictly an individual activity that can be eventually brought under voluntary control.[8] Naturalism becomes so attractive to the moderns, because it appears to be capable "of achieving a kind of disengagement from our world by objectifying it. To objectify it means to make it neutral, and effect the purposes which we determine ourselves."[9]

Again, the modern understanding of reason has given rise not only to skepticism and naturalism but also to utilitarianism and formalism. Because of modernity's grasp of reason as disengaged and its resultant skepticism, reason's task is no longer to articulate a vision of order independent of itself. The task of determining what order is now falls under the "subject's rational construct." Utilitarianism as a derivative of naturalism seeks to fill the void created by this skepticism. It recognizes a good that exists inde-

[6] Ibid., p. 19.
[7] Ibid., pp. 18–19.
[8] Taylor, *Sources of the Self*, p. 53.
[9] Charles Taylor, *Philosophy and the Human Sciences: Philosophical Papers 2* (Cambridge: Cambridge University Press, 1990), p. 4.

pendently of the person and this is called happiness. But as Taylor points out, instead of the higher or lower that belonged to older metaphysical views, "there is just desire and the only standard which remains is the maximization of its fulfillment."[10] Thus, once any notion of higher or lower is expunged from the position that reason is ordered to something other than itself, "the only rational procedure must be to sum *de facto* goods. The right solution, that which enjoys henceforth the aura of a higher or moral way is that which emerges from the rational procedure."[11]

Kant was acutely aware of the problem attached to this kind of moral procedure. He saw that the utilitarian position fails to take into account a hierarchy of motives: "There seemed to be no qualitative distinction left between moral and prudential."[12] And as Taylor has shown, Kant solved the inadequacies "in one stroke: to act morally is to act from a qualitatively higher motive than the merely prudential. . . . "[13] Kant's solution leads to what Taylor calls formalism. Formalism, "like utilitarianism, has the apparent value that would allow us to ignore the problematic distinctions between different qualities of action or modes of life, which play such a large part in our actual moral decisions,"[14] while simultaneously establishing universal principles. Therefore, the utilitarian answers the question "What should I do?" in terms of what would produce the greatest happiness for the greatest number; the formalist answers the question in terms of choices that treat "other people's prescriptions as if they were my own."[15]

Because the modern understands reason in terms of production, one is rational to the extent that one operates within a given standard. "To be guided by reason now means to direct one's action according to plans or standards which one has constructed following the canons of rational procedure, e.g., to be proceeding according to clear calculations, or to be obeying a law one has prescribed to oneself according to the demands of reason."[16] Because Taylor sees the epistemological chaos in which we have found ourselves, resulting in utilitarianism and formalism, we must extricate ourselves from this morass of rationalism by an act of overcoming epistemology. This means abandoning what he calls foundationalism. "In-

---

[10] Taylor, *Sources of the Self*, p. 78.
[11] Taylor, "Justice After Virtue," in *After MacIntyre*, p. 27.
[12] Ibid.
[13] Ibid.
[14] Taylor, "The Diversity of Goods," in *Philosophy and the Human Sciences*, p. 231.
[15] Taylor, *Sources of the Self*, p. 79.
[16] Taylor, "Justice After Virtue," in *After MacIntyre*, p. 26.

stead of searching for an impossible foundational justification of knowledge or hoping to achieve total reflexive clarity about the bases of our beliefs, we would now conceive this self-understanding as awareness about the limits and conditions of our knowing, an awareness that would help us to overcome the illusions of disengagement and atomic individuality that are constantly being generated by a civilization founded on mobility and instrumental reason."[17] To overcome epistemology, we need to recover the primordial fact that what is valuable or worthwhile can only be attained in terms of a "background of social interchange and in light of a certain vision of what being a human being is all about."[18]

Taylor takes his cue from certain insights arising out of structuralism "that any act requires a background language of practices and institutions to make sense; and that while there will be a particular goal sought in the act, those features of it which pertain to the structural background will not be objects of individual purpose."[19] Because the demands of total clarity are impossible to fulfill, modern epistemology has created an environment of skepticism which has all but obscured the structure or nature of human living. Taylor's concern to "overcome epistemology" finds a mid-point between total subjectivism and its opposite extreme, a strange Schopenhauerianism without an acting subject.[20]

Epistemology's treatment of reason as instrumental has skewed our understanding of our own subjectivity and has given rise to three dominant images. The first is the image of the disengaged subject whose self-understanding is defined purely from within; our identity is no longer tied to anything outside. Secondly, because of this "punctual" view of the self our stance toward ourselves and our world is sheer instrumentality. The subject calculates whatever is necessary in order to secure its own personal welfare. Lastly, society is now conceived in terms of an aggregate of self-contained monads.[21] For Taylor these images of the modern identity need to be overcome along with epistemology.

The question of identity may be looked at in two ways. First, the modern understanding of personal identity sees the *individual* as a natural being

[17] Taylor, "Overcoming Epistemology," in *After Philosophy*, pp. 479–80.

[18] Taylor, *Sources of the Self*, p. 55.

[19] Taylor, "Foucault on Freedom and Truth," in *Philosophy and the Human Sciences*, p. 173.

[20] Ibid., p. 172. Taylor sees Foucault as the best representative of the latter position. In other words, Foucault leaves us with the "will" of Schopenhauer without an acting subject.

[21] Taylor, "Overcoming Epistemology," in *After Philosophy*, pp. 471–72.

characterized by a set of "inner drives or goals or desires and aspirations. Knowing what I am really about is getting clear about these. If I inquire after my identity, ask seriously who I am, it is here that I have to look for an answer. The horizon of identity is an inner horizon."[22] The second approach is what Taylor calls the pre-modern. It regards persons as parts in a larger order. Without this order we would be less than human. Being situated within this defined order answers for us the deepest questions concerning who we are and what role we play in the drama of human existence. This horizon is external to us.[23]

For Taylor, the pre-modern understanding of identity is no longer tenable, but neither is the modern understanding. The subjectivism of modernity is a dead end. In order to overcome the modern and the pre-modern approaches to identity, Taylor offers an alternative: "To define my identity is to define what I must be in contact with in order to function fully as a human agent, and specifically to be able to judge and discriminate and recognize what is really of worth or importance, both in general and for me."[24]

For Taylor, identity refers to certain evaluations that are the indispensable horizon or foundation for personal reflection and judgment. Modernity's vision of the disengaged self, grounded on the model of self-clarity and control, contradicts that concrete being who grows and becomes. "I can only know myself through the history of my maturations and regressions, overcomings and defeats."[25] Our identity is defined by those things that deeply matter to us. They provide the framework or horizon out of which we can judge what is good and valuable; and more importantly, they reveal how we are situated *vis-à-vis* what really matters to us. However, the full definition of a person's identity involves not only "his stand on moral and spiritual matters but also some reference to a defining community."[26] The very possibility of our stand on what we consider to be an authentic identity is already constituted in "a social understanding of great temporal depth, . . . in a tradition."[27]

Reason as disengaged instrumentality disregards the rich human experience of desiring or craving to be in contact with something greater than ourselves. Not only do we desire to be in contact with this *other*, but more importantly, we want to know how we are placed with respect to this ideal,

---

[22] Taylor, "Legitimation Crisis," in *Philosophy and the Human Sciences*, p. 258.
[23] Ibid.
[24] Ibid.
[25] Taylor, *Sources of the Self*, p. 50.
[26] Ibid., p. 36.
[27] Ibid., p. 39.

whatever it may be. There is then an aspiration to wholeness, a basic need in all persons to be connected to "or in contact with what they see as good, of crucial importance, fundamental value."[28] Only by having an identity can we define what is and what is not important to us. Properly understood, self-realization presupposes the existence of goods or values independent of the self. It is the cultivation of these that ultimately makes our life rich, fruitful, and authentic.[29] In short, it is crucial to our identity to understand life in terms of a highest good, be it God or justice. The "assurance that [we are] turned towards this good gives [us] a sense of wholeness, of fullness of being . . . , that nothing else can."[30]

Taylor wants to overcome the epistemological quagmire of subjectivism which dominates much of modernity's self-understanding. It is a mistake to conceive our identity as an isolated solitary act of self-creativity; if our desire to be authentic is grounded in an aspiration to wholeness, which moves us beyond ourselves in order to be who we wish to be, then we need to know how we can avoid the pitfalls of subjectivism. Taylor does this by developing the idea of a framing epiphany.

For Taylor human existence is a quest for meaning and significance. Not to have a framework for this quest is to "fall into a life which is spiritually senseless."[31] Taylor's concern then is to find "moral sources *outside* the subject through languages which resonate within him or her, the grasping of an order which is inseparably indexed to a personal vision."[32] Here is where modern art comes into play. Taylor traces the idea of a framing epiphany to the rise of Romanticism in the nineteenth century. This Taylor calls the "expressivist turn."

Now it is important to note that the shift that takes place in nineteenth-century artistic and moral sensibilities occurred within a cultural context where there was the gradual fading of a believable notion of cosmic order, "whose nature could be specified and understood independently of the realization/manifestation of the current of nature in our lives."[33] The older order grounded in an ontic *logos* was no longer viable. This passing of the older order clearly had its effect on art. For instance, where once Alexander Pope in his *Windsor Forest* "could draw upon the age-old views of the order of nature as a commonly available source of poetic images,"[34] this

[28] Ibid., p. 44.
[29] Ibid., p. 507.
[30] Ibid., p. 63.
[31] Ibid., p. 18.
[32] Ibid., p. 507.
[33] Ibid., p. 380.
[34] Ibid., p. 381.

was no longer possible. Art was understood no longer as *mimesis*, the imitation of reality. Now art was conceived of as an expression of making that which is hidden manifest while simultaneously realizing it.[35] With the passing of a commonly shared cosmic vision, the artist then was burdened with articulating his or her own world of references. It is here where we can begin to look more closely at what Taylor means by the expressivist turn.

There is now no longer an esoteric order available to all upon inspection, this is especially true for the artist. What replaced the older "interlocking order" was the Romantic vision of a purpose of life coursing through nature. "Against the classical stress on rationalism, tradition and formal harmony, the Romantics affirmed the rights of the individual, of the imagination and of feeling."[36] Truth is to be found within the self. In other words, "If the order of things is not esoterically there to be imitated by art, then it must be explored and made manifest through the development of a new language which can bring something at first esoteric and not fully seen to manifestation."[37] Or to quote Shelly: "The poet strips the veil of familiarity from the world, and lays bare the naked and sleeping beauty which is the spirit of its forms."[38] The expressivist turn as found in Romanticism is in effect the idea of an inner voice. It is in and through this inner voice that we discover what is true, good, and beautiful within ourselves. To have a proper moral stance towards nature or the cosmos is to have access to this inner voice. Because nature is an intrinsic source, an inner voice, we cannot hope to find outside of ourselves models on which to pattern our lives. The search must be within. Given the fact that art no longer imitates reality and that there is no fixed ontic order, the romantic artist must articulate an original vision of the cosmos. Thus, someone like Hölderlin in his poem *Homecoming* no longer plays on an established gamut of references. He "makes us aware of something through nature for which there are as yet no adequate words. The poems themselves are finding the words for us . . . something is defined and created as well as manifested."[39] Implicit in this expressivist turn is the belief that each of us has an original path to follow, unique to us and because of this uniqueness we are obligated to live up to this originality.

This notion of creating something which manifests or reveals what is hidden is associated with the power of the creative imagination. The work

---

[35] Ibid., p. 377.
[36] Ibid., p. 368.
[37] Ibid., p. 380.
[38] Ibid., p. 378.
[39] Ibid., p. 381.

of art that results from this creative play of the imagination is a "revelation which at the same time defines and completes what it makes manifest."[40] It is an epiphany, a "locus of a manifestation which brings us into the presence of something which is otherwise inaccessible, and which is of the highest moral or spiritual significance."[41]

With the rise of modern art, however, there is again a certain shift in aesthetic vision. Art is still to be understood as epiphanic and non-imitative, but not in the same way as in the Romantic understanding. For the Romantics, the work of art is an expression of an inner voice, through which the creative imagination portrays something significant that would otherwise be hidden. The difference between the two forms of epiphany is that the expressivism of the Romantics sought to reveal "a greater spiritual reality or significance shining through the work of art itself."[42] Conversely, twentieth-century art shifts the locus of epiphany from something to which the work of art ultimately points, to the interior of the work itself. In other words, both Romanticism and modern art see art as a vehicle which manifests something morally significant that is hidden; what this significance is cannot be separated from the work of art. Yet for modern art, and here poetry is the best example, the epiphanic power of the work depends upon a break from ordinary discourse. For example, Wordsworth shows us the spiritual significance of things, whether people or places. But he does so using ordinary discourse, realistic descriptions. Through the power of ordinary and familiar discourse he opens us to something rich and more meaningful. Conversely, Mallarmé "speaks of the poet as ceding the initiative to words and allowing the poem to be structured by their inherent, interacting forces. . . . The poetic image is opaque, non-referential. Here the Romantic contrast between the symbolic and referential has intensified into the attempt to achieve epiphany by deranging reference. . . . "[43]

Most of the great Romantic artists, particularly poets, saw "themselves as articulating something greater than themselves: the world, nature, being, the word of God,"[44] which had been lost or had become debased. Now the moderns can certainly conceive of a "spiritual order of correspondences." But what they cannot conceive is having access to such an order without its being mediated through an epiphany brought about by the creative imagi-

---

[40] Ibid., p. 419.
[41] Ibid.
[42] Ibid.
[43] Ibid., p. 426.
[44] Ibid., p. 427.

nation.[45] Modern art and particularly poetry must be understood in terms of articulating what is real, but this articulation cannot be separated from the means (medium) of expressing that vision. This is the modern nature of epiphany.

Now it is clear that a certain subjectivism is inseparable from modern epiphanies because we cannot ignore the fact that an epiphany is mediated through the imagination. It is always a personal vision that is being articulated. But this does not necessarily imply the insidiousness of self-centeredness. This is not to deny that the very make-up of an artistic epiphany "can make it difficult to say just what is being celebrated: the deep recesses beyond or below the subject, or the subject's uncanny powers."[46] Because of this danger, guarding against or overcoming the trap of self-centeredness should be one of the primary moral and aesthetic projects of art.

Just as with the Romantics, inwardness is a significant part of the sensibility of modern art, but there is also something de-centering about the work. It is not reducible to merely the personal, even though our access to it can only be from within that framework. For Taylor, it is Rilke who best exhibits this de-centering and inwardness. For example, in the ninth *Duino Elegy* Rilke lays before us the task of transfiguring the world.

> And these Things,
> which live by perishing, know you are praising them; transient,
> they look to us for deliverance: us, the most transient of all.
> They want us to change them, utterly, in our invisible heart,
> within—oh endlessly—within us! Whoever we may be at last.
>
> Earth, isn't this what you want: to arise within us,
> *invisible*? Isn't it your dream
> to be wholly invisible someday?[47]

Someone like Rilke has taken us beyond mere subjective expressivism. He has placed us squarely within the primary issue of the nature of epiphany. It is not just a matter of *praxis* that is at stake. It is, rather, the "*transaction between ourselves and the world.*"[48]

In short, the epiphanic is genuinely mysterious, and it possibly contains the key to what it is to be human. The notion of epiphany identifies those sources which serve as the locus for one's authentic ideal. Epiphanies man-

[45] Ibid., pp. 427–28.

[46] Ibid., p. 429.

[47] *The Selected Poetry of Rainer Maria Rilke*, trans. Stephen Mitchell (New York: Vintage Books, 1984), pp. 201–02, quoted in Taylor, *Sources of the Self*, p. 482.

[48] Taylor, *Sources of the Self*, p. 482 (italics added).

ifest that which is other. They issue from the call of the "world," understood as an independent matrix of meaning, from which our idea of what it means to be authentic is revealed. An epiphany discloses something beyond us that makes demands upon us, or calls us. Again, for Taylor it is in modern art and poetry that we find the clearest expression of epiphanic events. Modern art and poetry seem to respect modernity's concern for the subject, without falling into an aberrant subjectivism. Modern art is at once inward, yet it involves the de-centering of the subject.[49] For Taylor, epiphany works against the idea that the *telos* of human existence is merely an inwardly generated activity tied to nothing beyond itself. An epiphany frees us from the debased mechanistic world, and it brings "to light the spiritual reality behind natural and uncorrupted human feelings."[50] An epiphanic event functions as a source of authenticity because it enables us to see the good, and thereby empowers us to orient our life in terms of this ideal.[51] In other words, epiphanic art completes us "through expressions which reveal and define"[52] what it means for us to be authentic.

"Since the era of the great chain of being and the publicly established order of references," nothing in "the domain of mythology, metaphysics, or theology stands in this fashion as publicly available background today."[53] Nonetheless, epiphanic art at some level encompasses some commonly held belief positions, but its stance towards these positions is much more tentative than in the old public creeds.[54] It is also what we can call their personal index that makes them a different kind of thing. "We know that the poet, if he is serious, is pointing to something—God, the tradition—which he believes to be there for all of us. But we also know that he can only give it to us refracted through his own sensibility. We cannot just detach the nugget of transcendent truth; it is inseparably imbedded in the work. . . ."[55] In the following poetic excerpts from Wallace Stevens, we find what Taylor sees as one of the clearest examples of the melding of the transcendent and the subjective:

---

[49] Ibid., p. 456.

[50] Ibid., p. 454.

[51] Ibid.

[52] Ibid., p. 476.

[53] Ibid., p. 491.

[54] For example, Taylor points to Rilke's image of the angel. There may be some general belief concerning this particular image, but as Taylor makes clear, Rilke is articulating a vision of angelic being that is radically outside of any traditional understanding.

[55] Ibid., p. 492.

> The world about us would be desolate except for the world within us.
>
> The major poetic idea in the world is and always has been the idea of God.
>
> After one has abandoned a belief in God, poetry is the essence which takes its place as life's redemption.[56]

We now live in an age where a common order of public meaning is no longer accessible. The only way we can understand the order in which we find ourselves is through a "personal resonance." Self-realization through an ideal of authenticity presupposes that some things are important beyond the self, "that there are some goods or purposes the furthering of which has significance for us and which hence can provide the significance of fulfilling life's needs."[57] Reading Rilke places us in a situation in which our desire for self-realization stands in relationship to something outside ourselves calling to us, making demands upon us. Rilke shows us that "the world is not simply an ensemble of objects for our use, but makes a further claim on us. . . . And this demand, though connected with what we are as language beings is not simply one of self-fulfillment. It emanates from the world."[58]

Each of us has an aspiration to wholeness that is only possible to the degree that we commit ourselves to something beyond our own desires. Epiphanic art discloses to us how self-determining freedom and our desire to be authentic depends on something noble, courageous, etc., that calls to us independent of our will. True freedom, therefore, means choosing between alternatives that either move us to a greater realization of our ideal of authenticity, or imprison us in a world that perpetuates a life of baseness, cowardice. Or in the words of Rilke:

> But because truly being here is so much; because everything here apparently needs us, this fleeting world, which in some strange way keeps calling to us. Us, the most fleeting of all. Once for each thing. Just once; no more. And we too, Just once. And never again. But to have been this once, completely, even if only once: to have been at one with the earth, seems beyond undoing.[59]

---

[56] Ibid., p. 493.

[57] Ibid., p. 507.

[58] Ibid., p. 513.

[59] The Ninth *Duino Elegy*, in *The Selected Poetry of Rainer Maria Rilke*, p. 199.

The Good, the Bad, and the Ugly: The Aesthetic in Moral Imagination

James P. Mesa

Maritain holds that methodological purposes determine the formal distinctions made and the vocabulary used in the analysis of different modes of knowing. For instance, the Augustinian concern with the person's concrete modes of activity divides the soul's higher faculties into three: *understanding*, *memory*, and *will*, while the Thomistic speculative and ontological analysis has a bipartite division of *intellect* and *will*.[1] He also maintains that we can distinguish a moral science midway between moral philosophy and prudence, a *practically practical science*. This science is not to be confused with prudence but is more closely tied to contingent circumstances than moral philosophy. It is the work of the practitioners of moral science—the moralist or moral counselor, and the psychologist insofar as the work is directed to the development and implementation of moral pedagogy.[2] There need be no conflict in different modes of analysis so long as the truth of the various distinctions made and relations identified are grounded in the complex unity of the object analyzed. In this paper no new distinctions are introduced, rather it is suggested that the division of imagination into the moral and aesthetic need not be strictly held for purposes of a practically practical science.

The fusion of the moral and the aesthetic is common in art, literature, and conversion experiences. A recent example that suits my purpose is taken from Bernard Nathanson's *The Hand of God*. There is nothing especially distinctive about what he relates, but rather its poignancy stems from

---

[1] Jacques Maritain, *The Degrees of Knowledge*, trans. Gerald B. Phelan, in *The Collected Works of Jacques Maritain* (Notre Dame, Indiana: University of Notre Dame Press, 1995), vol. 7, p. 35.

[2] Ibid. pp. 333–35.

the complex and incommunicable nature of concrete moral judgments. Formerly a leading proponent and practitioner of abortion, this autobiography
provides an account of his twenty-five year journey from "that *revolting* ex-
travaganza playing itself out on the bodies of pregnant women and their
slaughtered babies,"[3] to his acceptance of the value of unborn life. In that
moving passage, Nathanson expresses his dismay at his former uncritical
acceptance of the "shoddy" practices of "shabby" practitioners and wonders why these scenes of the "grotesque" did not lead to his recognition of
their evil. He reflects on Aquinas's teaching that Being is apprehended as
Oneness, Truth, Goodness, and Beauty. "The apprehension of each aspect
helps us uncover the others so that we can apprehend, for instance, the
Truth by its Goodness, or the Good by its Beauty. Why could we not trian-
gulate from the *shoddy* to the shameful?"[4]

A first response to his question is the perennially troubling Augustinian
one: you could not apprehend the evil and the ugliness because there was
nothing to apprehend; evil is the absence of Goodness, and ugliness the absence of Beauty. This is in keeping with a metaphysical account of the problem, but Nathanson's question is more psychological. It is, as Nathanson
recognizes, a matter of *seeing*. A move in his medical career, perhaps
through the hand of God, afforded him the opportunity to see through a new
lens of technology. "Ultrasound opened up a new world. For the first time,
we could *really see* the human fetus, measure it, observe it, watch it, and indeed bond with it and love it. I began to do that."[5] But these fuzzy, two di-
mensional electronic images are unlike the very real, solid, three dimen-
sional fetuses that he studied in anatomy and handled in the abortions that he
performed. It could not have been that he was previously unaware of what
he now saw on the ultrasound screen. Why did he now see?

In groping for some explanation of his prior blindness, he recalls an example of skewed vision from the history of medicine. Vigegano, a fifteenth-
century anatomist, who published the first illustrated anatomical text, "per-
sisted in drawing things he could not possibly have seen." He drew the liver
as having five lobes when it should have been obvious to him that it had
only four. "Vigegano did this because he viewed the human body—open as
it was to his objective and disinterested search—through the *lens* of
Galen,"[6] and ignored what was presented through the lenses of his own

---

[3] Bernard Nathanson, *The Hand of God* (Chicago: H. Regnery, 1996), p. 106
(italics added).

[4] Ibid. (italics added).

[5] Ibid., p. 125 (italics added).

[6] Ibid., pp. 145–46 (italics added).

eyes. It is as if both he and Galen had been mesmerized. There is some factor in concrete judgment that distorts seeing.

The emphasis on seeing is the central matter here. Thomism acknowledges that the senses are the foundation of all knowledge. But knowledge is not something, it is someone, *someone-who-knows*; there is no science without the scientist. Knowledge is, as Newman says, a "personal possession" and thus will be shaped by factors in the individual's history. These subjective conditions do not entail relativism. It is a personal possession of a *shared reality* that the human mind did not create. Knowledge is true by being obedient, by being personally submissive to that reality. "Creation is what it is by its correspondence with the 'standard' [of] God's creative knowledge; human cognition is true by its correspondence with the 'standard' of objective reality."[7] But human knowledge is always limited to being the *what-I-have-seen-so-far.*

The role of the senses, as Nathanson recognizes, is crucial to morality. The practical intellect's field of action is in the sensory encounter with a real and objective world in concrete, individual, and unrepeatable conditions. It is here that we have the incommunicable work of prudence and art, where the conditions of truth are relative to the person. In morality, the intellect is operating in the heat and stress of the situation and not in the comfortable cool of a conversation in a friendly pub.

> Man as conscious being, as intelligence making use of the senses, is at the center of the order of the *moral Good*, and it is with respect to him, with respect to the senses informed with intelligence that *acts* are divided into *good and evil*. This distinction between *the good and evil* applies *in all situations for action known* to the senses, but is relative to man as conscious center.[8]

A major difficulty in contemporary thought has been the reduction of moral judgment and rational action to propositional thinking. A rational act is considered to be one that has been preceded by a proper chain of principled propositions. As Ryle warned, our separately mentioning the "thinking" and the "being anxious" in a mother's *thinking anxiously* about her ill child, does not two distinct realities make. The anxious mother does not first dispassionately consider the truth of her child's illness and then, recognizing its rational appropriateness, generate feelings of anxiety and start

---

[7] Josef Pieper, *The Four Cardinal Virtues* (Notre Dame, Indiana: University of Notre Dame Press, 1980), p. 7.

[8] This passage is an alteration of a passage from Maritain. The changes are in italics. See note 21 for the correct quotation.

acting in an anxious fashion. "She thinks anxiously, and she is anxious enough to keep thinking about her child, and to think little of other things, unless as things connected with and *colored* by her child's danger."[9] Just as "separately mentionable characteristics" of a facial expression are not entities or parts distinct from it, so the anxiety is not a distinct entity apart from the thinking.

Neither Maritain nor the Thomistic tradition can be charged with reducing moral judgment to mere propositional thinking. This is notable in accounts of the moral virtues and the role of practical reason. Prudence's truth is the reality of the person in the existential situation. It is a *properly-discerning-reason-in-action*; it is "nothing less than the directing cognition of reality."[10] This requires the proper fusion of reason, appetites, and senses. The simultaneously *properly-oriented-appetites-here-and-now* provide focus for correct discernment of the situation and impetus for proper action. This is in marked contrast with the imprudent person who "sees the arena in which he must act through the *lens* of his disordered appetites."[11] The prudent person knows the arena of action by a special, concrete sensory knowledge which Aquinas calls the *vis cogitativa* and *ratio particularis*. In some unspecified way it partakes of reason, but nonetheless this sensory knowledge is so essential that by comparison the knowledge provided by the study of moral philosophy (or even practically practical moral science) is of little importance.[12]

The observations of the educational psychologist William Kilpatrick dovetail with the moral philosophy of Aquinas and Maritain. "It is nice to think that moral progress is the result of better reasoning, but it is naïve to ignore the role of moral imagination in our moral life. . . . The more abstract our ethic, the less power it has to move us."[13] Kilpatrick follows Edmund Burke and Russell Kirk in the employment of the notion of "moral imagination" and in so doing offers an additional insight into the working relationship between the senses and practical reason. Kirk described moral imagination as "that power of ethical *perception* which strides beyond the

[9] Gilbert Ryle, "A Rational Animal," in *Reason*, eds. R. F. Dearden, P. H. Hirst, and R. S. Peters (London: Routledge and Kegan Paul, 1975), p. 133 (italics added).

[10] Pieper, *The Four Cardinal Virtues*, p. 25.

[11] Ralph McInerny, *Art and Prudence* (Notre Dame, Indiana: University of Notre Dame Press, 1988), p. 106 (italics added).

[12] Cf. *Summa Theologiae* I, q. 78, a. 4; *De Veritate* q. 10, a. 1; *In II Ethicorum*, lect. 4, 284–85.

[13] William Kilpatrick, *Why Johnny Can't Tell Right from Wrong* (New York: Simon and Schuster, 1992), p. 142.

barriers of private experience and momentary events."[14] Kilpatrick adds a rich and multi-faceted description of "moral imagination" in contrast with what he calls "idyllic imagination." One could say that the contrast is between good moral imagination which is subordinate to *recta ratio* and bad moral imagination which is not. Idyllic imagination confuses fantasy with reality, pleasure with the good, and feelings with knowledge. Moral imagination is grounded in an already established reality and recognizes that there are goals that ought to be realized regardless of feelings. The moral imagination "recognizes that reality does not conform itself to our wishes but often thwarts them."[15]

Moral imagination is not explicitly in Aquinas, but it is in effect described by Maritain. He maintains that preceding conceptual and logical expression, reason and intelligence function in "a quasi biological way, as the 'form' of psychic activities and in an unconscious or preconscious manner."[16] In this originating prereflective state, reason "is enveloped, immersed, unconscious, embodied in images and inseparable from sensory experience, . . . [and] operates like a *pattern* for our inclinations."[17]

I would suggest that this pattern, this melange, is grounded in and held together by the power of memory, the receptacle of images, which is so necessary for such elemental matters as preserving personal identity and familiarity with our surroundings. We would have no continuity of conscious life without the presence of memory. And indeed, Aquinas identifies memory as one of the auxiliary virtues required for prudence. "[We] need experience to discover what is true in the majority of cases . . . experience is the result of many memories . . . prudence requires the memory of many things." Could we not say that experience requires a "pattern" of memories? And further, Aquinas's observations coincide with the call to shape imagination early in life because we "remember better what we saw when we were children. . . . [I]mpressions easily slip from the mind, unless they be tied as it were to some corporeal image, because human knowledge has a greater hold on sensible objects."[18]

It is reasonable to suggest that there is a connection between Kilpatrick's

---

[14] Russell Kirk, "The Perversity of Recent Fiction: Reflections on the Moral Imagination," in *Reclaiming a Patrimony: A Collection of Lectures by Russell Kirk* (Washington, D.C.: The Heritage Foundation, 1982), pp. 46–47 (italics added).

[15] Kilpatrick, *Why Johnny Can't Tell Right from Wrong*, pp. 208–09.

[16] Jacques Maritain, *An Introduction to the Basic Problems of Moral Philosophy*, trans. Cornelia N. Borgerhoff (Albany, New York: Magi Books, 1990), p. 53.

[17] Ibid., p. 56 (italics added).

[18] *Summa Theologiae* II–II, q. 49, a. 1, resp. and ad 2.

imagination, Aquinas's memory and Maritain's quasi-biologically operating intelligence. I would have us consider moral imagination as that undirected, spontaneous portion of memory as it relates to the goods known through inclination and the senses. The moral imagination is not preconscious but *conconscious*[19] intelligence shaping, texturing experience and seeing, but is itself unnoticed. It is a *pattern* which serves as a kind of concrete universal through which possible goods available to choice are recognized and made more or less interesting to the person. It highlights familiar features congruent with the person's full range of experiences.

Kilpatrick urges a return to more traditional pedagogy which presents moral values to children through lessons in history and literature. Memory is crowded not only with objects given in direct sense experience but also with those vivid images induced through the arts. Powerful signs and images in drama, storytelling, and literature provide a kind of dramatic rehearsal for the moral life. Such memories operating in imagination either aid or hinder moral life. The proper development of moral imagination enables the child to locate his acts within the context of traditions which have ennobled human dignity. In contrast with teaching which is abstract and propositional, this type of education promotes a *visualization* of the moral life: "[T]here is a connection between virtue and *vision*. One has to *see* correctly before one can act correctly."[20] The moral imagination is an essential element in the proper focusing of the moral lens and it is important that its adjustment begin early in life.

What follows aims to link the aesthetic to moral imagination through memory. I begin with the correct quotation from Maritain which earlier had been changed to apply to the knowledge of good and evil.

> Man as conscious being, as intelligence making use of the senses, is at the center of the order of the aesthetic, of Beauty, and it is with respect to him, with respect to the senses informed with intelligence that things are divided into beautiful and ugly. This distinction between the beautiful and the ugly applies to all things *perceptible to the senses*, but is relative to man as conscious center.[21]

The liberties taken in the earlier altered quotation are meant to highlight the similarity of the role of the senses in both moral and aesthetic experience. It is granted that in Aquinas there is a clear distinction between the good and

---

[19] I use this expression with a reverential bow to Maritain's use of *connaturality*.

[20] Kilpatrick, *Why Johnny Can't Tell Right from Wrong*, p. 133 (italics added).

[21] Maritain, *An Introduction to the Basic Problems of Moral Philosophy*, pp. 69–70 (italics added).

the beautiful with respect to appetite. "For the good, being what all things want, is that in which the appetite comes to rest; whereas the beautiful is that in which the appetite comes to rest through contemplation or knowledge."[22] The good pleases appetite whereas the beautiful gives pleasure in the mere apprehension. The apprehension of the moral good requires the assistance of properly ordered appetites but beauty does not. The apprehension of the beautiful is *"a kind of seeing or looking which is mediated by the senses but is of an intellectually cognitive order, and which is both disinterested and yet produces a kind of pleasure."*[23]

But what is known through the senses may be retained in the memory; thus the object, its beauty, and the pleasure experienced are preserved even if only vaguely. We then speak of an aesthetic imagination. But there are not two separate memories, two separate imaginations. Maritain was fond of diagrams, and in an interesting one he represents the powers of the soul as superimposed inverted cones sharing a common peak. Imagination penetrates into intellect and the external senses penetrate into both.[24] There are three distinguishable powers but only one soul. There is but one intellect with all its activities. And there is but one imagination. Aesthetic and moral knowledge, aesthetic and moral imagination are of different orders, but they are unified in the one knower. There is only the one person who remembers and who is presented with images from the distinct orders of goodness and beauty. It may be possible to separate distinct imaginations in philosophical analysis, but the separation cannot be realized in fact in the living person. And it is in this realm of the concrete living person that a practically practical moral science takes interest. In this science, the division of aesthetic and moral imagination may be usefully blurred.

Kilpatrick draws attention to the practical role that aesthetic experiences play in moral life. "Nietzsche saw that most people are convinced not by arguments but by aesthetics—by the force of beauty. Or more accurately, by what they perceive to be beautiful."[25] And this may be reinforced with Maritain's claim that our aesthetic delight is greater when the effects of human intelligence are present. The bay of Rio de Janerio is indeed beautiful he admits, but he is moved more profoundly by "the port of Marseilles, as it opens its man-managed secretive basins one after another, in a forest

[22] *Summa Theologiae* I–II, q. 27, a. 1, ad 3.

[23] Umberto Eco, *The Aesthetics of Thomas Aquinas*, trans. Hugh Bredin (Cambridge, Massachusetts: Harvard University, 1988), p. 58 (italics in the original).

[24] Jacques Maritain, *Creative Intuition in Art and Poetry* (New York: New American Library, 1954), p. 77.

[25] Kilpatrick, *Why Johnny Can't Tell Right from Wrong*, p. 165.

of masts, cranes, lights, and memories!"[26] This may seem odd at first, but it is consistent with Maritain's focus on the person who is the conscious center of the aesthetic. In perceiving beauty, intelligence recognizes its own indispensable role in the aesthetic experience, and in some fashion comes face to face with itself. "The intelligence delights in the beautiful because in the beautiful it finds itself again and recognizes itself, and makes contact with its own light."[27] We could add with any appropriate distinctions that the same would apply to moral experience.

Given the vagaries of memory, when aesthetic and moral images entwine the patterning power of the imagination is enhanced. The influence of imagination is most noticeable in children. In the child the imagination is preoccupied with visions of a future self. The child's interest is not set upon the distinctions given in moral philosophy to guide his life, but upon visions of himself as an actor set in a world yet to be lived. "The question for a child . . . is not do I want to be good but who do I want to be like?"[28]

What we want to be like is ourselves, but that knowledge is given to us incompletely, piecemeal, gradually over time. The desire, however, demands to be satisfied now, and it is here that the role of images/models enters, especially for the young. An image of a "man-managed" and aesthetically appealing life-style is the Sirens' call. The sturdy steed, shining armor, dazzling sword, the accoutrements of honor, courage, and chastity compete with Mercedes, diplomas, gleaming surgical steel, masking ambition, greed, coldness of heart; hot wheels, logo-ed jacket, blazing automatic pistols bound to group loyalty, power, and lust. "Style is of great importance in gang life."[29] Style, the beautiful life and its beautiful people, trump the arguments. Mother Teresa and Nietzsche knew this. But she was the wiser because when she said, "Do something beautiful for God," the beauty was always to be united to the separately distinguishable moral good.

[26] Maritain, *Creative Intuition in Art and Poetry*, pp. 6–7.

[27] Maritain, *Art and Scholasticism*, trans. Joseph W. Evans (New York: Charles Scribner's Sons, 1962), p. 25.

[28] Kilpatrick, *Why Johnny Can't Tell Right from Wrong*, p. 167. Kilpatrick is quoting Bruno Bettelheim, *The Uses of Enchantment* (New York: Vintage Books, 1977), p. 10.

[29] Kilpatrick, *Why Johnny Can't Tell Right from Wrong*, p. 169.

Is Medicine Today Still An Art?
Maritain and Managed Care

John F. Morris

Is Medicine today still an Art? Within the tradition of Hippocrates, Medicine was clearly considered an Art. And, throughout its history, Medicine has been known primarily as the "healing Art." However, the rapid technological explosion in America which has been gaining force for the last several decades, has just as rapidly been changing our contemporary understanding of Medicine. This boom of technological development and scientific discovery has contributed to the notion, stemming from the dualism of Descartes, that Medicine is not an Art—but a pure Science.

I will grant that we still hear Medicine referred to as an Art. However, claims made today that Medicine is an Art seem to be taken less and less seriously. As Carleton Chapman noted in the 1980s in his book, *Physicians, Law and Ethics*, "[S]ome physicians view medicine solely as bioscience."[1] Chapman goes on to estimate that this "scientific" mentality has dominated the statements of the American Medical Association for at least the last one hundred years. Furthermore, there is little doubt that Medicine is practiced in an increasingly "scientific" manner. Blood tests, CAT-scans, and MRIs are the technological tools that give evidence to the Science of Medicine. When the "Art" of Medicine *is* discussed, it is largely limited to those specific areas within Medicine which remain inexact, such as fighting Cancer and HIV\AIDS. It would seem that only in the face of such difficult problems, where scientific technology is not yet able to make much progress nor offer much hope, can Medicine be spoken of as an Art.

My contention is that the continued erosion of our understanding of

---

[1] Carleton Chapman, *Physicians, Law and Ethics* (New York: New York University Press, 1984), p. 147.

Medicine as an Art is problematic, and indeed dangerous, for contemporary health care. Considering Medicine purely as a Science fails to capture the essence of Medicine, and as a result blurs the true goals of Medicine. I am concerned with the impact that such "blurring" will have on the future of Medicine and medical practice in America.

And so, my purpose in this paper is threefold. I will first explore some basic reasons why one might consider Medicine today exclusively as a Science. Second, I will explain why this purely "scientific" understanding of Medicine is inaccurate, using the work of Jacques Maritain, *Art and Scholasticism*. I find in Maritain a clear argument for maintaining that Medicine is indeed an Art—albeit, an Art that relies heavily upon Science. The argument rests upon the distinction within the scholastic understanding of Art between Making and Doing. Regardless of how much Science and technology it may employ, Medicine always involves a "making"—the making of health—and so, Medicine must be an Art. Finally, I will discuss the importance of maintaining the distinction between Art and Science by exploring the impact that the "scientific" understanding of Medicine is having upon the changing delivery of health care in America. Managed Care Health Plans, such as HMOs and PPOs, are quickly becoming the preferred method of delivering medical care in this country. However, part of the "management" of these plans involves the establishment of predetermined courses of treatment for specific diagnoses. Attempts by physicians and therapists on the plan to deviate from prescribed treatment options are discouraged by various methods—including the use of financial incentives to remain within plan guidelines. It is my contention that such practices in Managed Care are built upon a "scientific" understanding of Medicine, and that these practices threaten to completely erode the Art of Medicine. If this erosion occurs, we will no longer have true Medicine, but will be left only with a "healing" Science.

MEDICINE, THE SCIENCE

It would be a surprising occurrence to find someone who would seriously question whether or not modern Medicine is "scientific." But if such an individual were to come forth, it would apparently be a simple task to convince him otherwise. Even the simplest doctor's office bears the mark of Science—from the traditional blood pressure cuff which reminds us of the science of blood circulation, to the bright red "bio-medical-hazardous-waste" containers mounted on the wall which testify to more recent discoveries in the cutting edge sciences of virology and bacteriology. A visit to any specialist will usually provide us with the opportunity to view anything from charts of muscles and bones to enlarged images of the various viruses a person may have the misfortune of being infected with. Since there is usually ample time to study such charts in the examining room, a diligent patient can obtain a mini-medical education—especially if you have one of those diseases that we can describe and illustrate on a poster, but which unfortunately takes several trips to various practitioners to actually find and diagnose. These comments may sound flippant, but they are actually quite serious. Anyone facing a major health problem in America today will quickly be engulfed by Science—and the effect, for any who have been through it, can simply be overwhelming.

In recent years, medical practitioners have begun to realize that the presence of too many scientific tools can become unsettling to patients. And so, the more elegant doctor's offices and hospitals have learned to disguise and hide the "Science" in nice cupboards and behind curtains. In September of 1997, my wife and I were ushered into a beautifully decorated and quite comfortable hospital room—complete with cable-TV—in which our son Kevin was to be born. When the "time" had finally arrived, cupboards were opened, curtains pulled back, and monitors, surgical trays, and various other items were extracted. Within five minutes (I actually timed this because I was still timing my wife's contractions which at this point were only two minutes apart—so in less than three contractions), the hotel-like room had been converted into an operating room—complete with the traditional operating room, "overhead light" which was mechanically lowered from behind a panel in the ceiling with the touch of a button. Even when you cannot see it—the Science is there.

In addition to these common ways of understanding Medicine as "scientific," a proper philosophical understanding of the nature of Art provides evidence for why Medicine, and so many other Arts similar to it, are often considered to be Sciences. In *Art and Scholasticism*, Maritain explains that an essential property of Art is that it proceeds in certain and determined methods.[2] This can be illustrated most easily in the mechanical arts:

> The art of the shipbuilder or of the clockmaker has for its proper end something invariable and universal, determined by reason: to permit man to travel on water or to tell time—the thing-to-be-made, ship or clock, being itself but a matter to be formed according to that end. And

---

[2] Jacques Maritain, *Art and Scholasticism and The Frontiers of Poetry*, trans. Joseph W. Evans (New York: Charles Scribner's Sons, 1962), p. 18.

for that there are fixed rules, likewise determined by reason, in keeping
with the end and with a certain set of conditions.[3]

Maritain immediately adds that in certain cases, "where the matter of the
art is particularly contingent and imperfect, as in Medicine . . . ,"[4] contingent rules and a kind of prudence are needed for the Art to operate effectively. Nevertheless, Maritain emphasizes that Art, at all levels, derives its
power and force most properly from its fixed and universal rules. Thus,
Maritain offers this conclusion: "That is why the arts are at the same time
practical sciences, such as Medicine and Surgery. . . ."[5] Any activity, then,
that qualifies as an Art will have a certain method of being applied. In the
case of Medicine, the application of the Art requires the use of various Sciences. Sciences such as anatomy, neurology, and pharmacology (to name
but a few) establish the fixed rules of Medicine. And so, the fact that Medicine does have a specific method of being applied that is largely scientific
further confuses the view of Medicine as an Art, since we commonly consider Art today to be the result of free expression, which runs in opposition
to fixed rules of application.

There is also a powerful philosophical basis from which Medicine has
been viewed as a Science—a basis that Pellegrino and Thomasma attribute
to the thought of René Descartes.[6] Descartes argues that there is a "real distinction" between the mind and the body. The mind, for Descartes, is the
realm of the "psyche" or "personality." The body, in sharp contrast, is simply a machine—a machine which can be disassembled, repaired, and re-
assembled like any other machine.[7] By mechanizing the human body in this
fashion, Cartesian dualism suggests that Medicine, if properly applied,
should be able to attain mathematical certainty. This Cartesian mentality
has had a lasting influence on the understanding of Medicine, an influence
which O'Rourke and Brodeur point out has created an "aura of infallibility
surrounding it."[8]

To summarize, there are a number of important reasons why Medicine is

---

[3] Ibid., pp. 18–19.

[4] Ibid., p. 19.

[5] Ibid.

[6] Edmund Pellegrino and David Thomasma, *A Philosophical Basis of Medical Practice* (New York: Oxford University Press, 1981), p. 99.

[7] René Descartes, *The Passions of the Soul*, Articles V–XI, in *A Discourse on Method and Other Works*, trans. E. S. Haldane and G. R. T. Ross (New York: Washington Square Press, Inc., 1965), pp. 239–43.

[8] Kevin O'Rourke, O.P. and Dennis Brodeur, *Medical Ethics: Common Ground for Understanding* (St. Louis, Missouri: Catholic Health Association of the United States, 1989), p. 6.

considered a Science. First, Medicine is deeply embedded with the tools of Science and technology. Second, Medicine, as all Arts, proceeds according to fixed and universal rules derived from various Sciences. Finally, the powerful mechanistic view of the human body which has overtaken many aspects of Medicine due to the influence of Cartesian dualism, has helped solidify the modern understanding of Medicine as being purely a Science.

MEDICINE, THE ART

The previous discussion suggests both common ideas and philosophical notions for recognizing Medicine as a Science. Is Medicine therefore a Science, and only an "Art" in some figurative or metaphorical sense? It is my contention that, whereas we can understand why Medicine may be considered purely "scientific," it is *not* in fact a Science. To demonstrate this conclusion, it will be instructive to examine more closely Maritain's *Art and Scholasticism*. In his brief first chapter, Maritain explains that while the Scholastics do not provide us with a specific treatment on the Philosophy of Art, we can "find in them a very profound theory of Art."[9]

The scholastic conception of Art is founded upon the distinction between the speculative intellect and the practical intellect.[10] Science, in its pure form, is the pursuit of knowledge for the sake of knowledge, and so it falls within the realm of the speculative intellect. This is as true of the Medical sciences as of any other, for the virologist and the bacteriologist are primarily pursuing knowledge for the sake of knowledge. Medicine, on the other hand, employs knowledge—scientific knowledge, as well as other types of knowledge—for the sake of action, and so it falls within the realm of the practical intellect.

Now, as Maritain explains, "[T]he practical order itself is divided into two entirely distinct spheres, which the ancients call the sphere of Doing . . . and the sphere of Making. . . ."[11] Doing, "consists in *the free use, precisely as free, of our faculties. . . .*"[12] Since Doing involves the exercise of our free will, it is also identified with the realm of Morality.[13] Making is defined as "*productive action*, considered not with regard to the use which we therein make of our freedom, but merely *with regard to the thing produced* or with regard to the work taken in itself."[14] Since Making is not di-

[9] Maritain, *Art and Scholasticism*, p. 3.
[10] Ibid., p. 7.
[11] Ibid.
[12] Ibid.
[13] Ibid., p. 8.
[14] Ibid.

rected toward the end of human life, but rather to a work produced, it is identified with "the sphere of Art, in the most universal sense of this word."[15]

Medicine, then, must be an Art, for the goal of Medicine—in its simplest expression—is the Making of health. The subject matter is a human being—ill, diseased, vulnerable, and sick—and the work produced is the restoration of wellness and wholeness. Science may require a certain amount of "creativity" in its investigation of problems, but no Science, purely on its own, is productive.

But the case is different for Art:

> The work of art has been thought before being made, it has been kneaded and prepared, formed, brooded over, ripened in a mind before passing into matter. And in matter it will always retain the color and savor of the spirit. Its *formal* element, what constitutes it in its species and makes it what it is, is its being ruled by the intellect.[16]

Consider for a moment how well this description of Art applies to the field of Medicine. A student of surgery, family medicine, physical therapy, or psychiatry will "think" many years before touching "matter." The student's knowledge is "kneaded and prepared" through a long and rigorous course of academic study. Then, as the formal academic training draws to a close, the knowledge gained by the student is "formed" and "brooded over" through clinical experiences, until the "thought" finally "ripens" in the mind of each student. Only after this process of formation is a student of Medicine finally ready to pass the knowledge acquired into the matter of patients—real people like you and me.

Recognizing that Medicine is an Art can also help to correct the common misunderstanding that the medical practitioner with the most scientific knowledge, and subsequent technological skill that accompanies scientific study, also makes the best healer. In an early scene from the film, *The Doctor*, the lead character—a cardiac surgeon played by William Hurt—comes upon his group of residents engaged in a debate about the value of caring for patients. The Doctor's advice: "If you have thirty seconds before some guy bleeds out, I'd hope that you cut straight and cared less."[17] The Doctor here expresses a clear preference for technical skill over compassion and caring. The irony of the film is that when confronted with his own impor-

---

[15] Ibid.

[16] Ibid., p. 9.

[17] From the feature film, "The Doctor," produced by Touchstone Pictures, 1991, screenplay by Robert Caswell. Based on the book by Dr. Edward E. Rosenbaum originally titled, *A Taste of My Own Medicine* (New York: Ballantine Books, 1988).

tant surgery to remove a tumor from his vocal chords, the Doctor asks the more "caring" of two surgeons to perform the delicate operation. A proper conception of Art helps clarify the misunderstanding related to technical skill. Maritain explains what was recognized by the Scholastics:

> Manual skill is no part of art; it is but a material and extrinsic condition of it. The labor through which the zither player acquires nimbleness of finger does not increase his art as such nor does it engender any special art; it simply removes a physical impediment to the exercise of the art . . . art stands entirely on the side of mind.[18]

Now we must be clear to point out that "technical skill" does not perfectly equate with "scientific" knowledge. Yet, the two are clearly associated with one another in the field of Medicine—the best technical experts receive the most research money, and in turn become the scientific experts in their discipline. But the Art of Medicine demands more than technical expertise. To think otherwise is to reduce Medicine to the purely mechanistic view of Descartes. The best technician may be the most efficient person to fix a machine—but how often does technical expertise fail the surgeon, the nurse, and the therapist? How often has a physician's technical expertise failed you or a loved one?

Undoubtedly, few would want to dispense with those practitioners of Medicine who are recognized as the experts in their fields, nor does the scholastic understanding of Art suggest any such thing. Yet, this view of Art reminds us in a powerful manner that in the restoration of health, technical ability plays but a small role, and one that is largely limited to physiological needs—not psychological, social, or spiritual needs. In practicing the Art of Medicine, then, the doctor ought indeed to "cut straight"—but he ought also to "care *more*" for the patient—the subject upon which the work of health is being imprinted.

A final point regarding Art. Recognizing that Medicine is an Art, and not a Science, helps us remember that the Making of health results in *Beauty*. Have you ever considered the *beauty* that is revealed in the person who has been restored to health and wholeness? The successful transplantation of a kidney, or the removal of a tumor, is not simply a "scientific" achievement. In the deepest possible sense, these are works of *beauty*. Although Maritain focuses primarily on the fine arts in his discussion of *beauty*, he notes that *beauty* is not exclusive to the fine arts. In a footnote, Maritain explains:

> To tell the truth the division of the arts into the arts of the beautiful (the fine arts) and the useful arts, however important it may be in other re-

[18] Maritain, *Art and Scholasticism*, p. 14.

spects, is not what the logicians call an "essential" division; it is taken from the end pursued, and the same art can very well pursue utility and beauty at one and the same time. Such is, above all, the case with architecture.[19]

I would maintain that Medicine is an even more appropriate example than architecture. Painting and sculpture, for all their *beauty*, can only capture in the barest sense the *beauty* of a living human person. Any claims that can be made regarding the *beauty* that human artists can effect in the fine arts can be applied more perfectly to the Making of health in the humblest human creature, and to the *beauty* that results from human wellness and wholeness.

To justify my claim regarding the *beauty* of health, consider the following passage from Maritain's discussion of *beauty*:

> Every sensible beauty implies, it is true, a certain delight of the eye itself or of the ear or the imagination: but there is beauty only if the intelligence also takes delight in some way. . . . Moreover, the higher the level of man's culture, the more spiritual becomes the brilliance of the form that delights him.[20]

Maritain acknowledges that at the most basic level of our understanding of *beauty*, we focus upon what is pleasant to sense and imagination. This notion is what is usually referred to as "physical *beauty*." In society today, the quest for, and admiration of, physical *beauty* is quite prevalent. We need only think of *People Magazine's* yearly tribute to the "50 Most Beautiful People" to find evidence of this fascination within human culture for physical *beauty*. And yet, true *beauty* must also delight the intelligence, Maritain tells us. The implication is that what delights the eye may not, in fact, be *beautiful*. To emphasize this point, Maritain adds the reference to the deeper meanings of *beauty* that will be found the higher the level of culture we attain. To my knowledge, *People Magazine* has never named a dying person laying on a street in Calcutta to its list of "*beautiful*" people. Yet, Mother Teresa reminded us that even the least of our brothers and sisters are still *beautiful*. Whose opinion should we value more—*People Magazine* or Mother Teresa? In this same vein, a walk through any hospital's Intensive Care Unit, or even just a regular floor, will more than likely not produce any candidates for *People Magazine* to select from for the year 2000. But I would contend that every living person restored to some level of health and wholeness possesses an immeasurable "spiritual brilliance" and *beauty*.

---

[19] Ibid, p. 158, n. 40.
[20] Ibid., p. 25.

And so, Maritain's explication of the scholastic conception of Art corrects the misconceptions that Medicine is purely "scientific," and enriches our understanding of Medicine by showing us that it is an Art. My discussion in this section has not attempted to explore the fine distinctions that arise in considering Medicine as "scientific" or simply as "technical." I have been considering all such views as being derivative, in some part, to the view that Medicine is purely a Science. Nor should this discussion be taken as anything akin to a full-fledged Philosophy of Medicine, such as can be found in the important works of Dr. Edmund Pellegrino. My purpose has been to draw upon the thought of Maritain, and his instructive discussion of the scholastic conception of Art, to argue that Medicine is, in fact, an Art. Calling Medicine an Art, then, is not simply a matter of semantics, or hair-splitting, or even a case of distaste for the use of the term Science. Philosophically speaking, Medicine is an Art.

ART VS. SCIENCE: DOES IT REALLY MATTER?
THE PROBLEM OF MANAGED CARE

Even if one were to grant everything that has been suggested thus far, the question might still arise, does the distinction between Art and Science in respect to Medicine really matter? What harm can come from considering Medicine a Science? I made the claim at the outset that considering Medicine purely as a Science was problematic—even dangerous—for contemporary health care. In this section, I will offer justification for this claim.

In recent years, there has been a growing concern expressed within American health care that Medicine is not being practiced in a "scientific" enough manner, despite the continued improvement of the scientific tools of Medicine. In an article on Managed Care which appeared in a 1994 issue of *Bioethics Forum*, Judith Wilson Ross explains this concern:

> It is seldom acknowledged that the vast amount of health care research in the United States has not led to improved medical outcomes for us as a society. . . . The U.S. wars on disease have been fought zealously, but with much less success than is generally acknowledged. The media do not tell us that only twenty percent of the medical treatment we use is supported by good scientific evidence of benefit, let alone more benefit than burden or risk. The wide practice variations that exist in the U.S. and other countries suggest a "system" of health care that is seriously lacking in science or rationality. . . .[21]

[21] Judith Wilson Ross, "Ethical Decision Making in Managed Care Environments," *Bioethics Forum* (Fall 1994), p. 25.

The cause, Ross goes on to suggest, of the wide variations in treatment across the country is the over-utilization of medical technology by physicians. The proposed solution is to move from the fee-for-service model of health care delivery (which has been particularly vulnerable to over-utilization) to Managed Care Health Plans.

A shared interest of all Managed Care Organizations is to standardize treatment protocols. This is evidenced in a special report produced in 1995 by the Midwest Bioethics Center of Kansas City, Missouri, which examined ethical issues related to Managed Care. The task force in charge of the project stated the following as one of their basic assumptions:

> Managed care plans determine when care is medically necessary and, thus, will be covered. This process assumes agreed-upon standards of care by which to measure appropriateness of care. There is only minimal consensus about the standards used to make these determinations by managed care plans at this time.[22]

Later in its report, the task force recognized that one of the many responsibilities of Managed Care Plans was to:

> Choose to cover or exclude treatments on the basis of appropriate clinical information, developed through objective measures of clinical research, where available, and cost effectiveness.[23]

The task force further charged Managed Care Plans to "engage in standardized data collection and reporting activities."[24] The call for better data collection to help develop standards of care, which can be applied throughout our system of health care, is recognized as one of the potential advantages of Managed Care—it will be able to reduce medical costs in part by reducing variations (and therefore, wastefulness) in the practice of Medicine. And so, Managed Care appears to be good both for individual consumers and for our health care system. It is no wonder, then, that Managed Care is becoming the dominant model of health care delivery in this country. But what is most noteworthy for our purposes is that the goals of Managed Care are achieved through a process that ultimately attempts to make medical practice more "scientific." Underlying this request for a more scientific ap-

---

[22] Joan D. Biblo, Myra J. Christopher, Linda Johnson, and Robert Lyman Potter, "Ethical Issues in Managed Care: Guidelines for Clinicians and Recommendations to Accrediting Organizations," *Bioethics Forum*, Special Supplement (Spring 1995), p. MC 11.

[23] Ibid., p. MC 16.

[24] Ibid.

plication of health care is the mistaken view that Medicine is purely a Science. Since Managed Care Plans represent the driving force behind the current pressure for more Science in Medicine, I will specifically address the practices of Managed Care in regard to standardizing health care and why they are problematic.

First, a key supposition behind the attempt to standardize treatment practices is that over-utilization is the result of *poor* Science. It is argued that standardizing treatment will decrease the wasteful application of scientific knowledge and medical technology, thereby improving the Science of Medicine. The problem with such a supposition is that it objectifies the patient, and distances the patient from the physician and other health care practitioners. In an insightful article published in the *Hastings Center Report* titled, "The Sorcerer's Broom: Medicine's Rampant Technology," Eric J. Cassell discusses this problem:

> Technological methods move the evidence employed in diagnosis away from the patient and reduce the impact of the patient's particularity on the physician. In using them, physicians mistakenly believe they can reduce uncertainty by changing the patient's problem to one for which there is a technological answer. They then reduce the problem from that of the patient to that of an organ or body part for which a technology exists, and they distance themselves from the patient by employing that technology.[25]

The danger with this approach is that scientific knowledge and medical technology are allowed to assume a role that is more important than the patient who is sick. Cassell notes later in his article that what results is a situation in which a patient's claim of pain and suffering is not believed until there is some scientific evidence to support the claim.[26] This problem will only be worsened through the standardization of treatment practices, which would direct a physician to provide treatment X for disease Y based on national, "scientifically" collected data—regardless of the patient's individuality and particularity. The subjective experience of each patient will become less relevant in health care the more that diagnostic tests and treatments become standardized, which in turn will inhibit the Art of Medicine.

A second problem associated with the attempt by Managed Care Organizations to standardize treatment practices involves the manner in which such standardization is enforced. As already noted, a basic assumption of

---

[25] Eric J. Cassell, "The Sorcerer's Broom: Medicine's Rampant Technology," *Hastings Center Report* 23, no. 6 (November–December 1993), p. 36.
[26] Ibid., p. 38.

Managed Care is that the plan—not the individual practitioners—sets the standards of care for the plan members. In fact, the key method for standardization of care, and thus for the more "scientific" approach to Medicine, is central control of medical treatment through pre-authorization requirements. It is well recognized that this is one of Managed Care's most difficult challenges, as Judith Wilson Ross points out in her article, "Managed Care: How Did We Get Here?" She writes:

> Managed Care's task is to provide less that is better. The fact that so much unnecessary treatment is provided in our system makes that task somewhat easier. The fact that there are so many inefficiencies built into the system will make that task somewhat easier. What will be hard is getting professionals to accept outside authority (even if only in the form of other physicians in the form of guidelines or authorizations for referrals) when making treatment decisions; getting physicians to understand themselves as members of teams rather than as commanding individuals (captains of the ship, lone professionals with sole responsibility). . . .[27]

I find this attitude regarding physicians troubling. I suppose that if Medicine truly were a Science, there would be no cause for alarm in a physician consulting an outside authority—there is no harm in one mathematician consulting another; the data, the numbers, the formulae are all identical. But patients are not identical. Two kidneys, in two different people, are not completely alike. Nor does it seem possible for an attending physician to convey to an outside authority, on a phone in some office, all of the nuances drawn from the personal encounter between physician and patient. In short, these practices of Managed Care Organizations which demand an outside consultation to review physician decisions regarding a patient whom the "authority" has never examined or spoken with, do violence to the patient-practitioner relationship that lies at the very heart of Medicine. Such practices also seem to comprise an assault upon the personal integrity of medical practitioners—the very thought that an administrator examining data on paper should have the final say regarding an attending physician or therapist's patient ought to be offensive and insulting to the medical profession. And so, these practices will further erode the Art of Medicine by often tying the hands of the practitioners involved in the actual healing process.

These are but two of the problems that have arisen from the mistaken view that Medicine is a Science. The practices of Managed Care provide an important illustration of the problems of "scientific" Medicine, and deserve

---

[27] Judith Wilson Ross, "Managed Care: How Did We Get Here?" *Ethical Currents* 346 (Summer 1996), p. 3.

careful attention since Managed Care is on the rise in this country. But the future of health care will be no better than its past if it rests upon mistaken notions of Medicine. To be fair, most supporters of Managed Care recognize that the movement towards more "scientific" standards of treatment needs to be balanced with caring and compassion at all levels of the Managed Care Organization. While this recommendation for balance is commendable, I contend that it is not enough. I do not mean to suggest that I think Medicine needs to be divorced from Science and technology—if that would even be possible. Nor do I intend to condemn the theory behind Managed Care and its effort to preserve our health care system. I would concur with the late Cardinal Bernardin that Managed Care can contribute significantly to the Common Good, provided we "manage" Managed Care itself.[28] My focus has been upon specific practices of Managed Care Organizations to control costs, which I contend are founded upon an understanding that Medicine is a Science. Establishing systems of Managed Care, or any model of health care delivery, that truly benefit the Common Good will require that we be clear about both what Medicine is, and what Medicine is not.

CONCLUSION

What we need to be mindful of, then, is that Medicine is an Art. Furthermore, the Art of Medicine is applied to individual patients who cannot be objectified or reduced to a mechanistic entity. This point is well illustrated by O'Rourke and Brodeur in a chapter of their medical ethics text titled, "Medicine: Not An Exact Science":

> [I]ndividuals are different in their physiological makeup. Thus, medical diagnosis and prognosis are not precise and exact. . . . The response of each patient to therapy cannot be predicted scientifically. The "art of medicine" is operative when science is applied to the individual. Because the physician assumes the responsibility to help the patient strive for health, medicine is a unique form of art because its "work" is a better human being, not merely an improved inanimate object.[29]

What we risk losing by maintaining the view that Medicine is only a Science is this unique "work" of Medicine—a better human being. The at-

[28] Joseph Cardinal Bernardin, "Managing Managed Care," An Address to the International Association of Catholic Medical Schools, 13 May 1996 (St. Louis, Missouri: Catholic Health Association of the United States).

[29] Kevin O'Rourke, O.P. and Dennis Brodeur, *Medical Ethics: Common Ground for Understanding*, p. 4.

tempts to turn Medicine into more of a Science through the efforts to standardize treatment practices are problematic and dangerous, because they do violence to both patients and practitioners. To counteract these problems, and to avoid further dangers, we must reaffirm today that Medicine still is an Art.

Art: A "Political" Good?

Jeanne M. Heffernan

Art is said to do many things. Among others, it gives visual expression to religious sentiment; complements the power of prose in telling a story; records the likeness of family members, preserving memories for the benefit of posterity; and generates passionate response to issues of public moment. Hence, churches commission sculptors, publishers hire illustrators, the wealthy retain portraitists, and governments employ propagandists. In each of these instances, the artistic product serves a distinct function designated by the sponsor; the monetary value of the work corresponds to its perceived utility. While some consider patrons of sculpture or oil portraits frivolous, most would grant that if churches or blue-bloods or the *nouveau riche* "get something out of it," they are free to spend their money as they wish.

It is less clear for most of us to recognize the public, indeed political, value of the fine arts; hence the fierce debate concerning its public funding. I shall argue that Jacques Maritain's aesthetic and political work sheds light on this difficult problem. It helps us to think analytically and comprehensively about three questions: What is art? What is politics? Is art a political good? Examining these issues serves a twofold purpose, theoretical and practical: to clarify the nature of the creative process and product and the relationship of these to social and political life so as to, in turn, clarify one of the more divisive issues of the day, public funding of the arts. In the course of his aesthetic and political work, I shall argue, Maritain provides the foundation for a contemporary Thomistic defense of publicly funded art far superior to the conventional defense offered by social liberals. Current varieties of liberalism, found on Capitol Hill no less than in the academy, are ill-equipped to answer such questions; their philosophical assumptions and related methods are, as Aristotle would say, inadequate to the object under study.[1] Liberal theories of politics, like John Rawls's, attempt to bracket comprehensive views of the good from their accounts of justice: justice, so the argument goes, is political not metaphysical. The persistence of value conflicts in the public square reveals the inadequacy of this conception. How does a polity adjudicate claims about the *value* of public art without a conception of the good life and the place of beauty within it? Unlike political liberalism, Maritain's aesthetic and political theory offers an alternative account of the nature of art and politics which yields not only a persuasive theoretical response to the question: Is art a political good? but provides practical guidance as to its concrete resolution.

WHAT IS ART?

In *Art and Scholasticism*, an early attempt to fashion a Thomistic aesthetics,[2] Maritain admits the difficulty of the task. St. Thomas and the Schoolmen did not articulate a philosophy of art *per se*. Thus, a Thomistic aesthetics must be synthetic, building upon the Scholastics' more general reflections concerning *techne* on the one hand and beauty on the other. Such a difficult synthetic enterprise has its benefits, for it reveals the narrowness of modern aesthetics which considers "under art the Fine Arts only and deal[s] with the beautiful only as it concerns art."[3] Maritain, by contrast, attempts a more holistic analysis by situating the fine arts within the larger category of art and identifying beauty as a transcendental reflected in works of art, but finally independent of them.

In laying out this holistic analysis, Maritain employs the scholastic distinction between the speculative and practical intellect. Art, broadly understood to include "useful" and "fine" art, pertains to the latter; it is a habit of the practical intellect which operates for the good of the work done specifically by sharpening the intellective faculty—hence the resemblance between the virtue of art and the virtues of the speculative intellect.[4] Yet, art sharpens the intellective faculty not for the sake of contemplation, but with a view to *doing*—hence its kinship to prudence. Yet, where prudence concerns the doing of moral actions, art concerns productive action or *making*. Maritain distinguishes the two thus:

[1] Aristotle, *Nicomachean Ethics* I.2, trans. Terence Irwin (Indianapolis, Indiana: Hackett, 1985).

[2] Throughout this essay I shall treat the term aesthetics rather specifically to refer to the beauty associated with the fine arts.

[3] Jacques Maritain, *Art and Scholasticism* (New York: Charles Scribner's Sons, 1937), p. 2.

[4] For a later statement of this relationship see Maritain's *Creative Intuition in Art and Poetry* (New York: Pantheon, 1953), pp. 44–52.

> Art, therefore, keeping Making straight and not Action, remains out-
> side the line of human conduct, with an end, rules, and values, which
> are not those of the man, but of the work to be produced. That work is
> everything for art,—one law only governs it—the exigencies and the
> good of the work.[5]

Art *qua habitus* is a "state of possession" or inner strength which perfects man in his making; it is "the proper virtue of working reason."[6]

This orientation of the virtue toward the object made holds for the useful and fine arts. The useful arts pertain to the satisfaction of a particular material need; the art of shipbuilding, for instance, pertains to the need for safe transportation. The fine arts, by contrast, pertain to the satisfaction of a spiritual need, the need for beauty. As Maritain insists, the intellect "strives to engender," to release its spiritual creativity in creating beauty. "The need of the intellect to manifest externally what is grasped within itself, in creative intuition, and to manifest it in beauty, is simply the essential thing in the fine arts,"[7] a category inclusive of poetry, music, and the visual arts. In each of these categories, the object produced is the material expression of the artist's creative intuition, that is to say, of his participation in beauty which yields an utterly singular work made for itself.

Inasmuch as the artist engages in contemplative contact with the transcendental beauty and discovers "a new way in which the brilliance of form can be made to shine upon matter,"[8] artistic activity can be described as "disinterested." It is personal and subjective, as the artist is an individual subject giving expression to his unique creative intuition, but the object of the intuition is transcendent. Maritain helpfully underscores this point, for it challenges the dominant twentieth-century view of art and artist. A culture like ours that has inherited a vulgarized Romantic notion of the artist as expressive individual and has lost an earlier notion of art as window into the transcendent and artist as mediator of the transcendent has special need of this corrective. Art, properly understood and practiced, is not the expression of a grandiose, neurotic ego.[9] On the contrary, Maritain insists, artistic

[5] Maritain, *Art and Scholasticism*, p. 7.

[6] Maritain, *Creative Intuition in Art and Poetry*, p. 49. Maritain later distinguishes the roles of "working" and "intuitive" reason in the fine arts. Intuitive reason, "in the obscure and high regions which are near the center of the soul," plays the major role: it yields the creative intuition. Working reason directs the artist in the material realization of the intuition (p. 63).

[7] Maritain, *Creative Intuition in Art and Poetry*, p. 56.

[8] Maritain, *Art and Scholasticism*, p. 46.

[9] This fact takes on special significance as it bears on the debate over public funding of the arts. If art is merely self-expressive, designed to gratify the personal preoccupations of the artist, then it would be difficult to see its intersubjective

creation "engages the human self in its deepest recesses—but in no way for the sake of the human Ego."[10] The artist reveals himself in his work, it is true, but he does more than this. As Maritain puts it, "The very engagement of the artist's Self in [artistic or] poetic activity, the very revelation of the artist's Self in his work, together with the revelation of the particular secret he has obscurely grasped in things, are for the sake of the work."[11] In this way, the artist is profoundly other-regarding, indeed open to the divine; he detects the spiritual "in the things of sense."[12] Maritain describes the artistic subject thus: "Poetry's *I* is the substantial depth of the living and loving subjectivity, it is a subject as act, marked with the diaphaneity and expansiveness proper to the operations of the spirit. Poetry's *I* resembles in this regard the *I* of the Saint, and likewise, although in other fashions, it is a subject which gives."[13]

Yet, it must be added, the artistic *I* has a particular way of giving that may pose difficulties for social life. As Maritain emphasizes, art is in a sense an "inhuman virtue," inasmuch as it strains after "a gratuitously creative activity, entirely absorbed in its own mystery and its own laws of operation, refusing to subordinate itself either to the interests of man or to the evocation of what already exists."[14] The temptation of art is to abstraction—to an isolation from everything not peculiar to its own laws and object—leaving the artist and his work "separate and exempt from, and perfectly disinterested in regard to man and things."[15] But art depends upon man and things, for it subsists in man and is nourished by things; the artist *qua* man thinks and acts as well as makes. He must take account of his moral and intellectual life and the state of his environment, lest his art destroy the very conditions of its own existence. If able to claim the whole man as its own, art will devour "the substance of the artist and the passions, the desires, the speculative and moral virtues which make it truly human, it [will also] devour its own subject of inherence."[16] Though in some sense an

---

meaning and, hence, social value. If, on the other hand, art has a transcendent object—that is at least in principle accessible to all men *qua* spiritual—then artistic activity can have an intersubjective value.

[10] Jacques Maritain, *The Responsibility of the Artist* (New York: Charles Scribner's Sons, 1960), p. 51.

[11] Ibid., p. 52.

[12] Jacques Maritain, "The Frontiers of Poetry," in *Art and Scholasticism* (New York: Charles Scribner's Sons, 1937), p. 96.

[13] Maritain, *The Responsibility of the Artist*, p. 51.

[14] Maritain, "The Frontiers of Poetry," p. 92.

[15] Ibid., p. 91.

[16] Ibid., p. 92.

"inhuman virtue," art is also *for* man, if not like prudence, then at least with respect to the way in which it is used. Art will decay if it rejects the constraints of prudence or the "service of our common culture, which requires it to make itself intelligible, accessible, open, to shoulder the burden of the inheritance of reason and wisdom by which we live."[17] The tension between art and prudence and the requirements of cultural longevity is perennial and comes to the fore when the topics of art and politics are brought into connection.

WHAT IS POLITICS?

Like his account of art, Maritain offers a comprehensive account of politics. Though Maritain freely uses the language of rights, his conception of politics owes more to the Aristotelian-Thomistic tradition than it does to classical liberalism. This becomes evident in Maritain's robust conception of the common good and the body politic.

In *Man and the State*, Maritain challenges narrow conceptions of politics that view the political task as essentially negative, that is, as the protection of individuals against the encroachment of others, reduce politics to interest group competition, and deny the existence of a common good. While acknowledging the importance of the negative function of political order, Maritain assigns politics a range of positive responsibilities, which suggests an understanding of politics as broadly conceived.

For Maritain, the body politic or political society exists not merely for the satisfaction of individual material needs, nor for the technical mastery of nature, nor yet for the domination of some over others. Rather, the *telos* of political society is:

> to procure the common good of the multitude, in such a manner that each concrete person, not only in a privileged class but throughout the whole mass, may truly reach that measure of independence which is proper to civilized life and which is ensured alike by the economic guarantes of work and property, political rights, civil virtues, and the cultivation of the mind.[18]

This rich conception of political society harkens to Aristotle and Aquinas for whom the moral and intellectual development of man is the end of politics. As Aristotle argues and Aquinas affirms, the city exists not for the sake of mere subsistence, but for the sake of the *good* life. The relationship

[17] Ibid.
[18] Jacques Maritain, *Man and the State* (Chicago: The University of Chicago Press, 1951), p. 54.

among citizens, therefore, differs from that of simple allies. Whereas in an alliance the parties concern themselves with mutual protection or economic benefit, in a city, the citizens concern themselves with the character of their fellows; indeed, the first task of legislation is the cultivation of virtue.[19] Maritain, working within a Thomistic framework of natural and supernatural ends, glosses Aristotle in this way: human life, he maintains, has an absolute ultimate end, namely, the "transcendent, eternal common good," which is the object of individual ethics, but it also has a "subordinate ultimate end," namely, the "terrestrial common good."[20] This is the direct object of political ethics. Politics considers (but does not have principal responsibility for) the absolute ultimate end as it carries out its own specific charge: "the good of the rational nature in its temporal achievement."[21] But insofar as man is a unity of body, mind, and spirit, the good of his rational nature temporally considered includes not only basic material goods, but also the cultivation of moral and intellectual virtues. Considered in this light, the political task may be viewed as essentially a task of "civilization and culture," of "making faith, righteousness, wisdom and beauty ends of civilization."[22]

IS ART A POLITICAL GOOD?

Maritain's rich understanding of art and politics holds promise for bringing the two into contact. They need not be alien, one from the other. Rather, if one regards art as a virtue of the practical intellect and politics as the ordering of communal life with a view to moral and intellectual excellence, then it seems reasonable to speak of art as a political good, that is, a good to be achieved in political association. Indeed, Maritain affirms, "Art is a fundamental necessity in the human state,"[23] for it plays a critical role in the life of virtue: art teaches man the pleasures of the spirit and frees him from a preoccupation with the pleasures of the flesh. Art points beyond itself to what is nobler than itself, and insofar as it does this, "it prepares the human race for contemplation."[24] Art thus bears on our temporal and eter-

---

[19] Aristotle, *The Politics* I.2.1094b8, III.9.1117b5–8, ed. Ernest Barker (London: Oxford University Press, 1958); *Nicomachean Ethics* II.2.1103b, X.9.1180a10.

[20] See also *Integral Humanism* in *Integral Humanism, Freedom in the Modern World, and A Letter on Independence*, ed. Otto Bird (Notre Dame, Indiana: University of Notre Dame Press, 1996), pp. 286–89.

[21] Maritain, *Man and the State*, p. 62.

[22] John U. Nef, *The United States and Civilization* (Chicago: The University of Chicago Press, 1942), p. 252 quoted in Maritain, *Man and the State*, p. 55.

[23] Maritain, *Art and Scholasticism*, p. 80.

[24] Ibid.

nal good. With respect to the former, the cultivation of art is, at least in principle, a proper concern of public life—even of the legislator.[25]

As Maritain anticipated, the achievement of this good in political society is difficult. Art and prudence reign in their own spheres, and the claims of each may conflict, or appear to conflict; the artist and the prudent man may be at odds, each with a tenable position. Maritain's description of such tension is apropos of our cultural situation in which the battle lines are often simplistically drawn between self-described "independent artists" and "concerned citizens." The difficulty of this problem, Maritain reminds us, stems from the fact that "by nature Art and Morality are two autonomous worlds, with no direct and intrinsic subordination between them."[26] There is an indirect and extrinsic subordination, however. Each party to the debate forgets one side or the other of this proposition. At the one extreme is the artist who claims complete autonomy for his art, denies any subordination of art to morality, and disregards the extrinsic and indirect subordination that does exist. At the other, is the totalitarian who views artistic activity as wholly subservient to morality (state defined) and under its direct control, thus neglecting the limiting fact that the subordination is only extrinsic and indirect. In short, the two poles disregard the fact that "the realm of Art and the realm of Morality are two autonomous worlds, but within the unity of the human subject."[27]

Several implications concerning the artist and political community follow from this profound observation. An artist is a man before he is an artist. As such, he ought to be disposed toward his comprehensive good, that is, charity, which "when it takes hold of [him], makes the entire subjectivity purer, and, consequently, the creative source purer."[28] If effective, this disposition gives rise to a sense of social responsibility. "If the artist loves truth and loves his fellowmen," Maritain affirms, "anything in the work which might distort the truth or deteriorate the human soul will displease him, and lose for him that delight which beauty affords. Respect for truth

---

[25] Certainly for Plato and Aristotle, who took the arts very seriously, this implication followed. Recall Plato's discussion of music and poetry in Books II and III of the *Republic* and the broad mandate Aristotle ascribes to the legislator in the moral and intellectual development of his citizens (*Nicomachean Ethics* X.9). It is important to note here, though, that Maritain does not reduce political society to the state and its actors; he has a broader conception, including mediating institutions. Thus, to say that art is a political good is to affirm that it is "of the *polis*," which includes but is not coextensive with government.

[26] Maritain, *The Responsibility of the Artist*, p. 22.

[27] Ibid.

[28] Ibid., pp. 60–61.

and for the human soul will become an objective condition or requirement affecting his virtue of art itself. . . ."[29]

The political community, including civil associations and the state, ought in its turn be guided by a true conception of the common good. This requires respect for intelligence and conscience, including artistic conscience. Society may, under certain circumstances, and the state, under rarer circumstances still, legitimately interfere with the free expression of artistic activity. (Such circumstances, like inciting vicious acts, are very limited for Maritain.) But art must not be pressed into the service of the people or regime. It cannot become an instrument of the state without being destroyed; socialist realist art comes to mind. Nor can it serve the public directly without losing its intrinsic focus (namely, the good of the work); various species of "uplifting" art come to mind, from public ad campaigns to religious kitsch. Political society owes to the fine arts respect, interest, attention, and engagement.[30]

RESPECTING THE ARTS

To recognize art as a political good, we ought to practice the duties to the artist Maritain outlines above. This requires difficult prudential judgments. Nowhere is the difficulty of these judgments more apparent than in the case of public funding of the arts. Nevertheless, Maritain's observations on art and the *polis* provide a framework for outlining a contemporary Thomistic defense of public funding for the arts.

Recall that for Maritain the common good entails the fulfillment of positive duties to the artist, as indeed to laborers, teachers, workers of all kinds. Now the essence of political authority is to will the common good formally *and* materially.[31] Enter the role of government in the arts. I would argue that insofar as government has responsibility for the common good materially considered, it ensures at least a tolerable justice in the way of compensation for work. Political authority, in my view, should guarantee that "respect for the arts" has practical meaning, and what we value, we pay for.

The fate of the artist, poet, and composer ought not be left to the vagaries of the market or the beneficence of private philanthropy. Other vital aspects of the common good, such as the technical arts of civil engineering

---

[29] Ibid., p. 60.

[30] Ibid., pp. 85–88.

[31] See Yves R. Simon's *Philosophy of Democratic Government* (Chicago: The University of Chicago Press, 1951) for a penetrating Thomistic analysis of political authority.

receive public compensation—we not only "respect" them, we fund them. Why should not the fine arts, which represent a related excellence of the practical intellect, receive similar recompense? One might object that the fine arts do, in fact, get funded both by government and private contributors. This is true, but the comparatively small sums of public support the arts currently receive are ever endangered by political squabbles and the technocratic designs of educational bureaucrats.[32] What is being established here is the principled case for public funding of the arts which, if compelling, would put the question of the amount and distribution of funding on the table as a serious question of equity.

The distinctly public nature of such funding, as distinguished from private donations, is central, for it attests to the proper end of politics: the cultivation of virtue. It is important that funding of the arts be done in the name of the whole. The arts are "ours." *Our* city has a community band, a symphony orchestra, a museum of fine arts. In an important sense, insofar as these are supported by public funds, we own them, in much the same way that public parks (as opposed to private gardens) signal our communal life and the importance of natural beauty. While public money is typically not the only financial support for these, it is crucial. It protects against the corporate cannibalism of the civic sphere which has degraded public life in our cities. (Imagine if the Cleveland Symphony were owned by Art Modell—it might join the Browns in Baltimore!) Public sponsorship of the arts has another important advantage: it can indirectly limit state power. The arts, as Maritain tells us, reveal to us something of the transcendent; they remind us that we are spiritual, as well as material, beings. They remind us that there is more than the state, that the material realm of taxes and tariffs does not comprehend our existence. The arts, as dissident poets and composers in totalitarian states teach us, speak of the indomitable spirit that will forever resist imperial power. In less dramatic fashion, in a technocratic democracy the arts remind the powers that be that meaning cannot be reduced to utility, that value cannot always be quantified. Art can, in other words, reinforce the distinction between the good of civil life and the absolute human good—a fundamental distinction, as Maritain reminds us:

> The common good of civil life is an ultimate end, but an ultimate end
> in a relative sense and in a certain order, not the absolute ultimate end.

---

[32] For a sobering account of the trend to privilege "computer education" over the fine arts—in some cases phasing out art and music requirements altogether—see "The Computer Delusion" by Todd Oppenheimer in the *Atlantic Monthly* (July 1997).

This common good is lost if it is closed within itself, for, of its very nature, it is intended to foster the higher ends of the human person. The human person's vocation to goods which transcend the political common good is embodied in the essence of the political common good. To ignore these truths is to sin simultaneously against both the human person and the political common good. Thus, even in the natural order, the common good of the body politic implies an intrinsic though indirect ordination to something which transcends it.[33]

For these reasons, there should be public support of the fine arts, from the national to the local level, whether through block grants, the NEA, or fine arts curricula in the public schools. Not only is this within the proper scope of political action, it is a positive duty entailed by the common good.

[33] Maritain, *Man and the State*, p. 149.

The Arts and Authority

Joseph W. Koterski, S.J.

The relation between the arts and civil authority can take various forms. There is, for instance, the strenuous brand of oversight and censorship which Plato proposes in the *Republic* as a way of controlling the arts for the good of the state. While that version of their relationship strikes us as manipulative in the extreme, even the standard policies actually practiced in ancient Athenian democracy raise certain questions. The occasion for the production of Greece's great dramas, for example, was always one of the state-sanctioned religious festivals, and the cultural significance of these plays was not lost on the authorities. Aeschylus's *Eumenides*, for instance, argues dramatically for the innovations then being made in the system for the administration of justice. The agora's ideological battles were often fought out in the theater by such rationalists as Euripides and such traditionalists as Aristophanes.

In chapter four of *Scholasticism and Politics* Jacques Maritain raises the problem of the relation of authority to modern forms of democracy, and his remarks can contribute to our understanding of the relation between authority and the arts, for distorted views of democracy (manifested, for instance, in the persistent confusions of equality with identity) and of freedom (often conceived of as the license to do whatever one wishes, except perhaps to injure others) frequently seem to have paralyzed authority from giving any moral guidance in matters of art. In this area authority has generally been operating on the defensive for generations and in many cases seems to have foresworn any positive, constructive role.

In part the problem comes about from authorities who have forgotten how to be true authorities and who instead understand themselves largely in terms of power. Granted, there have been figures in authority who have grown drunk with their power, but in regard to the arts civil authorities often seem terrified of using even the legitimate power at their disposal (sometimes, but not always, from a wimpish desire to be liked at all costs). The question readily gets cast as a matter of preserving artistic freedom from any external restrictions—it is not just an opposition to censorship in the strict form of a civilly enforced prohibition on production and display, but resentment even against the more restrained form of censorship by way of reasonable critical comment from recognized public authorities. In other quarters, of course, the issue is debated in terms of removing all financial support for the arts by the government. In the one case we find a liberal account of the complete license claimed as vital for artistic creativity, while in the latter it is as if an a-tonal sonata has been played, one that at first sounds conservative but is actually entirely libertarian in design and thus no more likely to inspire and uplift the soul than the abandonment of harmony in Schönberg. In the first case the anarchy (literally, the denial of any principle of authority) is masked by the appearance of "authority" in the form of a governmental force interested largely in the protection of certain privileged realms of "freedom." In the second, the anarchy is quite open ("let pure market forces weed out bad art by eliminating all public subsidies"). But in neither case is authority doing its job, that is, using its legitimate power in a restrained way for the genuine promotion of the common good according to the ethical principles that ought to govern authority in the use of the power at its disposal. Those with responsibility seem content to rest on the laurels of some previous generation's labor at building up humanistic culture. In making this assessment, we must, of course, admit that authority, particularly in the deeply regressive culture in which we presently live, will need to employ great caution in any use of its power, but this admission should not obscure the need for authorities to embark again on the prudent use of both moral suasion[1] and legal remedies in the effort to resume the needed leadership that authority is supposed to provide. After considering the topic of authority in itself, we will turn to Maritain's thoughts on democratic authority and the arts.

THE NATURE OF AUTHORITY

What sort of thing is authority? What sort of quality is it that lets us say that a person is acting with authority in a certain case? There are authorities

---

[1] For example, the statement passed at the annual meeting of the National Council of Catholic Bishops on June 19, 1998, urging Hollywood, for the sake of the common good, to reduce the vast amounts of sensational violence and sexual promiscuity in the production of new movies.

in many different walks of life, perhaps by virtue of the office held or by a factor such as knowledge or experience. Although academic authorities are quick to condemn arguments from authority as the weakest of arguments, their own efforts to be recognized as authorities by their peers do not arise from a desire to be the source of the weakest of arguments but from a latent sense of the real definition of authority: the connection of authority to some truth prior to and superior to the person who is giving witness to that truth and thus able to decide about the correctness of an assertion or the advisability of an action to be taken in light of that truth.

The chief task of authorities is to give witness to truths superior to themselves, truths by which they are to make the decisions they do and by which they are entitled to judge whether and how to use the power at their disposal. It is this intrinsic relation of authority to higher truths that allows authority to command obedience and prevents the decisions of authorities from seeming or being partial and arbitrary, whether or not the contingencies of the actual circumstances warrant the authority actually to provide an explicit justification for the decisions taken. This is the case whether it be the truths of physics on which someone like Stephen Hawking is a recognized authority and a competent judge of theories asserted about certain matters in physics, or the truths embodied in the founding documents of a nation on which a Supreme Court Justice is expected to be a juridical authority. We expect from such an authority a learned opinion, showing the chain of reasoning by which a decision was reached, and not the raw assertion of judicial will. If we disagree with a decision, the burden falls on us to point out the missing or misinterpreted premises, or to identify some faulty step in the logic, and to do it in a form that is reasonable, argued as cogently as we can for all to consider.

The questions in a given field may be subtle and hard to answer, but so they also seemed during the early years of our schooling. When we were in the third grade, our teachers needed to make authoritative judgments about how we handled the addition of fractions and to decide which of our answers were right and which were wrong (even if the answer was counter-intuitive, as when one-third and one-sixth were said to add up to one-half and not one-ninth!). But such authoritative judgments were only possible because there exists a truth with which the authority had experience as a truth to which every judgment handed down must give witness. Where the material authority of the truth of the arguments is not produced for our inspection, we must rely on the formal authority of the teacher, and in this situation there is danger of an arbitrary decision. Yet this very possibility points to the need for genuine authority to be related to some higher truth, and in the best of all possible worlds, to present the case for the decision made in a way that rests the burden entirely on the validity of the arguments.

Authority is something intrinsically relational. Some individuals, of course, seem to bear a kind of personal authority, such that they need only enter a room to become the center of attention and respect; their demeanor and gravity may shift the center of conversation in a particular direction; their cleverness or learning predominates. There is some quality within them that is the ground of the sociological authority they possess. But even here their authority is exhibited by the way others relate to them, and there are any number of cases where what we mean by the authority is not the individual person nor some personal quality but the office held, as when we speak of the authority of the office and mean to indicate the obligation of the governed to obey the governor, regardless of who occupies the office or whether any personal charisma is operating. A scholar with no personal magnetism by which to attract a school of disciples could thus have authority in a certain field (the sociological relation of knowledge), just as an air traffic controller whose personality would make him the kill-joy of a party deserves the complete attention of pilots approaching an airport (the sociological relation of action).

Family structure is one of the most natural cases of an authority-relation. Children need the guidance of parents, and we try to place orphans in the care of foster parents. The authority appropriate to parents comes from the special relation in which they stand to their children. The point is not that parental supervision of dependent children is the central paradigm for understanding authority, as if political authorities were simply *in loco parentis* for the general populace, but simply that the structure of authority is relational. This is true not only of natural associations like a family, but also of voluntary associations like a baseball team, where the manager has authority over who plays and what the strategy is going to be at any point in the game. Success is more likely if someone has special talent for the job, but the holder of the office is in charge regardless.

The relation involved in any sort of authority is a connection between the authority and some higher truth. This is not to say that all parents are natively gifted with knowledge of what it takes to be good parents any more than that all managers are good managers. The actual situation is sadly otherwise. But it is precisely by looking at health that we can discuss disease, and by looking at the example of successful family structure we have the grounds for diagnosing the problems of dysfunctional families where, among other problems, we find individuals unable or unwilling to exercise the authority proper to their parental roles, with unfortunate results for the children. Serious study of the sports page over the years reveals the wisdom of sportswriters in finding fault with managerial style for at least some of the disastrous seasons experienced by teams loaded with star athletes.

This same connection to truths superior to one's own preferences can be seen in other normal experiences of authority-figures, e.g., in the case of a person deemed an expert in some area of professional competence or someone holding public office. Were some experience to disabuse us of the conviction that a given person really had the knowledge claimed, our respect for the learning that constituted his authority would diminish as quickly as the respect for a person in high office found to have abused the power placed at the disposal of the office. Should the official retain the office, fear or even terror might fill the gap, but our moral outrage would make clear that authority had passed over into authoritarianism, and the naked use of raw power, instead of its tempered use in the service of a higher truth, would simply further the confusion between power and authority that gives authority its checkered reputation today.

It is often the case that the truths which authorities must inspect and respect in the proper use of their power are hard to formulate, or too complex to be stated in short compass, but sometimes they can come to be known by experience and common sense. What does it take to be a good parent or a good manager? It is not at all clear that the advice of the "experts" is always or regularly right. Whether we praise or blame the influential brand of nurture championed by the late Dr. Benjamin Spock, the basis for our evaluation will necessarily be the truths about child-rearing, so far as we can figure them out. In fact, the entire sphere of education has seen "experts" constantly challenging traditional authorities within family tradition with their advice about breast-feeding, quality-time, interpersonal skills, the best ways of dealing with siblings and young friends, etc. "By their fruits ye shall know them" applies to authorities in regard to art as much as to any other field of life—a claim that will certainly be doubted by those who see no intrinsic connection between art and truth, but admitted by those alert to truths about beauty and about the role of art and symbol in the formation of human individuals and human community.[2]

---

[2] Consider the following passage from Jacques Maritain's *Art and Scholasticism*, trans. J. F. Scanlan (London: Sheed and Ward, 1930), in a section entitled "Some Reflections upon Religious Art": "Sacred art is in a state of absolute dependence upon theological wisdom. There is manifested in the figures it sets before our eyes something above all our human art, divine Truth itself, the treasure of light purchased for us by the blood of Christ. For this reason chiefly, because the sovereign interests of the Faith are at stake in the matter, the Church exercises its authority and magistracy over sacred art" (p. 144).

THE ETHICS OF AUTHORITY

By observing the intrinsic relation of any authority to some truth outside and above itself, we can lay the foundation for an ethics of authority. Authority is present in all aspects of social life, including art, and the duties of a given authority help to define its purpose. Failure to live up to those duties perverts its effectiveness, either by letting down those it ought to protect with its power from the invasive assertion of other powerful forces, or by dominating those over whom it is supposed to rule for some private interests, often for the benefit of those in authority themselves.

It is precisely to avoid these extremes in politics that we prefer the rule of law to autocratic regimes. The rule of law suggests the predominance of impersonal and reasonable decision-making, whereas an autocratic regime suggests rule by force and decisions by the arbitrary use of power. But rule by law cannot escape making a place for authority, that is, the creation of offices which persons must occupy. Even when power is divided, (for instance, according to the tripartite scheme of the American experiment in democracy), there remains the problem of the power vested in authorities charged separately with making or executing or interpreting the law. The separation of powers has proved a wise strategy for balancing competing forces but should not be mistaken to have eliminated the need for an ethics of authority, for authority is an essential concomitant of liberty, an indispensable principle for holding liberty and order in balance.

The relationships involved in authority regularly involve the communication of something from the bearer of the authority to those subject to the authority. Systems of social life that operate by extensive dependence on persuasion and consent, good will, mutual understanding, or tolerance might seem to be able to do without authority, but deeper observation regularly reveals that it is only their smooth operation which conceals the presence of this other indispensable factor. It is only our distrust of abusive authorities, nurtured by the optimistic experience of living in the peace of a free society, that makes us blind to the vital role of authority. Even in societies blessed with a spirit of generous cooperation and goodwill that try to proceed by consensus whenever possible there is still a need for authority, and not just in societies whose members for one reason or another cannot be trusted to decide for themselves on what the best course of action is.

What is it that authority communicates? Ultimately, what it imparts is decision about how to proceed—a point that needs careful consideration, for it is precisely this prerogative of decision that makes authority suspect. To some extent it is a question of style: will the conduct of authority be authoritative or authoritarian? But to say that it is a difference in style is not enough. Even a gruff administrator can be fair and prudent in decision-making, and pleasant manners are no guarantee of a backbone firm enough to make the tough and even unpopular choices without which a society will flounder. The difference between authoritative and authoritarian conduct is founded, rather, on whether the authority makes decisions in justice and fairness and on the basis of the truths small and large that pertain to the area in question. Paradoxically, it is the intrinsic subordination of any human authority to a standard higher than himself that renders the bearer genuinely authoritative.

The relation between those who bear authority and those subject to it can be disrupted by various imbalances. Yves R. Simon lists possible conflicts in regard to justice, life, truth, and order as likely to give authority the bad name it often has today.[3] If, for instance, the relationship becomes primarily one of privilege and one's position bestows some right to goods and services or to lower prices—resentment will easily spring up, whether toward congressional junkets or *Politburo dachas*, for the fairness of exchange that generally characterizes justice seems to have been violated.

If authorities emit propaganda and expect quiet submission, our sense of truth is offended. The world of art and architecture provides some striking cases—the colossal statues of Mao, Lenin, and the ideal Socialist Worker, for example, or the Fascist buildings of Mussolini's Rome. There is often the temptation simply to believe our own government's version of a conflict, when we feel some need to express an opinion and find that the objective truth about the situation is hard to determine—patriotic songs have been known to abet this goal. On the other hand, cynicism can set in and make us suspect that "authority" is merely a pragmatic tool for pacifying or arousing the masses. If the mere decisiveness of authority becomes an attractively easy solution to the distressing inactivity of prolonged deliberation, the process of social decision may be short-circuited. We expect better of authority.

Likewise, authority can easily seem an obstacle to the exercise of freedom and the achievement of truth vital to the spiritual nature of the human person.[4] Inevitably the decisions of authority come from a source outside

---

[3] Yves R. Simon, *A General Theory of Authority* (Notre Dame, Indiana: University of Notre Dame Press, 1962), pp. 13–22.

[4] Maritain's *Art and Scholasticism* emphasizes the genuine needs of freedom for artistic creativity.

the person, and even if the actions commanded are objectively for the good, the mere fact of being commanded can appear to detract from the spontaneity and voluntariness we cherish as marks of our freedom. The case of teenagers may prove useful here, for with their increasing bodily strength, size, and energy come strong and healthy desires to make their own decisions. Their parents must walk a delicate line of guiding them decisively and leaving them room to act independently, even if they make some painful mistakes. It is not that authority will always look like the care of good parents, subtle but solicitous, but that any authority has to size up what the capacities and maturity-level of those subject to authority are in order to determine the proper mode of its exercise. For if an error in one direction leaves those who ought to be subject to authority untrained in self-control and eventually bored and restless with their energies unharnessed and uncultivated, an error in the opposite direction will keep those no longer children perpetual adolescents, unable to deal maturely with the legitimate decisions of authority and continually alienated by any demand for obedience.

By the vagaries of political history the change undergone by the term "liberalism" reflects this same ambivalence at the level of political life. Classical liberalism emphasized freedom and personal autonomy, and to this end developed a sophisticated theory of private property, a politics focused on personal autonomy and on popular self-determination, and the rhetoric of rights predominant in our political discourse; the claims of artistic license followed suit. But modern liberalism has swung from emphasis upon self-determination to enforced re-distribution and empowerment, highlighting *égalité* instead of *liberté*. The clash of desires here is evident even in the constraints liberals are willing to place upon one's disposable income by high tax rates to pay for social programs. Further, there is the problem with arbitrariness in governmental policies about which choices are to be given legal protection and preference, as evident in the tangled debates over the integration of schools and neighborhoods. Liberalism's attempt to "empower" some will mean for others a change in the type of education available, common living patterns, and the free use of goods and property.

At the root of the confusion about the idea of authority is the view that power alone guarantees the liberty that comes from equality of opportunity. There is considerable truth in the observation that freedom to act presupposes the power to act, but to judge the matter aright requires a profound sense of what freedom is and what it is for. In the mood-cycle of a given culture, there often comes a period of romanticism and the conviction that only activity that flows spontaneously from passion is worthwhile, but this is as debilitating to the spiritual nature of persons as the Stoic distrust of all passion.

THE DIFFERENCE BETWEEN POWER AND AUTHORITY

It may require the threat of a nightstick or even the use of physical force to cow a hardened criminal, and it may simply be fear of apprehension and punishment that keeps some people from breaking the law, but in people of even ordinary virtue respect for the value of social order and the common good testifies to the reality of moral authority distinct from the power of enforcement. The directives of a person whom we credit with moral authority, e.g., a teacher who has won the trust of his students, or an elder whom we consult for advice, have forcefulness not because of physical strength, but because of knowledge or character or proven ability. Where power implies some attempt to master the given, to have control over reality,[5] true authority suggests respect for the truth about things as they are given and the direction of activity in accord with that truth. If we attempt to make any application to art, it will be important to remember that it is not slavish imitation of nature that is crucial, or even right, but respect for the truths about nature, and especially the proper formation of human persons.

When operating according to the ethic here proposed, authority is rooted in discovering the truth about reality. It works by a kind of reverence for the truth about things. To some this will immediately suggest passive submissiveness to the *status quo*, but trying to be respectful of the fact that things have natures no more implies a stodgy reluctance to change than a meddlesome eagerness to tamper and adjust. What is required is the prudence to determine how closely the *status quo* is attending to the nature of things and how much pressure and disruption of the existing order would be required to bring about needed change. In any given sphere there is need for more specific rules on making prudential decisions, but here we need to make the general point that authority has a legitimate but restricted right— and sometimes the duty—to use the power at its disposal, but except for policing the incorrigible, it works best by issuing a call for moral respect, and this will be especially true in the realm of art. All power rests on the ability to bring control into effect, but genuine authority ought to evoke ready obedience, whether those subject to it fully understand or not.

The stress on the freedom vital to artistic creativity makes it important to

[5] Romano Guardini, *Power and Responsibility: A Course of Action for the New Age*, trans. Elinor C. Briefs (Chicago: Henry Regnery, 1961).

treat, if briefly, the relation of authority to liberty. Now, admittedly, etymological explanations go only so far, but here the roots of the word "authority" in *auctor*, author, suggest the need of present authority to look to a past founding event, whether it be jurists returning to the authors of our Constitution or moralists pondering the plans of the author of human nature and of creation as a whole. The root verb *augere* means "to grow, to increase," and what the *auctor* is supposed to do is to make what has been founded grow and increase. In our politics, for instance, it names those responsible for a free people, but this implies a careful cultivation of balance by preserving a genuine but restricted set of liberties, with neither anarchy and license nor the abolition of freedom and total conditioning. Political authority achieves this goal by the legitimate use of certain powers, not by the arbitrary use of the force at its disposal, which is a type of violence. The juridical power vested in a head of state, an individual, or corporate person, exemplifies this distinction, for the formal origin of the power is the legal constitution of the society. But history has shown the persistent need for checks and balances to be written into this constitution to help restrain accumulations of power in actual practice from becoming arbitrary and forgetful of the purpose to which they are ordered.

In contrast to the rule of law, rule by power is limited only by something outside the possessor of the power: another power which it fears. Instead of taking the measure of things, including the nature of human beings and of well-balanced social institutions, power-driven forms of government prefer to fashion things to the measure of their own liking,[6] whether for ideological reasons, say, the Marxist vision of man championed by twentieth-century totalitarianism, or for private aggrandisement, as has been the custom of tyrannies down the ages. Hannah Arendt correlates the difference between desiring to respect and to dominate reality with a difference in temporal focus.[7] Rule by power sees the past as a source of reality it wants to

---

[6] All too often taste in matters of art is reduced to *de gustibus non disputandum est*; while there certainly are legitimate differences in taste, the reduction of the entire question to arbitrary preference is forgetful of the equally important question of good and bad taste. Again, consider the general point about art in this quotation from Maritain's *Art and Scholasticism*: "Religious art is not a thing which can be isolated from art simply, from the general artistic movement of an age: confine it and it becomes corrupted, its expression a dead letter. On the other hand, the art of a period carries with it all the intellectual and spiritual stuff which constitutes the life of a period; and in spite of whatever rare and superior qualities contemporary art may possess in the order of sensibility, virtue, and innovation, the spirituality it conveys is not infrequently poor indeed and sometimes very corrupt" (p. 142).

[7] Hannah Arendt, *Eight Exercises in Political Thought* (New York: Penguin Books, 1977); see especially chapter 3: "What is Authority?"

control, and so looks to the present and future as opportunities where it can exercise domination. By contrast, authority governs present and future by fidelity to the origin, allowing the foundations to set limits to political power. To refuse to give assent to legitimate authority is ultimately to align ourselves with power, and the most radical existentialists end up in the same place as the totalitarian regimes they deplore, since both resort to a philosophy of will in denying the existence of natures and essences, higher truths to which present authority must be subordinate in order to preserve human freedom.

The recognition that there are higher truths which genuine authority must recognize allows us to make a useful distinction between an authority's "decisions" and its "determinations." I take "decisions" to refer to the choices, good or bad, an authority makes by its own power; I use "determinations" to refer to statements an authority makes not by its own choice but in recognition of the way things are. However easy it would be to lump together all the activities of authority under the same heading, it is better to recognize that there is a legitimate sphere of decisions, whose binding force comes precisely from the power at the disposal of authority to choose some course of action for the common good; they are binding wholly and entirely because so decided. On the other hand, there is also a sphere of determinations, whose binding force arises from a source higher than the authority, but which an authority may have to recognize, respect, or make known to those it governs.

DEMOCRATIC AUTHORITY AND THE ARTS

Let us turn finally to some of Maritain's comments on the relation of authority and democracy in *Scholasticism and Politics*.[8] Although he has few direct comments on the specific problem of art and authority, some applications may be attempted. Many of Maritain's views receive additional elucidation in *Man and the State*[9] and in *Integral Humanism*.[10]

In *Scholasticism and Politics*, after contrasting various forms of European democracy with the American version, Maritain turns to a discussion of

[8] Jacques Maritain, *Scholasticism and Politics*, trans. edited by Mortimer J. Adler (New York: Macmillan, 1940; rpt. Garden City, New York: Doubleday Image, 1960), esp. pp. 91–115.

[9] Jacques Maritain, *Man and the State* (Chicago: The University of Chicago Press, 1951), esp. pp. 126–39.

[10] Jacques Maritain, *Integral Humanism: Temporal and Spiritual Problems of a New Christendom*, trans. Joseph W. Evans (Notre Dame, Indiana: University of Notre Dame Press, 1973).

the relation between authority and democracy in terms of political function (that is, how to govern individuals and groups) and passes quickly over other aspects, such as the economic functions of government (the administration of things such as industry and commerce, considered in abstraction from concern with human beings as such). He offers a distinction between authority and power that is relatively standard within the natural law tradition. Authority is "the right to direct and to command, to be listened to or obeyed by others," whereas power is "the force which one can use and with the aid of which one can oblige others to listen or to obey."[11] Such a distinction will seem suspect to post-modern thinkers (especially those who have been made cynical by the corruptions of authority into authoritarianism) and to their Machiavellian forebears, yet it allows Maritain to distinguish the moral authority of a Socrates from the power of a gangster or tyrant. Further, it allows a role for a sound moral authority in the realm of art and what is morally good for culture, over and above (and perhaps also embodied in) the person who bears civil authority and who has the power of the law.

But Maritain's case for the legitimacy of distinguishing between power and authority in no way de-emphasizes the need for concrete connections between power and authority. All authority, insofar as it concerns actual social life, needs to be completed by power; without power an authority risks becoming useless and inefficacious. The proper limit to power comes from the ethics that governs genuine authority.

The general guidance Maritain offers here is that the amount of power legitimately at the discretion of authority should be measured by the duties of the office. As a way to assess what powers an authority has a right to employ, we need to consider what the truth is to which a given level of authority has the duty of being a witness and then to determine what sorts of decisions need to be made by that level of authority. For Maritain in *Scholasticism and Politics*, the dialectical relation between the concepts of power and authority is this: the degree to which authority has power is the extent to which authority has entered the physical order, while the degree to which power gains authority, it has risen into the moral and legal order. To separate them would be to divide force and justice. But authority always remains of superior importance. Gaining power will be important to anyone who wants to act upon the community, but to acquire authority is to gain the right to be followed by the minds and wills of others and the right to exercise power.[12] Granting that there are many matters of taste once we enter

[11] Maritain, *Scholasticism and Politics*, p. 93.
[12] Ibid., p. 94.

the realm of art, and thus considerable liberty, it would be merely anarchical and not truly democratic to deny a place for moral authority here, even if the burden of proof that authority should use its legitimate power in any given case remains on the affirmative. Even in democracies, authority has a role it may not ignore in the formation of the human person, and the cultivation of art and artists will play a role here. For an authority to renege entirely on the question of art would be to abandon its responsibility for this aspect of the formation of the human person.

Using the same distinction between *person* and *individual* which he articulated at great length in *The Person and the Common Good*[13] to resolve some of the problems about the duties and rights of human beings *vis-à-vis* the state, Maritain proposes a comparable distinction between a *democracy of the person* and a *democracy of the individual*. The prevailing ideology in the West has been the ideal of liberal democracy, which Maritain rightly traces back to Rousseau's model for preserving power even while suppressing authority. In Maritain's judgment liberal democracy is really a "masked anarchic democracy."[14] From the principle that each individual is born free, Rousseau deduced that an individual's dignity demands that he should only obey himself. Maritain observes in passing that Rousseau is being equivocal in his use of the word "free," for he uses it to designate both the free will with which each individual is born and a certain condition of existence, a freedom of independence. This equivocation, Maritain feels, is latent in the prevalent theories of liberal democracy, not to mention in the freedom claimed for artistic creativity. In such a social arrangement there would be no fixed principle of order, and even ordinary decision-making will become excessively complex. The expectations of a stable social order needed to live one's daily life, not to mention the need for order which the mercantile class has in order to prosper in business, will lead to a social contract, that is, the devising of some form of association through which everyone, though united with all others in specified respects, will only need to obey himself and remain virtually as free as before.

Whether any particular historical instantiation of liberal democracy explicitly appeals to Rousseau's mystical "General Will," Maritain argues that invariably there will be some comparable device to make it rhetorically clear that for a given liberal democracy, authority properly resides in the whole multitude. Such a device will reinforce the idea that authority not

[13] Jacques Maritain, *The Person and the Common Good*, trans. John J. FitzGerald (Notre Dame, Indiana: University of Notre Dame Press, 1966).

[14] Maritain, *Scholasticism and Politics*, p. 93.

only comes from the multitude but that authority is the "proper and inalienable attribute of the multitude."[15] For Maritain this is "a trick" to avoid granting that genuine authority needs to reside in certain responsible individuals; in fact, he finds it to be a formula that is likely to lead eventually toward totalitarian dictatorship, if only the tyranny of the majority which de Tocqueville feared. He regards it as a "trick" because it permits irresponsible mechanisms to exercise power over men without there being a responsible authority over them. The power of the state becomes, to one degree or another, a mask for anarchy. Such an arrangement, in Maritain's view, is actually a violation of nature, and there is an historical tendency for such accumulations of power to grow ever larger.[16] Despite the constant reassurances given in liberal democratic regimes that the power of the state emanates from the people, the actual arrangements favor the usurpation of power by allegedly neutral states in the vacuum of authority created by irresolvable conflict between comprehensive truth-claims.

The theory of authority which is presupposed by the natural law tradition locates authority in a person or an office defined precisely in terms of giving witness to a truth earlier, higher, or logically prior to the authority itself. Now this is the very feature missing in the ideology of liberal democracies and their attempts at working out a truth-neutral, purely formalistic basis for the regime (for example, in theories of equality that insist on identity blind to all sorts of significant differences as the principle of equality—in art, this means the claimed equality of taste).

In Maritain's analysis of the theoretical basis of liberal democracies, the mass that constitutes the populace is, by the social contract hypothesis, the proper subject of sovereignty, and yet it lacks political discernment in all areas except, perhaps, an instinctual drive to self-preservation, and even here it may well misjudge the proper means to the end. The result, he argues, is that those delegated by the multitude will actually direct the available power, but always under some myth about the sovereign multitude directing itself. In fact, the very category of "sovereignty" (he thinks) is presumably a myth,[17] and yet it may require that we have sufficiently strong theological lenses to see that all sovereignty is divine, and that human authority is only a borrowed commodity. Absent that foundation, liberal democracy can only work if it articulates a suitable myth about the law as the expression of number (majority vote). Gradually, the "mask" of

[15] Ibid., p. 94.
[16] Ibid.
[17] Ibid., p. 95.

power will become the only reality, for it will grow to fill the vacuum. Maritain dryly notes that in societies where the sense of authority has waned, there will be no surprise to find that the circles of opinion and of the press often tend to be in sympathy with certain totalitarian ideologies and aspire to a dictatorship of violence. A study of the history of the half century since Maritain's remarks would readily produce much support for his claim about the curious sympathy of the media and the arts-establishment for the totalitarian regimes of eastern Europe and for violent solutions to situations that are perceived as social problems, despite the evidence of raw manipulation of art and the press by those precise regimes.

Besides the cases of masked anarchy, Maritain also notes various forms of open anarchy that would suppress authority while at the same time suppressing organized power. The purely libertarian programs for the complete defunding of art risk falling into this camp. Maritain traces this vision of utopian democracy back to Proudhon, and one can see it relatively easily in those libertarians today who consider all power and all authority exercised by one individual over another or by the community over its parts as contrary to justice. In this schema there is a tendency to substitute an administration of things for the government of men, so as to put all "producers" on equal footing and to relegate governmental machinery, so far as possible, to a museum. In his more philosophically precise language, Maritain considers this the temptation to seek "a totality without hierarchy," a whole without subordination of any of the parts to the whole.[18] This form misses seeing the necessity of authority in the political community as something inscribed in the very nature of things, for it misses seeing that the political community, insofar as it is a whole, has its own unity, its own life, and its own existence. In some respects at least, it is superior to its parts, but therefore there is need of a hierarchical arrangement of those parts, in which some of the parts take on as their proper work the direction of common work and common life—in short, to take on authority over other parts in those things which concern the unity of the whole. Much like Yves R. Simon,[19] Maritain's argument here is the familiar one that the need for authority is not just negative (banding together to punish criminals and stop crime) but positive. In a world full of contingencies and historical singularities, a world where common goods cannot be achieved except by common effort, and yet where the identification of the exact means and proper inter-

[18] Ibid., p. 97.
[19] Yves R. Simon, *A General Theory of Authority* (Notre Dame, Indiana: University of Notre Dame Press, 1980).

mediate goals requires prudential decision and not just abstract impersonal calculation, there is need for authority even in the most well-disposed and well-prepared social groups. In art there is not only the work of individual arts, but the patronage of art that lets schools of great art flourish and that commissions the great works of art that are only possible by huge common efforts—the great Cathedrals, for instance. There has to be a place for authority to direct artistic energy and to supply artists who have the necessary vision with the resources of the community.

Let me summarize Maritain's point thus: democracies of the anarchic type, whether masked or openly anarchic, always seek a genuine good (whether they know it or not), namely, the increase of human freedom, and yet they tend to do so in an erroneous manner, that is, by "the deification of a fictional individual, shut up in himself"[20] and they refuse in principle the right of some men to be obeyed by others. And yet at the same time they seek political regulation of a community's affairs, something which can only occur with suitable organization, including a hierarchy of duties and freedoms. Rather, for mature persons to accept such regulation requires that the commands be of the sort suitable to free people and be of the sort that makes people more genuinely free.

What is the proper recourse for "a democracy of persons"? Presumably it will involve, among many other factors to be spelled out in a more elaborate theory, the judicious use of moral authority, backed up by the sparing but efficacious use of legitimate powers, especially in ways that are appropriately symbolic. It is a matter of letting the law serve its pedagogic function under the careful use of authorities who know how to use their moral authority for persuasion, as well as how to employ the powers of constraint at their disposal judiciously. Maritain calls this notion "the organic democracy of the person."[21]

Such a democracy will not simply efface the notion of authority from its self-understanding but will produce an appropriate structure of authority on the basis of its respect for the following pair of truths: (1) to obey a person who really has the right to direct action is in itself an act of reason and of freedom, and (2) to obey the person who genuinely fulfills the duty of directing the common work to the common good is to play the role of a free citizen.[22] This pair of truths allows one to make progress in understanding that the power of constraint is not the substance of authority, but merely

[20] Maritain, *Scholasticism and Politics*, p. 99.
[21] Ibid., pp. 98–99.
[22] Ibid., p. 101.

one attribute which authority needs in order to complete itself for the purpose of being efficacious within a human community, especially given that this community will invariably include children and those incapable of self-control as well as the criminal, the vicious, and the obstinate. The sanctions which an authority will decide to impose will only be good if they are sufficiently vigorous as to be efficacious, but the preliminary condition of their goodness will be the way in which these sanctions are part of the authority's witness to a truth higher than itself and thus intrinsically conformed to justice, and are not simply binding as the decisions of personal will or Rousseau's majority-will. In short, even sanctions can be a part of the pedagogy of freedom, if designed more and more to make constraint superfluous as a population is brought to maturity.

The whole issue, it seems to me, turns on the justice and prudence expected of true authority. An organic democracy will not involve the suppression of authority but an insistence that authority be just, that is, that it be an authoritative rather than authoritarian form of authority. From the point of view of a populace, the relevant point is that human nature can only be protected and preserved, let alone developed, within a well-ordered culture. While it is beyond the scope of this essay to offer specific proposals about the form that such an authority should take in matters of art, it does hope to have provided an account of some relevant principles. It allows us to conclude that knee-jerk rejections of any censorship[23] at all fundamentally misconceive the problem by forgetting the cultural matrix by which human maturation takes place, a process that is needed for large groups of people as well as for individuals. Mindful that the maturation of responsible freedom necessarily includes the development of a mature relation to authorities, Maritain's organic democracy still excludes paternalistic domination by any social class (e.g., by some elite who just "knows better"). What law and authority need to keep prominently placed before their minds is the freedom of mastery that can be achieved by maturing human beings and which makes individuals truly free as it is achieved. We do well, with Maritain, to describe the cultural version of this as the cultivation of civic friendship—civic friendship is not something ready-made any more than individual freedom is, but something that comes about by vigorous ef-

---

[23] The difficulties in practice for establishing a recognizable moral authority to give guidance in matters of art are enormous. For an interesting history of the Catholic Church's "Legion of Decency" as an attempt to give moral guidance in the sphere of motion pictures, see Frank Walsh, *The Catholic Church and the Motion Picture Industry* (New Haven, Connecticut: Yale University Press, 1998).

fort and at the price of considerable sacrifice and discipline. Artists need to be mindful of this, that their art, precisely by its visual, tactile, and auditory stimulation, has tremendous effect on individual and collective processes of maturation.

Naturally, Maritain also likes to remind us of the principle of subsidiarity, that authority needs to be distributed according to the ascending degrees of intermediate bodies that exist below the political community, starting from the naturally basic community of the family. Invariably, allowing so much place for varied levels of authority means some room for error in judgment. He also reminds us that the pluralism to be cultivated in democratic forms of government means that there will invariably be much foolishness and some evil. Nonetheless, this principle of subsidiarity is crucial to the workings of moral authority, for the authentic exercise of moral authority presumes realistic acquaintance with the actual state of development of persons and groups, and the closest level of the hierarchy of authority will be in the best position to judge the status of that development and to assess likely strategies for continuing individual and moral development. But most of all what is required is that these authorities, moral and civil, be mindful of what makes them authorities and not just powers and then be willing to exercise their authority in the diverse ways that are appropriate.

Social Justice as a
Work of Art in Action

Henk E. S. Woldring

According to Jacques Maritain, the final end of the state should be the common good. To achieve this end the enforcement of social justice is the primary duty of the state. Social justice is not the same as the common good but is an essential ingredient of it. We do not desire justice for itself, but for the sake of the common good. A similar point arises in Maritain's treatment of the relationship between beauty and the arts. He argues that the contemplation of beauty produces delight. The fine arts create beautiful works that are delightful, whereas useful arts not only produce delight but also satisfy practical human needs. We do not desire the useful arts for themselves but rather for the sake of satisfying human needs.

Maritain says that beauty is a kind of good which produces delight. The common good may be called something beautiful. In fact, social justice which is essential to the common good as something beautiful may be characterized as a work of fine art. In addition, since social justice serves to promote the common good and thus to satisfy a practical human need, it may also be characterized as a work of useful art.

To elucidate these thoughts on social justice, I shall examine first Maritain's theory of beauty and the relationship which the common good and justice have to this theory. Secondly, I shall discuss Aristotelian, Augustinian, and Thomistic ideas of justice to which Maritain's thought is much indebted, and I shall contrast these ideas with the ways in which some modern philosophers have dealt with the question of justice.

BEAUTY AS A KIND OF GOOD

In the classical tradition the essence of a work of art is called beauty. Although for many contemporary artists and aestheticians beauty thus understood has disappeared, Maritain's aesthetics follows classical thought. Maritain maintains that beauty produces delight: "Not just any delight, but delight in knowing; not the delight peculiar to the act of knowing, but a delight which superabounds and overflows from this act because of the object known."[1] According to Maritain, this delight in knowing does not depend on the delighted subject or viewer, but rather on the thing seen and known. Something is called beautiful because of its effect on the beholder, but this pleasing effect is the result of the very nature of the object seen.

Now since beauty fulfills the human need of delight, Maritain observes that beauty is a "kind of good."[2] However, the beautiful and the good differ logically: the beautiful relates to a cognitive power since it pleases when seen or known, whereas the good relates to appetite since all things desire the good. Desirability is not the very essence of the beautiful. Something beautiful is not necessarily an object of desire, but it is essentially delightful. Insofar as the beautiful assumes the aspect of the good, it is desirable; as such, the sight or knowledge of the beautiful allays the appetite.[3]

Following St. Thomas, Maritain mentions three characteristics of beauty: integrity, proportion, and clarity. Integrity refers to the "fullness of being," to "perfection" or "completion," which can be realized not only in one way but in a variety of different ways. Proportion means that a thing of beauty is characterized by "order and unity," "fitness and harmony." Integrity and proportion must be understood in relation to the clarity or the brilliance of the form.[4] Furthermore, Maritain argues that beauty produces love. Every form of beauty is loved for its own sake. Love in its turn produces ecstasy: the lover is in a real sense transported outside of himself. He is overtaken by the beauty of the work of art.[5]

After having seen what Maritain understands by beauty, we can now consider its relationship to art. This relationship can be analyzed by turning to the distinction between the fine arts and the useful arts. Works of fine arts are ordered to beauty; as beautiful works, they suffice of themselves and they give delight when seen. Useful arts, on the other hand, are ordered to the service of practical human beings and are therefore mere means.[6]

---

[1] Jacques Maritain, *Art and Scholasticism and The Frontiers of Poetry*, trans. Joseph W. Evans (New York: Charles Scribner's Sons, 1962), p. 23.

[2] Ibid., pp. 26, 167, n. 57.

[3] Ibid., pp. 23, 167–70. See John W. Hanke, *Maritain's Ontology of the Work of Art* (The Hague: Martinus Nijhoff, 1973), pp. 15–16.

[4] Maritain, *Art and Scholasticism*, pp. 27–28.

[5] Ibid., pp. 26–27.

[6] Ibid., p. 33.

Maritain acknowledges, however, that some arts can simultaneously pursue beauty and utility.[7] Although Maritain's work contains a more detailed analysis of beauty and of art, the distinctions discussed above are sufficient for my argument.

SOCIAL JUSTICE AS A WORK OF ART

We have already seen that beauty is a kind of good. Something beautiful may be called good not only because it gives pleasure when known but also because it fulfills a human need; thus, we desire what will satisfy our need. The common good may be described in terms of such a desirable good and consequently in terms of the beautiful. The common good is for the well-being of society and its citizens, and when known it produces delight. It is a good that is "common to the whole and to the parts."[8]

According to Maritain, the desired end of the state should be the common good and it is to be achieved by the strengthening of social justice.[9] The latter is not the same as the common good, but it is "essential to the common good."[10] Now since the common good may be called beautiful and since justice is essential to it, we may also say that justice is something beautiful. Like any other beautiful object, justice is characterized by integrity, proportion, and clarity.

In elaborating the essentials of the common good, i.e., the characteristics of social justice, Maritain enumerates three features which are compatible with the conditions of beauty: (1) the intrinsic morality or integrity of life, the perfection of the good and righteous life of human persons; (2) a proportionate or harmonious distribution of goods among persons; aid fitting for their development; and order, unity, and authority in society; (3) the highest possible realization of persons in their lives as persons (that is, the highest compatible with the good of the whole) and of their freedom of expansion or autonomy.[11] Such optimal realization of persons may be considered the splendor of the common good.

---

[7] Ibid., p. 158, n. 40. See Hanke, *Maritain's Ontology*, pp. 35–36.

[8] Jacques Maritain, *The Rights of Man*, in *Christianity and Democracy and The Rights of Man and Natural Law* (San Francisco: Ignatius Press, 1986), p. 94.

[9] Jacques Maritain, *Man and the State* (Chicago: The University of Chicago Press, 1951), pp. 14, 20.

[10] Maritain, *The Rights of Man*, p. 96. See also Jacques Maritain, *The Person and the Common Good* (Notre Dame, Indiana: University of Notre Dame Press, 1985), p. 55.

[11] Maritain, *The Rights of Man*, pp. 94–95. See James V. Schall, *Jacques Maritain. The Philosopher in Society* (Lanham, Maryland: Rowman & Littlefield, 1998), p. 145.

These characteristics determine the essence of social justice as an aesthetic-moral principle. Social justice may be characterized both as a work of fine art that produces delight and as a work of useful art that serves a human need, that furthers the common good. To explain my thesis that social justice is in effect a work of art, I shall compare and contrast the ideas of ancient and modern philosophers on justice.

JUSTICE AND THE GOOD LIFE

Aristotle argues that the *polis* exists for the sake of the good life, that is, the most exalted of all goods.[12] The good life is constituted by the practice of virtues, and in particular by the virtue of justice. Aristotle discusses justice in a general and in a particular sense. In the general sense, justice is the supreme moral virtue because it can be practiced for the sake of all citizens, and it brings about what is to the advantage of all citizens. For a legislator the virtue of justice means making just laws that are to the advantage of all, that promote the common good. For a citizen this virtue means obeying the laws of the *polis* and performing his civic duties.[13] Particular justice aims at giving to people their fair share. It is based upon the principle of the equality of citizens, that is, treating equals equally and unequals unequally but in proportion to their relevant differences.[14]

Particular justice is divided into distributive and corrective justice. Distributive justice is exercised in the distribution of honor, wealth, and the other divisible assets of the community, which may be allotted to its members in equal or unequal shares. In the distribution of common funds, the same ratio in which the contributions of the different persons stand to each other will be followed. What is just in such a distribution follows "geometrical proportion."[15] Corrective justice consists of a corrective principle in private transactions.[16] It is characterized by an "arithmetical proportion"; the law treats the parties as equals, merely asking whether one has inflicted damage and the other has sustained damage. The injustice here consists of the inequality due to the damage incurred and the judge endeavors to make both parties equal once again through the penalty he imposes.[17]

---

[12] Aristotle, *Politics* I.1.1252a1–9, trans. H. Rackman (Cambridge, Massachusetts: Harvard University Press, 1932; rpt. 1990).

[13] Aristotle, *Nicomachean Ethics* V.1.1129b1–1130a10, trans. H. Rackham (Cambridge, Massachusetts: Harvard University Press, 1926; rpt. 1990), hereafter cited as *NE*.

[14] *NE* V.2.1130a14–30.

[15] *NE* V.3.1131a20–25.

[16] *NE* V.2.1130b30–35.

[17] *NE* V.4.1132a1–35.

We see that justice in a general sense tends to promote the advantage of all citizens and the body politic at large. It serves to promote the common good or the good that is common to the whole and its parts. This characteristic of justice in a general sense is precisely what Maritain calls the intrinsic morality or integrity of life, the perfection of the good and righteous human life of the people. Aristotle employs mathematical arguments to express his conception of particular justice which effects a certain proportion. This argument is compatible with what Maritain calls a proportionate or harmonious distribution of goods among persons, which leads to their development and to order in society. Justice both in a general and in a particular sense brings about the ultimate end of the state, that is, the good life of its citizens. In other words, this ultimate end gives justice its brilliance. This corresponds to Maritain's third characteristic of justice: the splendor associated to the highest possible realization of the lives of persons and of their freedom of expansion.

Based upon these three characteristics, I call Aristotle's ideas of general and particular justice together social justice. Since I characterize social justice as an aesthetic-moral principle, I have to criticize the mathematical arguments used by Aristotle to explain his conception of particular justice. A distinction must be made between the essence of particular justice and mathematical arguments. The latter originally belong to the sphere of numbers and quantities and not to the essence of the aesthetic-moral principle of justice. If the discussion on justice is restricted to mathematical arguments, and man's dues, as it were, to mankind are determined by pure calculation, then in practice communal life would necessarily become inhuman.[18] Besides, in what respect are human beings equal and in what respect are they not equal? There may be damage that can never be restored despite the punishment inflicted. And in regard to distributive justice, excellence should certainly be recognized and given appropriate weight, but we should also acknowledge the claims of those less fortunate in society.[19] Mathematical calculations alone cannot adequately explain social justice, the essence of which is characterized by the intrinsic morality of human life and the proportionate distribution of goods, both of which are related to the splendor of the good life.

[18] See Josef Pieper, *The Four Cardinal Virtues* (Notre Dame, Indiana: University of Notre Dame Press, 1966), p. 113.

[19] See Yves Simon, *Philosophy of Democratic Government* (Notre Dame, Indiana: University of Notre Dame Press, 1993), pp. 197, 94. See also Ralph Nelson, "The Scope of Justice," in *Freedom, Virtue, and the Common Good*, eds. Curtis L. Hancock and Anthony O. Simon (American Maritain Association, 1995), p. 352.

A RADICAL SHIFT IN JUSTICE

Like Aristotle, Cicero argues that justice and the existence of the state are closely connected.[20] He also distinguishes between distributive and corrective justice which are based upon a rationally calculable distribution of goods in order to promote a harmonious society. However, justice was to be achieved only through the state as an institution of power.[21]

One of the most important critics of Cicero's idea of justice was Augustine. Still, like the classical Greek and Roman jurists, he is of the opinion that justice is the supreme virtue and that a true political society cannot exist without true justice. Again, like these jurists, he holds that justice is "the virtue which accords to each and every man what is his due."[22] However, his interpretation of true justice is very different from theirs. Augustine was motivated by the heroic and humane concept of virtue in late Roman ethics and culture, where the emphasis was on the promotion of individual and common well-being. He must have been fully aware of this conception of virtue when he developed his own alternative interpretation.

Although Augustine agrees with the general formulation of justice given by the Romans, he argues that justice transcends the sensible sphere and is related to God.[23] Justice may be illustrated by mathematical harmony and proportion, but Augustine does not deduce these from mathematical arguments. Augustine grounds his idea of justice in the Christian faith, and he relates justice to love of God and love of neighbor, both of which should produce moral integrity in relationships between persons and a harmonious society. The divine law should be the source of inspiration for the legislator.[24] According to Augustine, the state that achieves a moral and harmonious society would also promote true justice (although he was not optimistic about the possiblities of such a state in his time). If the state could achieve these goals, it would be considered neither an institution of power nor the highest end of human life but rather a means to serve the happy life of its citizens.[25]

[20] Cicero, *De Re Publica*, III, 22–23, trans. C. W. Keynes (Cambridge, Massachusetts: Harvard University Press, 1988).

[21] Cicero, *De Officiis*, I, 4, 11–14; IV, 14; VII, 7; XIII, 40, trans. W. Miller (Cambridge: Harvard University Press, 1990).

[22] Augustine, *The City of God*, XIX, 21, trans. G. G. Walsh and D. J. Honan (Washington, D.C.: The Catholic University of America, 1954).

[23] Augustine, *Confessions*, X, 33–34, 50, 53 (New York: Arno Press, 1979).

[24] See R. A. Markus, *Saeculum: History and Society in the Theology of St. Augustine* (Cambridge: Cambridge University Press, 1970), pp. 89–90.

[25] Augustine, *The City of God*, II, 19.

Augustine's conception of justice consists in promoting the moral integrity of human life and a proportionate distribution of goods. Moreover, integrity and proportion are related to love of God and love of neighbor and their purpose is the happy life of citizens which gives justice its splendor.

JUSTICE AND LOVE

Like Aristotle, Thomas Aquinas considers justice to be the supreme moral virtue for promoting the common good of the state and its citizens. Moreover, like Augustine, he argues that faith creates justice in us: "Just as love of God includes love of our neighbor, ... so too the service of God includes rendering to each one his due" [26]

Following Aristotle, Thomas holds that justice presupposes equality of human beings, that is, treating equals equally and unequals unequally but in proportion to their relevant differences. Our relations with other persons and the relations of persons to the political community should be guided by the general virtue of justice. Since the law should aim at the common good, justice should be achieved by law. The justice that is achieved by law is called "legal justice," which orders the relations of citizens to the political community.[27] Thomas discusses particular justice, which consists of commutative justice as ordering the mutual dealings between citizens, and distributive justice as ordering the relations between the community and its citizens.[28] In the case of commutative justice, Thomas, like Aristotle, applies geometrical proportion, whereas in the case of distributive justice the arithmetical proportion is applied.[29]

The general virtue of justice which orders the relations of citizens to the state for the sake of the common good pertains in Thomas's thought to the intrinsic morality or integrity of human life. Particular justice (including both commutative and distributive justice) pertains to the proportionate distribution of goods. Although Thomas's conception of particular justice is illustrated by mathematical arguments, the essence of justice transcends these arguments.

Like Augustine, Thomas begins his discussion on justice with the love of God, which includes love of neighbor; this love produces justice for the common good. The aesthetic characteristics of justice just mentioned are

---

[26] Thomas Aquinas, *Summa Theologiae* II–II, q. 58, a. 1 (Westminster, Maryland: Christian Classics, 1981), hereafter cited as *ST*. See Pieper, *The Four Cardinal Virtues*, pp. 43–113.

[27] *ST* II–II, q. 58., a. 5.

[28] *ST* II–II, q. 61, a. 1.

[29] *ST* II–II, q. 61, a. 2.

related to the service of God—a service which determines the meaning of human life and gives justice its splendor. The three characteristics that determine social justice as a moral-aesthetic principle correspond to the features Thomas enumerates of beauty: integrity or perfection, proportion or harmony, brightness or clarity.[30]

MODERN DEBATES ON JUSTICE

Modern philosophers rarely analyze the essence of justice. Their discussions of justice are derived from a discussion of other matters. I shall illustrate this briefly by some examples.

Thomas Hobbes holds that the origin of justice is produced through covenants which must be controlled by the coercive power of the state. Justice should be understood in terms of the commands given by law, which are the result of the formative power of the governor.[31]

John Locke argues that the government "is bound to dispense justice," based on the rights of private properties. To guarantee these rights, "men unite into Societies, that they may have the united strength of the whole Society to secure and defend their Properties, and may have *standing Rules* . . . , by which every one may know what is his."[32]

David Hume holds that "public utility would be the *sole* origin of Justice."[33] Utility is characterized by the strongest energy, and as such has the most complete command over our sentiments. According to Hume,

> It must, therefore, be the source of a considerable part of the merit ascribed to humanity, benevolence, friendship, public spirit, and other social virtues of that stamp; as it is the *sole* source of the moral approbation paid to fidelity, justice, veracity, integrity, and those other estimable and useful qualities and principles.[34]

Utility would be evident in a just society without excessive richness and extreme poverty.[35]

Jean-Jacques Rousseau acknowledges that God is the source of justice. However, he says that if we knew how to receive it from above, we would

---

[30] *ST* I, q. 39, a. 8.

[31] Thomas Hobbes, *Leviathan*, ed. C.B. Macpherson (Hammondsworth, England: Penguin, 1968), chap. 26.

[32] John Locke, *Second Treatise of Government*, in *Two Treatises of Government*, ed. P. Laslett (Cambridge: Cambridge University Press, 1965), paragraph 136.

[33] David Hume, "On Justice," in *Essays: Literary, Moral and Political* (London: Ward, Lock, and Warwick, 1915), p. 416.

[34] Hume, "On Justice," p. 429.

[35] See Hume, "Some Further Considerations with Regard to Justice," in *Essays*, pp. 489–94.

need neither government nor laws. Since this is obviously not the case, there must be laws to link the rights of citizens to their duties on the basis of a social contract. These laws will produce justice.[36]

Karl Marx argues that in the history of all societies the interpretation and application of a moral value such as justice has been determined through class antagonisms, antagonisms that assume different forms at different times. Whatever form they may have taken, one fact is common to the history of all societies: the exploitation of one part of society by another.[37] After the eradication of antagonistic economic and social relations, justice would be achieved in the socialist society of the future, a society which Marx describes as "a community of free individuals, carrying on their work with the means of production in common, in which the labor-power of all the different individuals is consciously applied as the combined labor-power of the community."[38]

The contemporary philosopher John Rawls argues that all people, whatever their world-view or philosophy may be, have an intuitive idea of justice. Rawls designs an imaginary social contract on the basis of which people want to be treated as equals. He formulates two principles of political justice: (1) Each person should have an equal right to the most extensive political liberties (compatible with those of others), and (2) Social and economic goods should be arranged so that they are both to the greatest advantage of the least advantaged and also attached to positions open to all.[39]

Unlike Rawls, the communitarian philosopher Philip Selznick maintains a procedural conception of justice, along with a material or robust conception of justice. Like Michael Walzer,[40] Selznick argues that justice is a principle that is at the basis of communities and that should be practiced within communities in order to improve the quality of life. Moreover, he argues that a just distribution of social goods occurs through differentiated communities. He does not agree with authors who interpret this principle as a minimalist conception of justice: to mitigate oppression and to avoid destructive conflicts. On the contrary, Selznick argues: "The process of doing

[36] Jean-Jacques Rousseau, *On the Social Contract*, II, 6 (New York: St. Martin's Press, 1978).

[37] Karl Marx, *The Communist Manifesto*, in Karl Marx, *Selected Writings*, ed. D. McLellan (Oxford: Oxford University Press, 1977), p. 236.

[38] Karl Marx, *Capital. A Critical Analysis of Capitalistic Production*, I, I, 4, in Marx and Engels *Gesamtausgabe* (Berlin: Dietz Verlag, 1990), vol. II/9, p. 68.

[39] John Rawls, *A Theory of Justice* (Oxford: Oxford University Press, 1972), pp. 302–03.

[40] See Michael Walzer, *Spheres of Justice. A Defense of Pluralism and Equality* (Oxford: Basil Blackwell, 1983).

justice stimulates moral and legal development. . . . Justice affirms the moral worth of individuals; sustains autonomy and self-respect; domesticates authority; and establishes a framework for moral discourse on public matters."[41]

Selznick demonstrates that justice is a comprehensive concept. Its meaning cannot be captured by a single element such as the impartiality of procedural fairness, or by an abstract formula comparable to giving to each his due. If we minimize justice, we lose a great deal of its resonance and promise. Selznick refers to Aristotle who argues that the *polis* exists for the sake of the good life. He is aware of the fact that many contemporary philosophers have resisted this idea, mainly because it is incompatible with the doctrine that moral value is an expression of will and an arbitrary choice. Furthermore, there is concern that the notion of the good life commits us to specific conclusions about which ends we should pursue. However, like Alasdair MacIntyre, Selznick argues that the notion of the good life does not necessarily specify means, ends, or outcomes. Selznick does not present a blueprint of the just society or of the good life, but he does maintain that justice gives a direction to human striving toward individual and social well-being.[42] This well-being is often called the common good. However, Selznick interprets the common good as neither the sum of individual goods, as libertarians often do, nor as the goods of the community as a whole, as socialists formerly defended it. Like Maritain, he argues that the common good is a normative idea that directs the process of the just distribution and redistribution of material and immaterial goods among individuals and groups participating in society.[43] In Selznick's theory the practice of justice is characterized by the moral development of human life, by a proportionate distribution of goods, and by a commitment to the good life. In contrast to other modern philosophers, Selznick acknowledges that various agencies are involved in bringing about social justice; besides the government and citizens, private associations should also participate in this effort.

EVALUATION OF THE DISCUSSION

There is an important difference between the ancient and modern philosophers on social justice. The former, and also Selznick, who is an ex-

---

[41] Philip Selznick, *The Moral Commonwealth, Social Theory and the Promise of Community* (Berkeley, California: University of California Press, 1992), pp. 430–31.

[42] Ibid., pp. 148–51. See Alasdair MacIntyre, *After Virtue* (London: Duckworth, 1981), p. 164.

[43] Selznick, *The Moral Commonwealth*, pp. 535–37.

ception among modern philosophers, are discussing social justice according to deontological and teleological arguments. They argue that both government and citizens ought to act according to the principle of justice in its general and particular sense. The practice of social justice should promote the common good. They begin their discussions on justice by focusing on the good life of the political community (Aristotle and Selznick) or on love of God and love of neighbor (Augustine and Thomas Aquinas) as foundational for their ideas of justice. Elaborating on these arguments, they understand the essence of social justice as an aesthetic-moral principle which is characterized by the intrinsic morality or integrity of human life, by the proportionate or harmonious distribution of goods, and by the splendor that is attached to the good life or to love of God and love of neighbor.

Many modern philosophers discuss social justice as a derivative of the coercive power of the state (Hobbes), of the rights of property (Locke), of public utility (Hume), of rational arguments borrowed from a social contract theory to guarantee certain duties and rights (Rousseau and Rawls), or of the eradication of antagonistic economic and social relationships (Marx). They do not analyze the essence of social justice.

Since these modern philosophers are presenting social justice only as a derivative of other factors, they reduce social justice to these factors, and in so doing they formulate strict deontological or teleological norms to uphold their speculations. However, their theories will effect a theoretical destruction of the essence of social justice, and consequently, social justice will lose its potential dynamism because its inherent mission and promise have not been acknowledged.

CONCLUSIONS

I have argued that the common good, and in particular social justice, is something beautiful. I characterized social justice as both a work of fine art that produces delight and as a work of useful art that serves human needs. I would also say that it is a work of useful art which produces love. By way of conclusion, I shall pose three questions: (1) What kind of needs are served by social justice? (2) What kind of useful art is social justice? and (3) What kind of love is produced?

To answer the first question, the concept of justice has traditionally been related to the legal duties and rights of citizens and to their material interests. Recently, more attention has been paid to justice in relation to needs and their satisfaction. It would be incorrect to confine the notion of needs to biological, physical, and material requirements, and to ignore education, public health care and popular morality.[44] Selznick discusses justice as directive of the distribution of material and immaterial goods. Attention should be given to the redistribution of immaterial goods for the sake of the less advantaged and socially vulnerable.

However, who will satisfy these needs? In contrast to ancient and many modern philosophers who argue that either the government or individual citizens are responsible, Selznick and Walzer argue that a variety of social agencies bear this responsibility together. Given the plurality of private communities which are characterized by their own autonomy, there would be a number of distributing agencies, so to speak, from the family to voluntary associations, from benevolent associations to public bodies.[45]

Now moving to the second question, we cannot assume that all works of fine art display the structure of things. This is obvious if we compare a painting or a sculpture to music or poetry. Works of art belonging to the realm of music or poetry lack the constant actual existence proper to things. They can only be constantly objectified in the structure of scores or texts. The latter are characterized by symbols that can only signify the aesthetic structure of a work of art in an objective manner and cannot actualize it. They give rise to a separate kind of art, the performance.

Social justice as a work of art is also objectified in the structure of its enumerated characteristics. We may compare the aesthetic structure of these characteristics of social justice to the score of a work of music or the text of a poem. With respect to this objectification, social justice as a work of useful art should not be separated from its end as a work of fine art. I have already referred to the fact that some arts, according to Maritain, can pursue both beauty and utility. Social justice is such a work of art; it has the characteristics of both. It is an aesthetic-moral principle that is characterized by integrity of life, proportioned harmony and splendor, and at the same time, it is meant to fulfill material and immaterial needs.

We may argue that the measure of the attainment of social justice in society, that is, the measure of the fulfillment of the material and immaterial needs of the people, corresponds to the measure of happiness and moral soundness of the people. Moreover, the practice of social justice varies within different socio-historical and political situations. Since a work of art is located within a socio-historical context, and its style differs

---

[44] See Yves R. Simon, *General Theory of Authority* (Notre Dame, Indiana: University of Notre Dame Press, 1980), p. 24.

[45] See Ralph Nelson, "The Scope of Justice," p. 351.

from one context to another, so the measure of the attainment of social justice can vary from one political situation to another. Therefore, in such concrete situations social justice as a work of art cannot be considered simply as an object of contemplation that gives delight to the intellect. Here the one-sidedness of Maritain's classical idea of aesthetics is evident because the work of art might then become an object of elitist contemplation.

Nicholas Wolterstorff argues that contemplation for the sake of delight is certainly an ingredient of aesthetics; however, the aesthetic-contemplative tradition often served to maintain unjust social relations. He argues that "all works of art are objects and instruments of action. They are all inextricably embedded in the fabric of human intention. They are objects and instruments of action whereby we carry out our intentions with respect to the world, our fellows, ourselves, and our gods. Understanding art requires understanding art in man's life."[46] Wolterstorff argues that works of art are meant to play many diverse roles in human life and that they are objects of human action. We may apply Wolterstorff's theory to social justice as a work of art: social justice plays many roles in a variety of unjust situations; it carries out our intention to change these situations, and it may be characterized as a work of art in action.

With respect to the third question, Maritain argues that beauty produces love, that is, we are captivated by something beautiful and we love it. We may love social justice as a work of art, and we certainly love this aesthetic-moral principle even more when it is attained in practice. Although there is a difference between justice and love, there is no opposition between the two. Since moral love has its own meaning and power, it strengthens our understanding and practice of social justice in order to promote the common good. In other words, moral love reinforces and directs justice. The latter should not be reduced to what modern philosophers see as the common good that is founded upon mathematical calculation, commands of law, rights of property, or rational organization by contract. On the contrary, social justice should be strengthened by love. Only in this way can social justice continuously take care of a multitude of needs and interests.

Finally, let us consider whether social justice guided by love implies a transcendental reference to religious love and justice. Like Augustine and Thomas Aquinas, Maritain answers this question in the affirmative. He ar-

---

[46] Nicholas Wolterstorff, *Art in Action. Toward A Christian Aesthetic* (Grand Rapids, Michigan: Eerdmans, 1980), p. 3.

gues that love of art produces ecstasy, such that the lover is beside himself: an ecstasy whose fullness we experience in the love of God.[47]

The teaching of the Old and New Testaments instructs the people of Israel as to their obligations in particular toward widows, orphans, strangers, the poor, and all socially vulnerable persons. The basis for these obligations, for the practice of justice, is the remembrance of God's love: the fact that God delivered the Israelites from slavery in Egypt. This remembrance changes the bipolar model of justice between the government (and other agencies) and citizens into a triangular model. Instead of the rule of the bipolar model of social justice, that is, "to give everyone his or her due," the rule of the triangular model reads as follows: "Do unto others as God did unto you."[48] The point of the triangular model is that the characteristics of social justice should be achieved especially by taking care of the needs of the socially vulnerable. Doing justice in this manner actualizes what the memory of God's liberating action promises and gives social justice its dynamism and splendor. Because of this dynamism social justice should be characterized as a work of art in action.

---

[47] Maritain, *Art and Scholasticism*, pp. 26–27.

[48] See Hans S. Reinders, "The Golden Rule between Philosophy and Theology," in *Ethik, Vernunft und Rationalität/Ethics, Reason and Rationality*, eds. A. Bondolfi, S. Grotefeld and R. Neuberth (Münster, Germany: Lit Verlag, 1997), pp. 163–66.

Contributors

Brian J. Braman is Director of the Perspectives Program at Boston College, a four-year interdisciplinary program centered on the humanities and the natural sciences. Besides his essay on Charles Taylor, he has also published on Martha Nussbaum and Bernard Lonergan on the question of religious desire. He is currently working on a book that puts Lonergan and Taylor in dialogue on the politics of authenticity.

Matthew Cuddeback received his Ph.D. from the School of Philosophy of The Catholic University of America in 1998. He is currently Adjunct Assistant Professor of Philosophy at Providence College in Providence, Rhode Island.

Christopher M. Cullen, S.J. did his doctoral studies in philosophy at The Catholic University of America and his undergraduate work in philosophy and European history at Georgetown University. He is currently teaching in the department of philosophy at Fordham University. His field of interest is medieval philosophy, both the Augustinian-Franciscan tradition and Thomism. He is also interested in contemporary Neo-Thomism.

Patrick Downey received a Ph.D. from Boston College in 1994, a M.T.S. from Harvard University in 1984, and a B.A. from Claremont College in 1980. He presently teaches at St. Mary's College of California. His publications include "Tragedy and the Truth," *International Philosophical Quarterly* (Spring 1999), and "Serious Comedy: An Investigation of the Philosophical and Theological Significance of Tragic and Comic Writing in the Western Tradition" (forthcoming). His research interests are in Plato, Kierkegaard, fundamental theology, biblical narrative, and literary theory.

Desmond J. FitzGerald is Professor Emeritus at the University of San Francisco. He attended the lectures of Maritain and Gilson at St. Michael's, University of Toronto, as an undergraduate in the 1940s. He holds a B.A.

and an M.A. from Toronto and an M.A. in political science and a Ph.D. in philosophy from the University of California at Berkeley. He taught at the University of San Francisco from 1948 to 1998.

Donald Haggerty is Professor of Moral Theology and Spiritual Director of St. Joseph's Seminary/Dunwoodie in Yonkers, New York. He received an S.T.D. in moral theology from the Accademia Alfonsiana at Rome in 1995. He has published articles on Jacques Maritain and connaturality, on St. John of the Cross, and on subjects related to spirituality in *The Thomist*, *New Blackfriars*, *The Linacre Quarterly*, *Faith & Reason*, and other journals.

Wayne H. Harter received his Ph.D. from The Centre for Religious Studies at the University of Toronto in 1993. He currently teaches in the department of philosophy at St. Mary's College of California. His research focuses on the relation of moral, theological, and intellectual virtues in Catholic higher education. His publications include "Acts Commanded by Religion," *New Blackfriars* (June 1994), and "The Privileged Task," a book-length manuscript on the integration of Catholic higher education, currently under review.

Jeanne M. Heffernan is a recent Ph.D. in Government from the University of Notre Dame, where she also served as Associate Director of the Erasmus Institute for two years. She joined the political science faculty of Pepperdine University in California in the fall of 1999. A specialist in Christian Political Theory, she has written book reviews on Thomism for *The Review of Politics* and has contributed an essay on Yves R. Simon and Reinhold Niebuhr for a forthcoming volume of the American Maritain Association on Thomist political thought.

Thomas S. Hibbs received his Ph.D. from the University of Notre Dame in 1987. He is presently Associate Professor in the department of philosophy at Boston College. He is the author of *Dialectic and Narrative: An Interpretation of the Summa Contra Gentiles* (University of Notre Dame Press, 1995) and editor with an introduction of *Aquinas on Human Nature* (Hackett, 1999).

Gregory J. Kerr is Associate Professor of Philosophy at Allentown College of St. Francis de Sales in Center Valley, Pennsylvania. He is editor of *The Maritain Notebook*, the American Maritain Association newsletter. He has published articles on Maritain's aesthetics and on education in volumes of the Maritain Association.

Joseph W. Koterski, S.J. is Associate Professor of Philosophy at Fordham University. He is Editor-in-Chief of the *International Philosophical Quarterly*. He is Chaplain and Tutor at Queen's Court Residential College of Fordham University. His teaching concentrations include natural law ethics and medieval philosophy.

Daniel McInerny is Assistant Professor of Philosophy at the University of St. Thomas/Center for Thomistic Studies in Houston, Texas. He received his Ph.D. from The Catholic University of America in 1994. He works primarily in ethics, with a concentration on Aristotelian and Thomistic themes. He has also published on Aristotle's psychology and scientific method.

Ralph McInerny has taught at the University of Notre Dame since 1955, where he is the Michael P. Grace Professor of Medieval Studies and Professor of Philosophy. A fellow of the Pontifical Academy of Saint Thomas Aquinas, he is a lifelong member of the American Catholic Philosophical Association, the American Philosophical Association, the Metaphysical Society of America, and the Fellowship of Catholic Scholars. He has written extensively on Thomas Aquinas, most recently the Penguin Classic, *Selected Writings of Thomas Aquinas* (1999). He gave the Gifford Lectures in Glasgow in October 1999 and February 2000.

James P. Mesa received his undergraduate and graduate degrees in philosophy from Saint Louis University. His primary research interest is in ethics and has presented papers in the area of his doctoral study "Moral Indoctrination and the Virtue of Prudence." He is currently Professor of Philosophy at Newman University in Wichita, Kansas.

John F. Morris received his Ph.D. from Saint Louis University in 1995. He is Assistant Professor of Philosophy at Rockhurst University in Kansas City, Missouri. His area of specialization is in ethics and in medical ethics, with a background in medieval philosophy and St. Thomas Aquinas. He is currently a member of the Ethics and Human Values Committee at St. Joseph Health Center in Kansas City, and a member of the American Occupational Therapy Association's Commission on Standards and Ethics. He has presented several papers related to natural law, the philosophy of Maritain, and medical ethics, and has published an article in *Ethics and Medics* entitled, "Which Principle: Autonomy or Respect?" (23, no. 4 [April 1998]).

Ralph Nelson taught philosophy and political science at the University of Windsor in Ontario, where he is now Professor Emeritus. He has published numerous articles on Jacques Maritain and Yves R. Simon, among which is an essay on Simon's philosophy of science included in *Acquaintance with the Absolute: The Philosophy of Yves R. Simon* (New York: Fordham University Press, 1998). His main interest in political science is in democratic theory and practice.

Katherine Anne Osenga received an M.A. in religion and the arts from the Graduate Theological Union at Berkeley and a B.F.A. from the University of San Francisco. She is currently a Ph.D. candidate at the Graduate Theological Union. She exhibits her icon work nationally and teaches icon making throughout the Bay Area. She is working on a book of her latest icon series of the Madonna and Child.

Alice Ramos is Associate Professor of Philosophy at St. John's University in Jamaica, New York. She holds a Ph.D. in French Literature from New York University and a Ph.D. in Philosophy from the University of Navarra in Spain. Her publications include a book written in Spanish on semiotics and a metaphysics of the sign, articles in the areas of Thomistic metaphysics, Kantian ethical theology, and Christian anthropology. Her present research focuses on the foundations of ethics and on the transcendentals in St. Thomas, especially beauty.

Carrie Rehak is a doctoral candidate at the Graduate Theological Union in Berkeley. Her main research interest lies in the relationship between spirituality and the arts. Her most recent work deals with representations of the landscape as model for the conduct or misconduct of American Western heroes (i.e., cowboys) in literature, paintings, and films.

Stephen Schloesser, S.J. received his Ph.D. in modern European history from Stanford University in 1999. He spent the spring semester of 1999 as a post-doctoral fellow at the Erasmus Institute of the University of Notre Dame. His dissertation, entitled "Mystic Realists: Sacramental Modernism in French Catholic Revival, 1918–1928," studied the role of Jean Cocteau, Jacques Maritain, and Georges Rouault in evolving a sacramental vision of reality which combined elements of the late nineteenth-century decadence and Neo-Thomism after the Great War. He has published articles in journals such as *Process Studies*, *Church Divinity*, and *The Heythrop Journal*.

Francis Slade is Professor Emeritus of Philosophy at St. Francis College in Brooklyn, New York, where for many years he was Chairman of the department of philosophy. His most recent publications are: "Rule as Sovereignty," in *The Truthful and the Good*, edited by John Drummond and James Hart (Boston: Kluwer, 1996); "Catholicism as Political Paradigm?" in *Telos*, no. 18 (Fall 1996); "Was Ist Aufklärung? Remarks on Maritain, Rorty, and Bloom," in *The Common Things: Essays on Thomism and Education*, edited by Daniel McInerny (American Maritain Association, 1999).

John G. Trapani, Jr. received a B.A. from Boston College and a Ph.D. from St. John's University in Jamaica, New York. He has written extensively on Maritain's aesthetics, including his dissertation: "The Interrelation of Poetry, Beauty, and Contemplation in The Philosophy of Jacques Maritain." He has also several published essays on various aspects of Maritain's philosophy. He is Professor and Chair of the philosophy department at Walsh University in North Canton, Ohio. In addition, he is active as a professional musician and bandleader.

Henk E. S. Woldring studied sociology and philosophy at the State University in Groningen, the Free University in Amsterdam, and the Goethe University in Frankfurt, Germany. He is Professor of Political Philosophy at the Free University in Amsterdam. In 1990–91 he was Visiting Professor at the University of Notre Dame. He has published several books in Dutch on the political philosophy of the Christian Democratic movement in Europe. In 1987 he published *Karl Mannheim: The Development of His Thought* (St. Martin's Press). Since 1999 he is a member of the Dutch Parliament for the Christian Democratic Party.

Index